The Good, The Bad and the Living Dead

Venture Capital Cases in the Healthcare Industry

Albert J. Henry
with **Glenn E. Bugos**

The Good, The Bad and the Living Dead

Venture Capital Cases in the Healthcare Industry

Albert J. Henry
with **Glenn E. Bugos**

Published by Essex Publishing

ISBN 0-9763888-0-4

For my mother and Joanne

12/20/04

To Carl —

Hope you enjoy the stories. MSO will join the "GOOD" in '05.

Best regards.

Al

Table of Contents

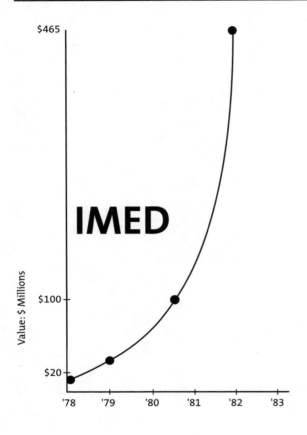

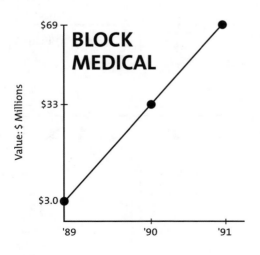

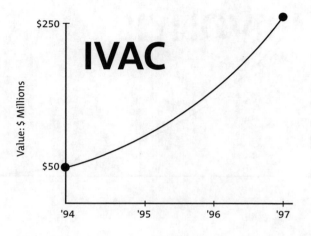

IVAC

Value: $ Millions

$250

$50

'94 '95 '96 '97

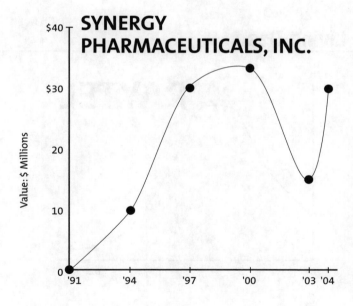

SYNERGY
PHARMACEUTICALS, INC.

$40

$30

20

10

Value: $ Millions

0

'91 '94 '97 '00 '03 '04

The **Bad**

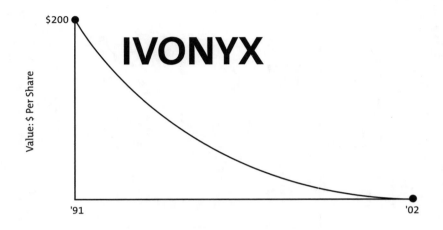

The **Living Dead**

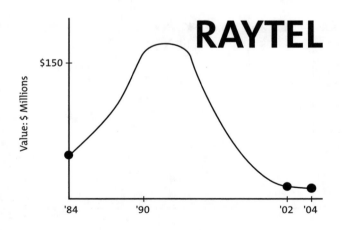

Introduction

IMED Corporation

Block Medical, Inc.

IVAC Medical Systems, Inc.

Synergy Pharmaceuticals, Inc.

IVoynx Group Services, Inc.

Raytel Medical Corporation

Approximately 25 percent of all venture funded start-ups are success stories. Almost one third of VC backed companies are abject failures which go bankrupt quickly and send their capital and technology up in smoke. One third to 40 percent of VC backed companies generally are break even investments. Their growth trajectory has leveled off, they remain mildly profitable, their executives start to leave, and the prospects of being acquired seem distant. These are the good, the bad and the Living Dead in venture capital parlance.

Henry Venture Funds invested in fifteen companies between 1980 and 2000. The six healthcare cases presented here were selected for their diversity of corporate events, which underline what can happen to a new company — both good and bad. The venture capitalist must deal with varied problems and opportunities to help create a successful company. These cases illustrate a wide range of problems and opportunities which require major action, and as such should offer a diversified learning experience.

Rather than highlight only successful illustrations we have chosen instead six case studies representing the good, the bad and the Living Dead. IMED Corp. is a phenomenal success story led by technological innovations which drove valuations higher and higher. IMED, a small private biomedical device company located in San Diego, became the first investment of the Henry Venture funds. It produced the world's first volumetric infusion pump, thus making infusions a viable way to deliver drugs. Henry served as IMED's CFO, and through extensive cost controls the company reported twenty-four consecutive quarter to quarter earnings increases. Subsequently, Lehman Brothers arranged the sale of IMED for $465 million cash. This represented a return of 23 times original investment value in 4.5 years for an IRR of 101 percent per year.

IVonyx, on the other hand, is an example of a bad investment. This was a home infusion company that began by franchising pharmacists. It became necessary to restart the business plan by emphasizing company-owned operations when franchise operations became unmanageable due to lack of compliance by franchised pharmacists. The company lingered for a decade with modest profitability causing repeated failures to find liquidity. In the end it was sold to drkoop.com in 2002. Unfortunately, drkoop.com faced financing problems itself and went bankrupt not long afterwards. Ivonyx was shut down in the ensuing bankruptcy.[1]

Raytel is an example of the Living Dead. It began with a technology for digitalizing x-rays in hospitals. Raytel was forced to abandon its original imaging technology when a patent infringement case against North American Phillips and AT&T disrupted operations. The case resulted in a $5 million settlement for Raytel. After the settlement, Raytel acquired CDI Medical, which monitored 25% of all cardiac pacemakers in the US. Raytel went public in 1995, fourteen years after its founding. Five years later, it had lost 93 percent of its equity value in the public market, as its business produced recurring losses, and it was acquired and taken private. Henry Funds sold their stock after the IPO and before the slide to show a 25 percent IRR.

The IMED success story also led to corollary investments in two other infusion pump companies that are discussed in this text. Both had excellent investment results. Shortly after the sale of IMED in 1982, the Henry Venture Funds provided seed financing to Block Medical which made elastomeric disposable volumetric pumps for home infusions. Block was successfully sold to Hillenbrand twenty-two months after startup for $69 million cash plus an earnout for a return of 14 times original investment value and an IRR of 298 percent per year.

The Henry Venture funds then provided the seed money for a third investment in the infusion market. This company was called River Medical and it was started by a management team from Block Medical. The company designed a disposable volumetric gas-driven infusion pump for antibiotic infusions. About one year after River Medical's genesis, Eli Lilly decided to dispose of its instrument division called IVAC through an auction process. Henry Venture funds teamed up with some other VCs as well as River Medical's management and purchased IVAC from Lilly and merged the entities. Henry became Vice-Chairman of IVAC, responsible for its operating performance. After a period of restructuring, IVAC was sold to IMED for $400 million cash. The original Henry Venture Fund investment had a return of six times original investment value in three years for an IRR of 84 percent per year.

The sixth case study to be discussed is a currently active biotechnology company which has already operated under three different names, and which has already advanced three distinctive and novel molecular platforms. Initially, the company known as IGX, Inc. developed an anti-diarrhea drug for AIDS patients based on an immunoglobulin compound. As this treatment methodology was overtaken by newer combination anti-AIDS products, the company shifted its strategy to develop an immunosugar drug as a therapy for Hepatitis C, and renamed itself <u>Synergy Pharmaceuticals</u>. Then, to better capture the value in the development of an azaspirane drug for multiple myeloma and to create more liquidity, the company merged with Callisto Pharmaceuticals, a public company. This is a good company and currently a work in progress. It is presented to give the reader hands on experience in the formation and development of a biotech company.

Henry Venture Fund

Henry Venture Fund began in 1980 with $21.465 million and raised another $10.7 million in 1987. The funds invested in approximately twenty companies over their life. All told, approximately $34 million in health-care investments from 1980 to 2002 resulted in gains of $151 million for institutional investors from the efforts of Henry Funds.

Henry graduated from Bradley University in Peoria, Illinois in 1960 with a Bachelor of Science degree in Civil Engineering and completed his MBA from the Graduate School of Business Administration at Northwestern University (since renamed the J.L. Kellogg School of Management).

Henry joined First National City Bank in 1962, now Citibank. In six years, he was head of one-fourth of its New York branch system for commercial and industrial loans, and had experience serving firms in electronics, health care and aerospace. In 1968, he founded his Wall Street firm to do securities research, investment banking and corporate finance. His clients included the major mutual fund money pools in Boston and Minneapolis, money center banks in New York, as well as pension funds and insurance companies in the United States and United Kingdom.

F. David Hare was recruited as president of Henry Funds and Dan R. Hendrickson as vice president. Hare had spent fourteen years with Irving Trust Company, and was previously IMED's banker. He opened Irving's first office in the western United States in Los Angeles, managed seventy professionals there, and had responsibility for all of its commercial banking west of the Rockies and around the Pacific Rim. Hendrickson was treasurer and CFO of offshore operations of IMED and was a CPA by training.

Market Cycles

Market cycles shape all facets of venture investing. They affect how much money a fund can raise, when it can disband, the valuations and shapes of investments and total returns on venture investments; all are interrelated. Business cycles in the venture capital industry are determined by the general economy and are described annually by the amount of funds raised, the numbers of IPOs, the average sizes of money raised in IPOs and the rates of return enjoyed by money invested with venture capitalists. The peaks and valleys of each indicator are fairly closely linked: venture returns to total amounts raised for funds (chart 1); returns to the numbers of IPOs (chart 2); returns to the total amount raised in IPOs (chart 3); and the average size of IPOs to the amounts raised in IPOs (chart 4).

The birth of venture capital in the United States is usually marked in 1946 with the formation of American Research and Development, which in 1957 invested in the Digital Equipment Company (DEC). Also, beginning in 1958 the Small Business Administration chartered Small Business Investment Companies (SBIC's) that provided capital mainly through loans guaranteed by the federal government.

The capital flowing into venture funds got a significant boost with the 1979 amendments to the Employee Retirement Income Security Act (ERISA). The amendments allowed pension fund managers to invest up to 10 percent of their capital in venture funds. Furthermore, tax law changes starting in 1978 reduced the maximum capital gains bite from 50 percent to approximately 20 percent for individuals, and the corporate rate from 30 percent to 28 percent. Between 1975 and 1980, the annual returns on venture funds ranged between 20 percent and 28 percent, so that many wealthy individuals and pension fund managers eager to invest in venture funds anticipated high rates of return.

Yet, between 1980 and 1986, the venture capital industry was at a low point in its industry cycle. There was a general economic recession in 1982 which affected the amounts raised by funds. Capital raised by venture funds, despite the ERISA amendments, actually declined from $2.3 billion in 1980 to $1.5 billion in 1981. The numbers of initial public offerings of stock were few because the recession scared investors away from equity markets. Returns also dropped from the 20 percent range in the late 1970s, to between 8.4 percent in 1981 to 10.98 percent in 1985. By 1983,

Chart I

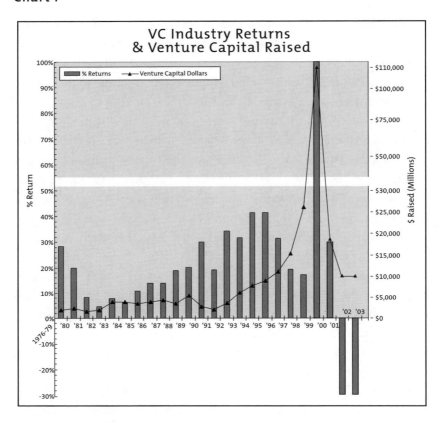

Source: Venture Economics, Venture Capital Journal

venture funds invested $3 billion in startups annually.

Returns then climbed back up, from 1986 to 1989, to range between 10 percent and 20 percent, then continued rising from 1991 to 1996. In fact, venture capital returns were excellent during the late 1980s, and even better in the 1990s. As a result, the amounts of capital raised for venture funds also increased. The number of IPOs grew apace the rising average rates of return. From 1985 to 1990, IPOs raised about $10 billion annually. Healthy returns from funds attracted more money into the funds throughout the 1990s.

The stock market crash of October 1987, though insignificant over the long term growth in the venture capital industry and in the stock market indices, was very significant in the short-term. Black Monday was a destructive sell-off in the liquid equity markets reflecting not so much bad economic times as it did psychological struggles with uncertainty. The federal government was failing to address the budget deficit and the trade deficit, so economists had trouble forecasting inflation or interest rates.

Market cycles affect venture fund returns, and so they also affect the ability to raise funds. During any recession, professional pension fund managers turn especially conservative. And during a bearish stock market, institutional investors sour on equity investments. Yet experienced venture capitalists know it is especially important to invest in new firms during a weak economy. Because new company valuations are depressed, good returns can eventually be earned with average companies. But, venture capitalists often find it hard to avoid the herd instincts during conservative times. Before they invest, they want to know who else is investing in some

Chart II

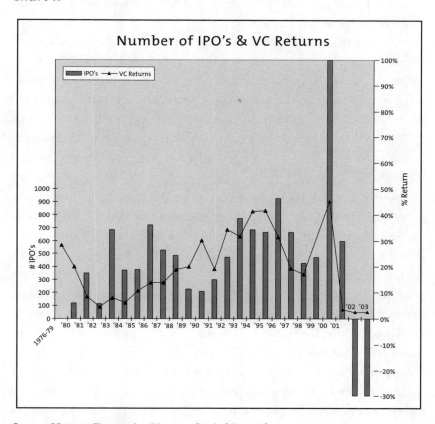

Source: *Venture Economics, Venture Capital Journal*

new industry segment or in some specific company. The first question they ask any entrepreneur is which other venture backer has already committed to financing the company. The company without early financing commitments may not get very far in the fund raising process.

In 1989, another recession occurred and uncertainty entered the markets. Soon the market for IPOs slowly returned and then surged. The most explosive era ever in venture capital came in the period between 1992 and 2001, when average annual returns never dropped below 32 percent. In two consecutive years, 1994 and 1995, the annual rate of return was 41 percent. It was also a period of record numbers of IPOs, which in turn recycled capital back into venture capital funds. IPOs in aggregate raised more than $50 billion annually. (*see Chart II, page vii*) However, in 2000 the industry had its highest annual rate of return followed by negative returns in 2002 and 2003 all due to first the boom of dot.com stocks followed by their disastrous bust.

Better returns make it easier to raise venture funds. Eventually there becomes a saturation point, where venture fund managers have too much capital. Returns drop because the pricing of new deals is driven up, weakening returns on successful deals. Also, newer venture fund managers fund weaker deals, driving up the failure rates and lessening total industry returns.

Toward the end of the 1990s, venture returns spike up in 2000 because of the numerous IPO's of dot.com stocks at huge valuations. Then, in 2001 and 2002, venture returns drop well off of their highs, largely because of the bust in many of the same dot.com stocks, along with numerous new dot.com and other investments going bust, such as biotechnology discussed below. There were also more venture capital fund management firms than ever before. In 1980 there were about 175 venture funds in operation. In 1990 there were about a thousand funds. A decade later, there were more than two thousand funds. And, because the average size of the funds also more than doubled, there was a tremendous expansion in the amount of venture capital under management. The result was a decline in venture capital returns with too many dollars chasing too few good deals as we entered 2001, 2002 and 2003.

In addition to broader market cycles, market cycles in individual industries dramatically affect the timing of initial public offerings. For example, in 2002, Synergy Pharmaceuticals, a biotechnology firm in the

Chart III

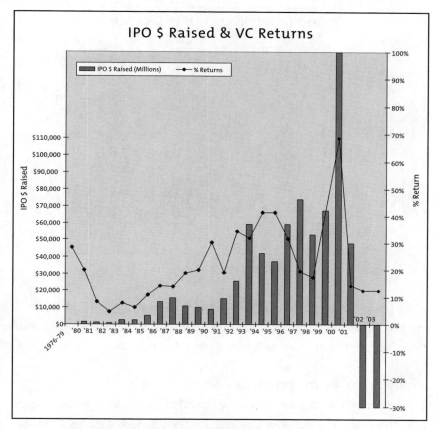

Source: Venture Economics, Venture Capital Journal

HVF II portfolio, was seeking both capital and a merger with a public company. However, in 2002, the valuations for public biotechnology companies were at a seven year low, and valuations for private biotechnology firms were even more depressed. Even though they continued to reach expected drug development milestones and demand for new drugs remained present in the financial community and in the general economy, from 2001 to 2002 the values of public biotech companies fell 70 percent in the marketplace. Depressed public markets killed the venture capital appetite for new investment in biotechnology even though many excellent technologies were available for investments. Dramatic breakthroughs in proof-of-concept Phase II clinical trials still drove up some biotechnology company valuations, over the course of a year, three times, sometimes

Chart IV

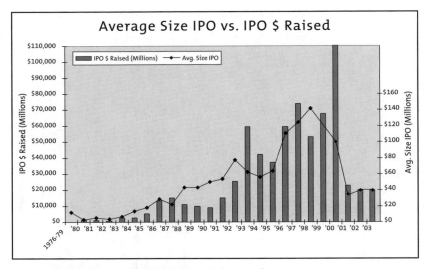

Source: Venture Economics, Venture Capital Journal

eight times. Such spectacular rises make biotechnology one of the most exciting areas for venture capital investment even as the herd of institutional investors remained negative toward biotechnology.

The Maturity of Venture Capital

Though it will always be affected by market cycles, the venture capital industry reached a state of maturity over the past two decades. There are more funds in operation, with greater degrees of specialization. There are broader sources of capital—like pension funds and institutions in addition to personal trusts—that provide a regular flow of capital into venture funds. Venture fund managers have an easier job today raising money for their funds than they did twenty years earlier. There is a routine to the structure of the industry, making it easier to form investing syndicates. Venture capitalists today have access to better information and training than earlier generations. And, the return from venture investments has been very good compared with the rates of returns from other equity asset classes.

Historically, there is an even larger economic cycle shaped by venture investing. Fortune 500 companies employed about 70 percent of American workers in the 1960's; by 2000 they employed about 25 percent or less. This shift in job formation from the largest firms to smaller firms is one of the best indicators of the importance of venture capital in the American economy. Each year during the late 1980s and 1990s, venture capitalists invested at least $3 billion in new company formation, and in some years as much as $15 billion. In 2000, approximately $100 billion was invested mainly because of the dot.com boom. Americans have always set a healthy pace in creating new firms, though in the past two decades the rate of new firm creation accelerated. And, compared with earlier types of new firms, these firms grew rapidly as employers. Skilled people—American and foreign-born--wanted to work for them.

The venture capital industry is an American invention, it has served the American economy very well and is the main reason that the United States is the world leader in developing technology. There is nothing quite like it in either Europe or Asia. Equally American, and equally crucial to that success, is the courage of individual entrepreneurs willing to take risks by starting a new company with new inventions. We now live an a world where young engineers and businesspeople work with the expectation that they can and should start their own firms, and they need not explain to their friends and families why they would chose to leave the comfort of the big firms. That cultural shift arose from more active participation by venture capitalists in those new firms.

Origins of These Cases

In 1994, Henry began accepting more invitations to lecture on venture finance at his alma mater, the Kellogg Graduate School of Management at Northwestern University near Chicago. He subsequently became Adjunct Professor of Finance at Kellogg. Venture capital then was at its peak, students wanted good courses, yet most of the faculty teaching venture finance were trained in finance or economic theory. Those who could lecture from experience, like Henry, were in demand.

Each of the cases is meant to be self contained. Each has a valuation and private placement chart that summarizes the structure and pacing of the deals. Questions are posed to the reader, and in the back of each case are the answers. Each case has footnotes to published sources, charts and a variety of attachments—most of which are original financing documents.

One theme common to all these cases, and which makes them unique among cases on venture capital, is the venture capitalist's persistence and ability to restart these companies as they confronted failure or irrelevance in their initial strategic direction. The discussion of management issues is very detailed and the structure of various deals is quite varied, which is a departure from the fictionalizing and sparse detail of many case studies. All of this, we feel, is good reading and education for those who expect to practice as a venture capitalist or for those interested in the rigors and complexity of venture capital.

Acknowledgements

Morton L. Kamien, PhD, the Joseph and Carol Levy Distinguished Professor of Entrepreneurship at the Kellogg School of Management, first introduced Bugos and Henry and provided encouragement throughout the project. Dean Emeritus Donald P. Jacobs, PhD, and Dean Dipak Jain, PhD, of the Kellogg School provided encouragement throughout. Jeffrey L. Wiese offered valuable advice on organization and content. Geoffrey P. Raymond, CFA, reviewed the text and made valuable suggestions. Both were excellent directors of Henry Venture Funds for eighteen years. June Knaudt was vice president of Henry Venture Funds for sixteen years and kept the business running smoothly. Duffy Design Works created the book jacket, and Donna Raymond designed the color combination. We thank them all for their help. Any shortcomings in the text are ours alone.

Citations

[1] Another case study on a rapid failure, that was not included in this book because it dealt with information technology rather than bio-medicine, is Albert J. Henry and Glenn E. Bugos, "Sydis and the Voice/Data Terminal Craze of 1984," *IEEE Annals in the History of Computing* 26/2 (April-June 2004) pp. 22-33.

The **Good**

The four case studies that follow are dramatic success stories. IMED and IVAC became great medical instrument companies and revolutionized drug delivery by marrying the microprocessor with mechanical fluid flow technology to create the first electronic infusion pumps. As a result, total parenteral nutrition (TPN) and chemotherapy were invented because the infusion of drugs could be done accurately. These instruments spawned development of the eventual $20 billion intravenous (IV) solutions and drug related business, which did not exist before their invention.

IMED Corporation

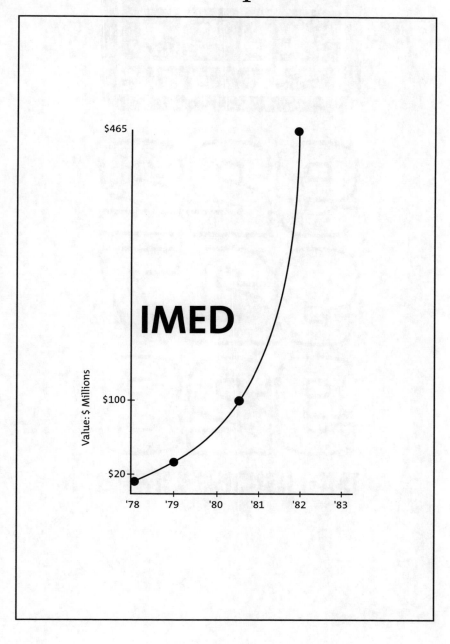

The following are pictures of the first three instruments invented by IMED, the 922, 927 and 928 electronic volumetric infusion pumps.

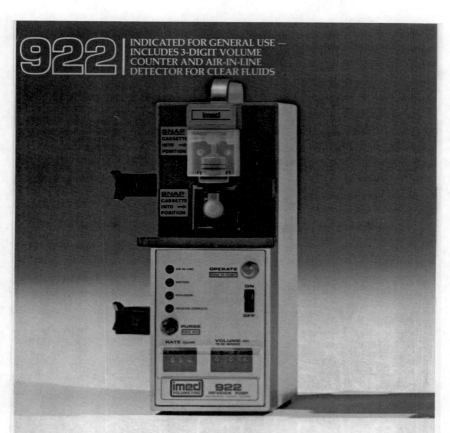

922 | INDICATED FOR GENERAL USE — INCLUDES 3-DIGIT VOLUME COUNTER AND AIR-IN-LINE DETECTOR FOR CLEAR FLUIDS

As the role of I.V. therapy in patient care becomes more complex, the need for simplicity, accuracy and safety are prominent in the criteria for infusion control. IMED Volumetric Infusion Pumps utilizing the sterile Accuset® disposable cassette provide that simplicity, accuracy and patient safety. The IMED Volumetric Principle allows a wide variety of I.V. fluids to be safely delivered at the rate and volume prescribed.

Imed Volumetric Infusion Pumps have numerous indications for controlled infusion: **total parenteral nutrition; enteral alimentation; intralipid fat emulsion; inter-arterial infusion; critical care fluid management; blood and blood products; pediatric fluid management during fluid restriction or during increased fluid requirement; continuous drug therapy; chemotherapy; oxytocic**

agents; regional heparinization; anti-arrythmic agents; closed wound irrigation; and a growing list involving both complex and simple solutions.

Once put in operation, Imed Infusion Pumps continue to deliver at the preset rate. Time required for repeated adjustment of "drop-rate" on conventional I.V.s and drop counters is eliminated. Easy to use, the Imed Volumetric Pumps are designed to save time, steps and worry during patient care and management of I.V. therapy.

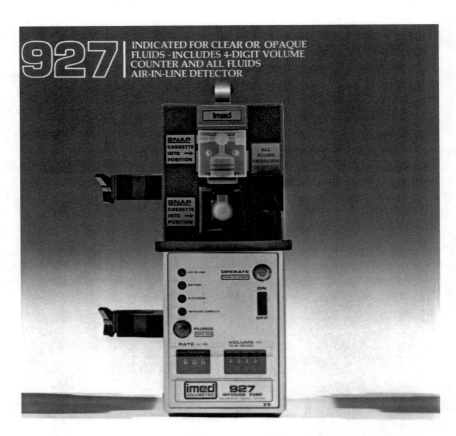

927

INDICATED FOR CLEAR OR OPAQUE FLUIDS – INCLUDES 4-DIGIT VOLUME COUNTER AND ALL FLUIDS AIR-IN-LINE DETECTOR

VOLUMETRIC ACCURACY The positive displacement principle of the unique Accuset® sterile disposable cassette used in the Imed Infusion Pumps insures that the patient receives a preset volume of I.V. fluid at a continuous and accurate rate. The stable construction of the Imed Accuset prevents expansion during the pumping cycle and assures accurate delivery. The Accuset® positive action valve virtually eliminates the possibility of "runaway" or "dumping" during I.V. administration. This unique valving system is designed to prevent a

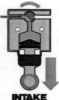

INTAKE

INFUSION

ACCUSET PRINCIPLE OF OPERATION

direct fluid pathway from the container to the patient — providing an added dimension of safety.

RATE (CC / HR) VOLUME (CC) TO BE INFUSED

CONTROLLED DELIVERY IN ML/HR The rate at which I.V. fluids are to be infused is simply dialed in ML/HR. No figuring or computation is necessary. The pumps will respond immediately to dialed-in rate changes.

The Accuset pictured below was a captive disposable to the IMED pumps. IMED recommended that every patient have at least one Accuset change per day for sterility reasons.

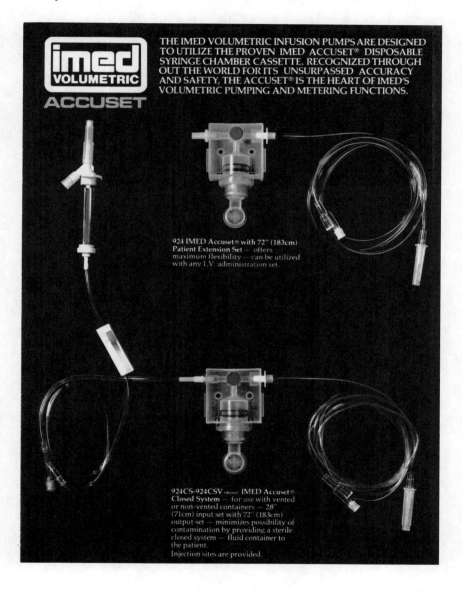

THE IMED VOLUMETRIC INFUSION PUMPS ARE DESIGNED TO UTILIZE THE PROVEN IMED ACCUSET® DISPOSABLE SYRINGE CHAMBER CASSETTE. RECOGNIZED THROUGH OUT THE WORLD FOR ITS UNSURPASSED ACCURACY AND SAFETY, THE ACCUSET® IS THE HEART OF IMED'S VOLUMETRIC PUMPING AND METERING FUNCTIONS.

924 IMED Accuset® with 72" (183cm) Patient Extension Set — offers maximum flexibility — can be utilized with any I.V. administration set.

924CS-924CSV (shown) IMED Accuset® Closed System — for use with vented or non-vented containers — 28" (71cm) input set with 72" (183cm) output set — minimizes possibility of contamination by providing a sterile closed system — fluid container to the patient. Injection sites are provided.

SPECIFICATIONS

WEIGHT — 12.6 lbs w/charger (5.7 kg)
DIMENSIONS — 7"x7"x14", (18cm x18cm x36cm)
POWER REQUIREMENTS — (Battery Charger)
  120 VAC/60HZ, 7 watts (max.)
TYPICAL BATTERY CAPACITY — 15 hrs at 299ml/hr
  25 hrs at 125ml/hr   30 hrs at 50ml/hr
OVERCURRENT PROTECTION — 5.0 ampere,
  SLO-BLO Fuse (Internal)
RATE RANGE — 0-299ml/hr, 1ml/hr increments
VOLUME TO BE INFUSED RANGE — 0-9999ml,
  1ml increments
AIR-IN-LINE DETECTION — Clear Fluids only
OUTPUT PRESSURE — 20 +5, -10 PSI
RECHARGE TIME — Battery Alarm to 80% charge,
  pump off — 24 hours Battery Alarm to 80% charge,
  pump operating at 125ml/hr — 30 hours
ALARMS — AIR-IN-LINE, OCCLUSION,
  INFUSION COMPLETE, LOW BATTERY
ELECTRICAL LEAKAGE — (Ungrounded with leads
  reversed) — Less than 10 micro-amperes

SPECIFICATIONS

Same as Model 922 except:
AIR-IN-LINE DETECTION — Clear or Opaque fluids

SPECIFICATIONS

Same as Model 922 except:
RATE RANGE — 0-799ml/hr, 1 ml/hr increments
AIR-IN-LINE DETECTION — Clear or Opaque
  Fluids

All models listed by The Canadian Standards
Association and The City of Los Angeles
Electrical Testing Laboratory

imed
VOLUMETRIC

IMED Corporation
9925 Carroll Canyon Rd.
San Diego, CA 92131 USA
Tel: 800/854-2033
In CA: 714/566-9000

IMED CANADA INC.
6535 Millcreek Dr.
Unit #11
Mississauga, Ontario L5N2M2
Tel: (416) 821-2212
TLX: 065-24578

IMED, LTD
57A Milton Trading Estate
Milton, Near Abingdon, Oxon
England OX14 4RX
Tel: (235) 83211
TLX: 837460

IMED GMBH
Gotenstrasse 57
D-6236
Eschborn/TS Germany
Tel: 06196-48718
TLX: 418-317 IMED-D

IMED S.A. GENEVA
4 Rue Du Mont-Blanc
1201 Geneva, Switzerland
Tel: (022) 32 69 38
TLX: 28 98 06 ADF CH

IMED SCANDANAVIA
Sandhamnsgatan 25
11528 Stockholm, Sweden
Tel: 60-31-20
TLX: 17996

EQUIPMENT POLE

The IMED 901 EQUIPMENT POLE has been designed
for use with IMED'S Volumetric Infusion Pumps and
Controllers, as well as related medical equipment.

At the top, the 901 accommodates two I.V. bottles or
bags. IMED'S exclusive "BOT-L-LOK"™ fixes the
neck of the I.V. bottles to prevent swinging and
possible breakage when the patient is ambulatory.
When not used to secure bottles, the "BOT-L-LOK"™
can be raised to function as a second cross arm for
hanging additional containers.

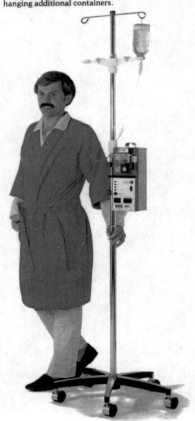

I MED offered a great new technology in 1975 — the first electronic, volumetric infusion pumps reliable and simple enough for hospital use. IMED had a good sales force which brought it to a level of $3 million in revenue by its third year. But the engineers running IMED lacked a sense of financial control. The company was out of cash, running steady losses on good sales, needed new manufacturing plant and equipment, and teetered on the brink of bankruptcy.

Five years after founding IMED, the company chairman finally convinced Al Henry, who had been a founding IMED shareholder, to leave his thriving Wall Street institutional research firm and take a much smaller salary as IMED's chief financial officer. He would bring venture capital and financial management to IMED. Five years after arriving, IMED was acquired at the highest price ever paid for a private firm in U.S. business history. Henry's institutional investors had put $4 million into IMED and earned back $44 million. How was it done?

The IVAC Proxy Fight

IMED's roots were in another company that had pioneered infusion technology. IVAC was founded in 1968 and led by a group of engineers headed by Richard A. Cramer, formerly chief engineer of the Sharp Laboratory Division of Beckman Instruments. From their headquarters in San Diego, the IVAC engineers hoped to apply revolutionary advances from California's microprocessor industry to new medical devices. IVAC made headlines in 1969 by introducing the electronic thermometer, which displayed temperatures accurately and unambiguously. A year later, they introduced one of the first peristaltic infusion pumps and a controller that counted drops through an IV tube. For three years in a row, Cramer was able to hire the top salesmen of Baxter Travenol, luring them with great stock and salary packages, large expense accounts, and the chance to sell products that were innovative and well-designed.

IVAC was led by engineers of imagination and skill, but with no expertise in business and finance. For example, IVAC had accidentally gone public. Under SEC Regulation A (since superseded) if a company exceeded a certain number of shareholders then the SEC considered it publicly-traded. In San Diego's untamed securities market, several IVAC shareholders had traded unregistered shares privately and IVAC unknowingly went public.

Significantly, IVAC chairman Cramer never took his financial forecasts seriously enough. So that IVAC had funds to grow its business, in 1970 Cramer completed an equity placement of $5.5 million with a New York-based investment banker, R.W. Pressprich & Co. Cramer concluded the placement on the basis of forecasted revenues of $30 million and pretax profits of $6 million. By year end 1971, however, IVAC had fallen far short of these estimates, reporting only $6.5 million in sales and a loss of $353,000.[1]

IVAC stock plummeted in the market and, ultimately, lost eighty percent of its value. Kenneth G. Langone, the president of Pressprich fomented a movement to oust Cramer, but Cramer won the first round. In February 1972, Cramer announced the resignation of two directors and three senior officers who had sided against him.[2] A week later, IVAC filed suit in U.S. district court against the dissident directors and Langone. The suit charged them with a conspiracy that "disparaged, unfairly" IVAC's top management and misrepresented IVAC's financial position, all in an attempt to drive down IVAC stock price so they could buy it cheaply and seize control.[3]

Langone responded to the mudslinging by launching a proxy fight, charging that Cramer certainly ran a spendthrift organization and probably misused corporate funds to inflate sales. Roughly sixty percent of IVAC's outstanding common stock was owned by major institutions, including banks, mutual funds, and pension fund money managers. At the regular IVAC annual meeting in May 1972, Langone reported that he voted 3 million IVAC shares while Cramer voted only 2.8 million. By a 3-2 vote of the new board, Langone replaced Cramer as IVAC chairman. Langone terminated Cramer and his supporters immediately.[4]

Langone returned to IVAC the corporate officers whom Cramer had fired, consolidated IVAC research and marketing efforts around the electronic thermometer and peristaltic infusion pump, and negotiated IVAC's acquisition by Eli Lilly & Co.

Bloodied but unbowed, Cramer and his associates founded IMED Corporation in 1972 largely with promissory notes secured by their personal savings. Yet IMED never fully escaped its history with IVAC. Cramer continued to have difficulty raising outside capital, haunted by his inaccurate forecasts and the disastrous proxy fight. However, the IMED engineers clearly understood the limits of the IVAC technology that they had helped create, and had already envisioned the next generation of infusion device. Like many first round venture firms, the new IMED focused on making and selling a technically-sweet product: the world's first volumetric infusion pump for use in hospitals.

The Volumetric Principle

In the early 1970s, physicians had two ways of getting drugs into the body — orally or injected. Drugs formulated into pills and syrups entered the body enterally. Drugs formulated as solutions were injected into the body in precise doses through a syringe and needle. Intravenous infusions were emerging as a third way of getting drugs into a body.

Intravenous infusion already worked fine for simple solutions — like the sterile water and glucose solution needed to keep a patient hydrated and from slipping into shock — but it was far too imprecise for the administration of drugs. Highly-trained teams of IV nurses monitored the infusions. They suspended the solutions bag on the pole, kept the connections sterile, eliminated air from the tube, placed the catheter in an appropriate vein, then started the drip. To regulate the flow rate, they placed a roller clamp on the tube coming from the bag, and tightened it by thumb so that the right number of drops fell against the second hand of a watch. Because the tube, made from polyvinyl chloride, had a memory and expanded back against the clamp, the nurse had to check the drip rate repeatedly. Errors in drip rate, however, were seldom fatal.

The IVAC system relieved the nurses of their constant monitoring of the drip. The IVAC controller had a photo-electric eye that counted drops from the bag and automatically adjusted a clamp to maintain the correct drip rate. Then the IVAC pump used a peristaltic motion — a row of fingers or a rotor mechanism driven by a motor — to massage solution through the tube at a measured rate. The IVAC system reduced the margin of error in the drop rate to ±2 percent. However, the error in the total volume infused hovered around ±20 percent, still far too high for infusion of more complex solutions.

IVAC's technology was sound; it counted the drops accurately. But its approach was flawed; the size of drops varied greatly. Adding chemicals changes the viscosity of a solution, altering the surface tension on the molecules and thus affecting the volume of each drop. Temperatures,

head height and flow rates also affected drop sizes. The drug streptoki-
nase, for example, contained flocculant fibers that increased drop sizes
up to fifty percent over the course of the infusion.

IMED's approach, therefore, was to count not the number of drops,
but the volume of fluid directly. In 1974 IMED introduced its first volumetric infusion pump, the Model 922. At the center of the pump was the
proprietary Accuset cassette, a disposable chamber much like a traditional syringe of fixed volume and made from sterile, medical-grade
plastics. Solution flowed from the bag into the chamber. Then a direct
drive motor flipped the chamber over at a constant, programmable rate.
This temporarily closed the connection back to the bag while a piston
expressed the solution down another tube and into the vein. By measuring
the fluid directly, the IMED pump reduced the total margin of error to
less than ±2 percent.

To this positive displacement approach, IMED added electromechanical controls to help IV nurses assure the efficiency and safety of the infusion. An "air in line" alarm warned nurses of embolisms; an occlusion
alarm sensed back pressures and warned nurses of catheters placed in
muscle tissue rather than veins or if a patient rolled over and crimped a
tube. Nurses used a thumbwheel to set the total volume to be infused,
and set the flow rate from one cubic centimeter (cc) to 299cc per hour.
Since prescriptions were written in volumetric measurements, nurses no
longer had to convert them to drop rates. When the infusion was complete, another alarm signalled and the pump automatically switched to a
very low flow rate, just enough to keep the line open. The pump ran for
25 hours on battery power and attached to a special IMED equipment
pole so it could be used as patients were ambulatory. The Model 922 was
reliable enough for regular use anywhere in a hospital and, because it was
made of seven distinct subassemblies, it was simple to service on-site.

In 1975, IMED introduced new pumps that detected air embolisms in
opaque fluids where they were not easily seen (IMED Model 927), or had
very high flow rates for wound irrigation (up to 799cc per hour on the
IMED Model 928). In 1976, IMED introduced its Model 929 "computer
pump" with circuitry that allowed an intensive care computer to automatically monitor and adjust the infusion rate. Cramer's forte was in see-
ing hospital infusions as a complete technological system. IMED's tech-

nology strategy, therefore, was to transfer to the pump the tasks that made infusions efficient and reliable.

Such precision and reliability opened up whole new fields of infusion therapy. Physicians could better control the level of drugs in the bloodstream over the course of the day. Pharmacists could formulate increasingly complex solutions for a variety of infusion therapies: antibiotics, anticoagulants, anesthetics, vasoactive drugs, blood products, oxytocic agents to induce labor, closed-wound irrigation, and morphine pain management. For patients with liver and kidney problems or congestive heart failure, the pumps allowed precisely measured fluid and electrolyte replacement.

Perhaps the most important new therapy was total parenteral nutrition (TPN), that is, feeding patients solely through the vein with a solution of electrolytes, amino acids, and trace elements. Only the positive pressure of a pump could push nutritional formulas and other viscous fluids through a decontamination filter and into the vein. Positive pressure also helped deliver chemotherapies that had to be infused into an artery, and enteral nutrition that had to pass through a nasogastric tube directly into the stomach. By creating a new way of delivering drugs to the body, the volumetric infusion pump was one of the most significant medical devices of the post-war period.

A Startup Venture Firm

Like many engineers in first stage venture firms, Cramer placed great stock in the power of salesmen to communicate the wonders of a new technology. When Cramer was forced from IVAC he persuaded his sales team to come with him. Promising even better stock and salary packages, larger expense accounts, and a superior product, Cramer continued to lure to IMED the leading salesmen from Abbott, American Hospital Supply Company, and Johnson & Johnson. IMED net sales grew rapidly, from $241,000 in 1973, to $655,000 in 1974, to $2.14 million in 1975, to $5.993 million in 1976, to $9.278 million in 1977.

IMED maintained a high level of investment in research and engineering, and held substantial patent protection on its pumps, cassettes and various alarms. IMED pumps proved very reliable in hospital use. Furthermore, IMED's competition emerged slowly. IVAC introduced a hurried response to the IMED volumetric pump in 1975, which it recalled soon afterward to solve persistent technical problems. IVAC reintroduced its pump in 1979, but it never overcame the stigma of the earlier recall. Abbott Laboratories also introduced a pump in 1975, that proved difficult to use, and sold mainly within smaller hospitals, Abbott's traditional market for its products. Baxter Laboratories and Valley Laboratories both announced they were designing pumps, but neither produced a marketable product until the Valleylabs pump appeared in 1978. For most of the decade, IMED held seventy percent of the market for volumetric pumps.

IMED made much smaller and more haphazard investments in manufacturing plant and equipment. IMED purchased seven basic parts for the pumps from vendors: circuit boards arrived fully stuffed, soldered and tested, and battery packs and direct current motors were bought off the shelf. At a small job shop in Scripps Industrial Park outside San Diego, IMED workers assembled the pumps, wired together the dials and circuits, calibrated them, and ran burn-in tests. Whenever problems arose, Boynton was good at building teams to solve them. Though IMED did a good job of manufacturing pumps, inventory levels fluctuated widely and unpredictably, routinely stressing its manufacturing capacity.

IMED's most pressing problem, however, was manufacture of the disposable cassettes. During IMED's start-up years, Marc Manufacturing, Inc. had performed all of IMED's injection molding on a contract basis. IMED then assembled them in a small clean room on-site, and contracted to sterilize them off-site. In 1976, IMED acquired Marc for $100,000 in IMED common stock and options to purchase 30,000 shares at $8.33. But as a division of IMED, Marc was still unable to invest in the molds and equipment needed to make enough plastic parts to extreme tolerances. IMED's scrap rate on the three molded plastic parts hovered around seventy percent.

Because of manufacturing inefficiencies and runaway sales expenses, even though IMED reported $6 million in sales for 1976 it also reported a loss of $110,000. The company was out of cash, surviving on infusions of personal cash from company officers, had no access to institutional capital on reasonable terms because of the discredit from the Cramer/IVAC proxy fight, had a net worth of only $125,000, and had trouble making payroll. It was a company on the brink of bankruptcy. As he had since IMED's founding, Cramer sought help from Al Henry.

A New CFO

Henry was then very successfully running his own Wall Street firm, Henry & Associates, to do securities research and corporate finance. He first learned of IVAC from Geoffrey Raymond, a former colleague at Citibank, just as IVAC introduced its new electronic thermometer. He contacted Cramer, visited San Diego several times, became a shareholder of IVAC, helped Cramer get some debt money, and placed with his clients about forty percent of the IVAC stock sold to institutional investors. Without taking sides during the 1972 IVAC proxy fight, Henry gave Cramer the chance to present his side of the story by arranging appointments with his institutional clients who owned IVAC stock. Cramer trusted Henry's advice, and when Cramer started IMED he asked Henry to serve as his chief financial officer, a request he repeated regularly over the next few years.

By 1978, Henry was ready to entertain Cramer's offer. His Wall Street business had done very well, and he was ready for a change. He considered the medical devices industry exciting, and IMED's product worth risking his career on. Cramer had kept the CFO position unfilled, even as finance became IMED's most pressing concern. He gave up his annual Wall Street income of $250,000 for just $42,000 salary and options on 85,250 (3.7 percent) shares of IMED stock. Later, he was given additional options. His job, above all others, was to raise venture capital and boost the total market value of those IMED shares as rapidly as possible.

Question 1

How would you find enough cash to keep IMED from going bankrupt? How would you characterize IMED as a company for financing purposes — seed, early stage, turn-around, or late stage. Why? What sources of financing would you identify to fit your characterization of company type? How much financing would you seek in debt, equity or both at this time? Explain your reasoning. Would you use an investment banker? Why or why not? What valuation do you seek for this financing and why? Describe your methodology for valuing IMED and why at this point in its life?

$1.1 Million for 3 percent Ownership

To survive IMED's cumulative loses, Cramer earlier had asked Paine Webber to help raise $2 million in equity financing. In early 1977, Paine Webber returned with commitments of $1.0 to $1.5 million in exchange for fifty to sixty percent of ownership on a total company valuation of $2.5 million. Henry, then still with his Wall Street firm, had persuaded Cramer to reject this financing. It would have diluted ownership by IMED management to about thirty percent, majority control would have passed to institutional investors, and they would have fired Cramer. As soon as he joined IMED as CFO, Henry had to find financing on better terms.

He had made some of his institutional investors a great deal of money during his Wall Street days. He wrote personal letters to twenty of his best clients, and asked them to support his new career by investing in IMED. The need for finance was acute, he explained. IMED's pump was establishing a hold on the market, receivables were growing, and he was turning his attention to cost controls. And IMED had just turned a profit. An explosion in sales between year end 1976 and 1977, from $5.9 million to $9.2 million, outpaced expenses growth so that IMED went from a $679,000 loss to $119,000 in net income. But none of his U.S. clients would invest with IMED's founding management in control. They still remembered Cramer's missed forecasts and the vicious proxy fight over IVAC.

Farther removed from the proxy fight, however, were two of Henry's former clients in the London institutional investment community, Lazard Brothers Limited, pension fund managers and merchant bankers, and Prudential Assurance, the largest insurance company in the United Kingdom. They trusted Henry enough to take a chance on IMED's "stiff stock," which they could not trade until the company went public or was sold. He convinced them that sales would grow thirty to sixty percent over 1978, to $12 million, and that IMED should be valued at twice those revenues. While IMED would make a profit on those revenues, it was still too young to base any valuation on a multiple of earnings. Henry charted the worth of other health devices companies to show that a valuation of two times revenues was fairly conservative. The London institutions made equity investments totalling $600,000, in exchange for three percent ownership, or a total company valuation of $20 million. This was remarkably better than what Paine Webber had arranged.

This infusion of equity doubled in importance because it was parlayed it into an accounts receivable line. As soon as he joined IMED, Henry had declared "open season" for banks. He invited proposals from Citibank, Bank of America, Security Pacific, Lloyds Bank of California and his own New York bank, Irving Trust. He got a range of rejections: one asked for personal guarantees, another said IMED was impossible to bank with its current operating losses. He asked Dave Hare, the head of Irving Trust's Los Angeles loan office to investigate the company from top to bottom. In spite of the primitive nature of IMED's accounting system, Irving decided that if IMED got an equity infusion of about $750,000 that Irving Trust would approve a $500,000 revolving credit line to finance accounts receivable. When the London investors injected their $600,000 in April 1978, Irving opened IMED's revolver.

Thus, by ten weeks after his arrival, Henry had raised $1.1 million dollars of fresh cash, had sacrificed only three percent ownership in the company, kept control in IMED management, had restructured its balance sheet, and started it on the road back from the brink. Henry had worked these deals quietly, and when the money hit IMED's bank account his reputation within IMED skyrocketed. He could now set about convincing his IMED colleagues that hard won cash should be closely kept.

Question 2
_____

What operational functions are needed in a small company with a new product? What controls does this company need to ensure reliable operating performance? How would you rate IMED's operating controls?

A Second Stage Venture Investment

Henry knew he had joined a company with a great market, a great product, and a great sales staff, but virtually no managerial controls. IMED compiled no monthly or annual budgets by which to measure its current results or projected performance. It measured success by the number of instruments sold. IMED watched its shipment tallies week by agonizing week, unaware that every increase in shipments resulted in a corresponding increase in costs. The IVAC experience taught Cramer that if he made a good product and spent as much as he could on sales, profits would take care of themselves. Cramer, like most first stage venture managers, had encouraged such a top line mentality.

IMED had almost no way of knowing its bottom line. It had no internal accounting system to indicate the cost of manufacturing the instrument or plastic chamber. It had no responsible financial officers: an accounting manager presided over a small staff of clerks whose principal task was preparing tax documents. IMED operated on a cash disbursement basis. Bills were paid only when vendors and suppliers screamed for their money. IMED only discovered the extent of its losses at year end when Arthur Young did its audit. IMED then made any necessary adjustments to inventory, receivables and other items.

IMED badly needed new tools for plastic molded parts and a new, expanded clean room for assembly of the disposable cassette. Yet capital expenditures were virtually impossible, because nobody knew whether cash would be available. Expense dollars, on the other hand, were easy to find. Cramer had given forty people authority to spend up to $5,000, and unilaterally decided all higher spending. Allowing his salesmen and engineers to spend, Cramer reasoned, built the loyalty he had lacked at IVAC. Similarly, Cramer eschewed organization charts, reasoning that rankings sowed the seed of dissent. Cramer thought it was his company, and resisted any efforts at financial or managerial discipline.

As soon as he arrived, Henry teamed with Dan R. Hendrickson, a CPA who had joined IMED in 1976. Hendrickson knew how money flowed through IMED and had solved a financial crisis in IMED's European operations. IMED promoted Hendrickson to treasurer, and they worked to tighten internal operations in all areas — sales and marketing, production and finance.

Henry and Hendrickson started with IMED's purchasing policy. Turnaround specialists often make the company burn rate their top priority, because cash reserves give them time to maneuver. They limited the number of people authorized to spend $5,000 from forty people to two — Henry and Cramer. Cramer continued to make off-line financial commitments for the company, and they only got him to show restraint by calculating how each expenditure affected IMED's bottom line, and thus Cramer's personal net worth. The strategy for restricting spending was to intentionally become a bottleneck for purchase orders. He would wait until somebody screamed and demanded that a purchase order be approved. If he heard no screaming within four weeks, he put the purchase order in the garbage. This strategy effectively conserved cash.

Henry and Hendrickson also closed the books at the end of each month (they had previously been left open). As they centralized all of IMED's record-keeping, they made the month the unit of time measurement within the company.

They devised a monthly forecasting system to temper Cramer's proclivity to promise too much to shareholders. The sales staff lived with unrealistic quotas, so they built up their own figures based on the number of hospitals a salesman could call on, the number of the beds in these hospitals, and an average chance for a sale. They devised max-min ranges that were constantly honed as the forecasting methodology became more exact.

Henry and Hendrickson then devised a cash flow forecasting system. They started with six month projections, and gradually refined them to monthly projections as the forecasts got more realistic. For psychological impact they always began with worst case scenarios, one of which clearly showed that at IMED's current rate of expenditure Cramer would have to lay off people or miss payroll. Cramer wanted to fire Henry two months after hiring him because the forecasts were used to suggest restraints on operations, which Cramer disliked. But Boynton, EVP of Operations and Cramer's close friend, convinced Cramer that Henry's cash flow analysis helped him plan inventory levels and control overhead costs. As Cramer became educated about the rudiments of cash flow analysis, Cramer and Boynton came to rely on his judgment about how much money the company had left.

Henry's importance within IMED became more obvious during the summer 1978 road show, when potential investors asked financial questions only he could answer. As his stature within the company grew, an executive committee was arranged to manage IMED. The committee reflected a good and genial division of interests — Henry spoke for finance, Boynton for manufacturing, and Cramer for engineering. All three decided issues of expansion and operations, but Henry had theoretical veto power over any decision that required a commitment of cash.

Though investors at the time often asked why IMED's CFO was not on its board, Cramer resisted appointing Henry an IMED director until

1980. After the IVAC fight, Cramer allowed only his personal friends on the IMED board: Boynton, Kevin P. Monaghan and John G. Davies partners in Cramer's long-time law firm, and real estate investor Christopher D. "Kit" Sickels was a friend who had lent money to IMED.

Redirecting Sales

With cost controls in place and its financial situation stabilized, IMED redirected its sales effort, improved its production efficiencies, and introduced new products. Finance never messed with IMED's engineering department so long as it kept to its budget, usually six to seven percent of net sales. In 1978 IMED had a staff of 25 full time engineers and technicians, and extensive relationships with consultants. IMED's three main inventors — Oscar Hyman, Larry Wilson and Clint Decker — often visited San Diego hospitals for insight on how to improve their pumps. IMED held thirty fundamental patents on infusion devices, then pursued a strategy of obsolescing its own devices. The IMED R&D effort was excellent.

IMED made a major leap forward in 1978 with its second generation of pumps, the Model 960. On the face of the 960 was a liquid crystal display that showed operating status, alarms, and a running total of the volume already infused. The more streamlined plastic case better resisted spills and bumps. An internal circuit indicated which parts of the pump might be malfunctioning. And the 960 used the same C924 Accuset disposable cassette as IMED's previous pumps.

Soon afterwards, IMED introduced its Model 965 Micro, based on the liquid crystal technology of the 960 but optimized for very precise, low rate infusions. With settings at 0.1 milliliter increments — ten times more precise than other pumps — the 965 Micro made infusions practical on neonatal, intensive care, obstetrical, oncology and anesthesiology floors. It used a proprietary C964 Microset plastic cassette that came in a variety of administration sets with microbore tubing. Trade periodicals praised IMED pumps when the 965 proved accurate enough for intravenous feeding of premature babies, and today IMED pumps are found in most neonatal wards.

With this new series of pumps, IMED consolidated its position on the cutting edge of infusion technology and doubled the average revenues per pump. Even though IMED had successfully boosted its

average prices on its mainstay Model 922 at ten percent a year, it sold at
only $759 per pump in 1979. IMED introduced the Model 960 with an
average price of $1,369, and successfully boosted that price ten percent
each year. Between 1978 and 1980, therefore, IMED boosted its total
revenues per pump by seventy percent, from an average $728 to $1029
per pump. Furthermore, IMED extended the product life cycle of its
C924 cassettes.

Concurrent with the introduction of new technology and the stabi-
lization of its finances, IMED redirected its sales. From a shotgun strategy of hitting every hospital and looking for the quick sales, IMED
focused on the major American teaching hospitals. Selling the big hospitals took cash: IMED's best salesmen had to camp out in the hospitals
while committees pondered purchases. Total sales might drop in the
short term, but if IMED cracked a major teaching hospital it would gain
tremendous credibility with other hospitals. IMED salesmen visited
every unit that might use infusion therapy, and sold the nurses and pharmacists as fervently as they sold the physicians.

Hospital pharmacists always formulated infusion solutions, and usually evaluated medical devices before purchase. Though few nurses had
purchasing authority within a hospital, they also had to be convinced of
the pumps' reliability and value. IMED salespeople appeared at nursing
conferences, especially those of the National Intravenous Therapy
Association which established standards of practice and training for specialized IV nursing teams. Focus groups were an expensive way to do
marketing research, yet IMED sponsored them to gain insight into nurses "wish lists" for a pump. Salesmen would place ten trial pumps on a
floor, stay near them in order to show nurses how efficient they were,
and be available 24 hours a day for in-servicing. Once IMED sold to a
hospital, the salesman stayed until each nurse was trained, since the
unwillingness of nurses to be retrained was the best guarantee against
penetration by competing pump companies.

This strategy paid off with an order for one hundred pumps from the
Johns Hopkins University Hospital, a leading teaching hospital, a pioneer in infusion therapies, and home to a renowned group of specially
skilled IV nurses. The $300,000 order was big for IMED. More important,
it validated IMED's technology and sales strategy. Houston Medical

Center, M.D. Anderson was the next big teaching hospital to buy IMED pumps, and would eventually install more than a thousand IMED pumps in a variety of wards. By 1981, 74 percent of IMED sales were to larger hospitals with 400 beds or more, a market IMED dominated.

To expand its sales outside the United States, in 1975 IMED started negotiations to acquire Tekmar, S.A., a Swiss company which had developed a sales force throughout Europe, the largest single hospital product market in the world. (In Canada, IMED pumps were distributed by a subsidiary of Cutter Laboratories, Inc. a leader in filters and other infusion supplies. Tokibo Co., Ltd. was IMED's exclusive distributor in Japan.)

IMED's Tekmar deal closed in July 1976, after Cramer paid $300,000 cash for 148,929 shares of IMED stock from one of Tekmar's principal shareholders. Jeffrey Frampton, Tekmar's other principal shareholder, remained as president of IMED's Tekmar subsidiary. Tekmar owned a small manufacturing plant in Milton, England, a service center in Germany, and a sales and engineering group in Switzerland. European hospitals had moved rapidly to adopt peristaltic infusion pumps, and Tekmar expanded rapidly. But Tekmar's peristaltic pumps faced serious competition from IVAC Corp. and Valley Laboratories (around the world), Braun A.G. (especially in West Germany), and Vial et Cie (especially in France).

IMED fairly easily converted the Milton plant to manufacturing volumetric pumps, but the rest of the Tekmar organization only slowly broke free from its focus on the original peristaltic pumps. Expenses mounted as Tekmar installed pumps in hospitals. In April 1977, IMED assumed a long term note for $1.15 million payable to Tekmar's Swiss bank, largely to finance Swiss operations. In December 1977, IMED received a telex from Frampton, stating that because of accumulating debt Tekmar would soon be declared insolvent under Swiss law. IMED renounced a debt of $1.8 million owed it by Tekmar, Frampton was dismissed in January 1978, and Douglas Rumberger relocated from San Diego to Geneva to continue IMED's European operations under the existing corporate structure. The subsidiary was renamed IMED S.A. Geneva, brought its operations under control, and set up a sales force in every major country. By end of fiscal 1978, ten percent of IMED sales were outside the U.S. though they contributed very little to corporate earnings.

At the same time IMED redirected their sales effort, it loosened its distributorship arrangement with the McGaw Laboratories Division of American Hospital Supply Corporation (AHS), the nation's largest distributor of hospital equipment and supplies. In the solutions industry, though, McGaw's ten percent share compared badly with Baxter and Abbott's forty percent shares. McGaw's catalog of hospital supplies included a range of infusion solutions and the Accumed collapsible IV bottle system, which worked well with IMED pumps. Soon after the introduction of IMED's first series of pumps, in 1975, IMED signed an OEM agreement (original equipment manufacture means that one company makes a product that another sells under its brand name) that made American Hospital its sole national distributor. A year later, IMED licensed American Hospital to manufacture the plastic cassettes for the IMED pumps, though it never did.

Both companies benefited because a major supplier of pharmaceutical solutions was offering a revolutionary new infusion technology. Though the pumps were sold under McGaw's name, the nameplate clearly stated "Manufactured by the IMED Corporation." IMED's credibility and market penetration soared through its ties with American Hospital. The arrangement was non-exclusive, meaning both companies could sell the same hospitals, and American Hospital had to buy a minimum monthly quota of pumps. By 1978, one-third of IMED sales were to American Hospital. Pleased with the relationship, in June 1978 American Hospital chairman Karl Bays authorized a major $1 million equity investment in IMED series C preferred stock convertible into common stock for five years. At a Chicago meeting with AHS top management and its investment bankers, IMED achieved attractive terms for the AHS investment. The AHS investment represented an important infusion of capital for IMED, and at an attractive total company valuation of $36 million. IMED's initial London institutional investors, in only nine months, made a 65 percent per share paper profit on their investment.

Question 3

Is the $1 million investment significant to IMED at this time? Why?

Gradually, the power relationship between the two companies shifted. Though American Hospital was much bigger, its salespeople represented more than 500 products, only one of which was electromechanical. Because the IMED sales force specialized in the pumps and had more flexibility in lowering prices, they proved more successful in selling the same hospitals once American Hospital made an initial call. Over time, American Hospital failed to purchase its monthly quota of pumps. In January 1979, IMED terminated the agreement, kept the equity place-ment, and continued building its direct sales force and dealer network.

In addition to the eighteen IMED "commandos" — its professional direct sales force — IMED built a network of 27 independent dealers. A characteristic of the medical devices industry then was that certain instrument dealers "owned" certain regional hospitals. Even though the dealers demanded discounts of up to 25 percent, if IMED could place its pumps in these dealers' lines then chances were good that these dealers would place some pumps in their hospitals. So while IMED salespeople focused on key accounts, its expanding networks of dealers tried to place pumps in hospitals of any size, and any place. From 1975 to 1981, sales split evenly between dealers and direct salesmen.

In 1980 IMED asked dealers to submit formal financial statements. By 1981, IMED learned that some of its dealers were suffering under rising interest rates. Since receivables from dealers proved only as good as their inherent financial condition, IMED tightened the financial requirements on the dealers and weeded out the weaker ones (see Exhibit #3, page 41). The transition from dealers to a larger direct sales force was gradual and well-planned but still depressed revenues about five percent in 1981. Between 1978 and 1981, IMED direct sales force grew from 18 to 48 very well-paid people. (IMED's top salesman earned $130,000 in 1981.)

To meet this growing demand without driving up costs, IMED shift-ed its focus to improving production. By 1978, IMED had leased eight buildings on Carroll Canyon Road north of San Diego of 110,000 square feet. The clean room occupied 40,000 square feet of this space, though IMED still lacked sterilization facilities. To bring this sterilization work in-house, IMED planned to acquire five acres of industrial land in San Diego, construct a 50,000 square foot building for a sterilization facility, and add tooling for manufacture and assembly. The total cost of expan-sion would be $1.75 million. To raise money for this expansion, which was still in the outline stage, IMED attempted to go public. Revenues were growing, the market continued to expand, its finances were well under control. The time looked propitious.

Does IMED qualify for an initial public offering (IPO) at this time? Why or why not? What issues does a seasoned manager assess when considering an IPO? What operating financial ratios are most important to the IPO process and why? Give a discussion of each ratio you deem important. If yes to an IPO, then what?

Red-Herring IPO

Cramer and Henry approached a number of underwriters, but chose Blyth Eastman Dillon & Co. Incorporated as its lead underwriter. Blyth had a solid institutional presence, connections with many individual investors of high net worth, and a prominent health care analyst named Fred Prunier. Blyth wanted to do the offering alone, but Henry picked Montgomery Securities as co-manager. Montgomery was a strong regional house, with New York institutional clients, and a prominent health care analyst named Bob Friedman.

In October 1978, Cramer and Henry did their road shows — New York, Boston, Chicago, Los Angeles, and San Francisco. They were well-received. High technology stocks were then riding high and, since IVAC had gone private, IMED would be the only publicly-traded company in the booming infusion devices industry. By mid-November, IMED was ready to go effective with the offering.

But Blyth seemed to be stalling, and IMED wanted to understand why. IMED encouraged its regional dealers and sales people to call local Blyth offices and ask, surreptitiously, when the IMED deal was scheduled on their calendar. To their amazement, they discovered that Blyth had not scheduled the IMED offering.

The Dow had dropped from 950 to 850 in early December 1978, and Blyth claimed they were holding back the deal for a better market. IMED believed, however, that Blyth was maneuvering for IMED to go public at a lower price than their filing range of $15 to $17 per share. IMED had calculated a valuation of $30 million using IMED forecasted earnings per share of $0.80 for 1979, which equated to $1,725,000 in after-tax earnings, up from only $118,000 the year before. IMED's P/E (price to earnings ratio) was twenty times its 1979 estimated earnings. Furthermore, IMED planned to keep some earnings in reserve so they could report earnings per share about fifteen percent higher than forecast. IMED had negotiated this offering price aggressively, and would not budge.

IMED argued that they were significantly ahead of projections, which would offset any general weakening in the market. Other companies were going public; there was no general terror in the market. After two weeks of negotiating, Blyth finally announced IMED could go public around 15 December 1978. Cramer and Henry went back to New York for visits with the growth fund managers at Morgan Guaranty, Banker's Trust and Chase, all former clients of his. Each institution made commitments for ten percent of the offering.

The next day, Cramer and Henry met with Blyth for one final pricing discussion. Blyth again tried to get IMED to accept a lower price. Blyth showed IMED its list of orders and prices, and polled its major offices nationwide on the squawk box. Blyth then recommended IMED go public at $12 per share, a 25 percent discount on the negotiated price and a valuation of $25 million based on data then nine months old. Henry had expected this. The night before, Henry had convinced Cramer that IMED could raise more equity privately. He and Cramer rose, shook hands with the Blyth staff, and left. Cramer had even rehearsed his parting: "Gentlemen," he said, "we are leaving the Big Apple to return to California and tend to our oranges." The Blyth staff were so shocked that Cramer and Henry would walk away from $5 million, that they followed them all the way to the elevator.

This was an important turning point in IMED's history. The funding would have kept IMED going for three years, though the depressed valuation would have diluted management's stock by about twenty percent. By walking away, IMED management kept the flexibility to manage their company.

Hard work was required to make sure private financing occurred after IMED said it could do better with another private placement. None of the U.S. institutions that had placed orders for the Blyth offering were now willing to invest in an IMED private placement. Officially they claimed they could not buy stocks in private companies. However, given

Cramer's reputation, they probably assumed that Blyth had uncovered something terribly wrong with IMED, which caused them to withdraw the deal.

Once again, Henry found interest amongst his institutional clients in London — Lazard Brothers and Prudential were joined by Sun Alliance, the third largest British insurance company. These institutions privately bought $1.5 million of common stock at $16 a share net to IMED, well within IMED's negotiated offering price range of $15 to $17 per share. In conjunction with steady growth in IMED's accounts receivable line, IMED now had sufficient capital to grow through 1979, and tighten its manufacturing operations. This investment would eventually show a return of 10 times or 1000 percent in three years.

Question 5

IMED walked away from its IPO. What major factors should be evaluated in the question of whether or not to crater an IPO?

Restructuring Manufacturing

When IMED first started selling pumps, it had trouble financing a logical expansion in its manufacturing capability. Plastics manufacturing, however, remained the biggest problem. To bring its seventy percent scrap rate under control, IMED commissioned expensive new multi-cavity molds, bought new Kawaguchi molding machines, and restructured IMED injection molding operations. But the cassettes continued to leak, so Robert Reiss, an expert in plastics manufacture with training from the General Motors Institute, was recruited. Reiss gradually rose to IMED president of manufacturing. Reiss in turn recruited a new generation of manufacturing experts, and brought sophistication to IMED manufacturing.

Infusion pumps fell under FDA Class II regulations for non-life supporting devices. IMED filed a form 510(k) — a disclosure form stating the pump was similar enough to existing devices that it did not need special tests — so the Food and Drug Administration could clear it quickly for sale. Because the FDA could inspect IMED's plant for adherence to good manufacturing practices, it was logical for IMED to expand its regulatory affairs program to include a quality control function. This regulatory affairs/quality control group was led by a pharmacist and reported directly to Reiss. It implemented test methods, sampling protocols, and quality specifications to assure that IMED machines always met the relevant federal standards.

Reiss also built an industrial engineering group to coordinate production and gauge efficiency against a set of learning curves. IMED invested in a $1.5 million Honeywell DPS 8/20 mainframe computer to track each part as a quality and inventory item. Within two years, IMED improved its inventory turns from 2.1 to 3.1, and forecast even higher turns. IMED's scrap rate dropped to less than three percent due to changes instituted by Reiss. As a result of improved manufacturing, in fiscal 1981 gross profit margin jumped four percentage points to sixty percent.

Disposables accounted for a steady two-thirds of IMED sales, which IMED protected strenuously. IMED's new experts in plastic molding devised a system of proprietary divots on the plastic cassettes. Hospital supply companies like Abbott and Baxter-Travenol, which sold IV solutions for use in IMED pumps, also tried to sell the disposable plastic tubing that the nurse had to change with every new infusion. Soon after they began selling a copy of the plastic cassettes. Abbott salesmen showed up at a hospital offering the cheaper cassette that they said would snap right into the IMED pump, only to find that IMED had changed the divots so only its cassettes would fit. Abbott abandoned their efforts after wasting $50,000 each on a series of useless molds of the plastic cassettes. However, in 1980, Baxter Travenol succeeded in making and selling an exact duplicate of the IMED plastic cassette. IMED brought suit alleging patent infringement and unfair competition, and Baxter Travenol countersued. IMED limited Baxter Travenol's penetration to three percent of the market, before they settled the suit in 1983.

IMED also built a new plant in Letterkenny, Ireland for manufacturing plastic cassettes for its overseas markets. IMED's financial group surveyed countries all over the world, but none beat the reliability of Irish workmanship and the receptiveness of the Irish government. The manager of a Baxter Travenol plant on Ireland's west coast considered his plant there the finest in the whole company. IMED negotiated the highest possible grant from the Irish Industrial Development Authority, which paid sixty percent of the total plant cost of $10 million. IMED also negotiated a term loan from Irish banks for an additional thirty percent of the plant cost, so that IMED put up only ten percent of the equity. IMED got a twenty year tax holiday on any earnings. Bob Renfroe, IMED general manager, built the plant on time and under budget. The plant was small when it opened in 1982, but it was completely integrated, including a cutting-edge nuclear sterilization facility to sterilize the finished products. The plant had tremendous long-term growth potential.

Question 6

What are the major determinants of value in any company? Name and discuss five or six major determinants of value in any company.

Boosting Total Market Value

IMED was moving further back from the brink. Throughout 1980, Irving Trust helped IMED to push some of its debt below the line, by restructuring some of its accounts receivable revolver as long-term debt. The debt agreement had covenants that would kick in if IMED's financial ratios worsened, so IMED monitored their ratios closely, though they were already among the best in the health devices industry (Exhibit #4, page 42).

IMED continued to tighten their controls on expenses. In 1979, IMED had divided all IMED operations into 67 chart-of-account departments. In these departments, IMED captured costs, did expense forecasts, and measured each company activity against a budgeted number. Each department head carefully prepared these budgets, and Henry and Hendrickson reviewed them carefully. Dave Hare, IMED's banker at Irving Trust, said it was the best internal reporting system he had ever seen in a company of IMED's size. These cost controls continued to pay off. IMED earned $800,000 dollars in the December 1979 quarter alone, on $6 million in sales.

IMED also improved its manufacturing statistics. Forecasting production and inventories of disposables was especially problematic. Because nurses were more likely to use machines they were familiar with, machines installed earlier consumed more disposables than newer pumps. Each pump consumed disposables at different rates: the nurse had to change the disposables at least every 24 hours, to maintain sterility, but sometimes changed them after infusing each bag. IMED devised several regression equations to forecast the geometric progression of disposable usage given the number of pumps placed in hospitals. As a result, its forecasts became more dependable.

Despite improved financial controls and strong market position, IMED still needed capital. In November 1979, IMED closed its first formal institutional private placement, using F. Eberstadt & Co., Inc. as its investment banker. IMED raised $3 million at a price of $23 per share — more than double the price of shares placed at $10.66 in March 1978.

In preparing for the Eberstadt placement, IMED had prepared some four year forecasts of operational performance. IMED worked hard to make these forecasts accurate, since they would be released widely to the institutional investment community.

IMED exceeded these projections for each of the next four years, and then exceeded each quarterly projection given to IMED shareholders and investment bankers. IMED beat its quarterly forecast of revenues and earnings for nineteen consecutive quarters from 1978 to 1982. IMED's forecasting prowess earned it the confidence of institutional shareholders and rejuvenated the reputation of IMED management. "Beating forecast," said Henry, "is vital to maintaining P/E ratios and equity values."

Healthy competition among bankers is another way to maximize equity values. IMED completed another limited private placement in August 1980, co-managed by Eberstadt and Lehman Brothers Kuhn Loeb, Incorporated. IMED raised $20 million, at $50 per share, at a total company valuation of $140 million. It was a solid valuation: for the previous twelve months IMED had reported $30 million in revenue and $4.5 million in after-tax earnings. Irving Trust had boosted IMED's line of credit to $18 million. Eberstadt initially resisted the valuation, but Lehman Brothers agreed to it, so Eberstadt was forced to go along or be displaced as IMED's lead investment banker.

The alliance with Lehman Brothers, a premier Wall Street firm, further raised IMED's stature. Henry developed a fine working relationship with Frederick Frank, then Lehman Brother's senior managing director of health care mergers and acquisitions, and one of the most prominent investment bankers in the health care field. (Over the next twenty years, Frank became Vice Chairman of Lehman Bros. and remained the most influential and effective health care investment banker on Wall Street. He later financed or sold six health care companies from the Henry Venture Funds.)

A Market Share Strategy

IMED introduced a new product in early 1981 — the Model 350 controller and associated Accudot set. The Accudot was a disposable, dial-controlled insert clamp that regulated the drop rate of gravity-fed solutions. The 350 was a gravity controller that counted drops through a photoelectric eye and automatically adjusted a clamp to maintain a precise flow rate. Nurses could use the Model 350 and Accudot together to double the reliability of the drop rate. Since the Model 350 and Accudot measured flow in drops, IMED researchers devised a flow rate chart to help nurses convert drops per minute into milliliters per hour at various fluid viscosities.[6]

IMED engineers, however, considered the Model 350 and Accudot a step backwards. They had introduced the first gravity controllers in 1971 when working at the IVAC company. IVAC updated the gravity controller in 1974 with more modern electronics, and quickly monopolized the controller market. IMED had thought its volumetric pumps would quickly render IVAC's controllers obsolete. By 1981, IVAC had placed over 50,000 units into hospitals, and the controller market appeared to be growing.

IMED's volumetric pumps, in some situations, required close monitoring because they applied positive pressure. Older gravity feed technology was safer for chronic infusions, which weaken blood vessels, or for infusing newborns who might die if a catheter slipped into body tissue and the pump alarm failed to detect the slighter back pressure. In addition, IMED estimated that one in five of all infusions were for simple solutions routine enough to be done without the more expensive pumps. The Model 350 and Accudot were cheaper, and suited for use on non-critical hospital wards. IVAC was vulnerable because it placed controllers on a "use basis," whereby a hospital used the controller for free but agreed to purchase a monthly supply of disposable sets that were not proprietary to IVAC. IMED's Accudot set worked well with the IVAC controller, and IMED expected that once hospitals started buying the Accudot sets they would switch to the IMED 350 controller. Accudot sales reached $183,670 for seven percent of IMED revenues in 1981, and IMED forecast annualized sales over $20 million by end of fiscal 1982.

Thus, the Model 350 and Accudot filled a void in IMED's line and offered a chance to quickly boost its share statistics in the total infusion devices market, which was growing exponentially. With a wider array of equipment, IMED began selling an Infusion System Program (ISP) to supply the entire infusion devices needs of a hospital. ISP customers could lease pumps or controllers for thirty months, during which IMED helped them plan disposables use and after which the customers owned the machines. Some IMED salespeople shifted their focus to national ISP accounts with the larger hospital chains. In 1980, IMED expected the ISP and Accudot to generate a third of its projected revenues for the coming five years.

IMED also planned to introduce new products to stake a claim in every segment of the industry. The Model 970, planned for a June 1982 introduction, would allow the nurse to adjust the positive pump pressure from nothing to the equivalent of eight feet in bottle height. (It responded to the Cutter/Quest infusion system, introduced in 1981, which measured fluid volume with a pump but delivered it with gravity so that there was no pressure.) IMED was developing an enteral pump with tougher and more expensive tubing to deliver nutrients directly to the stomach. IMED cooperated with the director of pharmacy at Massachusetts General Hospital to adopt its low level infusion pump for non-diluted drugs in small vials or bags. In two-thirds of all infusions the IV fluid served only to dilute the drug to work with the pump, and the higher volume of fluid boosted the chance of contaminants. IMED worked with clinical researchers at the University of Alabama to develop a closed loop system to deliver arrhythmia drugs and nipride to control a patient's blood pressure. IMED was developing a non-PVC tubing set to infuse nitroglycerine. IMED introduced its Model 911 peristaltic pump, derived from a pump sold by its European subsidiary, to compete directly with the IVAC 530 pump which still dominated the European pump market. And IMED built a new marketing department to help rationalize its future product introductions. These new products signalled a shift in IMED corporate strategy, from boosting earnings to capitalizing on its growing share in the total infusion market.

Question 7

What steps are involved in preparing a company like IMED for sale?

The Sale

By August 1981, as IMED entered its new 1982 fiscal year, all forecasts predicted that IMED would reach $125 million in sales and about forty per-
cent in pretax earnings. IMED had simply grown too big for management by committee to remain viable. Henry hoped to bring in a new
CEO, with experience in a major health care company, so that Cramer
could return to research and engineering such as had occurred at Cray
Research. But Cramer resisted any efforts to loosen his control. It was
impossible to go public with IMED's current management in place, and
with opportunities for a public offering thus limited, by December 1981
the IMED board began to sketch ways of selling the company.

IMED asked Lehman Brothers to serve as its sole investment banker
and show IMED to potential acquirers among major pharmaceutical
and health care companies. Fred Frank of Lehman suggested an auction
method that had recently resulted in some spectacularly high bids
for medical devices companies. IMED did not specify terms, but
specified a minimum asking price of $450 million. This was a premium
price at premium multiples, especially considering that stock markets
were depressed.

But IMED was in great financial shape: from 1980 through 1982, IMED
posted better financial performance than any public company in the U.S.
health care industry. Pretax profit margin averaged 35 percent, asset turnover
averaged 1.6, and after-tax return on equity averaged 49 percent. IMED held a
two-thirds share of the volumetric pump market (Exhibit #5, page 43). This
$450 million asking price was a multiple of five times revenue for the trailing
twelve months, and 29 times earnings for the trailing twelve months.

More important, the valuation anticipated an optimistic future
(Exhibit #6 and #7, pages 43 and 44). This $450 million price was three
times IMED's expected market penetration. From 1977 to 1982, IMED's
annual compound growth rate in revenues was 65 percent; its annual
compound growth rate in earnings was 103 percent. While IMED growth
might slow, IMED was expected to hold its share in a market that was
expected to continue growing beyond all earlier expectations.

IMED considered Abbott Laboratories the most logical acquirer
because of Abbott's strength in the IV solution market. Also, Abbott's
pumps sold well in smaller hospitals and IMED had kept Abbott out of

the larger hospitals. IMED heard rumors that Abbott was considering an offer of $350 million, but Abbott never made a formal offer because IMED refused to release proprietary financial data. Abbott had just introduced a competing infusion pump, and IMED suspected they were fishing for cost data.

Pfizer submitted an offer of $425 million, with $200 million cash, payable immediately. The remainder would come as a one-year earn out of $225 million if IMED reached their fiscal 1983 projections.

Warner-Lambert made the best offer — $163.81 per share, for $465 million in cash, payable on closing. Warner-Lambert had done due diligence for a month before chairman Ward S. Hagan and CFO George Hromadko arrived in June 1982 for one final inspection. The two company chairmen, Hagan and Cramer, toured the plant, returning occasionally to see the two CFOs, Henry and Hromadko, working page-by-page through Henry's blue binder of chart-of-accounts data. By the fourth time Hagan and Cramer returned from a portion of their tour, Hromadko had learned what he needed to know. "Ward," said Hromadko, a Hungarian refugee who had worked himself up to become CEO of a $4 billion company, "the financials are excellent." He walked out of the room and the deal was sealed.

At a meeting with Wall Street analysts on 12 July 1982, Warner-Lambert defended the timing of the IMED acquisition. "Warner-Lambert was just beginning to get its act together," noted analyst Ronald Nordmann of Oppenheimer & Co. "It looked to be heading for 10 percent to 15 percent operating earning growth."[7] In 1981, Warner-Lambert had a net loss of $97.5 million, which included a special write-off of $134.3 million for some of its discontinued consumer lines. Warner-Lambert was diversified and worldwide, offering pharmaceuticals, dental and optometric products, non-prescription drugs, and chewing gums and mints. It was strongest in shelf products — Listerine, Schick, Dentyne — that enjoyed great brand presence but slim margins. The previous week Warner-Lambert had sold the vision care, soft contact and safety glasses businesses of its American Optical Corporation. Hagan called the IMED acquisition "the first step in a plan to increase Warner-Lambert participation in high-technology health care."[8] Furthermore, noted Hromadko, IMED fit snugly with its Deseret unit, which marketed infusion supplies and had a strong international market.

Warner-Lambert also had to defend the price of its IMED acquisition. Most analysts questioned paying twenty times earnings for IMED, which expected to earn $23 million after taxes in fiscal 1983 on revenues of $125 million. But competition had recently driven up the price of high-technology firms, most doing worse than IMED. Smith-Kline paid nearly $1 billion, an estimated 29 times earnings, for Beckman Instruments. American Hospital Supply Company had paid 48 times earnings in bidding $246 million for Bentley Laboratories, which made disposable blood products.

Furthermore, Warner-Lambert defended the price on market share data. While it would be difficult to maintain IMED's fifty percent growth rate, it still held a 35 percent share in a market worth $300 million and growing. IMED's total liabilities to equity ratio — of 0.7 to one — made its balance sheet more conservative than Warner-Lambert's. Hromadko contended that a "strategic redeployment of assets" would keep Warner-Lambert earnings loss to only five percent by the IMED acquisition, and that IMED would start contributing to Warner-Lambert earnings by 1984. Throughout the two months that Wall Street analyzed the acquisition, Warner-Lambert stock kept trading at around $21 per share.

When the deal closed in August 1982 it became the highest price ever paid a private company in U.S. business history. And IMED was still very closely held: 120 shareholders held the 2.8 million IMED shares outstanding. The London institutions, who had less than five years earlier invested $4 million to save IMED for its management, gained $45 million on their investment. No American financial institution of any prominence, on the other hand, had an equity stake in IMED. Twenty IMED employees became millionaires.

Question 8

Did Warner-Lambert pay too much for IMED? Explain your answers based on financial and business analysis [see attached *Wall Street Journal* announcements on pages 45-54].

Epilogue
IMED had created an industry. Infusion therapy, with the exception of simple hydration, was virtually non-existent when IMED was founded

in 1972. Two decades later infusion therapy — solutions, pumps, catheters and services, in both the home and the hospital — accounted for a $15 billion annual U.S. market, with intense competition for new products.

IMED sold the company at its peak. Within a year IMED's compounded growth rate fell from 40 percent to 27 percent. Sales stagnated between $75 and $115 million while the headcount soared from 1,200 to 1,700, ruining earnings. As a division of Warner-Lambert, IMED assumed all the trappings of a big bureaucratic company. Warner-Lambert brought in a president with no experience in electronic devices, and a CFO who was preparing to retire. The human resources group grew from 3 to 45 people. The headcount in the engineering department tripled, though the older Model 960 remained IMED's best selling pump over the next decade. Most of IMED's best people, now richer than they ever dreamed, left to start new ventures.

IMED's early growth brought ample competition into the field. By the early 1980s several well-capitalized competitors succeeded in bringing working volumetric pumps to the market. In 1978, Valley Laboratories introduced a pump as sophisticated as IMED's, but IMED's better sales force kept Valley Labs out of the larger hospitals until the early 1980s. At a December 1981 trade show, Baxter Travenol showed a pump designed by Oxiometrics. Though Baxter delayed full-scale introduction, its traditional customers were the larger hospitals on which IMED depended. Under an onslaught of competition for lower-end devices, IMED's Accuset and Model 350 controller achieved only a fraction of the market penetration they had forecast.

In 1986, four years after acquiring IMED, Warner-Lambert sold its IMED division to The Henley Group, a U.K.-based holding company for health care firms, for $163 million. That was about a third of what Warner-Lambert paid for it.

Yet Warner-Lambert bought IMED at precisely the right time, even though raising the $465 million in cash had strained its balance sheet. Five months following the acquisition of IMED, the most prominent health industry analysts issued reports praising Warner-Lambert's move into high technology. They predicted Warner-Lambert's compounded annual growth would accelerate from eleven percent to sixteen percent. This growth rate placed it among such industry stars as Merck and

Eli Lilly. And it had a multiplier affect on Warner-Lambert stock. During the IMED acquisition, the stock had been trading about $21 per share, with 75 million shares outstanding, for a total capitaized value of $1.5 billion. One year afterwards, it was trading at $38 per share, almost double the price.

Furthermore, based on this improved capitalization, Warner-Lambert did a debenture offering with some warrants attached. The offering raised $500 million. Through imaginative financing, Warner-Lambert CFO George Hromadko added $1.5 billion in capitalized market value to Warner-Lambert shareholders by spending $500 million, and then subsequently replaced the cash W-L used to acquire IMED. The price of Warner-Lambert stock never came down, even after taking a $302 million accounting write-off on the divestiture of its IMED division.

By 1990, market share for IMED volumetric pumps had fallen even further — from a high of seventy percent in 1982 to 22 percent. In April 1990, Advanced Medical Technologies, Inc., a San Francisco-based holding company, completed acquisition of 93 percent of the IMED Division of The Henley Group for $106 million. Advanced Medical sold off the Irish operations for $3.7 million, tightened operating expenses, protected its patents on the Accuset disposables, focused on selling its Gemini line of peristaltic pumps, and struggled to raise cash in an industry depressed by talk of health care reform.

For IMED to have gone from near bankruptcy to a company worth $465 million in less than five years displays remarkable accomplishment at returning a company from the brink. IMED's story is one of inspired product design and the extraordinary direct selling effort characteristic of first stage venture firms. Into IMED's second stage, its story became one of poor management transformed into good management by recruiting experienced talent, adding rigorous financial controls, and applying creative finance to maximize the company's total market value.

Notes to Published Sources

[1] "IVAC Corp. Earnings Report," *Wall Street Journal* (31 January 1972) 14/4.

[2] "Ivac Corp. Dissidents Quit After Bid to Oust Chairman is Defeated," *Wall Street Journal* (29 February 1972) 3/2.

[3] "Ivac Files Lawsuit Against 4 Ex-Aides, Pressprich Official," *Wall Street Journal* (3 March 1972) 4/3.

[4] "Ivac Corp. Dissidents Win Control of Concern's Board," *Wall Street Journal* (4 May 1972) 20/2.

[5] "Imed Files Combination Offer," *Wall Street Journal* (13 October 1978) 37/3.

[6] Robert P. Rapp, "Comparative Accuracy of Five Intravenous-Fluid Controllers." *American Journal of Hospital Pharmacy* 41 (December 1984) 2634-2641.

[7] "Warner-Lambert Plan to Buy IMED Corp. Draws Cool Reaction by Analysts Due to Cost, Timing," *Wall Street Journal* (14 June 1982) 41/2; "Warner-Lambert To Acquire Imed For $465 Million," *Wall Street Journal* (8 June 1982) 2/2.

[8] "Warner-Lambert Co. Defends Its Proposal To Buy Imed Corp.," *Wall Street Journal* (13 July 1982) 38/3; "Warner-Lambert Co. To Buy Imed Corp.," *Wall Street Journal* (28 July 1982) 4/1; "Warner-Lambert Co. Completes Purchase," *Wall Street Journal* (23 August 1982) 27/3.

[9] "Advanced Medical to Buy 93% of Firm's Imed Unit," *Wall Street Journal* (24 January 1990) A4/6.

Exhibit #1

IMED Corporation: Private Placements and Company Sale

	March 1977	March 1978	June 1978	Dec. 1978	January 1979	Nov. 1979	June 1980	August 1982
Total Company Valuation	[$2.5m]	$20m	$36m	[$25m]	$37m	$60m	$140m	$465m
Price per Share	[$1.00]	$10.66	$16.67	[$12.00]	$16.00	$23.00	$50.00	$163.81
Amount of Placement	[$1.1 to 1.5m]	$0.6m	$1m	[withdrawn]	$1.5m	$3m	$20m	$465m
Percent of IMED Purchased	[50% to 60%]	3%		[25%]	4%	5%	14%	100%
Purchasers	[NY Inst.]	London Inst. Series B	AHSC Series C	[IPO]			NY Inst.	W-L
Investment Banker	Paine Webber [not closed]	Henry	Henry	Blyth [not closed]	Henry	Eberstadt	Eberstadt & Lehman	Lehman
IMED Sales *(Trailing 12 Months)*	$5m	$9m	$9m	$12m	$12m	$19m	$30m	$85m
IMED After Tax Earnings *(Trailing 12 Months)*						$0.5m	$4.5m	$16m
P/E *(Trailing 12 Months)*						120 times	30 times	29 times

Numbers in square brackets are for transactions that were proposed but not closed.

Exhibit #2

Selected Consolidated Financial Information
(In thousands, except per share data)

	Year Ended 31 December					Seven Months Ended 31 July	
	1973	**1974**	**1975**	**1976**	**1977**	**1977**	**1978**
						(unaudited)	
Operating Results							
Net Sales	$ 241	$ 655	$2,149	$5,993	$9,278	$4,618	$7,244
Operating Profit (loss)	(632)	(834)	(279)	1,028	1,278	768	1,098
Income (loss) before extraordinary credit for Tekmar, S.A.	(632)	(834)	(279)	(679)	119	704	615
Net income (loss)	(632)	(834)	(279)	(110)	119	704	1,015
Earnings (loss) per share:							
Before extra. credit	(.97)	(.78)	(.23)	(.45)	.07	.42	.31
Net	(.97)	(.78)	(.23)	(.07)	.07	.42	.51

Exhibit #3

Information on Distribution Channels
(per fiscal year)

	1978	**1979**	**1980**	**1981**
Sales Through Distributors*	76%	72%	59%	53%
Number of Distributors	25	19	14	10
Number of Direct Sales Employees	18	25	35	48

* Percent of total sales through distributors is based on an average of the percent mix in each of the four quarters of the fiscal year indicated.

Source: "Descriptive Memorandum," Lehman Brothers Kuhn Loeb (December 1981) 34.

Exhibit #4

Financial Ratios Comparison for Health Devices Industry

Fiscal 1979

	Current Ratio	Quick Ratio	AT ROA	Finance Leverage	AT ROE	Pretax Margin	After Tax Margin	Earnings Retention	Reinvest Rate	Capital/ Debt	Structure Equity	Asset Turnover	TIE Coverage
Industry Average	2.97	1.65	10.89	1.77	19.40	14.53	8.68	88.31	17.51	41.41	58.59	1.28	19.41
IMED	2.71	1.57	16.88	2.36	39.77	16.26	8.84	98.59	39.21	56.61	43.39	1.91	10.00
Hewlett Packard	2.29	1.44	11.70	1.43	16.80	17.10	8.90	90.80	15.20	31.50	68.50	1.32	50.33
Beckman Instruments	2.31	1.20	8.20	1.95	16.00	11.30	6.60	86.30	13.80	49.20	50.80	1.24	6.45
Tektronix	3.33	1.81	12.50	1.51	18.90	16.00	9.50	81.20	15.40	33.50	66.50	1.32	23.60
Perkin-Elmer Corp.	3.21	1.68	9.10	1.72	15.60	11.70	6.30	78.80	12.20	44.90	55.10	1.45	12.69
Valleylab Inc.	3.64	1.96	17.70	1.59	28.00	20.00	11.90	100.00	28.00	34.80	65.20	1.49	14.69
US Surgical	2.93	1.70	10.10	2.61	26.20	16.30	9.10	100.00	26.20	64.50	35.50	1.10	5.84
Cobe Labs	3.72	1.92	9.40	1.86	17.50	11.40	6.30	100.00	17.50	42.20	57.80	1.50	6.54
Cordis Corp.	2.35	0.96	13.50	2.07	27.90	18.10	11.70	100.00	27.90	48.20	51.80	1.16	9.12
Bentley Labs	4.43	2.79	10.60	1.26	13.30	17.70	9.20	100.00	13.30	20.90	79.10	1.14	117.00
Medtronic	2.46	1.63	10.90	1.48	16.10	15.30	9.50	82.50	13.30	32.30	67.70	1.15	14.42
Baxter Travenol	2.30	0.91	8.80	1.85	16.20	11.90	9.10	85.30	13.80	45.80	54.20	0.96	5.91
Abbott Labs	1.58	0.89	11.00	1.88	20.70	16.20	10.30	68.50	14.20	46.80	53.20	1.07	8.51
Becton Dickinson	3.76	2.16	9.30	1.50	13.90	13.50	7.70	74.10	10.30	32.70	67.30	1.20	13.01
Technicon	3.19	2.10	7.50	1.62	12.10	12.60	9.60	99.60	12.10	39.50	60.50	0.78	5.20
Narco Scientific	3.28	1.63	7.00	1.63	11.50	7.10	4.30	67.20	7.70	39.20	60.80	1.62	7.27

Sources: Company Annual Reports

ATROE = [AT Margin] [Asset Turnover] [Leverage]

$$\text{ATROE} = \text{ATN} = \frac{[\text{ATN}]}{\text{Average Annual Equity}} \quad \frac{[\text{Annual Sales}]}{[\text{Annual Sales}]} \quad \frac{[\text{Average Annual Assets}]}{[\text{Avg Annual Assets}]} \quad \frac{[\text{Average Annual Assets}]}{[\text{Average Annual Equity}]}$$

Exhibit #5

Volumetric Pump Market Share Data for 1981

Company	First Introduction	Percentage of 1981 Installed Volumetric Pumps
IMED *(6 models)*	1974	70%
Abbott *(3 models)*	1975	16%
Valleylab *(2 models)*	1978	9%
IVAC *(2 models)*	1975	4%
Baxter Travenol	1982 est.	0
Other		1%

Source: Data collected by IMED sales force, and reported in "Descriptive Memoradum," issued by Lehman Brothers Kuhn Loeb, December 1981.

Exhibit #6

IMED Corporation — Combined Income Statement for 1981

($000)

	1978	1979	1980	1981	1982*	1983*	1984*
Sales	11,904	20,078	35,448	55,539	84,052	135,484	218,593
Cost of Sales	5,265	9,755	15,825	21,931	32,963	53,265	86,954
Gross Profit	6,639	10,323	19,623	33,608	51,089	82,219	131,639
Total Expenses	5,032	7,069	9,720	16,263	21,296	36,984	58,256
Foreign Currency	(1,102)	(164)	35	—	—	—	—
Pre-Tax Income	505	3,090	9,938	17,345	29,793	45,235	73,383
Taxation	75	1,315	4,615	8,406	14,557	21,109	33,745
Net Income	430	1,775	5,323	8,939	15,236	24,126	39,638
Shares Outstanding		2,158	2,480	2,617	2,700	2,750	2,800
Earnings Per Share	0.16	0.85	2.15	3.41	5.64	8.77	14.16

* estimated

Exhibit #7

IMED Corporation — Combined
Common Size Income Statement

($000)

	1978	1979	1980	1981	1982*	1983*	1984*
Sales	100%	100%	100%	100%	100%	100%	100%
Cost of Sales	44.2	48.6	44.6	39.5	39.2	39.3	39.8
Gross Profit	55.8	51.4	55.4	60.5	60.8	60.7	60.2
Total Expenses	42.3	35.2	27.3	29.3	25.4	27.3	26.6
Foreign Currency	(9.3)	(0.8)	(0.1)	—	—	—	—
Pre-Tax Income	4.2	15.4	28.0	31.2	35.4	33.4	33.6
Taxation	0.6	6.6	13.0	15.1	17.3	15.6	15.5
Net Income	3.6	8.8	15.0	16.1	18.1	17.8	18.1

* estimated

Exhibit #8

Warner-Lambert To Acquire
Imed For $465 Million

The Wall Street Journal
Tuesday, June 8, 1982

Warner-Lambert To Acquire Imed For $465 Million
Purchase of Medical-Device maker to Continue Move To Nonconsumer Lines

By a Wall Street Journal Staff Reporter

MORRIS PLAINS, N.J.-Warner-Lambert Co. said it agreed in principle to buy closely-held Imed Corp. for $465 million.

The planned purchase price is equal to about $163 for each of Imed's approximately 2.8 million shares outstanding. Warner-Lambert, a health-care products concern, has already obtained options from Imed's management and from Imed that would, if exercised, give Warner-Lambert 51% control of Imed, the companies said.

Warner-Lambert said it would use cash and its lines of bank credit to obtain the funds for the proposed Imed purchase, which is still subject to definitive terms and approval by the Warner-Lambert board. Imed's board has approved it. Imed, founded in 1972 in San Diego, Calif., is a leading producer of electronic medical instruments to administer intravenous solutions to patients.

The purchase would continue a program during the past three years under which Warner-Lambert has been withdrawing from consumer products and expanding its pharmaceutical and medical instrument product lines.

Imed competes with Eli Lilly & Co. and Baxter Travenol Laboratories Inc. in this special equipment field, a market analyst said. Ward S. Hagan, Warner-Lambert's chairman and chief executive officer, said Imed expects to earn about $20 million after taxes this year, and an Imed source said this would be at least 50% above 1981.

Imed has more than 1,200 employees in plants in San Diego, Ireland and the United Kingdom. Richard A. Cramer, Imed's chairman and chief executive officer, is reportedly the largest shareholder: the company has 120 stockholders. Mr. Cramer, a principal founder of Imed, and other major officials of Imed would continue to operate the California concern, according to the Warner-Lambert announcement.

In the first quarter, Warner-Lambert reported profit of $41.3 million, or 52 cents a share. In the 1981 period, the company had a net loss of $97.5 million, including a special charge of $134.3 million for the write-off of certain businesses that Warner-Lambert decided didn't any longer fit its long-range profit goals. Under this program, Warner-Lambert last week sold the vision care, soft contact lens and safety glasses businesses of its American Optical Corp. unit to a private company in Greenwich, Conn.

Warner Lambert common stock closed at $21,875, down 25 cents in composite trading yesterday on the New York Stock Exchange.

Warner-Lambert Co. Defends Its Proposal To Buy Imed Corp.

The Wall Street Journal

Tuesday, June 13, 1982

Warner-Lambert Co. Defends Its Proposal To Buy Imed Corp.

By a Wall Street Journal Staff Reporter

NEW YORK-Warner-Lambert Co. defended its proposed purchase of Imed Corp., saying the maker of advanced electronic equipment for administering intravenous solutions will provide the company with "significant incremental sales and profit gains."

Speaking to a group of analysts, Ward S. Hagan, chairman of the health and consumer-products company, said the $465 million cash transaction isn't expected to dilute earnings more than 12 cents to 13 cents a share in 1982 and 1983. He added that financing the acquisition won't have any impact on earnings after 1983. Mr. Hagan also said that he expects Warner-Lambert's second quarter profit rose about 24% from $39.7 million, or 50 cents a share, the year earlier.

When the company announced its plan last month to acquire Imed, analysts reacted coolly, saying the transaction would cut sharply into earnings for several years. Some said that while Imed is widely considered to be a premier company in a fast growing segment of the medial-supply field, its purchase price about 23 times earnings, was too steep for Warner-Lambert. Analysts said the transaction might reduce projected 1982 earnings per share of $2.45 as much as 10%, and hurt earnings through 1985.

Mr. Hagan disputed such forecasts, saying analysts haven't been able "to make a complete, detailed judgment about the acquisition." He said an essential part of the company's "anti-dilution" strategy was a planned "redeployment of assets." He declined to specify what such moves might entail, but said the resulting capital gains will be sheltered by the capital losses the company had when it disposed of its American Optical unit and other businesses recently.

Mr. Hagan said the planned redeployment will "involve certain operations which don't meet the criteria delineated in our strategic plan." Over the past three years, and under Mr. Hagan's direction, Warner-Lambert has shed a number of businesses, especially those in the consumer-health field. While the sale of several of these operations have resulted in charges against earnings, Mr. Hagan said future actions won't result in write offs.

Mr. Hagan told the group that Imed's purchase would be "the first step in a plan to increase Warner-Lambert's participation in high technology health care." Joseph Williams, Warner-Lambert president, said Imed's sales in 1982 are expected to be about $100 million and are expected to rise about 46% annually to about $500 million in 1987. Imed's 1982 earnings are expected to be about $20 million, he added.

IMED here sold for $465 million

The San Diego Union-Tribune
Monday, June 7, 1982

IMED here sold for $465 million

By Janet Lowe

Tribune Financial Writer

In what will be the largest known acquisition of a San Diego based company, and one of the largest mergers in the history of corporate America involving a privately held company, IMED Corp. today announced it would be purchased by Warner-Lambert Co. of Morris Plans, N.J., for $465 million cash.

Warner-Lambert will acquire 100 percent IMED in a deal that is expected to become final within from one to three months.

Richard Cramer, IMED chairman and chief executive officer, said the company would continue to be operated by the current management team, and that IMED would remain headquartered at Scripps Ranch.

"I would like to emphasize our commitment to San Diego," Cramer said in an interview. "It is the infrastructure and strength of health sciences here that has allowed our success. We've been able to draw on that for growth."

When Cramer and 120 mostly local investors founded IMED, they paid $10 a share for their holdings. The stock, which has never been publicly traded, alter underwent a three-for-one split.

Under the agreement with Warner-Lambert, IMED investors will receive approximately $163 a share. About 25 percent of IMED stock is controlled by four principal shareholders.

Since its founding in 1972, IMED has emerged as the world leader in volumetric instrumentation, probably the most rapidly expanding area of the medical intravenous-feeding market.

IMED has had sales and earnings growth of more than 50 percent a year, and is expected to have operating earnings of about $20 million after taxes in calendar 1982.

A spokesman for First Boston Corp., the investment banking firm representing Warner-Lambert in the deal, said he believed the $465 million purchase price easily ranked among the five largest sums ever paid for a private firm.

It is the company's rapid growth, Cramer said, that led to merger discussions with several U.S. and foreign companies, and the subsequent agreement with Warner-Lambert.

"Our worldwide market-place is incredibly large," Cramer explained. "The faster we grow, the faster we can grow. The resources required to properly expand in that huge marketplace are enormous. At some point, we would have had to go public. We deliberately set forth to choose the best possible partner we could find for a merger."

Warner-Lambert's operations, he said, fit well with IMED's because the companies sell in many common markets and have complementary product lines.

Cramer founded IMED following a proxy battle in which he lost control of IVAC, electronics medical instrument company he founded here in 1967. IVAC was later sold to Eli Lilly Co. for slightly more than $60 million.

Sources report that when the IMED merger is complete, Cramer personally will receive a dollar amount larger than the entire sale of IVAC. In addition to his continued leadership at IMED, Cramer will join the board of directors of Warner-Lambert.

Pending the completion of the merger transaction, Warner-Lambert has an option to acquire 51 percent of IMED stock from the company and members of management.

IMED has more than 1,000 employees locally, and about 200 more workers in England, Ireland and Europe. Construction has started on a manufacturing facility in Vista, which Cramer said will further expand IMED's employee pool.

Warner-Lambert employs about 45,000 people in 140 countries worldwide. The company primarily produces the Parker Davis line of prescription drugs as well as diagnostic products, hospital supplies, scientific instruments and other health-care products.

The conglomerate, with sale of $3.4 billion last year, experienced a drop in earnings from $2.41 a share in 1980 to 12 cents a share in 1982.

Those earnings, said a Warner-Lambert spokesman, reflected expenses involved in the divestiture of several divisions, which was part of a restructuring of the company.

He added that the restructuring, designed to intensify Warner-Lambert's participation in high-technology health-care markets, has involved the closure of more than 30 Warner-Lambert plants worldwide.

The acquisition of IMED fits in with the Warner-Lambert's new approach, he added.

Reprinted with permission from The San Diego Union-Tribune

IMED Case Solution

Question 1, page 15

1. How would you find enough cash to keep IMED from going bankrupt? How would you characterize IMED as a company for financing purposes — seed, early stage, turn-around, or late stage. Why? What sources of financing would you identify to fit your characterization of company type?

(a) **Answer:**

IMED is an early stage company which has an unproved product that is possibly a revolution for I.V. administration, marrying the microprocessor with mechanical functions to result in fluid flow control. The company is early stage because the product is not widely used in hospitals; the company does not know whether it can make the product in volume and does not know what it costs to build the instrument. Because IMED is early stage, certain types of money pools will not be interested in investment. Institutional debt and bank debt will not be accessible to IMED because the company has no net worth, no collateral and deficit cash flow.

(b) Private Equity? A chance. Some startups or new technology companies are financed by high net worth individuals.

(c) Private Equity Placement Retail Wire House (NYSE member)? Perhaps.

A.G. Edwards just financed a new technology Internet company though its high net worth retail customers in a small private placement. Retail houses, both national and regional are looking for ways to earn fees in M&A/private placement work. Cramer's poor reputation removed this alternative.

(d) Institutional Private Equity Placement? Perhaps.

IMED's technology was new and compelling with possible growth implications in company and market development, longer term. These are prerequisite for an institutional private placement. Cramer's reputation would be a problem, but professional investors can deal with problems. Problems always affect price, and they did in IMED's case. Institutional equity is usually expensive.

(e) Mezzanine or venture level of placement?

Venture is many times more expensive. I used mezzanine level institutional investment for IMED. Buyers are sometimes less rigorous on due diligence regarding products and forecasts and usually do not negotiate valuation significantly downward.

Question 1, page 15

2. How much financing would you seek in debt, equity or both at this time? Explain your reasoning for amount and type of financing recommended.

(a) **Answer:**

Debt financing is not possible as described above. Equity financing will be the only available money for IMED because the company is so early-stage and not established.

Question 1, page 15

3. Would you use an investment banker? Why or why not?

(a) **Answer:**

An investment banker should definitely be used to broaden the coverage of accessing individuals and institutional equity pools. This money-raising job is too complex to be solved by company management. I was able to succeed because I had prior Wall Street experience and institutional contacts.

Question 1, page 15

4. What valuation do you seek for this financing and why? Describe your methodology for valuing IMED and why at this point in its life.

(a) **Answer:**

Forecasts of revenue and earnings for approximately one to three years should be prepared by IMED management from the bottom up (i.e., detail number of salesmen penetrating X number of hospital accounts to result in placement of Y number of instruments which would consume Z number of disposables result-ing in a revenues and earnings forecast that would be used on a basis of revenue multiples or P/E multiples to give a total capitalized value for IMED). If IMED sought to raise $1 million on a $20 million total capitalized market value, it would obviously then be selling 5 percent of the company.

(b) Discounted Cash Flow (DCF) valuation method would not work for an early stage company because a ten-year forecast would be completely unreliable and not believable to institutional investors.

Question 2, page 17

1. What operational functions are needed by every small company with a new product?

(a) Cost controls, inventory controls, careful headcount analysis, establishment of standard costs if volumes are significant enough to give reliable data, working capital analysis which includes rigorous accounts receivable and accounts payable management, and preferably MBOs (management by objectives) for each major company function, i.e., production, sales, marketing and finance.

Question 2, page 17

2. What controls does the company need to ensure reliable operating performance? Give your reasons for selecting each operating parameter.

(a) Answer:
Financial controls are especially critical to IMED at this time since it does not know the cost of its product and does not have an established accounting system to produce monthly financial statements, including P&L and cash flow statements. Also, manufacturing is not sufficiently established as indicated by the extremely high scrap rate. Analysis of inventory turns is a wish at this point and not reality. IMED does not know how much capital it needs to run its business for the coming two years, and it must find out.

(b) Control Costs. Limit spending. Are these the same? Not necessarily. Directives are often sent out for managers to "control costs." The only sure way I know is to limit spending authority. A purchasing policy is necessary in the smallest companies.

(c) Establish Itemized Budgets.
The more careful the preparation, the better the resulting understanding of the ups and downs of a business.

(d) Analyze Actual Performance to Budget Rigorously.
Depth of analysis reveals often obscured weaknesses in operations. Also reveals trends, both good and bad, in product sales, sales force or channel of distribution performance, inventory levels, production issues and R&D performance. Analysis should be on both a P&L and cash flow basis. Verify standard costs if they exist— actual performance vs. existing standard costs.

(e) Analysis & Review Must be at Regular Intervals
Trends are identified by regular scrutiny reviewing results compared to carefully prepared benchmark — the budget. Biweekly review is not too often. Major companies often do it.

(f) Management Must Accept a Critical Answer.
If careful, exhaustive preparation and a rigorous, regular review process is used, then the answer may be more obvious.

3. How would you rate IMED's operating controls? Does operating performance affect a company's ability to attract financing? Why or why not?

(a) IMED's operating controls are almost non-existent and should be rated poor. Institutional investors would be leery of investing in a company which has such lack of operating control. Poor operating performance or lack of control of operating performance always diminishes total company value when seeking a financing. Well-run companies, as exemplified by superior operating ration, always secure financing at relatively higher valuations. P/E multiples expand for well-run companies.

Question 3, page 23

Is the $1 million investment significant to IMED at this time? Please express your thinking in some detail.

Emphatically: Yes

Reason:
1. First major equity investment by a strategic investor which gives IMED visibility and standing in its industry and also the financial community. American Hospital has placed an industry-savvy valuation on IMED as viewed by Wall Street money pools. This valuation is more valuable to IMED because it comes from a prominent health care company, which has 15 percent market share of the US I.V. solutions market. The IMED valuation is $36 million.

2. This investment is more valuable to IMED than if it came from a venture capitalist because the strategic investor is "smart money" and impacts the institutional equity market.

3. The valuation given by the "strategic investor" validates the product, its standing in the industry and the potential for significant increases in future equity value of IMED.

Question 4, page 25

1. Does IMED qualify for an initial public offering (IPO) at this time? Why or why not?

(A) Yes. IMED has begun a turn-around in operating performance and appears to have operating controls in place to produce earnings if revenue growth occurs.

Question 4, page 25

2. What issues does a seasoned management assess when considering an IPO?

(A) Company standing in its industry and market. Leader or follower?

(B) Historical financial performance compared to public companies. (See comparative company ratios to IMED.)

(C) Standing in product development.
IPO market likes a growth story through product innovation.

(D) Financial size of company. Projected capitalized market value? Create proper float in after-market for investor participation without selling inordinate amount of company.

(E) Ability of company to meet its forecasts?
Degree of control or confidence level in future operating performance? Unpredictable or higher probability of success? These factors will determine investor interest — institutional or retail — and hence the capitalized market value of the company.

Question 4, page 25

3. What operating financial ratios are most important to the IPO process and why? Give a discussion of each ratio you deem important.

(A) The most important measure of superior operating performance is After Tax Return on Equity (ATROE). For companies without earnings, revenue growth and cash reserves versus burn rate are the two most crucial measures of company staying power. (IMED has the highest ATROE among instrument companies by 10 percentage points versus the next best — Valley Labs. Reasons for superior ATROE: (1) Great asset turnover (high level of sales generated per dollars of assets deployed in the business), (2) High profit margins, and (3) Modestly leveraged balance sheet.)

Question 4, page 25

4. If yes to IPO, what then:

(A) Select an underwriter(s) with industry knowledge and standing. They must have placing power.

(B) Get commitment for support in after-market, both research follow-up and market making. Underwriter sponsorship is necessary to tell company story to the market.

(C) Prepare an extensive road show, i.e. management, show products and market research on products. Give the market confidence in the company's future.

(D) Build a formidable financial case for an attractive valuation. IMED was valued on a revenue multiple and a price earnings multiple of projected future earnings. Discounted cash flow (DCF) is not a primary measure of company valuation in the IPO process.

Question 5, page 27

IMED walked away from its IPO. What major factors should be evaluated in this instance of whether or not to crater an IPO?

1. What amount of IPO funds are at stake? (In IMED's case it was $5 million, and while this would be $40 million in current dollars, it was not a great cash war chest for multiple acquisitions, but rather represented operating funds for a few years.) If the IPO will give funds which are greater than a company needs for many years, then think twice and perhaps take the money (i.e., Amazon and some other Internet IPOs).

2. At what valuation is the IPO taking place? If the IPO valuation is excessively high by traditional financial ratio analysis, then take the money. (Dilution would be minimized by the excessive valuation. IMED's valuation was not a huge boon to the company. Amazon's and other Internet IPO valuations make it impossible to refuse.)

3. Can a replacement financing for the IPO be completed at a similar valuation and for the same net cash to the company? (The same valuation was secured on the subsequent IMED private placement, and IMED was private and in control of its own direction, not to be interfered with by possible demands of the public market.)

Question 6, page 29

What are the major determinants of value in any company? Name and discuss five or six major determinants of value in any company.

A. Major determinants of value:
  1. Aggregate Earnings Level. Earnings growth and sustainability. Earnings predictability — probably of forecast being achieved. (Cost controls evident.)

2. Product Uniqueness and Market Share of Company. Oligopoly, near monopoly or many competitors?

3. Industry growth occurring overall?

4. Superiority of management demonstrated by superior financial operating performance.

5. Demonstrated new product innovation to sustain future growth in revenues, earnings and market share.

B. Premium price/earnings multiples to the industry average will occur if the above determinants of value are exceptional.

Question 7, page 32

What steps are involved in preparing a company like IMED for sale?

1. Retain a major investment banker.

2. Prepare comprehensive, bottoms-up, five-year forecasts: Pro forma income statements, cash flow statements and balance sheets. (These forecasts will demonstrate whether the business is self-financing in the future or needs capital infusions. A potential purchaser will be most interested in these factors.)

3. Seek any available third party studies to validate growth in industry market and company market share.

4. Show operating performance parameters consistent with prepared budgets.

5. Demonstrate manufacturing capacity and ability to achieve higher volumes with existing plant, if possible.

6. Can growth occur through further acquisitions? Are there potential target companies which could be merged to enhance product lines and growth rates of revenue and earnings?

7. Discuss R&D and new product development or second generation evolution of existing product line.

Question 8, page 35

Did Warner-Lambert pay too much for IMED? Give your analysis.

Answer:

1. IMED was purchased for 20 times 1983 estimated earnings. (Or, earnings 15 months away.) Other instrument companies were purchased for 29 times (Beckman) and 48 times (Bentley Labs).

2. IMED had a 5-year historic compound growth rate (CGR) in earnings of 105 percent and a 5-year CGR in revenues of 65 percent.

3. A 20-times P/E is conservative for these CGRs.

4. IMED had a 75 percent market share for electronic, volumetric infusion pumps. This dominant market share commands a premium P/E and company valuation.

5. IMED's financial performance (ATROE, Asset Turnover and Profit Margins) indicates a superior management, a leading product line and predictability of earnings (cost controls are evident).

6. The market is the best judge of whether Warner-Lambert paid too much for IMED. One year after the IMED deal closed, Warner-Lambert had added $1.5 billion to its total capitalized market value. The market liked the deal.

Block Medical, Inc.

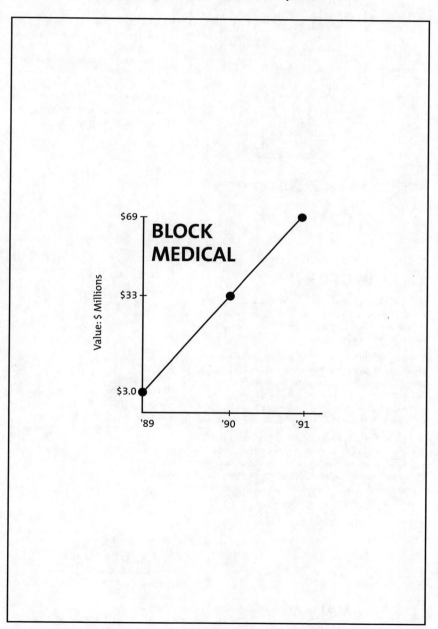

HOMEPUMP

DISPOSABLE ELASTOMERIC INFUSION PUMP

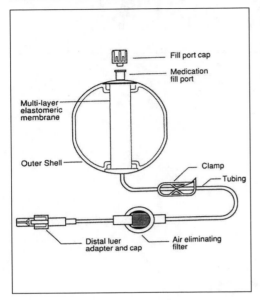

Labels: Fill port cap / Medication fill port / Multi-layer elastomeric membrane / Outer Shell / Clamp / Tubing / Distal luer adapter and cap / Air eliminating filter

FEATURES & BENEFITS:

- Elastomeric membrane made of highly biocompatible materials.
- Multi-layer membrane ensures flow continuity and protects against leakage.
- Homepump™ can be refrigerated or frozen.
- Pre-set flow, single-use disposable.
- Durable outer shell.
- Sterile, nonpyrogenic fluid pathway and areas under protective caps.

DESCRIPTION:

Block Medical's Homepump™ disposable elastomeric infusion pump is a cost-effective, portable system designed to administer antibiotic infusion therapy to the in-home patient.

The Homepump houses an elastomeric membrane consisting of highly biocompatible material. The membrane's multiple concentric layers furnish controlled drug delivery and safeguard against fluid leakage. The integrated filter removes particulate matter and protects against possible air in the line.

Block Medical developed the Homepump disposable infusion pump to make drug delivery simple and safe for the in-home patient and at the same time allow the patient greater mobility. Equally important, the Homepump has been carefully designed to administer fluids at a constant rate.

SPECIFICATIONS:

Capacity:	110mL
Fixed flow rates:	50mL/hr
	75mL/hr
	100mL/hr
	150mL/hr
	200mL/hr
Rate accuracy:	±15%
Positive pressure:	10 psi
Retained Volume:	Approximately 1mL
Weight filled:	6 ounces
Filter:	1.2 Hydrophilic
	0.2 Hydrophobic

BLOCK
MEDICAL, INC.
5957 Landau Court
Carlsbad, CA 92008
(619) 431-1501
(800) 444-8681

HOMEPUMP

HOMEPUMP
DISPOSABLE ELASTOMERIC INFUSION PUMP

Introducing the Homepump™
Disposable Elastromeric Infusion Pump

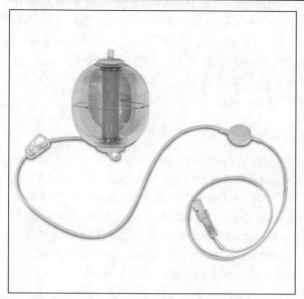

The Homepump™ is a disposable elastomeric infusion pump effective for the administration of IV antibiotics.

HOMEPUMP FEATURES:

• Small and portable	*– increases patient mobility*
• Single use disposable	*– easy for patient to use*
• Optional flow rates:	*– 50mL/hr*
	– 75mL/hr
	– 100mL/hr
	– 150mL/hr
	– 200mL/hr
• Multi-layer membrane	*– ensures flow continuity, safeguards against leakage, and is highly drug compatible*
• Elastomeric pressure	*– eliminates gravity flow problems*
• In-line filter	*– removes particulate matter and protects against possible air in line*

BLOCK
MEDICAL, INC.
5957 Landau Court
Carlsbad, CA 92008
(619) 431-1501
(800) 444-8681

B lock Medical showed one of the fastest and most spectacular returns in the Henry Venture II portfolio, the second fund Henry launched. An investment of $600,000 returned $7.5 million in cash after only 21 months from closing the Series A financing. "It's never this easy," effused Henry's co-investor, Robert Fleming of Orien Ventures, "this is a once or twice in a career kind of deal."[1] Block Medical's soaring value was a story of the expert development of a product idea to suit a new and growing market. How was the idea incubated?

Block Design

Gregory E. Sancoff was a Yankee tinkerer transplanted to San Diego's booming biomedical technopolis. He had earned an Associates Degree in Machine Design and Business from the Greater Lawrence Technical School in New Hampshire. Sancoff worked brief stints with Sega Electronics and Instrumentation Laboratories — a leading provider of blood gas analyzers — where he absorbed the excitement of building biomedical devices. He moved to San Diego in 1980 to lead project engineering on a high performance graphics projection system for the Hughes Aircraft Company's industrial products division.

In October 1986 Sancoff launched a consulting group called Block Design. He structured it as a sole proprietorship, funded by a $50,0000 bank loan. He hired a select dozen mechanical and electrical engineers, most of whom had yet to be tainted by big-company engineering. From a small laboratory in Carlsbad, near San Diego, they served as a think tank for hire to the biomedical industry.

Block Design promised speed to market. It guaranteed development of any new product — from conceptual research to prototype — in less than eighteen months and at a fixed cost. "Our turnaround time is one-third to one-half of what most companies take," noted Sancoff. "And it's really nice to know what your product costs are going to be."[2]

Block Design found clients quickly. Some clients were startups—"six guys and a venture capitalist" — who needed some piece to their technological puzzle in order to get their product to market. Some clients were more established biomedical firms that needed Block's fresh set of engineering eyes to debug a product, fine-tune a feature, or get past a bottleneck. Some clients were wrestling with a make-or-buy decision, and Block showed them how easy it was to look outside.

IVAC was Block's first client, looking for Sancoff's help in improving its volumetric hospital infusion pumps. Then Block started designing a vast array of medical devices. Block designed a tray container to store samples for Stratagene Cloning Systems, and provided engineering support to Thermoscan and to Robot Research Corporation. In 1988, the IMED division of Warner-Lambert commissioned Block to design a syringe pump for hospital use, as well as to design new features for its line of infusion pumps. Block helped design an adult ventilator for sale by Infrasonics Corporation. For Retroperfusion Systems Inc., Block designed a new device for a specialized method of angioplasty. Block led design and clinical studies for manufacture of a new orthodontics product sold by Johnson & Johnson as the Electronic Thermal Debonder. For Dr. Robert Fischell, a physician at Johns Hopkins Medical Center and a founder of Medinnovations, Block developed a mechanical atherectomy device used for cleaning leg and heart arteries. Block developed an optical diagnostic instrument for Gen-Probe Corporation, and a sonomicrometer for Sonotek Corporation.

Block Design grew expert in an extraordinary range of technologies and production processes. And as Sancoff made contacts throughout the industry and learned from his clients, Block Design also grew expert at discerning market trends in the biomedical industry. Gradually Block's work shifted— away from commissioned product design, and more toward developing products in-house then shopping for an established company to make and sell them. Block's policy was to stay away from products with no immediate market or those dependent upon risky new components. Block found partners for several of its brainchildren — like an electronic orthodontic instrument for measuring bite changes and tooth locations, and an integrated monitor for detecting early signs of premature contractions in pregnant women. "We became stimulators of ideas," claimed Sancoff. "We didn't just sit around waiting for the phone to ring."

In early 1989, though, Block invented two new infusion pumps specifically for use in the home infusion market. These designs prompted Sancoff to radically alter Block's way of doing business. Sancoff wanted to convert Block Design from a design bureau into a fully-integrated company that could also manufacture, sell, and support its own products.

Indeed, the new pumps were promising enough to support a new company. Block's patent position on them was virtually incontestable. More important, the major infusion pump firms — and two of the biggest, IVAC and IMED, were Block clients — had shown no interest in serving the burgeoning home health care market. Nor had they built any special expertise in manufacturing plastic or mechanical devices. Sancoff could more easily start from scratch. "Studies predict that in the next five years 700 hospitals will close. There will be a big need for products used for patients at home. The big players can't get involved fast enough."[3]

Question 1

What other steps could Sancoff undertake to be sure he had identified a valuable new product, and match it to its market?

After four years of a birds-eye view on the biomedical devices industry, Sancoff knew how to move quickly. What he needed most was a knowledgeable money pool — like that represented by Al Henry, with his background in the infusion instrument and home infusion services industries. The right venture backer would help time the equity placements and bring the right product to a new market.

Series A

On 6 October 1989, Sancoff incorporated Block Medical, Inc. under Delaware law. In exchange for 1,845,951 common shares, Block Medical acquired the entire assets of his sole proprietorship. Sancoff stopped accepting new contracts for commissioned engineering, and went looking for venture finance to launch a fully-integrated firm. Easing his way was the recent acquisition of Pancretec Inc., which was listed on NASDAQ, based in San Diego, and focused on manufacturing electronic infusion pumps miniaturized for home health care. In May 1989, Abbott Laboratories bought all outstanding Pancretec stock at $15 per share, or $54 million total, for a very attractive multiple of four times revenues.[4] This market was growing hot.

Sancoff found interest from Robert C. Fleming, managing partner of Orien II L.P. Orien Ventures was an $80 million joint fund of The Vista Group, an international venture group, and of Mitsui Bank of Japan.

Orien had just opened its west coast office and, following three months of due diligence, Orien's investment in Block would be its first investment out of that office. Fleming had planned to invest $1 million for a 29 percent ownership in Block, then valued at $3.45 million. Fleming and Sancoff expanded the offering to bring in Al Henry.

F. David Hare, president of Henry & Co., led the due diligence. Hare studied the business plan for an integrated company and called people Block had worked with. Hare especially hoped to discern whether Block was a one-man show or if Sancoff had a complete team of talented people. Thomas Edison's Menlo Park laboratory, remember, kept turning out new inventions very profitably without evolving into an integrated company. Kevin Kinsella, managing partner of Avalon Ventures, had hired Block to consult with several of his portfolio companies, and emphasized that Block's entire team was "honorable and capable."[5] Hare called the vice presidents of operations at two San Diego-based start-ups — Infrasonics and Retroperfusion Systems — and both were very complimentary about Block's understanding of what entrepreneurial firms needed to succeed.

Question 2

What was the pre-money valuation of Block Medical by venture capitalists Orien and HV II for the Series A financing? Show your calculations. Be prepared to discuss the merits and disadvantages of the attached term sheet (Exhibit #6, page 84) from the investor and the Block point of view.

Block Medical closed its Series A convertible preferred shares on 8 December 1989. Block raised $1.35 million, representing 36 percent ownership in the company. Henry Venture II Ltd. bought 350,000 shares at $1.00 per share and owned 10 percent, and Orien Venture bought one million shares for 26 percent ownership. Henry became a Block director.[6] An options pool representing thirteen percent ownership was allocated for top management. Sancoff kept the remaining common shares, vesting annually over three years.

"My whole philosophy," said Sancoff, "is that if you take investors' money you should be able to show a profit within a year."[7] Within this first year, Block Medical's extraordinary engineering group consolidated their patent position on seven new products. Mostly, though, Block used the fresh equity to bring its Homepump strongly to market.

Block's Homepump was a small, portable, and disposable infusion pump optimized for in-home infusions.[8] It looked like a plexiglass tennis ball with a tube attached. It had no moving parts, and no electrical components. The protective outer shell was a hard plastic sphere. Inside was a cylindrical tube, made of three layers of expansive, elastomeric polymer and latex. This tube ballooned up when a pharmacist filled it (through a self-sealing port at top, using a Homepump Easy Fill Fluid Dispenser) with up to 110 milliliters of an antibiotic fluid. By adjusting a capillary orifice to limit the flow, the pharmacist also preset the flow rate from 50 milliliters to 200 milliliters per hour. When the patient connected their catheter to the Homepump tubing and released a clamp, the elastomeric tube contracted at a constant pressure of ten pounds per square inch (psi), and the drug infused into the patient's vein.

The Homepump was very reliable. The tube materials were layered to prevent leaks, and were biocompatible with most antibiotic solutions. It could be refrigerated or frozen, for easier storage at home. The solutions infused at a rate accuracy of ± 15 percent which was fine for the most widely prescribed antibiotics, like Tobramycin and Gentamicin. The tubing had an integrated 1.2 micron filter to remove particulates or air from the line. Patient compliance improved because each Homepump was a single-use, self-contained disposable. It weighed six ounces filled, and included a carrying pouch worn around the waist or over the shoulder. With the small positive pressure, patient movement seldom caused significant canula blockage. Most important, the Homepump had an average price to distributors of $8.50, and an end price of $10.50 each. This low price made it very attractive to insurors.

Only one other mechanical pump could then compete with the Homepump — the Intermate manufactured by Baxter solely for home health care provider Caremark, Inc. But Baxter had not spent as much time selecting the Intermate's elastomeric, and used a material compatible with fewer drugs. Baxter planned to introduce the new Daymate pump for home chemotherapy, and Abbott/Healthtek planned to introduce their ADfuse pump to compete directly with the Homepump. But both were moving slowly.

Block moved from a cramped 4,000 square foot space in Sorrento Mesa into 30,000 square feet of leased office and manufacturing space in Carlsbad, which included 5,000 square feet of clean room (rated to the Class 100,000 standard) for Homepump assembly. Sancoff expanded Block's headcount, by hiring some top-notch manufacturing engineers, and adding sixty people to the Homepump production line. The first pumps off the line, on 19 April 1990, worked beautifully.

Series B

Block had burned through most of its Series A financing to get its manufacturing operations working, and now needed an infusion of cash to beef up its sales and distribution. In May 1990 Block closed on its offering of $1 million in Series B convertible preferred stock. With shares priced at $1.79, Block's pre-money valuation was $7.81 million. Henry Venture II Ltd. invested another $250,000, bringing its total investment to $600,000, for twelve percent ownership of Block. Orien also invested its pro rata share, maintaining its ownership to 31.3 percent.

Plus, that May the first revenues hit Block's books and by July they had made and sold more than a thousand cases of Homepumps. Block approached regional dealers who sold to the home care market, as well as national and regional home infusion companies like IVonyx and Total Pharmaceutical Care. Home health care nurses liked the Homepump.[9] They considered it very easy to "in-patient," that is, to teach patients how to use it themselves. "Children can stick it in a pocket or a fanny pack, and none of their classmates need to know," noted Michelle Dietz, coordinator of home nursing services for San Diego's Children's Hospital. "It's a lot easier than having them tied to an IV pole."[10]

The result was an explosion in growth. Within nine months of startup, Block headcount had grown from 12 to 120, with plans for 300 by the end of 1991. Secured by their growing backlog of sales, Block opened a $500,000 bank line of credit at prime plus 1.5 percent. Block forecast sales of $6 million to $8 million for calendar 1990. Because the Homepump earned a high gross margin, the company would be very profitable at this $6 million revenue level. Prospects got even brighter when Block signed an OEM agreement with McGaw Inc. McGaw had just shifted its strategy, and Homepumps would be a big part of its new direction.

What options are available to a new, small company with an innovative product to magnify its impact on the marketplace?

McGaw OEM

In October 1990, Kendall McGaw Laboratories, Inc. had been bought for
$200 million cash by health care entrepreneur James Sweeney. In 1979,
Sweeney had founded Caremark, Inc. and built it into the leading
national provider of home health services. Baxter Health Corp. acquired
Caremark in 1988 and replaced Sweeney, who went looking for opportu-
nities that didn't conflict with his non-compete agreement. Once
Sweeney acquired Kendall McGaw, he quickly spun-off the Kendall
Laboratories part of the company, and refocused McGaw on its core
strength in infusion products.

The refashioned McGaw, Inc. was privately held by Sweeney and a
small group of investors. McGaw was based in Irvine, California,
employed 3,000 workers at plants in Irvine, Dallas, and Puerto Rico, and
had annual sales of about $225 million. Sweeney changed McGaw's slogan
to "Changing Solutions." Sweeney promised an expanded sales force for
better customer service, a renewed entrepreneurial spirit, and innovative
products. The problem was that IV solutions had become a commodity
business, with price increases following the rate of inflation. Furthermore,
long-term purchasing contracts had fixed market shares, with McGaw at
the bottom of the big three. But the demand for higher-margin infusion
pumps seemed to be growing as fast as the technology matured.

Leveraging his experience in home health care, Sweeney promised
products for the alternate site market. The entire home infusion market
had grown from $1.5 billion in 1988 to $2.6 billion in 1990, and seemed to
continue growing at 25 percent annually. The antibiotic segment of the
market, which Homepump addressed, was growing at 30 percent a year.
And the customer base of home health care providers was mostly new
territory. Some hospitals had branched into home care programs, but so
did local pharmacists, visiting nurses associations, and physician clinics.
Sweeney promised he would never compete with his customers — those
who provided home health services — unlike the two other major suppliers of IV solutions and equipment. Abbott Laboratories had a home

health care division and Baxter had, of course, just bought Caremark. "Our customers," contended Sweeney, "will always have access to the most advanced products available."[11]

On 3 December 1990, six weeks after his takeover of McGaw, Sweeney announced in Las Vegas, before a national convention of pharmacists, that McGaw's new strategy was embodied in the Homepump.

Block had already, on 17 November 1990, signed a non-exclusive, four-year OEM agreement with McGaw Inc.[12] This deal looked much like the deal IMED had crafted a decade earlier, during Henry's tenure, whereby McGaw put its nameplate on IMED's new electronic infusion pump. The result, in the case of both products, was instant visibility and credibility in the marketplace. McGaw put its nameplate on the Homepump, stating it was manufactured by Block, and sold it through McGaw's 220 sales representatives nationwide. Block continued to develop its relationships with a dozen regional distributors, and to build its own nascent direct sales force, but agreed to let McGaw solicit business from national home health care providers like T2 Medical, Homedco, and New England Critical Care. Over the next few years, Block expected its revenue to come seventy percent from McGaw and thirty percent from its own distributors. Block promised to expand its Homepump line to include pumps in a range of fill volumes and flow rates, as well as a pump optimized for chemotherapy infusions. Most important, McGaw guaranteed minimum monthly revenues at a very profitable price for Block — which aggregated to $13 million over the coming eighteen months, and to $45 million over the coming four years.

With potential revenues from these promising new products, plus potential revenues from McGaw, plus actual revenues already arriving from the Homepump, it was time for Block's venture backers to seek liquidity. Block needed some fresh cash to bring the new products to market and build a direct sales force, and this provided the opportunity to arrange a mezzanine round of funding.

Series C

Block forecast some impressive numbers. On 30 September 1990, before the deal with McGaw, Block closed out its first fiscal year posting revenues of $1.4 million and a net loss of $1.2 million. Based on increased sales of Homepumps, Block drafted a plan which forecast revenues of

$17.2 million in fiscal 1991 with corresponding net income of $4.4 million. Revenues for 1992, 1993, and 1994 were forecast at $35.1 million, $55.9 million, and $69.3 million respectively, with net income forecast at $8.2 million, $12.7 million, and $15.4 million.

Based on these numbers, Block asked investment bank Berkeley International to syndicate its Series C convertible preferred shares among Berkeley's institutional investors. Berkeley had little problem closing the offering by 27 November 1990, ten days after Block closed its deal with McGaw. The Series C round looked liked a quasi-public offering, with some very solid institutional investors accepting a valuation for Block at $33 million. Block sold 597,015 shares at $6.70 each to raise $4 million in equity. These shares had a mandatory conversion if Block made a public offering at a price of at least $13 per share. Henry Venture II Ltd. did not invest in this round, but still owned ten percent of Block — bought at an average share price of $1.62 compared with a Series C price of $6.70 per share.

Block used this fresh cash wisely, especially to bring new products to market from its engineering pipeline. Block's second infusion pump was well on schedule for market introduction in February 1991. The Verifuse Ambulatory Pump was a miniaturized, electronic pump, with a peristaltic actuator, and powered by two 9-volt batteries. About the size of a Walkman, it was smaller and less expensive than anything else on the market. Block also optimized it for the home infusion market that most other companies ignored. Verifuse was as convenient as the Homepump, but allowed both higher volumes and more sophisticated infusions — like continuous, intermittent, and patient controlled anesthesia, as well as tapered infusions for total parenteral nutrition. Verifuse had an innovative programming protocol — using barcodes. The pharmacist attached a barcoded label to the bag of drug solution. The home patient then passed a light bar over the barcode, and the Verifuse LCD panel displayed its infusion program. The patient verified that the written and the programmed rates matched, then started the infusion.

For home patients getting more dangerous infusions the nurse or pharmacist could remotely monitor the infusion through a unit called the Homebase. The Verifuse slid into the Homebase, which was essentially a modem. The nurse could track boluses and alarms, and reprogram the Verifuse as needed. Block also introduced some innovative new accessories for its home pumps — like a needleless IV flush system and a protective connecting needle compatible with all IV lines.

Several other companies already sold miniature pumps that Verifuse would compete against. In United States markets Verifuse competed with Medfusion's Walkmed series of pumps and the Abbott/Pancretec Provider series. In European markets it competed with Pharmacia Deltec's CADD. But Block viewed these competitors as paving the market for home unit sales or rental. Once that market was pioneered, Block could more easily introduce its technically-superior product, at a premium unit price near $3,700.

Block brought to market a very different portable electronic device called the Accu•lab luminometer. The Accu•lab was used by culture assay laboratories to measure the small amounts of light emitted from chemical and biological luminescent reactions during mycobacteria testing. An OEM agreement with Gen-Probe, Inc. to sell the Accu•lab under its name plate had already begun to return revenues, and Block hoped to have four more distribution agreements in place soon.

In September 1991, Block ended its second fiscal year well over its seemingly optomistic forecasts. It reported revenues at $16.1 million and $2.47 million in net income. Staff had grown to 280 employees. Block added new production tools at its Carlsbad headquarters for assembling the Verifuse and opened a *maquilladora* in Tijuana to make the Homepumps. Block also built its own national distribution network. Block introduced Verifuse on schedule, and market acceptance was better than forecast. Block's monthly revenue run rate, in August 1991, was $2.5 million, which came equally from the Homepump and Verifuse pumps. For fiscal 1992 Block revised its forecasts upwards, to $45 million with after tax net income of $10 million. Block had quickly become the dominant player in a booming market.

Question 4

You work at HV II and your venture fund wants you to develop liquidity strategies for the Orien and HV II Block investment. How would you value Block in the fall of 1991? Discuss your methodology and show calculations. (Orien and HV II own convertible preferred in a private company.) What do you recommend to the Block Medical board of directors to give your fund liquidity on its investment in the fall of 1991? Block seems to be going well. Why are your partners in HV II thinking of a liquidity strategy at this point in time?

Plans had been to make an initial public offering as Block's revenues approached the $30 million annual run rate, which it had achieved. However, 1991 unfolded as a bearish year for biotechnology stocks, as promised products failed to appear, as well as for health care stocks, as managed care began to depress revenues. Instead, the Block board decided to seek an acquisition partner.

Hillenbrand Industries

The Block board retained Lehman Brothers and Fred Frank to look for an acquirer. The board sought $150 million in cash for complete ownership of Block, priced at $30 per share. Henry Venture II Ltd. for its ten percent ownership, would get a return between $12.5 million and $15 million.

Lehman Brothers quickly narrowed the short-list of potential acquirers to Hillenbrand Industries, Eli Lilly, and Johnson & Johnson — all major companies seeking to acquire new biomedical devices to position them in the home care market. Lehman expected a firm offer within four weeks, and completion of the transaction by mid-September.

Hillenbrand Industries, Inc. was a major conglomerate listed on the New York Stock Exchange. Its companies included Batesville Casket Company, American Tourister Inc., and Hill-Rom, a maker of hospital beds. It had 9,600 employees, annual sales of $1.2 billion, and earnings substantial enough to make the best bid. Company founder William A. Hillenbrand made his first fortune in the 1920s with Hill-Rom hospital beds, based on the revolutionary idea of bringing a homey atmosphere into the hospital by replacing the cold of white steel with the warmth of wood. An acquisiton of Block would represent Hillenbrand's first foray into home health care. On 30 November 1991 the Block acquisition closed.[13] The same day Hillenbrand announced plans to issue $100 million in unsecured 20-year debentures to be used for general corporate purposes and acquisitions. Terms of the Block deal were originally confidential, though later disclosed.

Just 21 months after start-up Hillenbrand bought Block Medical for $63 million cash plus an earn-out to $80 million. Henry Venture II Ltd.

received cash of $7.5 million (on an initial investment of $600,000) plus a continuing ownership interest in Block's earnings over the coming five years. The cash earnout to Henry Venture II could total $5.5 million, payable annually, though in fact nothing was ever returned.

Question 5

What was the CGR in valuation for Block Medical from the Series A to the sale to Hillenbrand? Did Hillenbrand pay too much for Block? What is your opinion? Please give your reasons.

Hillenbrand had a reputation for allowing local control of its companies, and that too appealed to Block executives. In a telephone interview at the time of acquisition, company president W. August Hillenbrand said he looked for companies with solid, aggressive management making products that were "not real high-tech." [14]

Sancoff left in June 1992, after Hillenbrand asked him to dissolve the OEM agreement with McGaw. McGaw had just announced a division that would provide home health services, called CAPS, and Block wanted to assure the customers that bought their equipment that they would not compete against them. [15] Block's growth slowed dramatically. Hillenbrand started actively seeking a buyer for Block. Block closed out its Carlsbad plant to make room for Callaway Golf and, in March 1996, moved to a smaller assembly facility in Rancho Bernardo. In November 1996 Block was acquired from Hillenbrand by another San Diego-based manufacturer of infusion pumps, I-Flow Corporation. I-Flow paid $17 million, about a quarter of what Hillenbrand had paid five years earlier. [16]

Sancoff had signed a non-compete agreement with Hillenbrand, to terminate in June 1994, by which Sancoff agreed not to compete in the home infusion devices market nor against Block's existing (June 1992) product line. This left the hospital infusion devices market wide open. Sancoff had another great idea and, with Henry's backing, would parlay it into River Medical.

Notes to Published Sources

[1] Sandy Hock, "Huge conglomerate buys Block Medical; Firm to remain here," *San Diego Business Journal* 12 (23 December 1991) 1/1.

[2] Paul Goethel, "A Better Mousetrap," *San Diego Executive* 9 (September 1989) 8-10.

[3] Sandy Hock, "IV pump designer raises cash to make its own product line," *San Diego Business Journal* 10 (18 December 1989) 1/4.

[4] Mary Hardie, "NASD reviews Pancretec's stock trading pattern," *San Diego Business Journal* 9 (27 March 1989) 1/13; Joel M. Graff, "Definitive agreement signed for Abbott Laboratories acquisition of Pancretec, Inc.," *Business Wire* (10 May 1989).

[5] Bradley J. Fikes, "Avalon Ventures plans to raise $50 million fund," *San Diego Business Journal* 12 (7 January 1991) 1/3.

[6] Sandy Hock, "IV pump designer raises cash to make its own product line," *San Diego Business Journal* 10 (18 December 1989) 1/4.

[7] "Block Medical, Inc." *The San Diego Union* (December 1990).

[8] "Disposable, Elastomeric Infusion Pump," *Home Health Care Dealer* 2 (November/December 1990); "The Homepump Elastomeric Infusion System," *Journal of Intravenous Nursing* 14 (January/February 1991).

[9] Doris Millam, "Homepump," *Central Line: Newsletter of the Institute for Home I.V. & Nutritional Services* 1 (November/December 1990) 1-2; *IVonyx Connections* 2 (June 1990) 1.

[10] Bradley J. Fikes, "Block Medical plans to double staff, quadruple sales in 1991," *San Diego Business Journal* 12 (14-20 January 1991).

[11] "Sweeney adds drug pump to McGaw line," *Orange County Business Journal* (10 December 1990).

[12] Cristina Lee, "McGaw signs distribution agreement," *Los Angeles Times* (4 December 1990); "Updates: McGaw Inc.," *Orange County Register* (4 December 1990); "McGaw Inc. signs distribution pact," *Orange Coast Daily Pilot* (5 December 1990); "Block Medical, Kendall McGaw Laboratories, Inc.," *In Vivo* 9 (January 1991).

[13] "Hillenbrand Industries closes agreement to acquire Block Medical, Inc." *Business Wire* (21 November 1991); Mike Bayer, "Hillenbrand buys Block Medical," *Cincinnati Enquirer* 151 (23 November 1991) C5.

[14] Sandy Hock, "Huge conglomerate buys Block Medical; Firm to remain here," *San Diego Business Journal* 12 (23 December 1991) 1/1.

[15] Donald E.L. Johnson, "Block Medical cancels contract with McGaw; Says it will never compete with its customers," *Health Industry Today* 55 (May 1992) 8-11.

[16] "Susan Gembrowski, "Medical company to move headquarter to Rancho Bernardo," *San Diego Daily Transcript* (7 March 1996) A1; Gayle L. Arnold, "I-Flow expects recent acquisition to drive strong improvements in results for 1997," *PR Newswire* (19 November 1996).

Exhibit #1

Block Medical, Inc.:
Private Placements and Valuations

	Dec. 1989	May 1990	Nov. 1990	Nov. 1991
Post-Money Valuation	$3.45m	$7.81m	$32.9m	$64m
Price per Share	$1.00	$1.80	$6.70	$14.72
Number of Shares	1,350,000	555,556	597,015	4,348,522
Amount of Placement	$1.35m	$1.0m	$4.0m	
Percent of Block Purchased	31.3%	12.8%	12.1%	100%
Purchasers	Series A	Series B	Series C	Hillenbrand
Investment Banker	Orien II L.P Henry Venture II	Orien II L.P. Henry Venture II	Berkeley	Lehman Brothers
Block Sales (Trailing 12 Months)	—	—	($1.4m)	$30m
Block Earnings (Trailing 12 Months)	—	—	($1.2m)	

Exhibit #2

Statement of Operations: Block Medical, Inc.
(years ended September 30)

	1990(a)	1991
Net Sales	$1,342,888	$16,187,199
Cost of Goods Sold	1,112,484	7,264,094
Gross Margin	230,404	8,923,105
Operating Expenses:		
Research & Development	693,783	893,904
Marketing & Sales	442,020	2,291,168
General & Administrative	410,335	2,559,990
Total Operating Expense	1,546,138	5,745,062
Income (Loss) from Operations	(1,315,734)	3,178,043
Interest Income, Net	45,430	106,561
Provision for Taxes		817,000
Net Income (Loss)	$(1,270,304)	$2,472,001

(a) For the period from inception (6 October 1989) through 30 September 1990.

Exhibit #3

Balance Sheet Data
Block Medical, Inc.

Assets	1990 Sept 30	1991 Sept 30
Current Assets:		
Cash and cash investments	$3,585	$1,123,238
Accounts receivable	516,103	4,592,271
Inventories	606,886	3,494,840
Prepaid expenses and deposits	74,931	326,508
Total current assets	1,201,505	9,536,857
Property:		
Equipment	273,609	1,099,284
Leasehold improvements	134,386	145,451
Furniture	55,859	150,452
Accumulated depreciation	(78,009)	(278,233)
Net total property	385,845	1,116,954
Other Assets:		
Certificate of deposit	200,000	600,000
Long-term deposits	63,087	76,649
Organization costs-net	27,002	17,708
Total other assets	290,089	694,357
Total Assets	$1,877,439	$11,348,168

Liabilities and Shareholder Equity	1990 Sept 30	1991 Sept 30
Current Liabilities:		
Note payable	$160,000	
Line of credit		$909,000
Accounts payable	368,823	1,410,562
Accrued liabilities	159,769	800,891
Income taxes payable		817,000
Capital lease obligations — current	16,764	16,764
Total current liabilities	705,356	3,954,217
Deferred rent	69,117	109,627
Capital lease obligations — long term	23,642	6,310
Shareholder's Equity:		
Convertible preferred stock, $.001 par value	1,906	2,503
Common stock outstanding, $.001 par value	1,846	1,877
Additional paid-in capital	2,345,876	6,386,219
Deficit accumulated	(1,270,304)	(1,270,306)
Net income	—	2,472,001
Total shareholders' equity	1,079,324	7,278,014
Total Liabilities and Shareholders' Equity	$1,877,439	$11,348,168

Exhibit #4

Statement of Cash Flows
Block Medical, Inc.

	1990(a)
Cash Flows From Operating Activities:	
Net Loss	$(1,270,304)
Adjustments to reconcile net loss	
to net cash used for operations:	
Depreciation and amortization	65,698
Changes in assets and liabilities:	
Accounts receivable	(516,103)
Inventories	(606,886)
Deposits and prepaid expenses	(74,931)
Certificate of deposit	(200,000)
Long-term deposits	(63,087)
Organization costs--net	(27,002)
Accounts payable and accrued liabilities	528,592
Deferred rent	68,117
Total adjustments	(824,602)
Cash used for operating activities	(2,094,906)
Cash Flows From Investing Activities:	
Acquisitions of Property	(384,925)
Cash Flows From Financing Activities:	
Advance on line of credit	160,000
Principal payments on capital lease obligations	(10,789)
Net cash contributed in exchange for common stock	23,636
Net proceeds from issuance of preferred stock	2,310,569
Cash provided from financing activities	2,483,416
Net Increase in Cash and Cash At End Of Period	$3,585
Supplemental Disclosure of Cash Flow Information:	
Cash paid during the period for interest	$8,989
Supplemental Schedule of Noncash Investing and Financing Activities:	
The Company entered into capital lease obligations of	$51,195
for new equipment and furnituare during the period ended	
September 30, 1990.	

(a)   For the period from inception (6 October 1989) through 30 September 1990.

Exhibit #5

Block Medical, Inc.:
Actual and Pro Forma Income Statements
($000)

(for the fiscal years ending September 30)

	Unaudited	Act	Estimate		
	1990	**1991**	**1992**	**1993**	**1994**
Total Revenues	1,357	17,174	35,109	55,852	69,301
Cost of Goods Sold	878	6,064	12,640	20,933	27,076
Gross Profit	479	11,110	22,469	34,919	42,225
Operating Expenses:					
Engineering	367	633	1,299	2,067	2,564
General and Administrative	489	1,471	2,984	4,747	5,890
Sales and marketing	869	2,151	4,389	6,982	8,663
Total Operating Expenses	1,725	4,255	8,672	13,796	17,117
Operating Income	(1,246)	6,855	13,797	21,123	25,108
Net Other Income/(Expense)	51	26	585	1,103	1,908
Income Before Taxes	(1,195)	6,881	14,382	22,226	27,016
Provision for Taxes	0	2,445	6,184	9,557	11,617
Net Income	(1,195)	4,436	8,198	12,669	15,399

Exhibit #6

Summary of Terms

1. Amount: $1,000,000

2. Instrument: Series A Convertible Preferred Stock convertible into 29% of the common stock of the company.

3 Capitalization After Closing:

Management:	Existing:* 52%	
	Option Pool:** 19%	
Orien II, L.P.:	Series A:	29%

*   Shares of existing management employed by the company for at least one year prior to closing will be vested over a three-year period, with 25% vested upon closing, with the exception of Howard Barr and Greg Sancoff. Greg Sancoff's shares will vest as follows:

Upon closing	33 1/3%
After 12 months	33 1/3%
After 24 months	33 1/3%

Howard Barr's shares will vest 33 1/3% upon closing, with the remainder over three years.

** Shares granted from the option pool will be vested over at least a four-year period. Unvested shares will be returned to the option pool.

In the event that the company is sold, proceeds from unvested shares will be held in escrow and continue to vest as long as the employee is employed by the acquirer.

4. Liquidation preference:

The Preferred will be a Participating Preferred such that proceeds from any sale, merger or liquidation will be distributed first, to redeem the Preferred then, secondly, to distribute $1 million to the common shareholders on a pro rata basis, and, finally, based on total ownership to all stockholders, including the Preferred on an as-if-converted basis.

5. Conversion: a. Optional: At any time at the election of the holder.

b. Mandatory: Upon the earlier to occur of (i) the election of the holders of at least 2/3 of the Preferred, or (ii) an IPO of at least $10 million at a net price of at least 5 times the then effective Series A Conversion Price.

6. Redemption: Upon a vote of 2/3 of the Series A Preferred and subject to legally available funds, the Company must redeem the convertible preferred in two equal installments on the sixth and seventh anniversary dates of the closing. The redemption price is the higher of cost or fair market value as determined by independent appraisers, mutually agreed upon.

7. Dilution Protection:

Weighted average anti-dilution formula with customary exclusions.

8. Preemptive Rights:

Pro rata right of first refusal based on total ownership for any new equity financing with the customary exclusions.

9. Ownership Retention Agreement:

Until the holders have received 125% of their total original investment from the sale of the Company securities, each member of management must retain 90% of stock held as of closing. This registration is eliminated upon a "qualified IPO," as defined in paragraph 5, or upon the conversion of 100% of the Series A to common. Transfers to immediate family are allowed.

10. Public Sale and Registration Rights:

> The investors, upon the request of the holders of 2/3 of the Series A, are entitled to two long form demand registrations (S-1) at the Company's expense unless the offering is withdrawn by the investors, in which case the investors offering their shares pay the costs pro rata, and two additional long form demand registrations to be paid pro rata by the selling shareholders.

> The investors will also have unlimited first priority "piggy back" registration rights and short form (S2 and S3) demand registration rights, subject to underwriters' limitations. The investors agree to defer any registration for up to 120 days upon good faith determination by the board of directors.

11. Voting Rights/Board of Directors:

> The Preferred will have the same voting rights as common shares on an as-if-converted basis. The board of directors will consist of the five following members:
> 2 Nominees from common shareholders
> 2 Nominees from the Series A investors
> 1 Mutually agreed upon outside member.

> The board will meet no less than six times a year, with no more than 90 days between meetings. Board members will be reimbursed for all expenses incurred in attending board meetings and working on other special projects.

12. Covenants: a. Affirmative: The Company will furnish the investors with the following:

> 1. Monthly financial and operating information compared to budget within 45 days after the end of each month. In addition, the CFO will send a certificate of compliance stating whether any event of noncompliance exists.

2. Yearly budget and operating plan prepared on a monthly basis for the following year at least 30 days prior to the new fiscal year.

3. Audited, unqualified (other than a "going concern" or similar qualification) financial statements by a major national accounting firm within 90 days of the closing of the fiscal year and a copy of the Management Letter.

4. Copies of any communications with shareholders and/or the financial community, government, or any group who may receive information which is of interest to the investors.

b. Restrictive: The Company may not do any of the following without the prior written consent of 2/3 of the investors and the approval of the board, including the affirmative vote of the investor representative.
   1. Pay any cash dividends.

   2. Issue any security or note which has any equity-type feature, profit participation feature, or may be purchased as part of an investment unit if such security also ranks on a parity with or is superior to the convertible preferred stock in either terms or conversion price.

   3. Sell or issue any common stock for which the consideration is other than cash, unless approved by the board, including affirmative vote of the investor representative.

   4. Make any loans, guarantees, or joint ventures, or invest in partially owned subsidiaries in excess of $250,000, in any 12-month period.

5. Create any subsidiary other than wholly owned subsidiaries.

6. Amend the certificate of incorporation or By Laws materially affecting the rights of the Preferred stock.

7. Merge, consolidate, or dispose of all, or substantially all of the Company's assets unless the Company is the surviving corporation. The Company may not on its own dispose of more than 10% of its assets in any 12-month period, other than product inventory in the normal course of business unless approved by the board, including the affirmative vote of the investor representative.

8. Engage in any business other than those presented in the business plan, or approved by the board of directors, including the affirmative vote of the investor representative, as a change in the business plan.

9. Repurchase any common shares or options other than those repurchased under existing buyback and/or vesting agreements unless approved by the board, including the affirmative vote of the investor representative.

10. Engage in any insider transactions which may be considered less than arm's length transactions and/or may adversely affect the Company.

13. Life Insurance:

So long as the Preferred is outstanding, the Company will use best efforts to maintain life insurance on the life of Al Henry in the amount of one million dollars.

14. Assignments:

> The Convertible Preferred may be freely assignable by the investors.

15. Events of Noncompliance:

> An event of noncompliance will occur if:
>
> a. The Company materially breaches any of the covenants or provisions in the Purchase and/or related agreements and it is not cured;
>
> b. Any mandatory redemption, interest payment and/or dividend is overdue;
>
> c. All of the Company's material representations and warranties are not substantially true as of closing;
>
> d. Any defaults on material debt agreements;
>
> e. The Company files for bankruptcy, makes an assignment for the benefit of creditors, materially compromises debt with material creditors or suffers acceleration of a material debt instrument.

16. Remedies for Events of Noncompliance:

> Immediately upon the occurrence of any event of noncompliance listed previously as c, d, and e, or after 30 days of continuous noncompliance described as a or b:
>
> a. A dividend will immediately come into existence on the Convertible Preferred Stock at a rate of 10% and will increase by one percent of each successive 30-day period of noncompliance to a maximum of 16%.
>
> b. Any unpaid dividend may be converted into common stock at the existing conversion price.
>
> c. The investors will have the right to elect the majori-

ty of the board. Once the event of noncompliance has been cured, then the composition of the board will revert back to the pre-default group.

d. The foregoing remedies are not exclusive, and other available legal remedies may be pursued.

17. Amendments and Waivers:

With the consent of the company and the holders of at least 2/3 of the Series A Preferred.

18. Investors' Expenses:

Upon the earlier to occur of (i) written notice from Orien that the conditions to closing will not be met, or (ii) closing, the company will reimburse Orien for all third party expenses incurred in the closing and/or evaluation of the anticipated round of financing. Third party expenses will, among other things, include travel expenses, consultants' fees, and legal fees for an investors counsel selected by Orien. Total expenses will not exceed $30,000. In the event that closing does not occur, the company will not be liable for Orien expenses incurred prior to October 4.

19. Other Terms:

Other terms traditionally contained in purchase agreements of this type, including representations, warranties, etc., shall be contained in the Purchase and related Agreements. Block Medical agrees not to pursue or accept alternative financing for a period of 30 days following written notification that all Investor Due Diligence has been satisfactorily completed. Due diligence is to be completed by October 10.

20. CONDITIONS TO CLOSING:

     a. Satisfactory completion of due diligence.

     b. No material adverse change.

     c. Satisfactory completion of legal documents.

The above terms are hereby agreed to by Block Medical, Inc.

_____   _____

General Partner   President
Orien II, L.P.

_____   _____

Date   Date

Block Case Solution

What other steps could Sancoff undertake to be sure he had identified a valuable new product and match it to its market?

1. Test efficacy of product-user acceptance.
   a) Build prototypes and conduct focus groups with nurse users.
   b) Have clinicians conduct patient studies and publish papers recounting experiences. Preferably clinicians of standing.

2. Any competitive products in existence? Have market research validate the size of the home market and have the companies using the newly-invented product researched to establish:
   a) standing with competitive products
   b) adaptability and ease of use of new product
   c) intent to use new product.

3. Establish sales price that the market will bear. Make a pricing survey of both users and reimbursement companies (HMOs & insurance payers) regarding acceptable maximum price for a home infusion antibiotic instrument, and willingness to reimburse users. The industry has a user/payer structure wherein user does not buy the product.

4. Verify that estimated manufacturing costs will produce acceptable gross profit margins. Have product consultants validate estimated standard costs of volume manufacture. Crucial to make sure product can be made in volume at estimated costs.

5. Test and validate prospective sales channel of distribution. Will the channel handle the instrument? At what incremental cost?

6. Have VC firms validate uniqueness of technology under confidentiality agreements.

What was the pre-money valuation of Block Medical placed on the company by venture capitalists Orien and HV II for the Series A financing? Show your calculations.

Pre-Money Valuation	=	Financing Amount	÷	Percent of Company Purchased	—	Amount of Financing.

$$X = \$1,350,000 \div 0.36 - \$1,350,0000$$
$$X = \$2.4 \text{ million}$$

Regarding the Block Medical term sheet, unusual elements to protect the VCs include the following:

1. Note that the shares of management and the founders are not completely owned by them until after 24 to 36 months of company founding. The principal founder, Sancoff, vested ownership of his shares at the rate of 2/3 after twelve months of company operation and 100 percent after 24 months of company operation.

2. The liquidation preference does not entirely go to the venture capitalists. Rather, $1 million is allocated to the common shareholders because the founders own a considerable amount of the company, post-financing.

3. The preferred stock purchase agreement calls for redemption on the sixth and seventh years after initial closing. Many venture capital preferreds now have redemption features.

4. Anti-dilution protection is present.

5. Affirmative covenants are standard.

6. Restrictive covenants are standard.

7. Principal founder has a $1 million life insurance requirement.

8. Events of non-compliance and remedies are standard.

9. Other terms-the venture capitalists required a stand-still agreement from Block Medical upon signing of the term sheet.

Question 3, page 72

What options are available to a new, small company with an innovative product to magnify its impact on the marketplace?

1. Get major product distribution deal with high profile corporate user or vendor.

2. License technology to a corporation with established sales force and large market share and let them manufacture product.

3. Outsource manufacturing for volume production and emphasize sales and market share development either direct or with distribution help.

Block Liquidity Strategy

Question 4, page 75

You work at HV II and your venture fund wants you to develop liquidity strategies for the Orien and HV II Block investment. How would you value Block in the fall of 1991? Discuss your methodology and show calculations. (Orien and HV II own convertible preferred in a private company.)

A. Valuation Methods for Block Liquidity Strategy
 1. For IPO determine comparable company multiples of revenues and after-tax income for similar industry growth rates and product lines. Develop database of comparable ratios of public healthcare device companies with high growth rates and of similar size (i.e. $20 to $50 million revenues).

 2. For sale to a corporate acquirer,
 a. Develop a database of comparable EBITDA multiples of healthcare device company acquisitions with similar growth rates. (We use EBITDA because it is possible that not all device companies would be reporting net income i.e. to have a P/E ratio.)

 b. Do a discounted cash flow (DCF) analysis of three years and five years of Block Medical P&L and Cash Flow Forecasts using a matrix of discount rates. Compare the DCF analysis to comparable company multiples of EBITDA for healthcare device company deals actually closed.

 c. Do a cost-based estimate of dollar amount to establish comparable market share in the home care market. What cost and time would be required to invent a new product placed in a market of comparable size to Block's home care market?

Question 4, page 75

What do you recommend to the Block Medical board of directors to give your fund liquidity on its investment in the fall of 1991? Block seems to be going well. Why are your partners in HV II thinking of a liquidity strategy at this point in time?

1. Liquidity sought by venture shareholders in fall 1991 because considerable value had been created in twenty months of Block operations since startup, with sales being $1.4 million and $16 million in years one and two, and $45 million

forecasts in year three. Business experience dictated that it is difficult to sustain a 100 percent growth rate with a start-up company, so partial liquidity (IPO) should be sought.

2. But, 1991 became a bearish year in the IPO market for health care and biotech companies. The venture investors then decided to cash out through a company sale for cash with an earnout. An earnout is appropriate for seller to seek because of very high forecast growth rate for years three, four and five (1992, 1993, and 1994). Total sale would only be made if multiples were very attractive (Block ultimately sold for $63 million cash plus earnout which was 5 times trailing 12 month sales and 32 times trailing 12 months after tax net income and 10 times net worth).

3. These are high multiples of value. A business fear of the venture capital shareholders at the time was the pressure being created by managed care to reduce health care costs. Block HomePump was somewhat expensive for home intravenous (IV) infusions and some managed care payers would not reimburse home IV companies using the HomePump. Reimbursement pressures could inhibit Block growth in sales and earnings in the future, which is in fact what happened. Block revenues never grew about $20 million annually after acquisition by Hillenbrand, which eventually sold Block for $17 million in 1995.

Question 5, page 77

What was the CGR in valuation for Block Medical from the Series A to the sale to Hillenbrand? Did Hillenbrand pay too much for Block? What is your opinion? Please give your reasons.

See Exhibit #1

The annual compound growth rate in per-share value for Block shareholders was 283 percent (i.e. value $1 per share on Series A and $14.72 per Block share on sale to Hillenbrand). The compound growth rate in aggregate post-money valuation was 352 percent (i.e. $3.12 million on Series A and $64 million Block value on sale to Hillenbrand).

Did Hillenbrand pay too much for Block?

As indicated, Hillenbrand paid 6 times the earnings forecast for the coming year, fiscal '92 of $10 million after tax net income. Also, Hillenbrand paid 4 times fiscal '92 EBITDA forecast. Neither of these multiples is high, if we assume that the fiscal '92 forecast can be achieved, which was not the case. The trailing twelve months' P/E multiples of 26 times is not high for the Block growth rate in sales and earnings, nor is the EBITDA multiples high, given the Block growth rate.

IVAC Medical Systems, Inc.

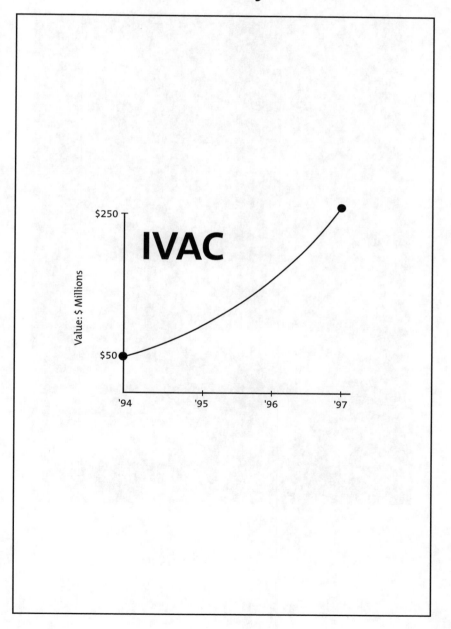

The following pictures depict the basic instruments of IVAC, along with its new products.

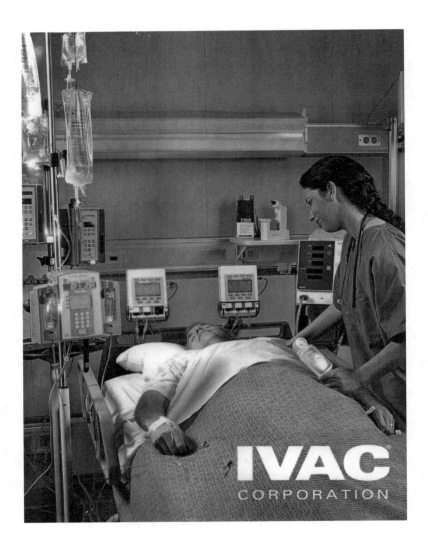

The Good, The Bad and the Living Dead

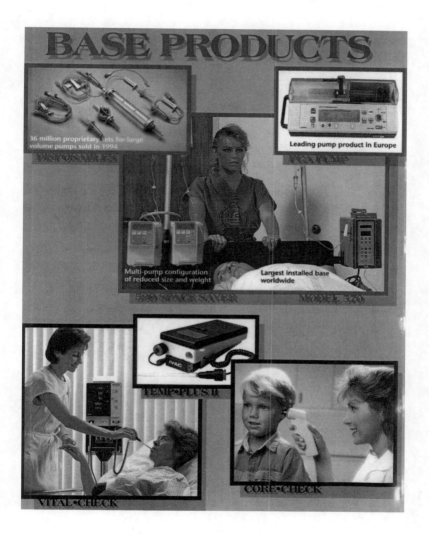

BASE PRODUCTS

36 million proprietary sets for large volume pumps sold in 1994

DISPOSABLES

Leading pump product in Europe

PCA PUMP

Multi-pump configuration of reduced size and weight

Largest installed base worldwide

599 SPACE SAVER

MODEL 570

TEMP•PLUS II

VITAL•CHECK

CORE•CHECK

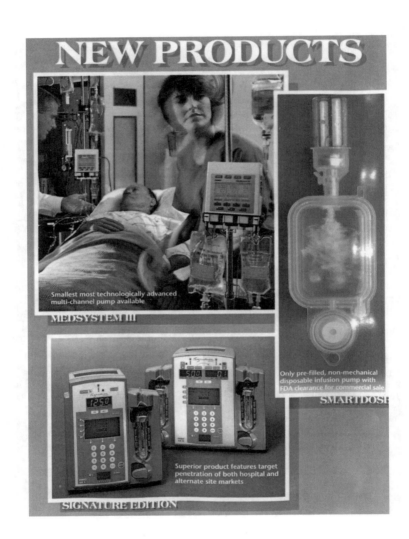

The following diagram shows how the River Medical instrument was designed and how it works.

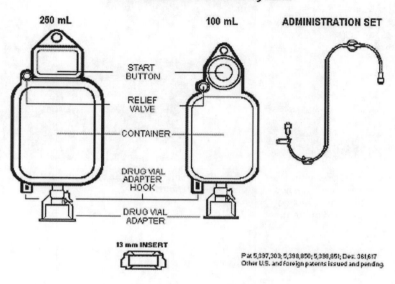

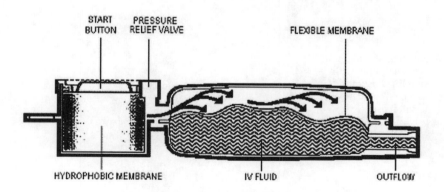

THE FLEXIBLE MEMBRANES ARE PUSHED DOWNWARD BY THE CO2 PRESSURE, FORCING SOLUTION OUT OF THE CONTAINER AT A CONSTANT PRESSURE.

100ml SmartDose, with standard drug vial attached and antibiotic drug mixing with the prefilled dilutent.

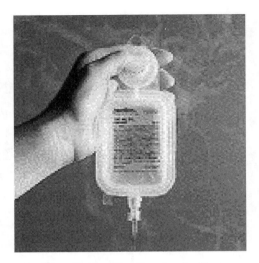

100ml SmartDose, with a thumb poised to press the start button.

IVAC Signature Edition™ compact pump with simplified user interface, designed for general hospital use.

I nfusions are good medicine, but tough business. Technology moves rapidly, opening opportunity for new products, but cost-conscious customers demand ever slimmer margins for instrument producers. Cash-strapped new companies get little time to generate revenues on their investment in engineering. Companies, both new and old, live and die by the alliances they build because market shares are controlled by the large solution and instrument companies that have been selling infusion products (solutions, instruments and disposables) to the same hospitals since the early 1970s.

IVAC had invented the world's first electronic infusion pump in 1969, and the company was acquired by Eli Lilly in 1974. Lilly is a major U.S. pharmaceutical company, and they wanted to participate in the growing market of instrumentation for infusion therapy, since they already owned an extensive portfolio of FDA-approved drugs.

Disposable Pumps

"Alternative site" infusions — at home or outpatient clinics — were the fastest growing segment of the infusion therapy industry, but hospital infusions were much greater in number. The size of the hospital market was most evident in antibiotic infusions. For every dose of antibiotics infused at home, thirty were infused at the hospital. Every patient recovering from surgery needed antibiotics, often for weeks. So did "compromised host" patients — those with AIDS or those undergoing chemotherapy, as well as patients with aggressive infectious diseases. (See Table #5, page 144.) Also, advances in pumps with sterile lines made infusions far less risky, so more physicians prescribed infusions as routinely as oral or injected antibiotics. Just in the U.S, and amongst adult patients, this hospital market equalled 300 million antibiotic doses per year. By 1993 the annual hospital market for infusion equipment stood at $2 billion, half of which was equipment for antibiotics.

This growth in hospital infusions strained the technical system for delivering them. Every morning, hospital pharmacists mixed antibiotic solutions for every patient for the entire day, and the nurses had to keep track of them. This was labor-intensive, also wasteful. Mixing the drug with the diluent started the clock on a short shelf life; if medication plans changed, the pharmacists had to dispose of any solutions the nurses did not end up infusing that day. A large 650 bed hospital could mix a thousand IV antibiotic doses per day then throw out 30 percent of those due to spoilage.

Furthermore, electronic pumps used to deliver most infusions became increasingly more sophisticated, bulky, and expensive. Few machines could be set up quickly enough to be useful in a trauma center. And in a cost-cutting environment, hospitals grew less willing to make the capital investment in sophisticated multi-purpose machines. Sancoff never hoped to design a pump to completely replace the installed base of electronic pumps, but hospitals replaced 10 percent to 15 percent of that installed base each year. This replacement market cried out for less capital-intensive alternatives.

In theory, this market for hospital infusion devices was so huge that any start-up might succeed by capturing a small market share. In reality, landing even a slender beachhead of market share would be a hard fight for any new company with a new product. Well-established purchasing alliances of hospital groups, as well as market dominance by a few major hospital supply firms, made this market extremely tough to penetrate. Sancoff had to offer some very promising new technology, and he approached Al Henry to finance his new company, River Medical, after their notable success together in Block Medical.

What Sancoff proposed was a disposable pump optimized for hospital usage. The pump fits in the palm and has three parts, all of plastic and all welded together. The most radical part is the motor. To start an infusion, the nurse presses a small sealed tablet — much like an Alka-Seltzer tablet — through a plastic membrane so that it mixes with water. This bubbles into a carbon dioxide gas at a constant 10 psi for ten full hours. This gas, rather than gravity or the mechanical force used in volumetric pumps, is the motive force behind the infusion. The gas moves through one precise aperture, and presses against a non-permeable plastic membrane in the second, larger, chamber of the pump. This chamber holds the most common diluents — like dextrose or saline in a sterile water solution. Because the chamber was prefilled in a sterile manufacturing environment, the solution and the pump has a shelf life of 12 months.[1]

The second part of the pump is a small port where the nurse attaches a standard 13 mm or 20 mm drug vial. Other pump makers used a proprietary vial attachment so that drug firms had to license the vial technology to sell their drugs. Because Sancoff's pump needed no special adapter, hospital pharmacies could save money by buying generic drugs or proprietory drugs in standard vials. Significantly, the vial attaches without needles, since OSHA was making needle sticks a major issue in hospital employee safety. Thus, in the large chamber, the drug and solution mix together, just before infusing into the patient.

The third pump part is the administration set — the lines going into the patient's veins. The nurse attached one of five different, color-coded lines so that the drug admixture flowed at the prescribed, volumetric rate. Thus, in one small, cheap package, came a complete ambulatory, volumetric infusion pump. Just before infusing, the nurse inserted the drug vial, shook the pump to mix the drug with the solution, attached the right administration lines, pressed the tablet to start the gas, then hooked the pump to the patient's gown. When the infusion finished, the nurse tossed the whole thing.

Because it simplified the whole infusion process, nurses would drive pump sales. A teaser advertisement would show only the equipment Sancoff's pump replaced. "No powercords! No batteries! No repairs!" — because it was non-electric. "No complicated programming!" — because it had a single start button. "No IV poles!" — because it was gravity-independent. "No risk of needle sticks!" — because of the generic drug vial attachment. "No IV bags!" — because it was prefilled. "No bulky machines!" — because of its stackablity and compactness. Unfortunately, few hospital purchasing departments bought new equipment just to spare nurses trouble.

To succeed, Sancoff's group would need to neutralize the concerns of hospital pharmacists. Those pharmacists without enough work to do would resist such de-skilling, by pre-filled containers that nurses could mix on the floor. Those pharmacists with too much work to do would object to keeping track of one more peice of equipment. Also, pharmacists liked that the pump delivered one exact unit dose of antibiotic, but considered the rate-control precision built into the pump as overkill for most antibiotics. The most common antibiotics — penicillin and cephalosporins — needed rate control only for patients with liver or kidney deficiencies. One focus group pharmacist claimed, "if the drug is not listed in hospital policy for rate control, I won't fill it with a rate-controlled device." Many pharmacists preferred the flexibility of IMED or IVAC volumetric pumps, were they could set variable dosages and volumes as well as flow rates.

Hospitals had already begun buying competing products that extended the shelf lives of solutions — like Abbott's ADD-Vantage and Baxter's Minibag Plus — from big companies that could put real price pressure on Sancoff's new pump. These competitor pumps were made from non-inert plastics that reacted with certain drugs, whereas Sancoff's pump could be used across the entire spectrum of antibiotics. Or the waste plastics produced toxic gases when incinerated, whereas Sancoff's polypropelyene burned cleanly into carbon dioxide and steam. Or the prefilled diluents had shelf lives no longer than a month, or they had to be frozen, whereas diluents in the new pump lasted a year at room temperature. Most important, the ADD-Vantage and Minibag Plus were only bags, not complete pumps.

Efforts at making complete disposable pumps — for emergency use on trauma victims — used complicated assembly of small plastic parts which rendered the pumps too expensive for routine use. Block Medical's elastomeric HomePump, for example, had just dropped in price from $9 to $7 each, still nowhere near Sancoff's target price of $4.50 each. And while HomePump was gravity-independent and easy for nurses to set up, it took so much pharmacy labor to fill that it never found its way into hospital use. No competing product integrated the complete package like Sancoff's disposable pump.

On the basis of his patent applications, Sancoff founded River Medical in January 1993. By March 1993, after spending $50,000 of his own money on product design, Sancoff asked Henry for the funding and expertise to move the pump into manufacturing.

Series A Funding

Sancoff's original business plan stated that he intended to raise $1.5 million in a first round from no more than three investment partners. By the end of 1993 River would burn $99,000 per month in salary, totalling $651,000 for the year. Add in $700,000 for product development and manufacturing equipment, and the $1.5 million total would be spent.

Assuming FDA product approval in late 1993, by January 1994 River would need an additional $1.5 million for operational capital. And Sancoff wanted this first round financing at a $5 million pre-money valuation.

Henry saw a great opportunity coming — a great product for a neglected market, offered by a skilled engineer-entrepreneur who had once before generated real profits for his fund. Henry Venture II Limited became lead financier on River Medical, expecting to make an investment of $1.0 million in River's Series A convertible prefered stock in exchange for 20 percent of the company. Sancoff then lined up funding from Kevin J. Kinsella who ran Avalon Bioventures, a La Jolla-based venture firm which had helped start more than thirty companies. Avalon would invest $500,000 for a 10 percent ownership. At the same time, Sancoff issued 3.24 million shares of common stock in addition to $50,000 paid-in capital. Total funding now stood at $1.55 million, enough for a year of good growth and enough to cover Sancoff's estimate of the cash needed to reach profitability.

Upon finishing his due diligence, Henry got Sancoff to accept a lower pre-money valuation. On 16 March 1993, HVF II and River executed their term sheet. Series A shares were convertible into one-third of the common stock of the company. On closing, River would create a 6 percent option pool for distribution to employees. As a result, Sancoff would initially own 60.67 percent of the Company, HVF II would own 22.22 percent, and Avalon Bioventures would own 11.11 percent. Redemption price was 150 percent of the original purchase price with payment begining on the seventh anniversary of the closing. The shares would convert automatically with an IPO of at least $10 million at a net price of at least two times the then effective conversion price.

Then Institutional Venture Partners (IVP) came into the round. IVP was a privately-held family of venture capital partnerships with deep roots in Silicon Valley and over $400 million in committed capital. Since 1974, IVP had invested in over 100 companes, with market values now over $8 billion, and mostly in the software, communications, and life sciences industries. Like the Henry Funds, IVP invests in new companies, helps them round out their expertise, and makes money on the sale.

IVP learned of River through Kinsella, since the $500,000 Avalon Bioventures invested originated with IVP. IVP urged Sancoff to expand the financing to $2,250,000 and give IVP a direct investment of $750,000 in addition to its indirect investment of $500,000 through Kinsella. Henry knew River would benefit from IVP's excellent contacts. Furthermore, Sancoff just found an excellent manufacturing space and the lease would boost River's burn rate. Since selling shares to IVP would lower Sancoff's ownership, the decision was ultimately his.

In a second closing, on 22 April 1993, Sancoff sold an additional $500,000 in Series A shares to the Institutional Venture Partner V fund, bringing the grand total raised to $2.25 million.

Question 1

How do you calculate the pre-money valuation of River Medical for its Series A financing if HV II received 22.22 percent for $1 million invested, and Avalon received 11.11 percent for $500,000 invested? Show your calculations.

Manufacturing

The day before meeting with IVP, Sancoff reported to Henry about potential manufacturing facilities. Since River expected quick FDA approval of the disposable pump — before fourth quarter 1993 — they very early began hiring manufacturing and quality control staff. First, concurrent design of a precision, sterile manufacturing line was a critical part of pump design. Second, River needed lots of pumps for the clinical trials. Third, River needed a launch price below $4.50 each. And finally, River wanted to make a big splash by offering bulk lots as early as January 1994.

So while River engineers fine-tuned the pump design, Sancoff searched all over San Diego for a proper manufacturing plant. River had already outgrown its leased 2500 square foot office, with simple wet lab and machine shop. He had found a building close to their existing office — 4,000 square feet that would cost $750,000. The landlord agreed to contribute $300,000 for building a class 10,000 cleanroom as soon as he arranged a bank loan.

Sancoff put together a team that quickly looked like a company. River spent its salary money up front, hiring the best people to serve as vice presidents. Tad Vaughn led construction of the clean room. Vaughn had worked at Block Medical as director of disposable operations, with IVAC as an industrial engineer, and with Pacific Device, a contract manufacturer of disposables. Mark C. Doyle led River's research and development as director of disposable engineering. Doyle was a mechanical engineer with vast experience in manufacturing plastics, who had most recently worked for APEX Medical setting up a completely automated facility for manufacturing condoms and rubber gloves. Frederic P. Field left Block Medical to become River's manager of biomedical enginering and direct pump design, product validation, and the test protocol.

The pump and manufacturing space developed well enough that at the River Board meeting of 6 July 1993, they considered tradenames. The working name had been A-Dose, since the pump delivered a single dose cheaply. The board discussed how the name also needed a meaning in Spanish — like Uno-Dose — since markets south of the border would be important and since California would be 40 percent Spanish by 2000. The board's confidence in a bright future became more apparent as the conversation turned playful — Dose-Off, Dispos-a-Dose, Mersi-Dose and Dose á Dose. When the vote came around, they adopted SmartDose™ for the prefilled pump and SmartDose II™ for the empty pump.

Series B Funding

By the summer of 1993, River had assembled a first-class team of people to lead the company. They were very far along in fine-tuning the manufacuring process as they awaited FDA approval. By September 1993, River needed extra capital for equipment — about $3 million, they estimated. Furthermore, Sancoff wanted to expand the option pool to 540,000 common shares (8.16 percent ownership) diluted from his shares of common stock. This next round of financing would prove painless, primarily because Henry remained committed. Henry asked that Series B shares issue at a $20 million pre-money valuation and that the Series B hold the same terms as Series A. He offered to invest up to $1.5 million in the Series B — the HVF II pro rata share of the Series B was 51.1 percent so that his fund maintained a 25.6 percent ownership in River.

Sancoff wrote to IVP, on 14 September 1993, to discuss a second round of financing. Sancoff suggested he might fund River through bridge loans with warrants until product launch. With a product on the market, River could then offer stock to an investment company like Berkeley Medical

Investment Limited, which would likely pay a significant step-up valuation. But IVP responded quickly, and very favorably.

IVP still desired to boost its investment in River. IVP had committed $1 million for the first round but were cut back to $500,000 — a small amount hard to justify considering the size of the fund. IVP now commited its pro-rata share of $1.5 million and by 3 Novermber 1993, the second round had closed.

As due diligence, IVP hired a marketing consultant to sit in on River's focus groups — of 10 hospital nurses and 14 hospital pharmacists — and recalculate the market and pricing potential for SmartDose. More importantly, IVP wrote to Sancoff describing a special conversion formulae for the Series B shares in case River did not make its 1994 plan. Sancoff's plan was for $16 million total sales at year-end 1994, plus FDA approvals to sell SmartDose to U.S. hospitals, plus $10 million in backlog and OEM orders. IVP proposed restating the terms for the second round financing. The pre-money valuation would remain $20 million if River acheived $16 million in gross revenues, if they got FDA approvals, and if they signed $10 million in backlog agreements. Or, the $20 million valuation was automatic if River signed a letter of intent to sell the company at a $50 million valuation. Otherwise, Series B shares would convert at a more favorable rate. The $20 million pre-money valuation would be adjusted downward on a linear curve — $5 million in total sales meant a $10 million valuation upward to $16 million in sales resulting in the $20 million valuation — plus discounts of 25 percent for lack of FDA approval or orders backlogs. Sancoff's ownership, and that of the option pool, could drop as much as 7 percent if they failed to make plan.

FDA Approval

Increasingly the FDA bureaucracy loomed larger on River's strategic horizons. By October 1993, River was crunching final test data so they could begin manufacturing the SmartDose. With the assistance of a contract laboratory named Fresenius, Inc. River accelerated their material compatibility tests, toxicity tests, and shelf-life stability tests. By November, they put finishing touches on their prototype production line, and earned certification as a pharmaceutical grade manufacturer under FDA Good Manufacturing Practices. So River could make the product, just not yet sell it.

The FDA at this time promised to approve biomedical devices more deliberately as a way of making the FDA more activist. At the same time, America's biomedical firms accelerated their pace of innovation thus lengthening the queue of products awaiting review. Political activism by disease-based interest groups plus a user-fee experiment begun in 1992, whereby the FDA hired 600 new inspectors by charging a $100,000 fee on each new drug application, marginally sped approvals for drugs, especially for the big drug firms. But the biomedical device review process remained a regulatory quagmire.

The FDA began regulating devices in 1976, but then only for engineering performance rather than clinical results. The FDA had approved 47 brand-new medical devices in 1990; in 1993 it approved only 12. Newt Gingrich called the FDA "a bully and thug" for constipating the innovation that made America's small biomedical start-ups the envy of the world. Increasingly these companies moved operations abroad. Congress passed the Safe Medical Devices Act of 1990 which nominally eased red tape for 510k approvals, but also allowed the FDA to demand more detailed data on safety and efficacy. Satisfying FDA data requirements doubled or tripled the cost of developing new devices. Higher capital costs during development, of course, made companies more dependent on quicker approval for sales. The FDA claimed a median backlog of 98 days for device approvals, only 8 days over the legislative requirement. But the Health Industry Manufacturer's Association noted the average backlog was 160 days, with the smallest, capital-starved companies clearly getting strung out the longest by the FDA.[2]

Not until December 1993 — after seven long months of waiting — did River receive any indication that the FDA was even looking at its SmartDose. River got an FDA review letter asking for raw data not included in the original application.

Fortunately, the FDA letter indicated that the FDA was inclined to consider SmartDose as a 510k device. Section 510(k) of the Food, Drug and Cosmetic Act allows firms to simply tell the FDA that they intend to market a device that is essentially the same as a product already on the market. The FDA could force a lengthy review, however, by raising two objections — that the device is not in fact a device, or that the device is not in fact similar to previous devices. Mark Shannon, hired in July 1993 as River's vice president of quality and regulatory affairs, had submitted both the unfilled and prefilled SmartDose for 510k approval.

The FDA letter allowed the empty SmartDose to proceed as a 510k device with approval, in principal, coming in three to five months — perhaps as early as March 1994. River responded quickly to the FDA letter. River never skimped or delayed the testing for SmartDose, and the total regulatory compliance and quality testing bill ran $313,000 in its first year. But given the FDA's constant alterations to the process, the approval date was highly unpredictable. Furthermore, the FDA held out the prospect that the prefilled SmartDose would still be approved as a drug product. River summoned forth substantial legal argument to convince the FDA that the prefilled SmartDose also fit 510k guidelines. Writing 510k applications — piggybacking product descriptions and evoking lineage to past products — was an art oftentimes unfamiliar to start-ups marketing their product as breakthrough innovations.

First, River had to define the prefilled SmartDose as a device, even though it contained a liquid that would infuse into the body. The FDA defines a drug as any material that acheives its advertised function within the body or through human metabolism. River argued that the liquid in SmartDose was simply an inactive diluent with no medicinal effect. Never before had the FDA regulated IV pumps as a drug simply because a drug passed through them. SmartDose would never embody the finished drug product like other new medical packaging — transdermal patches, nebulizers, or prefilled syringes. It simply reconstitutes the drug product before infusion. The only "drug" issues with SmartDose, River argued, were with material biocompatibility and product stability; River had already submitted ample data to satisfy those reviews.

Second, River had to define SmartDose as essentially similar to existing devices. River claimed SmartDose was a very closely integrated set of three existing devices — an infusion pump, a fluid container, and an administration set. Only one part of the device was really new — the gaseous propellant. The plastic it used, the saline or dextrose diluents it contained, and even the principle of the gas-driven pump had all long enjoyed FDA approval and hospital usage.

If the FDA considered SmartDose a device, review would be completed by the FDA Center for Devices and Radiological Health which had a reputation for efficiency. Only 60 other devices stood in that review queue. Best case scenario was approval in May, with exports as early as February. River spelled out why its review should remain with the CDRH: "In simple arithmetic terms, the product is three parts sophisticated device, 1 part inactive diluent." If defined as a drug, SmartDose would be reviewed instead by offices having a serious backlog of applications, and complicated drug testing. Best case scenario was approval no sooner than 28 months, plus formal FDA licenses required for exporting.

Now River had to rebuild its business plan around an empty Smart Dose that would be a product impossible to sell. River's first step was to cease all hiring and conserve operating capital until FDA approval came in whatever form it might come. That January River's burn rate hit $200,000 per month with $2.9 million left in the bank.

Perhaps the only good news was that with the delays, Sancoff's non-compete agreement with Block Medical expired and River would not need to take extraordinary legal steps to assure that its disposable pump would find its way into the home infusion market.

In April 1994, five months later than their worst-case scenario, River finally got 510k approval on its empty SmartDose. This limited approval altered River's strategic outlook. Hospital pharmacists were less likely to buy a SmartDose they had to fill themselves — it was easier to fill the generic bags that connected to electronic pumps — so River had to forge alliances with larger drug firms or hospital supply firms. Of these, Abbott Laboratories, Inc. showed the most intense interest.

Abbott Due Diligence

Abbott had first approached River as early as February 1994. Abbott suggested several options ranging from licensing of SmartDose manufacturing, to exclusive marketing rights, to acquisition of River Medical itself in order to protect the Abbott ADD-Vantage product line.

In four short months following FDA approval of ADD-Vantage approval in 1985, twelve major drug companies signed on to use the bags.[3] ADD-Vantage annual revenues reached roughly $500 million by 1992. Baxter had threatened Abbott's revenue stream with its MiniBag Plus, which offered all the shelf-life advantages of the ADD-Vantage bag plus an adapter for standard drug vials. By buying River, Abbott would bolster the ADD-Vantage product line with a rate-controlled disposable pump, extend its product life cycle, and encourage more drug companies to license Abbott's proprietary drug vial, which already commanded a 25 percent share of antibiotic sales to hospitals. Furthermore, Abbott CEO Duane Burnham had committed the company to a lean, centralized operation dedicated to maintaining market share in its core businesses. Abbott's competitors — Eli Lilly, Merck, SmithKline Beecham — had lavished more than $12 billion in 1994 acquiring drug benefit managers. Abbott invested instead in research and product acquisition on the assumption that the market will beat a path to the company with the best products.[4] Abbott especially hoped to break the stagnation in IV solution pricing — as it struggled to maintain market share against Baxter — by focusing on packaging.

In March 1994, Abbott sent to San Diego a team of operations experts for detailed due diligence of River. They concluded that River's product was outstanding, then recrunched and confirmed all of River's numbers. Abbott could price SmartDose at a premium, they figured, to maximize profit and keep it from cannibalizing sales of ADD-Vantage bags. Abbott could price SmartDose as high as $6.00 per unit — still 30 percent less than existing elastomeric disposables and 20 percent below the per dose cost with an electronic pump. With ADD-Vantage bags getting price pressure at $1.30 each, Abbott still had plenty of incentive to encourage hospitals to shift to the premium SmartDose container.

The product might be good enough to capture the entire market of 300 million doses per year for hospital antibiotics. These 300 million doses did not even include international, alternate site, chemotherapy, pediatric, or premixed drug sales, which a low-priced SmartDose could also capture. Furthermore, SmartDose had an even better chance of capturing the 80 million (27 percent) of these doses delivered by rate-controlled pumps either by drug protocol or hospital policy. River's business plan had conservatively called for capturing only 3 percent of that 80 million doses. If Abbott penetrated 5 percent of that market in the first year, at a possible unit price of $4.50, it could generate revenues of $67.5 million. If Abbott propelled unit sales to 80 million doses within three years, they would generate annual revenues of $360 million, not including additional revenues from administration sets and drug vials.

But the time to buy was now. If River moved ahead with their plans and launched SmartDose with a standard vial, Abbott could never re-launch SmartDose with its proprietory vial.

The fit between River and Abbott was excellent. In June, Abbott offered a deal. Abbott would have its crack 460-person sales force sell SmartDose on a one-year exclusive deal with a volume commitment. Abbott hinted at signing a non-compete agreement. First, however, they wanted to address some issues raised in their focus groups, and get better information on River's manufacturing process. Abbott expressed wonderment that River could manufacture to the price and high quality standards they claimed.

The River board, however, urged caution. River needed to protect their trade secrets on manufacturing. River had a lock on their technology. No other company was developing a competing disposable. River had six major patents pending, plus an agreement on the only potentially competing patent which was issued to an independent inventor for a gas pump built from a flexible IV bag. Abbott was developing its own CO_2 cuff-type pump, called the Abbott Energizer, that would likely only be approved for very low volume infusions to keep veins open.

Abbott's overtures were keeping River from getting more serious about its own sales force. Any agreement must allow River to hire ten regional distributors within the United States and sign a separate deal for sales abroad. Otherwise, three months would pass before Abbott could train its sales force, and three more before Abbott returned any revenues to River. Henry envisioned a traditional instrument sales approach for River, with a small, highly focused direct sales force — five people calling on national home infusion accounts and twenty calling on hospitals — complemented by a network of proven distributors working the large regional hospitals. River's vice president of sales had a hard-driving, commando style that could make this approach flourish. Not only would a direct sales force boost revenues quickly, but it gave River the flexibility to pursue various types of relationships.

Once River got FDA approval for the empty SmartDose, and a trickle of revenues, River set a 10 June deadline for Abbott to offer a unit price. Abbott let this deadline slip, then gradually their display of interest disintegrated. Abbott sent River a videotape of a focus group in Philadelphia that raised doubts about the marketplace perception of

SmartDose. (Abbott had asked nurses to compare the simplicity of setting up SmartDose versus the ADD-Vantage bag merely by looking at them.) River had already gained much from this dance with Abbott: they had a report from the top experts of a major pharmaceutical firm proclaiming that River had passed detailed due diligence with flying colors. River could make Abbott wait.

By August, Abbott feared they had lost basic access to SmartDose, and returned offering terms very favorable to River. Abbott asked for a three year, non-exclusive distribution deal, across Abbott's entire North American hospital and alternate care sales operations. Abbott wanted access to River's entire product line, on an OEM basis, and wanted pumps to accept both proprietary and standard drug vials. Abbott committed minimum volume purchases at good margins. By then, however, other firms had offered sweeter distribution deals for SmartDose.

Pharmacia, for example, hoped to use SmartDose to package a blood expander for its trauma subsidiary. Pharmacia also offered to pay a licensing fee and royalties for secured and exclusive rights to market the entire line of SmartDose products anywhere outside North America. River's San Diego plant already was moving toward ISO 9001 certification, and River could also use Pharmacia's pharmaceutical regulatory license to launch the prefilled SmartDose in Europe in less than 4 months. Biomedical device markets in Europe and the Pacific Rim were growing at a much faster pace than the U.S. Of all device firms responding to a survey by the Health Industry Manufacturer's Association, 61 percent stated that, because of endemic FDA delays, they introduced products overseas prior to FDA approvals for U.S. sales.[5] Doing so, however, often prompted retaliation from FDA bureaucrats. River also had competitive reasons to let international sales drive early revenues on SmartDose. European nations with nationalized or socialized medicine often prefer the cheaper syringe-type pumps over expensive electronic pumps. And SmartDose did not use the DEHP plastics, prohibited by European law, which are used in many American IV products.

After two months of negotiating, with Abbott, Pharmacia and others, River was finalizing a deal whereby IVAC Corporation, one of the oldest and best-established names in the infusion business, would buy $80 million of SmartDose pumps over a three year period for resale in the U.S.

IVAC needed River's technology to offer the full range of devices and remain the U.S. leader in pump sales. River balked at an exclusive agreement with IVAC only because the company did not have an alternative site presence as strong as its hospital presence and, since IVAC was for sale, it was unclear if the new buyer would lean that way.

Question 2

Discuss the positives and negatives of River becoming a captive OEM manufacturer for Abbott or for any other large health care company. Also discuss the effect of an OEM agreement on River's profit margins, its ultimate valuation in public and private equity markets, and restrictions on an IPO or other liquidity options. Do venture capitalists generally want to fund OEM companies? Why or why not?

Series C Funding

But first, River still needed cash for short-term operations. Henry remained tremendously enthusiastic, and was prepared to invest $500,000. IVP remained equally enthusiastic and saw an opportunity to boost his stake in River. IVP was prepared to invest $2.5 million, plus bring in associates from the Sand Hill Road venture finance community. IVP suggested that Menlo Ventures do due diligence and set valuation, but made it clear they choked at a $25 million pre-money valuation.

As the round closed, IVP put up $2.25 million (its direct and indirect investments now stood at 30.97 percent of River ownership). Menlo Ventures also put up $2.25 million, with smaller amounts from Avalon Bioventures. By 25 July the $5.125 million Series C Round had closed, setting a premoney valuation of $23 million. With this cash and valuation in hand, Sancoff proposed a bold stroke to which the River board agreed. They would use the value built into River Medical to leverage the acquisition of IVAC Corporation.

The State of IVAC

Henry knew plenty about IVAC. He had been an investment banker to IVAC in 1975, just prior to a proxy fight for control of the company. It was launched in 1967 by the same engineers who left to start IMED following a proxy fight. IVAC stayed in the San Diego area, where it dominated the local biomedical devices industry. Over 25 years, IVAC pioneered the first electronic thermometer, the first infusion controller, the first variable pressure monitor, the tympanic infrared thermometer, and the first closed-loop drug delivery system to control hypertension. Eli Lilly & Co., in shifting its strategy toward biomedical instrumentation, bought IVAC for $60.5 million in 1977, with IVAC annual sales at $25.2 million. Under Lilly, IVAC sales surged — to $181.3 million in 1985. (see Table #6, page 144)

Gradually, however, corporate gigantism clogged the arteries of this once nimble high-tech company. By 1993, annual revenues had slumbered up to $213.8 million. IVAC's product line diffused — it offered four families of infusion pumps, various disposables, and vital sign instruments — without breaking any new ground. IVAC's best selling product remained the 560/570 family of acute care pumps — which measured variable pressures at the catheter tip to prevent muscular infiltrations — a technology twelve years old by 1994. IVAC's entire product line was electronic (except for plastic infusion lines) and ignored new advances in biomedical materials. Iterations of the IVAC 590 Flow Stop pump were late to market, and some national account customers were losing faith in the company. IVAC was very slowly developing only one new pump-platform — called Signature Edition.

IVAC bought most of its new technology from other companies. In 1992 IVAC had acquired Welmed, a British firm that designed a very promising P Series of variable pressure syringe pumps for the European market. Syringe pumps work on small volumes, for neonatal or patient-controlled medication, and American hospitals have long suggested they would use more. In September 1993 IVAC acquired Siemens Infusion Systems, Ltd. and its MedSystem III, a complex three-channel volumetric pump suited for critical care floors.[6] IVAC was trying, with limited success, to move MedSystem manufacturing into the excess space at its San Diego campus and certify it to Good Manufacturing Practices. And IVAC kept looking to acquire a manufacturer of disposable pumps — like River — to move itself into alternate site infusions. While struggling to bring all these acquired products on-line, IVAC cost of product sold as a percentage of sales increased from 55 percent in 1991 to 66 percent in 1994. (see Table #8, page 146)

IVAC's facilities could best be described as hopeful. In 1981 they built a shining 38.5 acre campus in La Jolla, with a single 368,000 square foot, two-story research and manufacturing building. The next year they spent $125 million on a plant in Creedmoor, North Carolina for auto-mated disposables manufacturing. By 1994 this plant operated at only half capacity, with plenty of unused land surrounding it. They held long-term leases for space in Hampshire, United Kingdom, where they made syringe pumps, and in Tijuana where contract workers made disposable sets. IVAC was hastily opening up new dealerships abroad — during 1994 in Estonia, India, Pakistan, Sri Lanka, Lithuania, Latvia, and Russia.

In 1994, after years of never peaking over 12 percent, IVAC EBIT fell to a discouraging 2.3 percent of revenues. IVAC margins were so slim it had trouble generating the capital needed to remain competitive. IVAC head-count remained bloated, having risen by 300 in the past three years to 1800 employees, of which 62 percent were in manufacturing. IVAC offi-cers, however, continued to convince Eli Lilly, their corporate parent, to fund their floundering efforts at research and development.

That IVAC revenues did well at all testified to the drive and expertise of its 260-person sales force. IVAC's sales training process included 240 hours of classroom and field training in the first year. Sales people were incented by open-ended commissions and a recognition plan. Supplementing this sales force were nine people working national accounts and 150 field service technicians under contract with Lilly's Physio-Control defibrilator division. IVAC's sales staff was especially capable in selling to hospitals, the market River most needed help in cracking. And IVAC's sales force, working from Lilly's offices, was espe-cially strong in Europe, where it was the only American company with significant market share in each European country. In fact, what IVAC did best was manage its market share to build critical mass. (see Table #9, page 147) It had the largest installed based of IV equipment worldwide, controlled the largest share of the ongoing U.S. disposables revenue stream, and led the American market in hospital thermometry.

Question 3

What has been happening to IVAC's business over the past several years? Is IVAC a good candidate for acquisition? Why or why not? Would IVAC be more valuable to a certain type of buyer as compared to another?

In January 1994, new Lilly chairman Randal L. Tobias announced he would spin off and split off its nine device and diagnostics units — each a market leader or close second — to form a new public company called Guidant Corporation. Lilly would then refocus on its global pharmaceuticals business and boost the number of products in its pipeline.[7] That June, Lilly announced that it would separate four of its device companies — IVAC, Physio-Control, Hybritech, and Pacific Biotech — from the formation of Guidant then apply the proceeds from the sale of each to its $4 billion purchase of PCS Health Systems, Inc., a fast-growing drug benefits manager then owned by McKesson Corp. Lilly announced that "the opportunity exists for a partner that could enhance IVAC's competitiveness more than would be achieved with Guidant, which will focus on cardiovascular and minimally invasive systems. Thus, Lilly will continue to evaluate offers for IVAC."[8]

Question 4

What synergies do you see between River and IVAC? Based on the attached unaudited financial statements for IVAC Corporation, what amount should River Medical and any equity partners pay Lilly to acquire IVAC? What method do you suggest for calculating the valuation?

IVAC Acquisition

Lilly wanted cash, an offer for the entire assets of IVAC, and a good buyer. River wanted a good buyer for IVAC, too. River was, after all, negotiating an $80 million distribution deal with IVAC, and an IVAC owned by somebody else would make a much less attractive strategic ally. River well knew IVAC's promise and problems and thought of ways to make their own bid. Henry wrote to Chemical Bank to arrange leveraged financing of up to $150 million and to identify potential equity partners among the typical Wall Street money pools which participate in leveraged acquisitions of mature health care firms.

On 27 July, River submitted to Morgan Stanley, Lilly's broker, its nonbinding bid: cash of $180 to $200 million, structured as an asset acquisition for tax purposes, so River absorbed no restructuring or special charges. River would raise $85 million in bank debt, $50 million in private debt, and $50 million or more from its current and new institutional equity investors. The bid was good enough to get River on the list of acceptable bidders. Morgan Stanley made River one of four finalists and invited them to commence due diligence.

In August 1994, Bill Hawkins and his colleagues made a presentation to potential buyers. There, Henry and Sancoff learned who else were preparing final bids — Warburg Pincus, DLJ Merchant Banking, and Bain Capital. IVAC management wanted to be acquired by River. River technology excited them, and River refused to give their technology to an IVAC acquired by someone else. IVAC management knew River really needed IVAC's entire resources, and that Henry and Sancoff really understood how the infusion devices industry worked. Traditionally, Lilly protected their loyal employees and preferred that its divested companies keep their essential culture; personnel policies were an important part of the bid package. River found itself in a controlling position as the bidding progressed and with new financing options.

Sancoff and Henry continued to line up banks willing to syndicate acquisition debt. Bain Capital, Inc., for one, was a Boston-based private investment firm that had been quietly buying up medical products and services firms. Bain, for example, had just acquired Physio-Control Corporation from Lilly. And Bain bought the nine manufacuring businesses of Baxter International Inc., while crafting an exclusive agreement with Baxter's diversified distribution organization.[9] Bain understood that IVAC management favored a bid that included River. Bain and River could create a new company ("Newco") that would acquire the assets of IVAC. Bain suggested that River shareholders would contribute all their stock in exchange for 30 percent of Newco, with an option to purchase 10 percent more on closing. This split was not attractive to River. Bain would add $45 million cash in exchange for 60 percent of Newco (Bain also wanted a yield equal to 15 percent per annum) and would arrange debt financing to complete the purchase.

It took less than a week of faxing term sheets for River and Bain to realize how far apart they were. Henry would become chairman of Newco and Sancoff its CEO, but Bain would control the majority of the board. Bain basically asked River shareholders to just hand over their ownership. Bain evinced an LBO mentality with no understanding of the obvious synergy between River and a revived IVAC. Bain asked for high closing and management fees, as if this were a high risk acquisition. Most damaging, Bain saw IVAC as a fire sale and wanted to low-ball the bid at between $125 to $160 million. Henry and Sancoff knew they would lose in the effort to purchase IVAC from Lilly.

Question 5

How would you recommend that Henry and Sancoff structure the equity partnership between River and any money pool partner? Bain's recommendation of a $160 million bid to Lilly will not succeed. Give reasons for your proposed structure including incentives for success to both the River and money pool sides. Know that Henry and River management will run the merged company.

Waiting in the wings were other investment firms, and IVAC hardly cared which equity partner River brought to the table with them. DLJ Merchant Banking Partners was a $1 billion pool, founded in May 1992, and managed by Wall Street investment banking and securities firm Donaldson, Lufkin & Jenrette, Inc. Backed by a top-ranked research staff, DLJ specialized in junk bonds and merchant banking, businesses that allowed it to focus on quick returns and a sparing use of equity.[10] River brought its equity to the table, along with a plan and industry know-how. DLJ brought deep pockets to the table, matched with a faith that the management team of Sancoff and Henry could turn around IVAC.

As a stand-alone company, IVAC looked pretty far gone; indeed, a real turn-around challenge. The only clear conclusion was that Lilly should have sold IVAC 18 months ago. The first half of 1993 generated 75 percent of IVAC 1993 revenue; and 1994 opened with further erosion in IVAC gross margins. By June IVAC was well behind its 1994 plan. Six more months of operating profits at $2.5 million would hardly service the debt needed to acquire IVAC.

River could better go it alone, skeptics argued; $200 million was a lot to pay for distribution. Furthermore, IVAC's sales people, despite their superb reputation for selling capital goods, "probably won't even know their way to the pharmacy," commented one critic, "won't know how to pitch disposable pumps, nor how to find the alternate site market." Baxter and Abbott will fight them fiercely for market share in hospitals.

Plus, Lilly gave its employees benefits quite generous by industry standards, and these would burden any acquirer. And IVAC's "new" pumps were at best evolutionary.

But, Henry and Sancoff argued, even assuming no new IVAC products and diminishing growth rates in IVAC's existing infusions product line, the company still generated $225 million in annual revenues, held a very stable 22 percent market share, and represented the largest installed base of IV instruments in the U.S. This base generated money: disposables earned IVAC an average 53 percent gross margin (in 1994, compared with a 17 percent gross margin on its existing IV pumps and 25 percent on its newer electronic pumps). Furthermore, River was a technological engine that could power a reinvigorated company — adding $20 million revenue in year one and $40 million in year two (see Table #10, page 148). Abbott's due diligence, done conservatively, had projected River at $300 million revenues over a 30 month period following product launch into the hospital marketplace. IVAC's hospital sales force could have a great success with the River SmartDose.

Meanwhile, business slowly improved for River Medical. In October 1994 they reached $42,000 in total sales, with backorders of $21,000, from the efforts of only seven sales people. Manufacturing also improved. Each day, River put out 2000 of the 100 ml units. Labor content in manufacturing was dropping, and a leakage problem in relief valves disappeared. The number of shippable units per production run had grown from 60 percent that summer to over 90 percent. Together, Henry and Sancoff formed the most experienced operating team in the infusion industry. Their historic reputations would likely add several points to IVAC's P/E ratio if it were turned around and brought public. Henry and Sancoff believed IVAC-River synergy could create a capitalized market value of $750 million in three years.

Henry and River's chief financial officer, Dennis Mulroy, who had learned Henry's style of internal operating analysis while controller at IMED, looked over IVAC's numbers. They calculated a normalized EBIT of $20 million to $30 million (by eliminating one-time restructuring and research projects and other excessive staffing throughout IVAC that depressed 1993 EBIT to $7 million). Also identified were $10 million in selling, general and administrative cuts to corporate expense that could get EBIT to $30 million to $40 million. Chemical Bank agreed that this normalized EBIT of $30 million would support a $200 million valuation, with $150 million an appropriate level of debt. Chemical committed to syndicate this debt, if necessary. Henry and Sancoff used this banking commitment as a catalyst to close the IVAC purchase.

As things stood, DLJ could unilaterally submit a bid to Morgan Stanley for IVAC, claiming River its partner, with some potential deal-breakers still unresolved between DLJ and River. The River board opened a telephonic conference by noting: "We are now with DLJ where we got to with Bain." They then passed resolutions ratifying and approving the term sheet discussed with DLJ, and authorized Henry and Sancoff to serve as an Acquisitions Committee with full authority to submit a bid and close a deal.

DLJ wanted to motivate River shareholders to turn IVAC around, and wanted to protect their shares against dilution. In addition to one series of preferred stock (15 percent accreting, non-voting, non-convertible shares in exchange for $30 million cash), Newco would issue two classes of common stock. DLJ got 60 percent of class A common shares (in exchange for $20 million cash). River got all class B common shares (in exchange for the entire equity of River Medical, valued at $40 million). Initially, these shares converted to 40 percent of class A shares, so that HVF II would own 10 percent of Newco. However, after creation of an option pool and under a performance plan — essentially an earn-out as an incentive to keep River on track — River shareholders could boost their ownership to 58 percent of the combined company. At an equity liquidation event — IPO, stock swap, or recapitalization (defined as an extraordinary cash dividend to shareholders in excess of $100 million) — all of River's class B shares converted to class A. The value at liquidation was to be calculated as common equity valuation, which is gross sale price less expenses, corporate debt and minority interest. (see Table #11, page 149).

DLJ was delighted that Henry and Sancoff would take day-to-day management roles in IVAC. Sancoff would devote his full time to IVAC; Henry would prepare and implement the restructuring business plan while still running his venture investments. Sancoff would become chairman and CEO; Henry as vice chairman would personally oversee and monitor operating performance.

On 21 October 1994, River made its bid for IVAC in conjunction with DLJ Merchant Banking as its equity financing partner. The joint River/DLJ bid, though a Newco called River Acquisition Corp., was for $180 million in cash. DLJ committed $50 million in equity ($20 million common equity and $30 million in 15 percent pay-in-kind prefered stock) and a $75 million subordinated bridge loan to complete the acquisition. River Medical committed its entire equity (valued at $40 million) and a $125 million commitment from Chemical Bank (a senior secured term loan for $100 million plus $25 million in senior secured revolving credit for working capital needs during the transition from Lilly). With financing of $150 million in debt and $50 million in equity, River shareholders would continue owning a major portion of the new company. Now they all waited to see if Lilly would accept it.

In late October, River learned that they had to bid up the price of IVAC. Someone had outbid them by at least $10 million. To make their bid look more attractive River offered to remove $10 million worth of vacant land in La Jolla, and agreed to structure the transaction as a stock purchase, which would cost River $3 million, rather than as a 338H10 tax election, which would have cost Lilly $12 million. River revoked its right of first refusal for Lilly to package its drugs in River technology. Lilly had excluded this right from River's purchase bid because they were unable to value it, and River was sure they could market the right for more than $10 million. Also, River learned that recent improvements to MedSystem III and the Signature Edition pumps justified adding $5 million to their bid. The deal closed with the price at $200 million.

On 29 November 1994 Lilly announced a definitive agreement to sell its IVAC unit to River Acquisition Corporation.[11] At the press conference Bill Hawkins promised bounding sales: "Our customers are getting bigger, and they're now demanding that suppliers like IVAC provide them a broader array of technology and products."[12] As health care firms evolved to a continuum of care concept, only IVAC offered a product line that followed the patient as he transitioned from critical care (with multichannel MedSystem III pumps) to general hospital floors (with standardized Signature Edition and Model 570 volumetric pumps) to home care (with SmartDose). "An important criterion in selecting a buyer for IVAC was their approach to the IVAC employees," added Lilly executive Ronald Dollens. "River Medical has a philosophy that is consistent with Lilly's, including personnel policies and programs that recognize the value of employees."[13]

On 1 January 1995 River Acquisition Corporation became a new entity — IVAC Holdings. IVAC Holdings had two wholly-owned subsidiaries, IVAC Corp. and River Medical, which operated and reported earnings independently. As soon as the deal closed, IVAC CEO Bill Hawkins left to return to work with his former colleagues, now with Guidant Corp.[14] Sancoff became chairman of IVAC Corp., and Henry vice chairman. Sancoff took responsibility for evaluating IVAC's research and development effort. Henry, in taking responsibility for measuring IVAC's operating performance, drafted a 1995 business plan which included the required headcount and cost reductions. Henry then supervised implementation of the business plan, of a budgetary process, and personally directed the monthly performance review of each IVAC department to assure that IVAC would make its plan.

Question 6

What steps would you take to restructure IVAC? What are the most important measures of improvement in operating performance? Outline a restructuring plan for IVAC at this point in its evolution.

1995 Plan

Henry devoted two months to drafting IVAC's 1995 plan. His first task was getting better numbers than Lilly had collected on what was going on inside IVAC. He asked new CFO Debbie Crawford to expand upon the financial ratios used to measure operating performance — especially asset turns, working capital turns and inventory turns. And he tasked senior manager Laura Kilmer to break down all expenses by department, especially labor costs, so he could map out budgets and incentive programs.

By February 1995, the business plan was put in place (see Attachment #1, page 154). If IVAC made its 1995 plan, estimates showed its total capitalized value might approach $400 million. The plan called for IVAC to report year end 1995 revenues of $238 million, with $48.5 million in EBITDA, $36 million in operating profit, and net free cash flow at $24.8 million post-interest expense and debt service (which would be substantial in the first year). By comparison, IVAC had closed calender 1994 with revenues of $226 million and operating profits of $5.8 million. Thus, Henry's plan called for a six-fold boost in profits on a 5 percent rise in revenue.

He would accomplish this by drastically curtailing IVAC expenses, for a total reduction of $35.5 million over the year. Both Crawford and Kilmer proved indispensable to Henry's understanding of IVAC's cost structure. Henry, with Crawford's help, met several times with each department head. Eventually all agreed how to cut a required total of $23.4 million from departmental expense, an amount fully 30 percent of 1994 IVAC operating expenses. He expected additional savings of $6.5 million in material costs, and a $5.6 million reduction in manufacturing labor.

There were some new expenses. IVAC would spend $2.5 million to minimally rebuild the international infrastructure that Lilly had previously given it (for which they charged corporate allocations worth $8 million per year). Another $5 million was budgeted in severance costs, the parameters of which had been negotiated with Lilly. On 3 February 1995 IVAC announced lay-offs of 226 employees (16 percent of the 1,450 person workforce that IVAC Holdings acquired), mostly office staff.[15] Said one San Diego business observor, "when you're owned by a major pharmaceutical firm that has a no-fire policy, you end up with a lot of deadwood over the course of 20 years."[16] More layoffs came two months later, bringing the total to 400 jobs lost and 1,000 jobs saved.

The 1995 business plan brought focus to IVAC's entire operations. IVAC consolidated its supply and warehousing and rationalized manufacturing lines. Using what they had learned with River, Sancoff led IVAC through ISO 9001 certifications. And River adapted its needleless, latex-free I.V. administration set to work with IVAC pumps, introduced in February 1996 as the IVAC SmartSite Needless System. They cancelled still-born and high risk research programs — such as an $8 million effort in tonometry and the iVision vital signs measuring unit. IVAC under Lilly occupied 98 engineers on twelve major research and development programs running concurrently. After restructuring, IVAC's engineering headcount stood at 38 people who focused on two major programs and on improving the quality of existing products.

MedSystem III especially needed to be turned around. Seimens had spent $150 million developing the MS III and sold 5,703 units in three quarters. IVAC bought MS III in September 1993 and in their first three quarters of ownership sold only 2,011 units. Sancoff and Henry restructured engineering leadership to finish a redesign of MS III and bandage the red ink flowing as warranty costs. (Meanwhile, IVAC prepared claims against Seimens for misrepresenting design problems and witheld $12 million in royalty payments until they were resolved.) Next, the director of manufacturing was told to increase MS III assembly, to improve disposables manufacture at the Mexican facility, and to commit to numbers so IVAC could relaunch MS III in March 1995. Manufacturing committed to shipping 1,000 pumps per month, at a profitable standard cost, and with disposable costs reduced so that MS III could sell to the hospital general care floors. (Every new account that MS III opened would make it easier to introduce IVAC's Signature Edition when it completed final design and testing.) Then IVAC launched a marketing blitz for MS III, especially at nursing conventions. By October, IVAC engineering had reduced warranty costs on MS III to an all-time low, rendering it profitable. With a new sales bonus program, by year end IVAC had sold over 4,000 MS III pumps, making it their best selling pump.

This marketing initiative, called MS III FastAttack, was designed with input from the IVAC pricing and sales departments. MS III FastAttack was extremely important to IVAC sales force morale at a time of uncertainty over the ownership change and following five consecutive years with no new instruments being introduced by IVAC engineering. MS III FastAttack tided over the IVAC sales force until Sancoff could fix and relaunch the often-delayed Signature Edition line of single and dual channel pumps.

IVAC calculated severe worst case scenarios for cash flow in the first two quarters. If they could make it through June IVAC would not need to ask for a cash infusion. The finance department, under Crawford's direction, worked hard to produce a $14.6 million improvement in working capital. By stretching accounts payable and reducing accounts receivable from 75 to 67 days, IVAC generated $8.6 million more. The company generated another $6 million by tightening inventory turns. IVAC finance pressured Lilly to expedite returns of about $6 million per month in overseas sales. And IVAC prepared a statement of assets asking Lilly for a $15 million adjustment in the acquisition price to recoup misstatements in disposable yields, incorrect bills of materials, engineering defects in products, and service contracts that IVAC didn't know existed. (Lilly , however, calculated that IVAC owed them $13 million, so they submitted the matter to arbitration.) On 31 March, IVAC finished its first quarter of 1995 at 224 percent over plan in operating profit, on a 5 percent boost in sales over same quarter 1994. Operating income was 15 times greater than the same quarter 1994.

The turnaround was well established and continued through the next quarter. IVAC and Health Services Corporation of America (HSCA) signed a new five-year $60 million national account agreement. The U.S. Defense Department allowed IVAC to particpate in the DOD Prime Vendor Program so that military facilities could purchase the bulk of their infusion disposables through IVAC. Purchase Connection, a group purchasing organization, named IVAC its new manufacturer of choice.

The IVAC board now looked to bring in an outside executive with big company experience, someone to "caretake" IVAC's well-established turn-around. A recruitment firm found William J. Mercer, then a senior vice president with Mallinckrodt Group Inc. who was head of its veterinary division and former head of Mallinckrodt's Opti-Ray medical imaging line.[17] When Mercer became president of IVAC Corp., on 25 May 1995, the IVAC board tied his compensation to achieving plan. Mercer reported to the IVAC board of directors and an active director-level operational committee made up of Karl Wyss of DLJ, Henry and Sancoff. Henry continued to meet, each month for several days, with each IVAC vice president and with Mercer to review IVAC operating performance as compared to its 1995 budget.

Perhaps the most pleasant surprise of the year was customer accept-ance of the Signature Edition (SE) electronic pump. Starting in 1989 with extensive focus groups, IVAC embarked on a very ambitious customer-driven design process that resulted in a drastically simplified user inter-face. A single, intuitive flow control eliminated the danger of missetting, especially important for a pump that would be marketed for every floor of a hospital. SE had other real advantages. It was reliable, with only 100 parts. It had a new dynamic monitoring protocol. Following a long IVAC tradition of packaging performance in small boxes, SE was the lightest and most compact pump on the market.[18]

When River took over IVAC, however, SE was deep in debugging, and things looked bad. They discovered standard costs so high that each unit would ship at a loss. Shipping 3600 units as planned might generate $15 million in first year revenues to achieve a 5 percent revenue gain for the year, and the new plan had already built into IVAC's 1995 numbers the full negative impact of inventory build-up, re-engineering, and accounts receivable costs. Yet it was imperative that IVAC get Signature into the marketplace. IVAC's in-house research and engineering efforts had not generated a new infusion pump in more than six years. St. Joseph's Hospital got the initial launch order in November 1995; and of the first 190 units shipped only 6 were returned for trouble shooting. The merger of American Health Systems/Premier created an organization that covered 25 percent of the hospital beds in America. IVAC held the largest installed base in the new company, and the success with SE allowed them to expand their inroads. By year end — with MS III, Signature Edition, and SmartDose filling out its *continuum of care*-oriented product line — IVAC had captured some major accounts long held by Abbott. IVAC also lost some accounts because of many broken promises about Signature Edition's introduction. The net tradeoff between accounts lost and gained was roughly equal. Most importantly, IVAC had introduced to market its first new instrument in six years.

IVAC's financial department evaluated options for its 38.5 acre Campus Point facility. IVAC might sell it and lease it back for three or ten years, sell it and move all manufacturing to North Carolina, or keep it and move River into the excess space. At the July board meeting IVAC decided an outright sale would contribute most directly to cash generation to pay off bank debt. In November 1995, IVAC sold its Campus Point headquarters to telecommunications firm Qualcomm, Inc. for $26 million cash and announced that they had leased office space in Sorrento Valley and manufacturing space on Activity Road only fifteen minutes away.[19] River Medical stayed put.

River Medical benefitted as IVAC became a stronger partner firm, but only slowly recovered from the months of neglect when River officers fixed their attention to the IVAC acquisition and turn-around. River's 1995 business plan called for $13 million in SmartDose sales, turning positive cash flow in July, and finishing the year with $1.5 million in total operating income. But, it remained well off those marks. Once again, River was forced to ease its burn rate which was running at $500,000 per month. Marketing and production of the empty SmartDose atrophied as they anticipated FDA approval of the prefilled SmartDose. Jim Lierman joined River in April, from Abbott, but by August he was gone without having made a dent in River's problems because the FDA still witheld important approvals.

River finally got FDA approval to sell its prefilled SmartDose in May 1995, a full year after approval for the empty SmartDose. River took this opportunity to launch it as a new product. Temporarily, River would cede the hospital market to Abbott. At the annual meeting of the Intravenous Nurses Society, River recast the prefilled SmartDose as an alterative site pump, one so easy to use that patients could store it at home and set it up themselves.[20] River solicited Coram, America's largest home infusion company, and General Medical, which supplied outpatient clinics. Sancoff called on drug companies — like Pharmacia — to put their antibiotics into SmartDose so that River could re-announce each one as a new product. River expected SmartDose to capture 60 percent of the home IV disposables market, have the lowest costs on the market, and still return a 45 percent gross profit margin. But as they scaled up production, they had to resolve problems with leaky seams and sticky valves. By October 1995, River had only $629,000 in SmartDose sales for the year, with negative $7.5 million in EBITDA. River got cash infusions from IVAC as both continued to grow, but lagging sales made it clear that SmartDose needed a redesign, cost reductions, and repositioning in the market at a lower price.

Every month Henry did his performance reviews of each IVAC department. Every month he was able to approve the incentive bonuses for hitting plan. Company morale was excellent. In September 1995, IVAC became the first infusion pump maker certified to ISO 9001 quality standards, which immediately bolstered its sales prospects in Europe. IVAC also prepared additional $8.7 million in cuts — primarily in manufacturing and selling expenses — while boosting revenues at year end.

Question 7

As it became more clear that IVAC would make its first year business plan of $46 million in EBITDA, what would you do to further restructure IVAC for the 1996 Operating Plan? After EBITDA targets are achieved, balance sheet restructuring becomes possible. What are the general benefits from IVAC restructuring its balance sheet? Would restructuring enhance the reputation of IVAC in the public equity or debt markets? Why is this important?

Senior Notes

IVAC began to look at ways of taking out the bridge loans sooner rather than later. (Bridge loan interest was at prime plus a spread, beginning at 500 basis points, then jumping 100 basis points at six months, and 50 more points every three months thereafter.) DLJ advised the IVAC board that a public offering of high yield debt would find good market acceptance. Preparing the IVAC S-1 registration package would be useful if IVAC should decide to do an initial public offering of equity in the near future. Plus, a public offering would close more certainly than a private placement, at much lower fees. With $100 million in new senior secured notes, plus $22 million in excess cash, IVAC could pay off its entire $80 million bridge loan from DLJ Bridge Finance, Inc. They could also prepay half of their $60 million in term loans from Chemical Bank. ($26 million from the La Jolla property sale also paid down the bank facility.)

Furthermore, a bond offering presaged a public offering of equity. With IVAC debt now publicly traded, the company had a better idea of how it was perceived in the investment community. And it was perceived well. IVAC easily got a BB credit rating by Standard & Poor's and a B3 rating by Moody's, an interest rate of 9 1/4 percent and a three-year non-call provision. When the bond issue went effective on 3 November 1995, the offering was oversubscribed by 300 percent, with institutional orders for $300 million.

Thus, IVAC finished out calender 1995 on a strong note. The investment community had validated IVAC's plan for turning around the company. IVAC Corporation changed its name to IVAC Medical Systems, Inc. to reflect its desire to serve customers with its continuum of care concept. Furthermore, IVAC finished its year slightly better than plan — with revenues at $240.9 million ($2.1 million more than plan), $46.6 million in EBITDA ($2 million less than plan), and net free cash flow of $24.5 million post interest expense and debt service. With shares valued at about $10, IVAC had about $350 million total capitalized value.

Writing to the IVAC board in January 1996, Henry revised the 1996 plan (see attachment #2, page 159). Forecasting a modest 5 percent to 8 percent growth in revenue (to a range of $250 to $258.1 million), a 1996 EBITDA range of $61.6 to $65.5 million was forecast. IVAC could acheive this EBITDA by further squeezing cost-of-product-sold from 57.2 percent to 53.9 percent, and by keeping operating expenses around $69 million. The revisions kept incremental increases in those operating expenses at $4.9 million over 1995, but reweighted them to shift $1.7 million from expansion abroad and advertising into Group A account discounts like the MS III Fast Attack program.

The IVAC board also allowed for radical change at River Medical. For 1995, River reported $9.7 million *negative* EBITDA on revenues of only $800,000 (1995 plan called for $400,000 *negative* EBITDA on revenue of $13.2 million). To remain a viable company River needed three SmartDose drug deals in the first half of 1996 to reach year end revenues of $6 million, and thus limit River's EBITDA loss to $5.6 million. River subsequently failed to close these sales. (Despite the drag from River, in first half 1996 IVAC reported EBITDA of $20.6 million on net sales of $112.8 million.)

On 25 July 1996 IVAC announced that it would close its River Medical subsidiary, take a $17.4 million restructuring charge, and divest its assets — its strong patent position on disposable pumps and its 40,000 square foot fully FDA/GMP licensed facility at Kenamar Court. Over the past year, 33 River employees had transfered to IVAC; the remaining 42 would get severance. IVAC announced that SmartDose "no longer fit the overall strategic direction of IVAC."[21]

Yet Henry and Sancoff had done a remarkable job of leveraging their original investment in SmartDose. Sancoff's disposable pump and construction of a sterile manufacturing facility, along with venture capital help created value in River Medical. The company was then able to acquire IVAC by using very creative financial techniques, and with the considerable help of DLJ. After acquisition, IVAC was turned around and restructured in record time. Significant value was created for the shareholders of IVAC. However, liquidity was not achieved because IVAC was still a private company. Once again the histories of IVAC and IMED intertwined.

Question 8

What exit strategies are available to get liquidity from a mature, private and leveraged company?

Acquisition by IMED

After Henry had financially positioned IMED for its sale to Warner Lambert in August 1982 for $465 million, the company entered a long decline. The Henley Group, a U.K.-based holding company, bought IMED in 1986 for $165 million, then sold it in April 1990 for $106 million to another holding company for struggling health-care businesses, Advanced Medical, Inc.[22] Market share for IMED volumetric pumps had slipped from 70 percent in 1982 to 22 percent in 1990, then kept declining into a narrower market band of high-end hospital sales.

IMED management sold its Irish plant to its European distribution partners. IMED tightened operating expenses, protected its patents on the Accuset disposables, and struggled to raise cash in an industry depressed by talk of health care reform. Seventy percent of IMED sales came from sales of disposable administration sets for its installed pump base, though the average price of disposables was dropping and hospitals were changing protocols to make them last longer. IMED's Gemini line of peristaltic pumps was well-positioned to pick up sales as hospitals stopped buying IMED's older piston cassette pumps. Still, IMED competed at the top of the price range with a new product pipeline based on purchased technology.

By 1995, IMED had won limited stability. Revenues rose in 1995, after three years in decline; cash flow from operations had risen from $531,000 in 1993 to $18.5 million, and net borrowings had declined from $105 million in 1993 to $60 million in 1995. In June 1996 Standard & Poor's upgraded its rating on Advanced Medical's subordinated debt from CCC- to B- due to debt restructuring and improved sales. S&P tempered this optimism with concern about "the company's limited product diversity and reliance on the highly competitive domestic market."[23]

Product diversity and expansion abroad were two advantages IVAC offered. Advanced Medical had tried to buy IVAC from Eli Lilly two years earlier, but the DLJ/River investors beat them out. Now, with IVAC turned around and the efforts at SmartDose played out, the IVAC investors welcomed purchase offers for cash. Furthermore, Advanced Medical, though well turned-around, reported a lackluster first half of 1996: with EBITDA of $11.4 million on $53.9 million in revenues. On 26 August 1996, following two months of quiet negotiation, Advanced

Medical, Inc. announced that its principal operating unit, IMED Corporation, would merge with IVAC into one company.

Advanced Medical bid $400 million for IVAC, in cash. Advanced Medical financed the acquisition with $315 million in new debt and $125 million in subordinated notes. No one would speculate on the size of the restructuring charge, nor when the new company would become profitable. Following regulatory and shareholder approvals, IVAC will start contributing to Advanced Medical results in first quarter 1997. Advanced Medical stock edged up 13 percent on the news, though S&P placed its debt on CreditWatch with negative implications.

"This combination of two great names in infusion therapy," proclaimed Mercer, "will mean new opportunities for our employees, and will benefit shareholders by accelerating strategies to profitably grow the business into a world-class health care company."[24] The merged entity, combining companies with the third and fourth largest market shares, would be a global leader in infusion therapy devices with combined revenues over $353 million based on 1995 results. With consolidation sweeping through the health care industry, Mercer declared the new company big enough to compete with the likes of Baxter International and Abbott Laboratories.[25] The merged entity would be even stronger abroad. The two combined currently derived one-third of revenues from overseas: IVAC had sales in 120 foreign countries, and IMED had sales in 38 countries. By growing in Japan, Latin America, Russia and Southeast Asia, the merged company expected to earn half its revenues by sales abroad. The new Advanced Medical management team also announced they would make additional acquisitions to expand the range of products.

The new company would continue without direction from Henry and Sancoff. They had cashed out well. With help from DLJ, they had bought IVAC for $200 million in December 1994, and sold it for $400 million only 23 months later. As the deal closed on November 26, 1996, the Henry Venture Fund II investment in IVAC/River showed a 635 percent return on investment of $2.6 million for an IRR of 84% per year.

Question 9

Did IMED pay too much to acquire IVAC? Give reasons pro and con. What should IMED have paid to acquire IVAC?

Notes to Published Sources

[1] SmartDose technical specifications, as of August 2003, could be found at http://www.smartdose.com

[2] Peter Brimelow and Leslie Spencer, "Just call me 'Doc,'" *Forbes* (22 November 1993) 108-110; Jennifer Reingold, "Under watchful eyes: What's behind the sudden improvement in the FDA's notoriously slow drug approval process," *FW* (1 August 1995) 40-41; "Is the FDA hooked on caution?" *Business Week* (30 Jaunary 1995) 72-74.

[3] William D. Pratt, *The Abbott Almanac: 100 Years of Committment to Quality Health Care* (Elmsford, N.Y.: Benjamin, 1987) 208.

[4] Marcia Berss, "Aloof but not asleep," *Forbes* (29 August 1994) 43-44.

[5] Reingold (note 2) 41.

[6] "Eli Lilly unit to buy assets of Siemens Infusion Systems," *New York Times* (26 May 1993) C4.

[7] Thomas M. Burton, "Eli Lilly plans sale or spin-off of device units: Move to shed subsidiaries indicates fresh course under new chairman," *Wall Street Journal* (18 January 1994) A3.

[8] "Lilly To Form New Public Company, Guidant Corporation: IPO Scheduled for Fourth Quarter," Press Release, 20 June 1994, Eli Lilly and Company; "Lilly to Purchase PCS Health Systems from McKesson for $4 Billion," Press Release, 11 July 1994, Eli Lilly and Company.

[9] "Baxter pursues restructuring plan with sale of diagnostics business," *Health Industry Today* 57 (November 1994) 1, 10.

[10] Ida Picker, "The perils of prosperity at DLJ," *Institutional Investor* (August 1994) 27-32; Anne Schwimmer, "A peek at DLJ's financials: junk, merchant banking rule," *Investment Dealer's Digest* (4 September 1995) 9.

[11] "Drug Concern Agrees to Sell Ivac Unit to River Acquisition," *Wall Street Journal* (30 November 1995) B6; "Lilly in Deal to Sell Its IVAC Unit," *New York Times* (30 November 1994) C3; Craig D. Rose, "River Medical will buy IVAC," *San Diego Union-Tribune* (30 November 1994) C-1, 2; "Eli Lilly & Co.," *New York Times* (7 January 1995) N19.

[12] Bradley J. Fikes, "IVAC purchase assures that firm will stay in S.D.," *San Diego Business Journal* (5 December 1994).

[13] "River Medical to Purchase IVAC from Lilly," Press Release, 22 November 1994, Eli Lilly and Company.

[14] David W. Pomfret, "William A. Hawkins named a Guidant Vice President and President of Devices for Vascular Intervention, Inc." *BusinessWire* (17 January 1995).

[15] Craig D. Rose, "New owner of IVAC axes 140 jobs here," *San Diego Union-Tribune* (4 February 1995) C1,2; Craig D. Rose, "Pumped up for profits," *San Diego Union-Tribune* (28 February 1995).

[16] Bruce Ahern in Bradley J. Fikes, "Biosciences jobs decline for first time," *San Diego Business Journal* 17 (19 February 1996) 1.

[17] Bradley J. Fikes, "Making a difference for the common good," *San Diego Business Journal* 16 (16 October 1995) 1/8.

[18] Signature Edition specifications, as of August 2003, could be found at http://www.alarismed.com

[19] "Smaller IVAC moves to new home in Sorrento Valley," *San Diego Business Journal* (11 December 1995) 1/3.

[20] Kathi Gannon, "A good fit," *Drug Topics* (9 January 1995) 48; "River Medical aims at alternate site market with pre-filled infusion pump," *Health Industry Today* (June 1995) 4.

[21] "IVAC Closes River Medical Subsidiary," Press Release, 25 July 1996, IVAC Medical Systems.

[22] John R. Hayes, "Rescue Team," *Forbes* (22 April 1996) 100.

[23] "Advanced Medical Inc. Ratings Raised," (18 June 1996) Standard & Poor's Rating Group via *NewsEDGE*.

[24] *News Release for 26 August 1996*, Advanced Medical Inc. "Advanced Medical to acquire Ivac Medical," *New York Times* (27 August 1996) D4; Andy Pasztor, "Advanced Medical is acquiring Ivac for $400 million," *Wall Street Journal* (26 August 1996) B6.

[25] Kathryn Kranhold, "Advanced Medical Acquisition of Ivac Seeks Overseas Link," *Wall Street Journal* (27 August 1996) B6.

Table #1

River/IVAC Placements and Valuations

	April 1993	November 1993	July 1994	December 1994	November 1995	August 1996
Total Company Valuation (*pre-money*)	$3.5 m	$20 m (readjusted to $10.5 m)	$23 m	$40 m	$350 m	$400 m
Price per Share	$.8286	$3.0242	$2.705		$10	
Shares Placed	2,715,422	991,996	1,894,640			
Amount of Placement	$1.75 m (1st) $0.5 m (2d)	$3 m	$5.125 m			
Percent of River Purchased	44.44%	13.04% (readjusted to 22.22%)	18.22%	100%		
Purchasers	HVF II/Avalon (1st) IVP (2d)	HVF II IVP	Menlo Ventures IVP			
Investment Plan	Series A	Series B (plus new option pool)	Series C	Contribution to IVAC Acquis.	IVAC/River Senior Notes	Sale to IMED
HVF ownership (*post-money*)	22.22%	25.6% (readjusted to 28.15%)	23.03%	9.2%	9.8%	9.3
Product Revenues (*Trailing 12 Months*)	$0 m	$0 m	$0 m	$0.1 m	$239 m	$229 m
Company After Tax Earnings (*Trailing 12 Months*)	—	($1.2 m)	($3.2 m)	($5.5 m)	$36.9 m	$13.7 m

Table #2

River Medical, Inc.
Statement of Cash Flows

(year ended 31 December)
(dollars in thousands)

	1993	1994	[Inception] [to 1994]
Cash flows from operating activities:			
Net loss	$(1,234)	$(5,507)	$(6,741)
Adjustments to reconcile net loss to net cash used in operations:			
Depreciation and amortization	32	423	455
Change in:			
Accounts receivable	—	(51)	(51)
Inventories	(16)	(596)	(612)
Prepaid expenses	(33)	(3)	(36)
Other assets	(277)	(162)	(439)
Accounts payable	417	1,064	1,481
Accrued liabilities	62	10	72
Net cash used in operating activities	(1,049)	(4,822)	(5,871)
Cash flows from investing activities:			
Purchases of short-term investments	(3,787)	—	(3,787)
Sales of short term investments	3,787	—	3,787
Purchases of property and equipment	(1,937)	(1,877)	(3,814)
Payment for patent costs	(14)	(100)	(114)
Net cash used in investing activities	(1,951)	(1,977)	(3,928)
Cash flows from financing activities:			
Proceeds from issuance of common stock	50	—	50
Proceeds from issuance of Series A, Series B, and Series C convertible preferred stock, net	5,180	5,090	10,270
Principal payments under capital leases	719	706	1,425
Net cash provided by financing activities	5,896	5,519	11,415
Net increase (decrease) in cash	2,896	(1,280)	1,616
Cash at beginning of period	—	2,896	—
Cash at end of period	$2,896	$1,616	$1,616

Prospectus F-37

Table #3

River Medical, Inc.
Statement of Operations
(year ended 31 December)
(dollars in thousands)

	1993	1994	1995
Product Revenue	$0	$100	$842
Operating expenses:			
Cost of goods sold	—	111	4,492
Manufacturing start-up costs	475	3,196	
General and administrative	385	761	2,194
Research and development	239	542	726
Selling and marketing	144	906	2,813
Total operating expenses	1,243	5,516	6,500
Loss from operations	(1,243)	(5,416)	(10,900)
Interest income	31	55	0
Interest expense	(21)	(145)	(119)
Loss before income taxes	(1,233)	(5,506)	(20,407)
Provision for income taxes	1	1	
Net loss	(1,234)	(5,507)	(16,576)
Accretion of mandatorily redeemable stock	219	465	
Net loss allocable to common shareholders	(1,543)	(5,972)	

Prospectus F-36; IVAC management package.

Table #4

River Medical, Inc.
Balance Sheet
(at 31 December)
(dollars in thousands)

Assets

	1993	1994	1995
Current Assets:			
Cash and cash equivalents	$2,896	$1,616	$0
Accounts receivable	—	51	185
Inventories	16	612	1,311
Prepaid Expense	33	36	(10,076)
Total Current Assets	2,945	2,315	(8,580)
Property and equipment:			
Manufacuring equipment	1,364	2,970	
Leasehold improvements	258	267	
Furniture and fixtures	177	207	
Scientific equipment	113	280	
Computer equipment	25	90	
	1,937	3,814	5,939
Accumulated depreciation	(32)	(455)	(1,193)
Property and equipment, net	1,905	3,359	4,746
Patent costs, net	13	114	3,612
Other assets	278	440	429
	5,141	6,228	207
Liabilities and Shareholder's Equity			
Current liabilities:			
Accounts payable	417	1,482	78
Accrued liabilities	63	73	0
Current portion of capital lease obligations	161	316	
Other current liabilities	—	—	566
Total current liabilities	641	1,871	644
Non-current portion of capital lease obligations	505	779	1,856
Mandatorily redeemable convertible preferred stock			
Series A	2,306	2,441	
Series B	3,092	3,272	
Series C	—	5,240	
Shareholder's equity:			
Additional paid-in capital	50	50	13,331
Deficit accumulated during development stage	(1,453)	(7,425)	(15,624)
Total shareholder equity	(1,403)	(7,375)	(2,293)
	5,141	6,228	207

Prospectus. F-35; IVAC management package.

Table #5

Medical Conditions Potentially Requiring IV Antibiotic Therapy
(1988)

Condition	Number of Discharges
Cancer	4,974,000
Nosocomial infections	1,572,000
Cellulitis	456,000
Chronic pyelonephritis	129,000
Osteomyletis	91,000
AIDS	40,000
Cystic fibrosis	30,000
Bacterial endocarditis	26,000
Urethritis	26,000
Septic arthitis	23,000
Total	**6,912,000**

Table #6

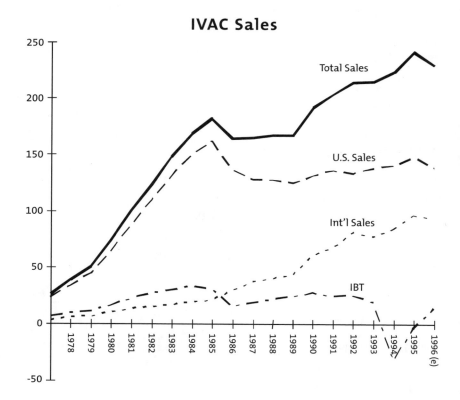

Table #7

Selected Consolidated Data for IVAC Corp.

(year ending 31 December)
(dollars in thousands)

	1990	1991	1992	1993	1994	1995
Income Statement Data						
Net sales	$191,080	$203,301	$213,430	$214,244	$223,227	$240,971
Cost of sales	101,802	111,431	123,487	125,542	146,659	157,869
Gross profit	89,278	91,870	89,933	88,702	76,568	83,102
Selling and marketing	38,383	40,428	41,395	40,190	45,055	43,994
General and administrative	13,445	13,808	16,348	16,032	21,586	28,381
Research and development	16,488	17,171	15,938	18,742	18,504	12,083
Restructuring	3,300	5,000	1,307	3,967	13,143	5,944
Parent company allocations	8,273	8,024	7,411	6,416	7,480	—
Other expense (income)	(3,324)	724	2,013	269	3,560	24,380
Operating profit (loss)	12,713	6,715	5,521	3,086	(32,760)	(31,680)
Interest income (expense)	5,541	5,193	4,729	4,040	700	(20,502)
Income tax expense (benefit)	6,268	3,595	4,755	1,710	3,793	(378)
Net income(loss)	11,986	8,313	5,495	5,416	(35,853)	(51,804)
Ratio of earnings to fixed charges	41.4x	22.4x	5.9x	7.2x	—	—
Other Data						
Adjusted EBITDA	33,362	29,634	24,501	23,718	4,674	32,871
Depreciation and amortization	9,076	9,895	10,262	10,249	15,119	20,950
Capital expenditures, net	12,261	11,293	8,324	9,920	9,000	(13,752)
Net cash from operations	14,463	7,640	18,618	8,115	6,502	38,213
Net cash used by investing activities	11,829	11,291	8,482	36,721	9,000	179,287
Net cash provided (used) by financing	(2,008)	—	(1,551)	30,217	—	(157,535)
Balance Sheet Data						
Cash and cash equivalents	5,299	2,112	5,400	4,683	3,226	18,308
Working capital	38,881	46,924	52,734	119,457	74,124	41,780
Total assets	209,210	222,333	230,012	248,909	174,144	215,995
Long term debt	—	—	—	12,000	11,621	131,824
Shareholder's equity	165,972	181,689	185,173	192,511	129,981	13,376

Prospectus p. 28; Amd. 1 to IVAC 1995 S-1 filed 20 September 1996.
Because the 1994 acquisition was accounted for as a purchase, data on the predecessor company through 1994 may not be consistent with 1995 data. 1995 data consolidates River Medical.

Table #8

IVAC Financial Data as a Percentage of Sales
(year ended 31 December)

	1989	1990	1991	1992	1993	1994	1995
Net Sales	100%	100%	100%	100.0%	100.0%	100.0%	100.0%
Gross profit			45.4	42.1	41.4	34.3	34.4
Selling and marketing			21.0	19.4	18.8	20.2	18.2
General and administrative			6.0	7.7	7.5	9.7	11.7
Research and development	8.5	8.6	8.6	7.5	8.7	8.3	5.0
Other expense				0.9	0.1	1.6	12.5
Operating profit (loss)			5.9	2.6	1.4	(14.7)	(13.1)
Interest income (expense), net				2.2	1.9	0.3	(8.5)
Provision for income taxes			1.9	2.2	0.8	1.7	(0.1)
Net income (loss)			3.9	2.6	2.5	16.1	(21.5)
Adjusted EBITDA				11.5%	11.1%	2.1%	25.5%
Return on assets	9.5	11.3	9.9	9.0	5.9		
(excl. interest & cash)							

Prospectus p. 31; Amd. 1 to IVAC 1995 S-1 filed 20 September 1996.
1989 and 1990 data from August 1994 IVAC roadshow overheads.
1995 data consolidates data for River Medical.

Table #9

1993 Market Shares
Infusion Therapy — U.S.

	Instrument Installed Base: 622,000 Total Channels	Drug Infusion Disposables: 271 million total units
IVAC	24%	31%
McGaw	22%	10%
Abbott	19%	12%
Baxter	22%	37%
IMED	7%	3%
Other	6%	7%

MDI Audit (Instruments) and IMS Audit (Disposables)

Table #10

Projected Performance Estimates IVAC and River Combined

COMPILED: AUGUST 1994
(dollars in millions)

	1993	Year 1	Change	Year 2	Change	Year 3	Change
Sales	214	245	14.4%	276	12.6%	323	17.0%
Cost of Sales	124	126	1.9	135	7.1	138	2.2
Gross Margin	90	119	31.3	141	18.5	185	31.2
Research and Development	19	16	(14.4)	14	(12.5)	14	0
Sales and Marketing	40	36	(10.4)	35	(2.8)	36	2.9
General and Administrative	15	13	(13.9)	12	(7.7)	11	(8.3)
Total Operating Expenses	74	65	(12.2)	61	(6.2)	61	0
Operating Income	16	54	225.3%	80	48.1%	124	55%

Table #11

Equity Adjustment Agreement
Between DLJMB and River

	Common Equity Value[a] Threshold through Year Four		
	$135 m	$235 m	$385 m
Adjustment[b]	-10%	0%	+10%
Adjusted River Ownership	30%	40%	50%
DLJMB Multiple of Investment	3x	4x	5x

(a) Common equity value is after accreted value of Paid-In-Kind preferred stock.
(b) Adjustments will be pro rata for common equity value thresholds greater than
$135 million and less than $385 million.

Table #12

High, Historical Multiples Paid
for Infusion Devices Companies

Company	Year	Sales Price	Company Sales
IVAC	1977	$60m	$20m (est.)
IMED	1982	$465m	$100m
Pancretec	1988	$54m	$7m (est.)
Omniflow	1989	$52m	$4m (est.)
Block Medical	1992	$54m*	$17m (est.)
IVAC	1996	$400m	$239m

*Includes earn out estimated at $30 to $50 million.

IVAC Case Solution

Pre-money valuation is a common denominator. It is the way VC's compare deals. It's like a golf handicap. You can compare a healthcare deal with an Info Technology deal. Two VC's discussing their respective deals will always note the pre-money values.

Pre Money Valuation Calculation

Question 1, page 108

What is the pre-money valuation for River Medical established by the Series A financing? Show your calculations.

Series A Financing from HV2 & Avalon	$1,500,000
Percent Ownership: HV 2 + Avalon	33.3%
Post Money Valuation	$4,500,000
Less: Series A Financing	$1,500,000
Pre Money Valuation	$3,000,000

Amount of Financing – Amount of Financing = Pre-money Valuation
  Percent Ownership

Question 2, page 117

Discuss the positives and negatives of River becoming a captive OEM manufacturer for Abbott or for any other large health care company. Also discuss the effect of an OEM agreement on River's profit margins, its ultimate valuation in public and private equity markets, and restrictions on an IPO or other liquidity options. Do venture capitalists generally want to fund OEM companies? Why or why not?

Answer:

Postitives and Negatives:

River shareholders would be guaranteed a return on their investment just because an Abbott deal would be profitable. However, Abbott would cap the upside to a financial return consistent with equity market returns (15 percent) because Abbott is the captive buyer of product and River post contract would only have the risk of correctly producing product.

The River venture capitalists made the investment because they are looking at hurdle rates of return of 500 percent to 1,000 percent return in three years (5x to 10x in 3 years). VC's usually do not want to turn our exciting new technology into an OEM supplier for a large company. It is not why VC's are in business.

Question 3, page 119

What has been happening to IVAC's business over the past several years? Is IVAC a good candidate for acquisition? Why or why not? Would IVAC be more valuable to a certain buyer as compared to another? Why?

Answer:

1. IVAC is a 25-year-old stagnate company with very limited to negligible new product introduction.

2. The company could be a decent acquisition candidate at the right price, which would be a lower end multiple of EBITDA, say 5 to 6 times EBITDA, because IVAC has recurring and relatively predictable revenue coming from disposables which are under contract in many instances.

3. IVAC would be more valuable to a company in the infusion industry which could leverage upon the extensive and competent IVAC sales force, and its brand name recognition in hospitals for reliable infusion products.

Question 4, page 120

Are there synergies between River and IVAC?

RIVER/IVAC SYNERGIES

PRODUCT AREA
1) Both infusion device companies.
2) IVAC has no disposable infusion devices.
3) River has no electronic devices as Block — a small company — did. River is a one-product company. Needs more product line breadth.

MARKET AREA
1) Both companies target the hospital market.
2) IVAC established in major hospital accounts. River totally new in hospital market- unknown. Hard to penetrate established accounts.
3) IVAC has broad based US and international sales force that needs new, innovative product. Can give excellent coverage for River product.

PERSONNEL
1) No similarities. IVAC big company, bureaucratic culture. River entrepreneurial and inventive.
2) IVAC sales force professionally trained and experienced. River sales force small and untested in marketplace.
3) Management very different.

Question 4, page 120

If IVAC were to be acquired, what would you pay for the business? Show how you value IVAC.

Answer:

IVAC Valuation Methods

1. Multiple of current (trailing 12 months) EBITDA and projected EBITDA.

2. Multiple of Revenues. Use comparables of medical device company transactions within the past 12 to 24 months using companies approximately the same size in revenues, market share or geographical coverage for product line and EBIT.

3. Multiple of after tax net income (P/E multiple).
4. Discounted cash flow (DCF) value of a 5 or 10 year IVAC forecasted P&L.

5. Estimate the value of IVAC percent market share and translate to total company value.

6. Because IVAC is a no-growth business which will require the injection of new products, a low-end multiple of EBITDA would be paid, say five to six times if possible. IVAC is unlikely to grow on its own which argues for an EBITDA multiple at the low end of the range.

7. A hypothetical examination of EBITDA post-acquisition should be done to see what upside would be available in an IVAC acquisition. (Our analysis indicated that IVAC could produce in excess of $40 million EBITDA in the first year of restructuring, which allowed River/DLJ to pay five times, or #200 million.)

Question 5, page 122

How would you recommend that Henry and Sancoff structure the equity partnership between River and any money pool partner? Know that Henry and River management will run the merged company.

Answer:

IVAC Acquisition — Deal Structure

1. River has limited net worth and limited ability to access debt to buy IVAC.

2. River has exciting new technology which could accelerate IVAC's stagnant growth and might attract outside equity to a merger with IVAC.

3. River needs a partner with financial muscle, not necessarily industry expertise. (River should seek a money pool as financial partner and provide management

expertise and product development itself. River shopped the IVAC deal to DLJ, Bain Capital and other LBO funds.)

4. IVAC has some cash flow or EBITDA which could be attractive to lenders to service new debt, but only if a substantial outside equity infusion takes place. The combination of new debt and new equity infusion combined with a merger of River and IVAC could accomplish the acquisition.

5. The objective of Henry and Sancoff was to value River in the post-acquisition merged company as high as possible to gain as large a percent ownership as possible.

6. In actual fact, DLJ put up $50 million of new equity, Chemical Bank and DLJ Bridge Fund lent $150 million, and this provided $200 million cash to acquire IVAC from Lilly. IVAC's cash flow was expected to service the acquisition debt, and the loans were made to IVAC, not River.

7. River was able to establish a sliding scale of pro forma ownership which ranged from 40 percent to 50 percent based upon consolidated EBITDA of the merged River and IVAC, post-acquisition.

Question 6, page 126
What steps would you take to restructure IVAC? What are the most important measures of improvement in operating performance? Outline a restructuring plan for IVAC at this point in its evolution.

Answer:
1. Eliminate unproductive R&D projects and cut corresponding expense.

2. Reduce headcount commensurately.

3. Bring instrument to market which is closest to Beta market testing (Signature Series Pump). Focus most, if not all, R&D expense and manpower on introducing the next generation electronic infusion pump.

4. Evaluate and trim inefficiencies in sales force and production departments. Reduce human resources expenses. Streamline same functions in international operations.

5. Increase EBITDA and working capital. See Exhibits 1-1, 1-2, 1-3, 1-4 for the outline of the restructuring plan.

Attachment #1

Finance Agenda

March 8, 1995

Board Meeting

Laura Killmer

❑ **1995 Budget Review**
(P&L Balance Sheet, and Cash Flow)

❑ **February YTD Financial Results vs Plan**

Exhibit 1-1

IVAC CORPORATION ONLY
1995 BUSINESS PLAN

Assumes Signature
Launched in 1995

Income Statement

($000)	1995 Plan	1994 Actual	Projected Growth/(Savings)	
			$	%
Sales				
U.S. Drug Infusion	$110,024	$105,324	$4,700	
U.S. Vital Signs	32,352	29,964	2,388	
U.S. Service	7,700	8,824	(1,124)	
International	88,204	82,842	5,362	
	238,280	226,954	11,326	5%
Cost of Sales	137,174	143,914	(6,740)	
% of Sales	*57.6%*	*63.4%*		
Gross Margin	101,106	83,040	18,066	22%
% of Sales	*42.4%*	*36.6%*		
Operating Expenses				
Selling	30,328	35,361	(5,033)	
Marketing	6,160	9,019	(2,859)	
R&D	10,868	17,977	(7,109)	
Admin	13,008	14,874	(1,866)	
Severance	5,000	—	5,000	
Total OPEX	65,364	77,231	(11,867)	(15%)
	27.4%	*34.0%*		
Operating Profit	$35,742	$5,809	$29,933	5.2x
EBITDA	$48,500	$20,522	$27,978	136%

Exhibit 1-2

IVAC CORPORATION ONLY

Reconciliation 1994 EBITDA to 1995 EBITDA

($millions)

EBITDA 1994		$20.5
1995 Saving Departmental Spending	$23.4	
1995 Material Cost Savings	6.5	
Additional Gross Margin on 1995 Forecasted Sales	5.6	
Total Savings		35.5
One Time Reductions in 1995 Forecasted Savings:		
New International Infrastructure	(2.5)	
Severance Expense	(5.0)	
Total Reductions		(7.5)
EBITDA 1995 Forecast		$48.5

Exhibit 1-3

IVAC CORPORATION ONLY
1995 Business Plan

Departmental Spending

($000)

Department	Officer	1995 Plan	1994 Actual	Projected Savings
US Marketing	Adams	$2,612	$3,605	$993
Operations/Service	Conn			
DL/Overhead		34,483	37,618	3,135
Facilities		5,405	5,083	(322)
Mat'l Costs Savings				6,508
		39,888	42,701	9,321
Finance/Systems	Crawford	7,221	7,333	112
Quality	Grigoriev	7,146	9,010	1,864
Human Resources	Lintvedt	883	1,093	210
Employee Benefits		9,253	13,453	4,200
		10,136	14,546	4,410
International	Mirando	18,144	21,284	3,140
Administration	Sancoff	500	426	(74)
Legal		821	1,591	770
		1,321	2,017	696
Research/Development	Semedo	5,891	12,837	6,946
US Sales	St. Philip	17,995	20,421	2,426
		$110,354	$133,754	$29,908

Exhibit 1-4

IVAC CORPORATION ONLY
1995 Business Plan

Working Capital Improvement Plan

(millions)	1994 Actual Average	1995 Estimated Average	Working Capital Improvement
Accounts Receivable DSO Reduced	75	67	$2.6
Accounts Payable Stretched	$5.9	$11.0	$6.0
Inventory Reduced — Raw Material	21.0	17.7	3.3
Work-in-Process	7.4	6.1	1.3
Goods	19.4	18.0	1.4
	$47.8	$41.8	$6.0
TOTAL Working Capital Improvement			$14.6

Question 7, page 131

As it became more clear that IVAC would make its first year business plan of $46 million in EBITDA, what would you do to further restructure IVAC for the 1996 Operating Plan? After EBITDA targets are achieved, balance sheet restructuring becomes possible. What are the general benefits from IVAC restructuring its balance sheet? Would restructuring enhance the reputation of IVAC in the public equity or debt markets? Why is this important?

Answer:

See Albert J. Henry memo dated January 5, 1996 (page 161) regarding the 1996 restructuring. Also, certain land and buildings were sold to generate cash to pay down the debt from acquisition. Reducing debt service post acquisition is very important in leveraged buyouts so assets are always sold to do so.

Question 8, page 133

What exit strategies are available to get liquidity from a mature, private and leveraged company?

Answer:

1. The possibility of an IPO should always be examined for an LBO emerging from a turnaround as a private company.
2. The IPO can be attractive to investors because growth may have been rekindled in the target company, management improved and possibly new products added. Many times LBO target companies are successful names from the past with industry and stock market recognition, which helps the IPO.

3. Private or public merger is the second liquidity opportunity for an LBO. Mergers may be difficult because of the large amount of debt that the LBO company carries. With the IPO approach, the equity infusion is used to pay down debt, and the IPO market accepts that.

Question 9, page 135

Did IMED overpay for IVAC? Why or why not?

Answer:

1. IMED probably paid the top end of the EBITDA multiple range for IVAC at 8 times EBITDA, which was just restructured to be at its maximum.

2. Today's market multiples are higher than those which existed in 1996; however, IVAC EBITDA subsequently dropped, post-merger, under new management.

3. The HV II return on its River Medical/IVAC investment was $16.495 million on a $2.60 million investment for a 72.3% IRR per annum compounded over four years.

Attachment #2

IVAC   *Teamwork for Excellence*

Memorandum

To: Board of Directors, IVAC Corporation
From: Albert J. Henry
Date: January 5, 1996

I have reviewed the draft financial plan for 1996, which was prepared on December 15, 1995, and have the following recommendations and observations.

1. To better understand the proposed plan I have used the 1995 original plan ($48.5 million EBITDA — IVAC only), prepared 3/8/95, as the initial benchmark. The revised 1995 plan ($46.6 million EBITDA — IVAC only), prepared 9/95, is shown for comparative purposes along with our best estimate for 1995 actuals. A 1996 forecasted revenue range of $250 million to $258 million is used for IVAC only, to which is added a $6 million revenue estimate for River products. The corresponding 1996 EBITDA estimates for IVAC only are $61.6 and $65.5 for the low and high revenue range, with IVAC and River consolidated EBITDA $56.0 million and $59.9 million, respectively. Estimated 1995 IVAC only EBITDA is $46.6 million, with 1995 IVAC and River consolidated EBITDA of $36.9 million.

    The $250 million IVAC only revenue forecast for 1996 appears achievable to me, while the $258 million may be a stretch. I believe that River needs three SmartDose™ drug deals in the first half of 1996 to reach $6 million in revenue for the year.

2. I have increased the anticipated gross profit in the 1996 plan by $3 million over that proposed in the 12/15/95 first draft because I believe manufacturing operations can and should contribute to this incremental gross profit. (In 1995, manufacturing operations produced approximately $2 million in materials cost savings versus 1994 after forecasting a $6.5 million saving. Direct labor and overheads savings in 1995 were forecast at $3 million and came in at $5 million in savings. For 1996, I expect that materials cost savings of $4.5 are achievable versus $3 million forecast in the 12/15/95 first draft plan. I also believe that an additional $1.5 million in direct labor and overheads savings are achievable in 1996 where no additional savings were forecast in the 12/15/95 final draft version. These accomplishments would produce the gross profit I recommend, which is $3 million higher than the 12/15/95 first draft version.)

3. Proposed operating expenses for 1996 include $5 million of expense from new areas and not incurred in 1995. These expenses are part discretionary and part unavoidable. The 1996 incremental operating expenses are:

| | 1996 Proposed Plan | |
	12/15/95 Management First Draft Version ($ millions)	AJH Recommendation ($ millions)
Discretionary:		
Advertising (including SE launch, needleless & other)	$1.85	$0.85
Group A Account Discounts	$1.00	$2.70
Southeast Asia/Latin America	$1.00	$0.30
Unavoidable:		
Business Development (Drug/Device Deals)	$0.40	$0.40
All Other (Facilities, Commissions, etc.)	$0.75	$0.75

I have recommended a different distribution than the 12/15/95 first draft of this approximate $5 million incremental operating expenses. I belive that the Group A account discounts could have been the biggest impact on preserving and increasing IVAC revenues and market share in 1996 and have heavily weighted discretionary money for this purpose (recall that the MSIII Fast Attack program increased both channel and instrument placements in 1995 by 28 percent over plan and this was in effect for a partial year). Aggregate incremental OPEX expenses proposed for 1996 do not decline with my recommendations.

4. The overall 1996 IVAC consolidated forecast does not anticipate any expense savings from a restructuring of IVAC International, such as occurred over 1995 with IVAC domestic. I believe that there should be approximately $5 million in expense savings from a rigorous restructuring of IVAC International, which could be a fertile source of incremental EBITDA for 1996.

5. I understand that $6 million has or will be spent on leasehold improvements for our new facility which seems excessive to me. The entire River Medical facility on Kenamar Court was converted from a bank building to an FDA-approved plant with approximately $1.6 million in expenditure budget, however, the projected net cash flow generation of $10 million is not enough for 1996 in my opinion. I would prefer to reduce the capital expenditures by $5 to $10 million dollars including leasehold expenditures if possible.

The attached two pages summarize IVAC only and River Medical P&L projections for the periods discussed. Also included is a reconciliation of EBITDA for IVAC only itemizing the new incremental savings and expense areas anticipated in the 1996 plan.

AJH:jmk
Attachments

Synergy Pharmaceuticals, Inc.

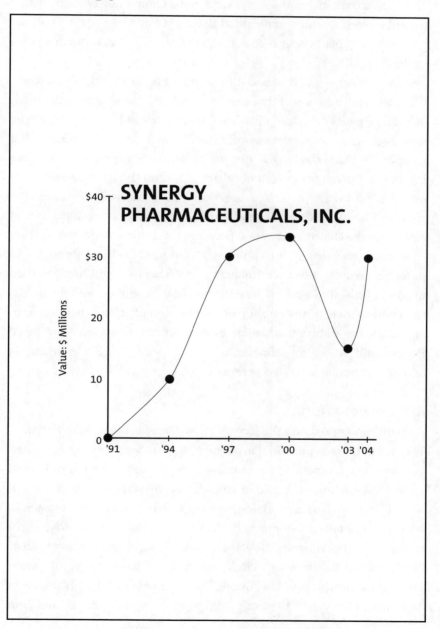

SYNERGY PHARMACEUTICALS, INC.

I magine starting a biotech company around a specific drug platform, raising $19 million and investing $17 million of that to develop a drug that worked. Then, in the midst of the final trials, you see the disease state you are attacking simply disappear because of a new therapy from a company you never considered a competitor. Leaders of successful biotech startups understand that they can never envision all the potential therapeutic approaches that, in effect, could make them second or third to market.

When blind-sided, the easiest thing might be to shut down the company, let academia absorb back the researchers, and shore up the intellectual property in case the disease state should return. However, seasoned venture capitalists understand that a smoothly functioning company is not something to dispose of lightly. Successfully repositioning the company around a new drug platform, though, requires keen intuition on possibilities. Nor is repositioning cheap. Three times the company considered here came within ninety days of running out of cash; once the chairman invested personal funds to meet payroll. During its start-up and restart, the company raised $29.27 million through five different financings — each financing was conceived and implemented to address specific issues in the evolution of the company and the industry. Institutional enthusiasm for private biotech offerings always fluctuates with the public market for biotech stocks. Knowing how to be flexible and where to define value in a quickly moving company is another mark of a seasoned venture capitalist.

IgX Corporation

Al Henry incorporated IgX Corp. as a Delaware corporation in February 1992 as HVII made the initial investment to start the company. The name IgX was derived from Ig for immunoglobulin and X for the unknown variable. A picture of a golden egg was on its stationery because IgX would develop drug candidates from eggs laid by hyperimmune hens.

Throughout the development of electronic infusion pumps and the total parenteral attrition enabled by IMED and IVAC instruments, scientists learned about the immunological importance of the presence of certain foods in the human gut. Also, through development of IMED, Block, River and IVAC, Henry saw the exploding population of AIDS patients who depended upon parenteral nutrition to maintain body weight because of persistent diarrhea.

In 1992, Henry assembled a group of thirteen clinical researchers associated with seven leading universities, teaching hospitals or medical research institutions.[1] All had medical or doctorate degrees and were experts in such fields as gut derived-sepsis, the effect of oral immunoglobulins, and the biology of diarrhea-inducing bacteria and parasites. Henry asked them to serve as principal investigators in conducting animal studies on various parasites that cause illness in humans, especially those patients with Acquired Immune Deficiency Syndrome (AIDS). Their mission was to discover food-derived biologics that delivered specific antibodies into the digestive tract.

One of these researchers was Charles R. Sterling, who co-invented what would become the IgX technology platform. Sterling had been professor of veterinary medicine at the University of Arizona since 1983, and was formerly a professor in immunology and microbiology at the Wayne State University school of medicine and an expert on malaria immunology. Sterling's lab gained fame in the late 1980s by identifying the monoclonal antibodies for *C. parvum* and *Giardia*, the two major water-borne pathogens causing diarrhea. The University of Arizona licensed Sterling's monoclonal antibody technology to Meridian Diagnostics, Inc. of Cincinnati, on which they based their popular Meriflour series of diagnostic kits. Sterling began work on *C. parvum* immunotherapy using monoclonal antibodies, and funded by $3 million worth of grants from the National Institutes of Health. Additional basic research was funded by the U.S. Department of Agriculture, the Environmental Protection Agency, and the American Water Works Association. Sterling's lab also began work, funded largely by Bristol Meyers-Squibb-Mead Johnson, on countering *C. parvum* infection with hyperimmune bovine colostrum (the antibody rich milk secreted for a few days after a calf was born). Then a more promising vehicle for therapy arose.

A postdoctoral fellow, Vitaliano A. Cama, arrived at the University of Arizona in 1988. Cama's doctorate was in veterinary medicine from the Universidad Nacional Mayor de San Marcos in Lima, Peru, and he brought a wealth of experience in avian pathology. Not only was his academic research on chickens, but he had worked as a veterinary supervisor with AVI-NET poultry farms in Lima, Peru. Together, Sterling and Cama developed a polyclonal avian drug platform, specifically to attack intestinal parasites.[2]

The idea behind the polyclonal avian technology was that hens injected with pathogen-specific antigens would produce antibodies in their eggs that could cure humans. This is called passive immunity — using an antibody produced by one animal or person to treat another. Breast feeding is the most familiar type of passive immunity delivered through the gastrointestinal tract, in that the mother provides natural protective antibodies to her infant through her milk. The hen yolk IgY antibody is structurally similar to the human IgG antibody. Yet it is a larger molecule, with 160,000 molecular weight, so it is not absorbed across the human intestine. Since the antibody does not cross into the serum, the human body does not make an antibody against it. It remains active only in the human gut — at the specific site of a parasitic infection. When enough of these hen yolk antibodies are present in the gut, the parasites will bind with it instead of attaching to intestinal epithelial cells. If the parasite cannot invade a cell, it cannot reproduce. It dies and is swept from the intestine. The infection then subsides with time. Passive immunity works directly against the pathogen so it is much faster than active immunization, in which a drug prompts production of antibodies in the patient's serum. Because these antibodies are polyclonal (as opposed to monoclonal), they bind with many different surface features of the pathogen so that the pathogen is less likely to develop resistance.

In July 1991 Henry approached Sterling, realizing the medical importance of his approach. Henry had incorporated IgX to organize the research being conducted at the many institutions, to hold license to any invention disclosures, and ultimately take the most promising discoveries into the clinic. In May 1992, soon after incorporating, IgX executed a forty-year technology license with the University of Arizona. Scientists from the eight laboratories peer-reviewed each others' results, and IgX consolidated its research contracts into the three most productive centers. Researchers at the University of Illinois and the University of Chicago continued research on treatments of C. difficile and E. coli, though all under the supervision of Sterling who continued to lead the research into C. parvum. Sterling remained a University of Arizona employee and became chairman of the IgX scientific advisory board; Cama was hired as IgX vice president of research and development.

HV II provided seed funding for this network of research through loans, which Henry expected to convert into Series A preferred shares when it was possible to close that round. In 1992, IgX funded Sterling's lab for $277,790 to study how a drug might be developed from this interesting in vitro laboratory data, and in 1993 IgX added an additional $74,406. From inception through 1998, IgX would fund $2.4 million worth of research at the University of Arizona, funding which employed on average four scientists with Ph.D.s, five doing masters' work, and four technicians. IgX would hold five exclusive licenses pertaining to the avian technology, based on patents applied for, and agreed to pay the university royalties of five percent of net sales of the drugs.

Cryptosporidiosis

As CEO, it was Henry's responsibility to select the first drug candidate to develop from this technology platform. As lead product he and the IgX scientists selected IGX-CP, an orally-administered antibody to treat *C. parvum*, specifically in patients with AIDS. *Cryptosporidium parvum* is a sporozoan protozoa parasite — similar to the malaria parasite except that it reproduces inside the colon. As it reproduces, it generates a toxin which the colon expels as diarrhea. The protozoa was first identified in 1900 and thought to only infect livestock until it was identified in a human in 1976. It remained underreported because there was no easy diagnostic for it (a pathologist had to identify the oocyst in a stool sample under a microscope). Between 1976 and 1982 there were only seven reported cases of cryptosporidiosis, five in immune-compromised patients. In 1982 the number of cases skyrocketed in proportion with the boom in AIDS patients.[3] Diarrhea became a leading cause of hospitalization among AIDS patients. A complete diagnostic workup cost $3,000 — including cultures and colonoscopy but excluding admission charges.[4] Once diagnosed, however, there was no way to treat it. Physicians simply managed the symptoms with parenteral nutrition and fluids. In 1994, total parenteral nutrition to put weight back on AIDS patients suffering "the wasting syndrome" cost $10,000 to $15,000 per patient per month. AIDS patients infected with cryptosporidiosis cost about $800,000 more to treat than uninfected AIDS patients. Without a treatment for the under-lying infection, the parenteral nutrition might continue for months — often terminating only with death.

For those with advanced AIDS — whose immune system could not stop the infection — cryptosporidiosis turned chronic and fatal. There were reports of AIDS patients passing 23 liters of stool in a day. For those infected, life came to a standstill. They could not function at work, sleep through the night, or eat enough to have any energy. When *C. parvum* invaded the biliary duct, as it often did, the nausea and vomiting got even worse. Others reported AIDS patients who died of heart attacks while sit-ting on the toilet, their diarrhea leaching from their bodies the essential minerals needed to regulate the beating of their hearts. Twenty percent of AIDS patients in the United States and Europe showed some cryp-tosporidial infection, and these AIDS patients were forty percent more like-ly to die. Cryptosporidiosis was implicated in a quarter of all AIDS-related deaths, becoming the second largest killer of AIDS patients.

Moreover, cryptosporidiosis was not limited to AIDS patients. *C. parvum* oocysts (the female germ cells — essentially eggs) are less than four microns in diameter, yet only a few need to be swallowed to start a full-blown infection.[5] They are found in virtually all of the surface water in the United States, and most municipal water systems cannot remove them. Chemicals like chlorine will not kill the oocysts. (In fact, to get a pure suspension of *C. parvum* bench scientists usually mixed a stool sam-ple with undiluted Clorox, which killed everything else.) And filtration systems fine enough to capture them must be backwashed very careful-ly. (Boiling water is the most effective way to kill them.) Once physicians knew what to look for, cryptosporidiosis outbreaks were reported more regularly — in Texas in 1984, in Georgia in 1987, in Oregon in 1992. Some smaller outbreaks were linked to tainted food or recreational water. The biggest outbreaks were linked to contaminated drinking water, all in areas where the water utilities met state and federal standards for water safety. In April 1993 the entire population of Milwaukee was exposed to *C. parvum*, more than 400,000 people were infected, and perhaps 110 died from the infection — prompting action by the Centers for Disease Control.[6] The cost of health care, litigation, and water treatments totaled more that $150 million. Those hit hardest were children. In the United

States each year as many as 200,000 children were hospitalized for diarrhea and about 500 children died each year from diarrhea-related dehydration or malnutrition. An EPA report had documented the high levels of *C. parvum* in the New York City watershed.[7] As the New York City water department continued to delay construction of adequate filtration, the Wall Street investment community grew personally aware of the danger that IgX addressed.

The situation was even more dire in the developing world. *C. parvum* was found more often in drinking water, was passed more often from livestock to humans, or transferred more easily among family members suffering inadequate sanitation. Cryptosporidial diarrhea is a self-limiting infection in immune-competent patients, in that a healthy body would usually cure itself without pharmacological intervention in about twelve days. Children who were already malnourished could not always last that long. In tropical developing areas in Asia, Africa and Latin America, diarrhea of all types killed 4.6 million children each year. More than 55 percent of AIDS patients in developing countries presented with some cryptosporidial infection; most who had that infection died from it. Throughout the early 1990s, IgX found itself developing a product for a disease state that the world cared a great deal about.

Question 1

Imagine you are the CEO of a biotech company that has some interesting in vitro and animal data for a compound, derived from a broad technology platform you own and against a specific disease indication. How much capital do you seek in your first round of funding? What issues guide your estimation to that amount? How does the stage of a biotech company's development influence its ability to attract funding?

Series A

Before IgX could shift from discovery to development, it needed to be capitalized. Despite this clear public health threat, little government money was available for firms to develop a drug against cryptosporidiosis in AIDS patients. To validate its private investment in this research and to support valuations for IgX equity financings, IgX needed to define a sizable potential market for its efforts. The company compiled vast numbers of research articles on the causes, spread and severity of *C. parvum* infections around the world. To estimate a treatable patient base by country, they identified the incidence of AIDS infection in the total population by country and the incidence of AIDS patients infected with cryptosporidial diarrhea. They narrowed their estimated market to those AIDS patients already infected with life-threatening cryptosporidiosis, though many might take the drug as prophylaxis against infection. They then estimated a conservative penetration rate for their therapy and a market price substantially lower than what insurers then paid to treat the symptoms. The bank of scientific, market and financial data behind the business strategy of the young IgX was impressive.

IgX next needed to estimate the cost of bringing the drug to market, with the first step being Phase I/II clinical trials. To generate statistical validity, IgX needed to estimate the number of patients to enroll in the study and how many study sites IgX needed to set up to find that many patients in a reasonable amount of time. Prompt completion of trials, once begun, was important to maintain investor confidence. IgX needed to produce enough of the drug candidate for use in the trials and estimate this cost of production. IgX also needed to estimate the ramp-up of personnel as they generated documentation for the FDA and oversaw the complicated task of running trials. At that projected monthly burn rate, IgX then needed to estimate how much cash would sustain them until they had results to justify a next round of funding.

To get IgX to the point it could begin Phase I/II trials, by September 1994 HV II had already funded IgX through loans and Series A equity totalling $1.2 million. Of that amount, $882,650 was in unsecured notes. As seed round funding, beginning in August 1992, HV II and its nominee had purchased 710,000 common shares and 370,000 shares of Series A preferred stock, for total proceeds of $370,000. The approaching Phase I/II trials as planned would cost at least $2 million, and Henry calculated that IgX would need a war chest totalling $5 million to $7 million. Henry's plans were to complete the Series A round of financing to bring the total raised to $5 million (and in completing this round convert his notes into equity). Based on the potential market, and the status of the IgX platform, Henry estimated he now could approach the equity market with the pre-money value of IgX at $15 million.

Question 2

HV II had invested $1.2 million as seed money in IgX, and was seeking to establish a $15 million valuation for the Series A round of funding. What multiple returns was HV II seeking over its own cost? Is it usual for founding or seed investors to seek a multiple return at the Series A round of funding? Why or why not? Give examples.

With the IgX animal data in hand, Henry began visiting venture firms and institutional investors to generate interest in a Series A round of funding. Yet 1992 marked the end of a bull market for biotech stocks, and the start of a three year span of unfavorable investment interest in preclinical biotech firms. Firms with drug candidates in Phase III tests could attract money. Valuations for biotech companies historically doubled upon moving into Phase III trials, even in bear markets.[8] Yet because of investor uncertainty about how expeditiously the FDA of the new Clinton administration would review drug applications, preclinical biotech firms were less attractive to private equity investors. Preclinical firms could not get bridge loans, not even with equity attached as warrants. Institutional investors were excited about the technical promise of the polyclonal avian platform, but not at the valuation Henry estimated for his company. Furthermore, for every important indication of interest, the presence of both Henry and Sterling was required to add weight to the business and scientific presentations. They traveled to San Francisco, Los Angeles, New York and London, and eventually they spent so much of their time trying to raise funding that drug development suffered. After five months of effort, IgX abandoned efforts to raise third party capital with Series A equity funding.

HV II decided to finance the trials itself. If efficacy was proven, IgX could raise funds at a pre-money valuation higher than $15 million, Henry thought, and possibly as high as $30 million. So HV II continued to advance funds to IgX through unsecured promissory notes accumulating interest at nine percent per annum. Debt financing allowed Henry to more carefully time investments to the cash needs of the company. Through the conclusion of the trials in November 1995, HV II would lend IgX an additional $900,000. With funding in place, IgX was able to conclude pilot production and move the drug candidate into trials.

Into Trials

Throughout the summer of 1994 IgX set up an IGX-CP pilot production facility in leased buildings in Tucson and had it certified to FDA good manufacturing practices. There the White Leghorn hens were monitored and the hyperimmune egg yolks processed. The eggs were collected every day and the egg yolks pooled. Lipoproteins were precipitated out, partially purifying the active ingredients. Then the lipid content (a fat) was reduced by half, leaving the antibodies in liquid form, and the antibodies were concentrated by cross-flow filtration. The product underwent 0.22 micron filtration to reduce the microbiological load, and sucrose was added to improve the taste. Then the solution was frozen for transport. It had a shelf life of eighteen months, and was easy to transport and prepare. A course of treatment was five doses per day for 28 days. When taken orally, patients would also take famotidine (Pepcid) or omeprazole (Prilosec), standard gastric acid blockers, to reduce the chance that the immunoglobulin would be ripped apart by gastric juices. Many patients took the drug through a nasoduodenal tube (a plastic tube through the nose into the intestines) or through a percutaneous gastrostomy (a tube directly into the abdomen). Soon IgX had enough of the drug to begin Phase I/II clinical trials.

Randolph Steer had joined the IgX scientific advisory board in 1993 to prepare its drug candidate for trial. Steer was formerly medical director for Ciba-Geigy and a prominent consultant to biotechnology companies on regulation and business development. In February 1994, two years after incorporation, IgX submitted its Investigational New Drug Application for IGX-CP to the U.S. Food and Drug Administration. Phase I/II trials began in September 1994 and ended in November 1995. These trials were run by the division of infectious diseases at the New York Hospital-Cornell Medical Center with physician supervision from Dr. Rosemary Soave. Since 1985, Soave had managed eleven trials and was widely regarded as the leading clinical expert in the United States on treating cryptosporidiosis in AIDS patients. Phase I trials evaluate the safety and toxicity of the drug candidate; Phase II trials generate preliminary data (to be verified in Phase III) on efficacy, or how well the drug candidate worked against a specific disease. The trial was open-label (Soave had stopped doing placebo-controlled trials in 1993 largely for ethical reasons) and ascending dose, with two dose levels. Of the 24 patients enrolled, 16 were evaluated after completing two weeks at the lowest dose level before advancing to the next. Eight of the patients withdrew from the study during the first three weeks for various reasons. Compliance with the protocol was worse at the higher dose, with those patients claiming the drug produced satiety, or a bloated feeling.

Both dose levels proved safe. There was no toxicity, as expected, since the active ingredients are commonly found in eggs, which are widely consumed. IGX-CP also proved effective. Six of the eleven low dose patients showed a decrease in the daily frequency both of bowel movements and of liquid stools — which the FDA declared to be the two primary measures of efficacy. Eradication of the oocysts occurred in one patient after one week, and two patients experienced near-total eradication at the end of the two-week treatment. However, the frequency of diarrhea worsened with patients taking the higher dose. IgX attributed this to the high lipid content of the formulation, since lipids sometimes induce diarrhea as well as a bloated feeling. The third measure of efficacy was stool oocyst quantitation — a measure of the density of the parasite in the stool. One-quarter of the patients showed improvement on density, though IgX did not believe that measure was as important since density increased with the decline in stool frequency — the more important measure.[9]

Based on what they learned, IgX reformulated IGX-CP to reduce the lipid content by half and formulate it as a powder rather than as a liquid. It was renamed IGX-CPL$_3$ (L$_3$ for low-lipid lyophilized) with the trade name Stercamacim (derived from STER-ling, Cama, and CIM for chicken immunoglobulin). After purifying the yolks, the bulk liquid was lyophilized (freeze-dried to a powder at low heat inside a vacuum) then packed as unit doses for easy reconstitution with 100 ml of pathogen-free water. IgX redid the animal studies and found that a high dose with this formulation would prove very effective.

Question 3

How would you evaluate the results of the Phase I/II clinical trial at Cornell? What do you do next based upon your assessment of the Phase I/II results?

HV II invested more money into IgX to fund this reformulation and the necessary animal studies. From September 1995 to July 1996, HV II lent IgX an additional $2.14 million, which in August 1996 it converted into Series A convertible preferred shares. IgX now had paid in equity of $4.913 million in its Series A shares, and had accumulated a deficit of $5.18 million. Apart from a small percentage of stock options granted, HV II owned all of IgX, having supplied all the capital. Yet following completion of the Phase I/II trials, IgX now needed a second financing to begin Phase III trials to test efficacy in a broader population.

Question 4

At this point, what value do you place on IgX to raise the Series B round of funding? What are the major factors to consider in estimating a pre-money value for IgX? What amount of funding should you seek? Can any form of debt be used in the financing, and at what mix of debt to equity? Give your reasoning throughout.

Competitive Therapies

As IgX prepared plans for the next series of trials it seemed to have a healthy lead on its competitors. Other companies were trying somewhat similar polyclonal approaches to battling cryptosporidiosis — each with orphan drug status from the FDA.[10] ImmuCell had completed Phase I/II trials of CryptoGRAM — an oral polyclonal antibody harvested from the milk of immunized cows. Yet Univax Pharmaceuticals, which had funded the trials in exchange for marketing rights, withdrew funding in June 1995 because ImmuCell had trouble producing sufficient uniform quantities of CryptoGRAM from cows. Protein Technology developed Immuno-C, a refined protein derived from milk that also contained lactoferrin to aid the transfer of immunoglobulins into the bloodstream. GalaGen had a proprietary process for producing polyclonal immunoglobulin in the colostrum of dairy cows. On this drug platform they had developed Sporidin G, an anti-cryptosporidiosis candidate. In April 1996, Montgomery Securities brought GalaGen public, raising $25 million at a pre-money valuation of $45 million. Sporidin G began Phase III trials in July 1996.

Yet each of these bovine drug platforms suffered production problems. By contrast, the IgX hens were pure and regular workers. The antibody produced by one cow every fourteen months was the equivalent to the antibody produced by thirteen chickens in one year. One cow consumed ten times the feed of thirteen chickens and took considerably more space. It took three years before cows produced the best colostrum, and at six years of age they were past their peak. Hens produce constantly from 25 weeks of age to 80 weeks. Furthermore, the bovine colostrum is not sterile, whereas under normal conditions egg yolks are. IgX had a superior technology platform, and its polyclonal approach was especially effective against cryptosporidiosis.

Other competitors developed more conventional chemical therapies. Janssen developed oral letrazuril which looked promising in early trials in Belgium. Unimed Pharmaceuticals had licensed nitazoxanide (NTZ) from Romark Laboratories and was sponsoring its FDA approval. NTZ was the anti-diarrhea drug of choice in the AIDS buyers clubs, which smuggled it up from Mexico. GelTex developed a series of oral, non-absorbed hydrogel polymers designed to bind to *C. parvum* spores in the gut. Preclinical trials began in January 1995. And Shaman Pharmaceuticals, Inc. derived a product from the croton plant found in Latin America which might treat the cellular mechanism behind diarrhea (but not the underlying infection) by blocking chloride secretion. In addition, the AIDS Clinical Trial Information Service was testing three established drugs for their effectiveness against cryptosporidiosis — azithromycin, clarithormycin and thalidomide. The FDA was being very lenient in allowing the open-label testing of these drugs on a compassionate use basis in AIDS patients, but was upholding strict standards for clinical results before formal licensing. Still IgX knew, based on the results of its early trials at the Cornell Medical Center, that it had a significant competitive lead over the other polyclonal and chemical approaches.

The race that IgX was losing, however, was not against its competitors for a polyclonal treatment. Rather it was against the waning of the disease state due to newer therapy. Early in 1996 the "triple cocktail" began to dramatically reduce the impact of AIDS symptoms in HIV-infected patients. A strict protocol of three drugs, including a reverse transcriptase inhibitor and a protease inhibitor, disrupted the replication of HIV inside the blood stream. When on a regular dosing regime of the triple cocktail, the amount of virus in a person infected with HIV often dropped by as much as 99 percent. The result was less virus to destroy CD_4-T lymphocytes — the white blood cells needed to start the body's fight against fungi, bacteria, and parasites like *C. parvum*. With more CD_4 cells, the HIV-infected person stayed immune-competent longer and stayed resilient to cryptosporidiosis longer. Even AIDS patients already infected with cryptosporidiosis could begin taking protease inhibitors to resolve that infection, as IGX-CPL_3 was meant to do.[11] Within months of the introduction of combination therapy, there was a dramatic drop in the number of advanced AIDS patients in the United States with chronic cryptosporidial diarrhea.[12]

A couple of years passed before the full public health impact of the triple cocktail was known. It remained unclear if drug companies could manufacture the massive amounts required, if patients could take so many pills at such precise times, or if insurance companies would pay for all that. Once these socioeconomic issues were resolved some scientific issue remained. The side effects became known gradually, though persistent side effects were diarrhea and weight loss. Further, by the end of 1997, it looked as though HIV had mutated to develop resistance to the protease inhibitors. As the number of active AIDS patients slowly climbed back up, physicians varied the triple cocktail protocol to fend off drug resistance. Active AIDS among HIV-infected patients again declined. Though hardly eradicated, HIV in the United States and Europe now appeared to be controlled.

The public health threat of cryptosporidiosis in the general population also started to wane. In September 1994, the Centers for Disease Control targeted cryptosporidiosis as an emergent infectious disease posing a global health threat.[13] The Council of State and Territorial Epidemiologists in January 1995 approved a measure to make cryptosporidiosis reportable to the CDC, providing legal authority for collecting data. The emergence of a reliable fluorescent monoclonal antibody test, costing only $5, made it more likely physicians would test for cryptosporidiosis in patients with diarrhea. The EPA required more regular testing of municipal water for *C. parvum* and, once identified, water could be more carefully filtered. A Working Group on Waterborne Cryptosporidiosis — with representatives of the American Water Works Association, the EPA, the CDC, and state health departments — met biweekly to trade data on where the parasite was found and how it was eliminated. As a last resort they set standards for issuing boil-water advisories. Also, with the flurry of press attention, physicians grew more aware of the infection, parents learned to wash their hands more carefully after changing diapers, and consumers learned to buy heat-pasteurized juices and ciders. As a result, while outbreaks continued on a small scale — typically around day care centers or among family members — the 1993 outbreak in Milwaukee would be the last major epidemic of cryptosporidiosis in the United States.

Irish Operations

Henry made plans to move the IgX Phase III trials to Europe because the lower quality of European drinking water could make it easier to enroll patients there as compared to the United States. The Medical Control Agency approved the IgX application to begin Phase III trials in Britain. The newly-created European Medicines Evaluation Agency, which centralized trials for all European Union nations, then reviewed and approved the IgX protocol for a Phase III double-blind placebo-controlled multicenter trial. Trials sites in France and Denmark were added to those in England. To run the trial, IgX contracted with two clinical research organizations, LCG Bioscience Limited and PRSI International, which expected to enroll a total of ninety patients at sixteen study sites in the three countries. Since FDA regulations prohibit export of biologics for use in foreign clinical trials, IgX could not use its Tuscon plant to supply IGX-CPL$_3$ as it had for the Cornell trials. So IgX looked to build a new plant in Europe.

Ireland was a clear front-runner for a European plant. In 1980, Henry financed and Robert Renfroe managed the construction of an IMED Corporation medical devices plant in Donegal. This plant had created more than 900 jobs, and cemented cordial relations between Henry and Irish business and political leaders. Robert Renfroe was the one person whom Henry later would trust with the complex and isolated job of constructing an Irish plant for IgX in Granard, County Longford and certifying it to FDA good manufacturing practices. In October 1996 the pilot plant begin to produce IGX-CPL$_3$ for use in clinical trials outside the United States.

To oversee the plant and European regulation, in September 1995 Henry had reorganized IgX Corp. to become a wholly-owned subsidiary of a new corporation, IgX Limited, organized in the Republic of Ireland. The reorganization took advantage of certain Irish tax benefits, resulting in a corporate tax rate of ten percent, and secured a grant from the Irish government to build a manufacturing plant should the Phase III trials succeed. The grant would equal IR£12,000 per job created, for a total of $2.28 million, or roughly half the cost of building the production plant. Furthermore, if IGX-CPL3 were successful in trials, the Irish Medicines Board would sponsor the marketing authorization application to the European Union to bring the drug to market. For IgX, this was the ideal corporate structure bringing financial advantages unavailable anywhere else.

All outstanding shares of the Delaware corporation, IgX Corp., were converted into shares of the Irish company. In August 1996, HV II cancelled all of its outstanding notes, and accumulated interest, in exchange for equal shares of Series B and Series C mandatory redeemable convertible preferred stock in IgX Limited, at a company post money value of $5 million. Robert Renfroe, who had worked as IgX senior vice president of operations since April 1994, was named managing director of IgX Limited. Henry had earlier hired Renfroe to build a medical disposables plant in Letterkenney for IMED Corp., and this would be the fourth plant Renfroe had built in Ireland. Renfroe was critical to the success of the project. Tony Geoghegan, an Irishman whom Henry had long known in an audit capacity, was named IgX financial controller.

IgX opened an office in London in April 1997. IgX had become a European biotech company with global aspirations, and had redesigned itself in the face of a changing market and financial environment.

IGX PRODUCTS IN DEVELOPMENT

Product	Disease Target	Stage of Development
IGX-CPL$_3$ (Stercamacim)	Cryptosporidium parvum-associated diarrhea in AIDS patients	Phase I/II trial completed November 1995. Phase III European double-blind, placebo-controlled human clinic trial begun January 1998.
IGX-CDL$_3$	Clostridium difficile-associated diarrhea arising from antibiotic therapy.	Laboratory studies in hamsters completed in 1997.
IGX-HPL$_3$	Peptic ulcers due to Helicobacter pylori infections	Basic research. Animal studies commenced late 1998.
IGX-EC	Escherichia coli-associated diarrhea arising from antibiotic therapy.	Laboratory studies in mice completed 1998.
IGX-M	Malaria infections caused by Plasmodium falciparum	Laboratory studies in mice completed in 1997.

IgX was also actively developing other drug candidates from its polyclonal platform. Each of these drug candidates originated from IgX-funded work at the University of Arizona department of veterinary science. IGX-CDL$_3$ and IGX-HPL$_3$ both used the polyclonal avian technology to produce antibodies against specific bacteria in the human gastrointestinal system. Since they developed no drug resistance, they were designed as alternatives to antibiotics. IGX-CDL$_3$ was designed to resolve diarrhea associated with the bacterium *Clostridium difficile*, especially problematic among newborns, the elderly in nursing homes, or surgical patients whose colonic microflora was disrupted from taking broad-spectrum oral antibiotics. When the existing flora are diminished, *C. difficile* can flourish and produce a toxin that damages the intestinal cells and causes diarrhea, vomiting and abdominal pain. *C. difficile* colitis was the fourth most common nosocomial infection (meaning acquired in a hospital), in the United States, so hospitals would be especially receptive to the drug as a way of reducing length of admission. IgX collaborated with BioSite Diagnostics to develop a fifteen-minute test to diagnose *C. difficile*, on the assumption that identifying the disease will make physicians more inclined to treat it. Total cost of pharmacotherapy for a patient presenting with C. *difficile* diarrhea was $2,155, in addition to hospital admission costs. In the United States 2.3 million patients per year suffer from C. *difficile*-associated diarrhea. Ophidian Pharmaceuticals, Inc. developed a recombinant protein from hen eggs that neutralized the toxins created by C. *difficile*. However, Ophidian's drug candidate did not attack the underlying infection.

IGX-HPL$_3$ was designed to reduce peptic ulcers due to infections of *Helicobacter pylori*. Four million new incidences of *H. pylori*-related ulcers were reported every year in the United States, and there was a growing statistical association between these ulcers and gastric carcinoma. *H. pylori* infections were being treated with their own combination therapy — bismuth, acid blockers, and several antibiotics. AMBI Inc. was in Phase III trials of Nisin, an antibiotic specifically designed to counter *H. pylori*. While four-fifths of patients responded well to this combination therapy, it was expensive, complicated, and *H. pylori* was beginning to show resistance to the available antibiotics. Astra Merck Inc. had just entered Phase III studies of perprozole and Eisai Co. had just begun selling rabeprazole in Japan. Both drugs, however, attempted to create an acid-poor environment hostile to H. pylori rather than directly blocking the urease receptors on the bacteria, as did IGX-HPL$_3$.

IgX had also begun animal studies on IGX-EC, an avian polyclonal antibody targeted against enterotoxigenic *Escherichia coli*. Not only is *E. coli* implicated in diarrhea, it also induces sepsis following trauma to the abdomen. A fifth potential product was IGX-M, a vasoactive peptide developed by Sterling and targeted at malaria infections caused by *Plasmodium falciparum*. IgX funded animal studies, completed in June 1997, that proved the concept. Since the peptide was outside its core polyclonal avian technology, IgX decided it would out-license any further development of IGX-M.

So even if cryptosporidiosis did wane, there was still much value in the IgX polyclonal avian platform. The overall market for monoclonal and polyclonal antibody products — both diagnostic and therapeutic — had grown 9.4 percent each year in the 1990s to being a $2 billion market by the end of 1997. The top ten companies in the antibody market in 1997 included some of the strongest global pharmaceutical firms: Abbott

Laboratories, American Home Products, Baxter International, Becton Dickinson, Hoffmann-La Roche, Eli Lilly, Miles, Organon Teknika (Akzo), Warner Lambert, and Johnson & Johnson. Antibody therapy would likely grow more prevalent with increased bacterial resistance to chemical antimicrobials In November 1997, IgX learned that its patent on hyperimmune egg yolk antibodies had been allowed by the U.S. Patent Office. IgX now controlled the avian platform for producing antibodies and creating drug candidates. It now had remarkable leverage in the antibody market.

A Forced Global Strategy

Meanwhile, IgX's lead product, IGX-CPL3, continued to confront delays. In Europe, as in the United States, the number of qualified AIDS patients was declining rapidly. In France, for example, protease inhibitors were first licensed for sale in March 1996. By May 1997, 64 percent of HIV patients were on combination therapy, which mapped to a 60 percent decline in reports of cryptosporidiosis. In May 1997 IgX trials began at the sixteen European sites, but recruitment of patients was negligible. Enrolled patients had to discontinue using any medication but the trial compound, and few wanted to give up their protease inhibitors.[14] Even those patients who failed to respond to the initial mixes of protease inhibitors preferred to self-medicate with a street drug than risk being assigned the placebo and suffering through months of diarrhea. By the fall of 1997, IgX had largely abandoned its efforts in Europe and refocused its strategy on its secondary market — countries in Africa and South America. There, cryptosporidial diarrhea was generally more widespread and AIDS patients did not yet have access to combination drug therapy.

IgX then launched a full-blown effort to find licensees or marketing partners for the IgX platform. IgX intended to maintain control of its proprietary manufacturing processes, and produce bulk materials for sale or distribution by other pharmaceutical firms. IgX added staff, bringing the total to 31 employees — eight in research, sixteen in manufacturing, and seven in administration and business development — working at a head office in London, a research laboratory in Arizona, a production plant in Ireland, and a new marketing and licensing office in New Jersey. IgX established a headquarters in Summit, New Jersey.

The IgX office in New Jersey printed up a business development plan, a corporate brochure, and a library of Power Point slides to facilitate the process of making presentations to potential strategic partners and institutional investors. They then contracted with Technology Catalysts Inc. of Falls Church, Virginia — one of the leading technology transfer agents in the United States — to set up initial meetings with the most promising licensees. The most promising licensing partners were the global pharmaceutical firms, with strong sales operations throughout the developing world. In addition, IgX looked for strong regional pharmaceutical firms in countries that seemed especially promising — including Argentina, Australia, Brazil, Canada, France, Germany, India, Italy, Japan, South Africa, South Korea, Spain, Sweden, and Switzerland.

Series B

IgX had used all the cash raised so far to build its Irish plant, file regulatory submissions in Europe, and organize the European trials. To fund this marketing effort and to prepare for the next phase of trials, Henry reorganized and recapitalized the company. From November 1996 through December 1997, HV II had lent IgX an additional $5,328,546, which gave the company its only cash. IgX estimated it would need between $3 million and $6 million more financing to complete its Phase III trials. Henry decided it was time to make a second attempt to access institutional equity in a Series B convertible preferred financing, now at a higher valuation.

Question 5

Review the Series B term sheets [Attachments, Question 5, page 219]. From the company's point of view, is this an attractive financing? Why or why not? From the investors' point of view, is this an attractive financing? Why or why not? From both points of view, which terms would you recommend be changed? Based upon the NPV analysis in the *Stercamacim Business Review* is the valuation proposed for the Series B satisfactory to IGX? Explain why or why not?

IgX stood as a transformed company with a strong story. Its science was on track, the Irish production plant showed good business development, and Phase III trials were imminent. Henry had anticipated that IgX would be worth double its $15 million valuation at the Series A round if it established efficacy for its lead compound. Indeed, following four months of presentations to various venture capital firms, Henry was able to start the Series B negotiations in late 1997 with a pre-money valuation of $35 million. New England Partners (NEP), a Boston-based private equity firm that managed NEGF II, the New England Growth Fund, served as lead investor. In December 1997, IgX raised $2.8 million in new cash by selling 436,672 shares of Series B preferred shares at $6.41 each. NEGF invested $1 million for 155,955 shares. Two of Henry's institutional investors also bought in: English and Scottish plc took 155,955 shares and Meriken Nominees took 109,168 shares. To maintain its ownership, HV II took almost as many shares (311,910 shares) by exchanging $2 million in outstanding debt for Series B shares. The $2.8 million in new cash was a fairly small amount, intended to fund only six months of operations until a public offering and keep the Phase III trials on track.

As a condition of NEP's investment, in December 1997 the company was reorganized so that IgX Limited became the wholly-owned subsidiary of IgX Corp., the Delaware corporation. Though NEP appreciated the long-term benefits of an Irish structure with tax advantages, it did not want to invest in a non-American company. NEP also outlined an equity ratchet to overcome investor fears about volatility in the biotechnology sector and to circumvent protracted negotiations over pre-money valuations. The ratchet allowed flexibility in the terms and timing of a future IPO or merger, while both protecting the Series B investor on the downside and providing unlimited upside. NEP based the ratchet on a formula that gave NEGF II and other Series B investors a rather high 75 percent internal rate of return at the time of a liquidity event. Series B shareholders got additional shares if IgX did not complete future financings at valuations that exceeded the Series B valuation by 75 percent per year, compounded. The mechanics of the adjustment could be through conversion price, escrowed stock or warrants. Edwin Snape Ph.D., the principal in New England Partners responsible for its health care investments, became an IgX director and chaired its newly formed Executive Committee for Corporate Development. Snape gave Henry considerable help in the subsequent development and financing of the company.

In January 1998, IgX trials started in South Africa, where it would be easier to enroll patients and the medical system was good. South Africa followed regulatory procedures approved by the E.U., so trial results would be recognized. Recruitment in South Africa was acceptable. The biggest difficulty was the exclusion criteria for patients, like having other opportunistic infections or other conditions known to cause diarrhea. To accelerate its trials in the race against protease inhibitors, in March 1998, IgX expanded the trial to Mexico City. IgX had every reason to expect that IGX-CPL3 would prove effective and fuel the growth of a profitable company. To prove that point, at least ninety patients needed to complete the trial.

Question 6

How important is going public to the corporate development of a young biotech firm? What are the major considerations in selecting an investment banker for your company's IPO?

Henry and Snape proceeded with plans to take IgX public. In January 1998, just as IgX went silent about the status of its lead compound with the start of Phase III trials, Henry and Snape started exploratory discussions with investment banks. They approached more than a dozen mid-size investment banks, each capable of doing a public offering in the $20 million to $30 million range. This was a fairly small placement, but they figured IgX did not have a high enough total valuation to warrant a public offering in the $50 million range. Most major firms, like Lehman Brothers, would not accept a offering of less than $50 million.

In case an IPO could not be quickly accomplished, Henry and Snape kept open the option of IgX merging with a much larger strategic partner. Vector Securities International, Inc. agreed to accept IgX as a merger candidate. Vector, located near Chicago, was one of the largest and most respected investment banks focused exclusively on health care companies. Its work divided fairly evenly between public offerings, private equity, and mergers and acquisitions. IgX felt validated that a firm of Vector's stature would take it as a client. In March 1998, Vector prepared a presentation on IgX and its polyclonal platform, and contacted 35 companies.

By May 1998, just as the South Africa trials had enrolled about half the patients needed, IgX was again low on cash. Entering 1998, the public market for biotech stocks began to cool, and by mid-1998 all stock market indices would be in decline. Vector Securities grew discouraged, and by May had stopped looking in earnest for a merger partner for IgX. Henry and Snape quickly settled on Josephthal & Co., Inc. to take IgX public. Josephthal was an old-line Wall Street firm, with a seat on the New York Stock Exchange and branch offices in Manhattan, Long Island, Florida and Texas. It had a strong, dedicated and traditional customer base. Josephthal's drug company analyst, a medical doctor, had made several successful recommendations on biotech company shares to the firm's customers.

IgX had an investment bank of sterling reputation representing it in merger discussions, and another bank planning ahead a possible IPO. Once plans were in place for the next big round of funding, NEGF II boosted its investment in the Series B round. In May 1998, NEGF II made an additional $2 million investment in Series B shares which kept IgX working until its next round of financing.

IgX licensing efforts slowly bore fruit. In August 1998, IgX and Laboratorios Sintofarma S.A. of Brazil agreed to form a joint venture named Sintofarma IgX Biotech Ltda. The venture was owned sixty percent by Sintofarma and forty percent by IgX. IgX granted this venture license rights to its three drug candidates, and Sintofarma would bear all the costs of getting them through clinical trials and marketing them in Brazil. Once the drug was approved, the venture would build a manufacturing plant in Brazil to make bulk ingredients for sale around the world. That same month IgX also licensed to Gador S.A., the second largest pharmaceutical firm in Argentina, the rights to two of its drug candidates for Gador to manufacture and market throughout the rest of Latin America. IgX or its Sintofarma venture would supply raw ingredients to Gador, and Gador would oversee regulatory approvals. Both Sintofarma and Gador agreed to return a royalty of ten percent on all product sold.

Initial Public Offering

IgX then asked Josephthal to finalize a prospectus. At that point, only a public offering could raise in excess of $20 million to exploit the opportunities facing the company and cover the burn rate for the coming two to three years.

Review the April 1998 fact sheet on IgX prepared by Vector Securities, and the consolidated financial statements from the IgX Corp. red herring of 30 September 1998, and the Results of the Phase I/II clinical trials written by Rosemary Soave, MD, New York Hospital, Cornell Medical Center, [Attachments, Question 7, page 264]. Suppose you are the IgX CEO and you want to convince a Wall Street underwriter to take your company public. First, address the qualitative issues in favor of an IPO. Second, show how you justify a valuation for the IPO. This might require a lengthy answer since you are approaching one of the most critical events in the evolution of your company.

Based on rigorous analysis, IgX and Josephthal agreed to do the IPO at a $65 million pre-money valuation as of September 1998. IgX ran the calculations to convince Josephthal of the value of its multiple potential products for broad potential markets. IgX estimated the United States and European markets for its *C. difficile* and *H. pylori* products at $400 million each. The licenses with Sintofarma and Gador brought into reach the South American markets for IGX-CPL$_3$. Most important to setting the valuation, companies with drugs in Phase III trials then routinely commanded pre-money valuations in excess of $50 million.

As Henry and Snape finished drafting the IgX prospectus, they believed that IgX was at the end of its money troubles. Henry and Snape made plans to convert their outstanding notes into equity. Underwriters routinely require companies going public to consolidate all preferred stock ownership into common stock, and most term sheets for preferred stock contain provisions for automatic conversion of shares into common stock upon completion of an IPO. That way the common shares are more attractive to the public, since no preferred shareholder has rights superceding the rights of the new class of common shareholders. Previously, Henry Venture II had converted its debt into preferred shares as financing rounds were closing. So near the IPO, though, it made more sense for HV II and NEGF II to convert their debt directly into common shares. Henry converted notes and accumulated interest worth $4,092,815 into 584,688 shares of common stock priced at $7.00 per share. NEGF II likewise converted its $1 million promissory note into 147,859 shares of common stock. As a result, HV II owned 71.2 percent of IgX and NEGF II owned 11.8 percent. English & Scottish plc and other HV II shareholders owned the remainder. The 1993 stock option plan for employees and consultants was superceded by a 1998 plan.

On 30 September 1998, IgX filed its S-1 with the Security and Exchange Commission. Plans were to sell 2.3 million shares priced between $8.00 and $10.00 for net proceeds of $18.1 million, or $26.4 million with the full oversubscription. This was easily enough to fund operations through December 2000 at the high burn rate generated by clinical trials. Josephthal & Co. Inc. were the underwriters, and the stock would trade on NASDAQ as IGXC.[15] The percentage of shares floated in the public market would be 25.65 percent; after the public offering HV II would still own 60 percent of IgX subject to a nine month lock-up.

However, in the fourth quarter of 1998 the market for biotech stocks soured. Scheduled biotech IPOs were being withdrawn across the board, and Josephthal turned timid. More importantly, biotech industry analysts following the companies that produced parts of the triple cocktail realized that the potential market for IgX could disappear. Henry delayed the IPO, and in December 1998 IgX again ran low on cash.

With this cash crunch, IgX could not support the $600,000 monthly burn rate associated with the $IGX-CPL_3$ Phase III trials. Nine months into the trial, as IgX was filing for its IPO, the rate of patient enrollment in South Africa slowed. Enrollment was only slightly better in Mexico. After screening 450 patients, IgX was still able to enroll only 40 patients, only 26 of whom completed a course of treatment. Results from the trials would be largely academic anyway, since IgX could not easily use them to raise more capital. Institutional equity investors were largely unimpressed by drugs targeted at non-US or non-European markets. IgX had emphasized the global problem of cryptosporidial diarrhea, but its market studies only assumed revenues from the developed world. In many developing nations drug companies have trouble getting reimbursements for novel drugs. The years it takes to establish cash flow from developing countries would strain the resources of any biotech startup. Without the American or European parts of the global equation, institutional investors saw little short-term promise for IgX.

Reluctantly, but realistically, in February 1999 IgX shut down its two pilot production plants, stopped the Phase III trials and broke the blind. In double-blind random trials no one knows which patients get a placebo and which get the prospective drug. For the EU or the FDA to have accepted the results and declared the prospective drug efficacious, the trials would have to continue blind — at great cost to IgX. There were no partial trials. In May 1998 the FDA had denied a drug application from Unimed for NZT against cryptosporidiosis. Unimed also had trouble enrolling patients — only ten of sixty after fifteen months effort — and was asking the FDA to approve the drug based on a curtailed trial, using historical data for the placebo controls. In urging statistical flexibility from the FDA, Robert Dudley of Unimed testified that "the conduct of placebo-controlled trials in this population has become impossible."[16]

But to IgX, it no longer mattered if their drug was approved. The potential market for the drug had literally dried up. By breaking the blind, IgX could evaluate those patients who got the drug, and the results could be published in a peer-reviewed journal. With published results IgX would no longer need to search out potential licensees; interested partners could find IgX. IgX competitors had fared no better. All told, the drug industry had spent more than $200 million in search of a cure for cryptosporidiosis. Even as late as January 2001, there would still be no FDA approved treatment for cryptosporidiosis. Work had ended on the bovine polyclonals. Only oral paromomycin, in combination with azithromycin, was allowed to be used on a compassionate plea basis for AIDS patients. However, it was only known to treat the symptoms of the infection.

IgX also stopped work on other drug candidates derived from its polyclonal avian drug platform and prepared scientific packages for potential licensees. IgX had spent $17 million and six years to discover that the drug indeed worked as promised, but that its business plan for cryptosporidiosis failed. The IgX drug had been eclipsed by AIDS therapy using protease inhibitors.

New Technology Platform

Monsanto Corp., through its the wholly-owned pharmaceutical subsidiary G.D. Searle, had invested more than $100 million since 1989 to develop several compounds aimed at treating HIV and hepatits.

However, in Phase I/II trials, although patients tolerated the compound well, it did not raise serum concentrations compound enough to completely block HIV infectivity. Monsanto abandoned its HIV indications. Hepatitis B remained a possible disease state that could be treated with the new technology. The woodchuck, *marmota monax*, is the gold standard of animal models for hepatitis B. In a woodchuck model of hepatitis B, treatment with one iminosugar compound led to no detectable amounts of the enveloped woodchuck hepatitis virus after three weeks. These results were first published in *Nature Medicine*.

Question 8

Review the woodchuck results from *Nature Medicine* [Attachment, Question 8, page 281]. What information does the article contain that supports the development of a drug candidate?

Despite the promise of these iminosugars, Monsanto decided instead to focus its corporate strategy on diseases where glycotherapy is more direct — like arthritis, cardiovascular diseases and cancer. So they out-licensed their work in antivirals. IgX was invited to select the most promising compound to develop further.

IgX signed a series of strategic partnerships, to start in September 1998 and continue through September 2013 to develop a hepatitis drug. The objective was to secure from Monsanto an exclusive license to the compound N-nonyl-DNJ, its patented method of manufacture, and to develop it as a treatment for hepatitis B and then hepatitis C.[17] Josephthal, because the market for biotech stock was getting choppy, felt that a successful IgX public offering depended upon signing a deal with Monsanto. Even though IgX had good Phase I/II data and was in the middle of Phase III trials for its avian HIV product, with the general weakening of the stock markets Josephthal thought IgX had a much stronger story with a second drug platform and a major license with big pharma. Even while preparing IgX for an IPO, Henry accelerated negotiations with Monsanto. An agreement was signed on 20 September 1998 and new paragraphs were added to the prospectus to give the IgX story more depth. Josephthal filed the S-1 with the SEC on 30 September.

Monsanto was entitled to a 1.5 percent royalty on any hepatitis B treatments sold, as well as 25 percent of any up front fees paid to license the product. Monsanto retained exclusive rights to commercialize or further develop the compound for hepatitis B. Its first right of first refusal was exercisable at the start of Phase I trials and its second at the end of Phase II trials. Monsanto would then pay all further clinical and commercialization costs, would reimburse research expenses to date, and pay a fee equal to the net present value of the license.

In December 1998, out of cash following the withdrawn IPO, Henry and Snape arranged a Series C round of financing to fund IgX through 1999 and into 2000. HV II and NEP joined the round by converting into Series C shares the common shares they had received in exchange for $5.1 million in debt, just prior to the S-1 registration in September 1998. A second closing, in April 1999, brought in an additional $2.132 million from a broad group of institutional investors. With the Series A, B, and C fundings, IgX now had $24.17 million of paid-in capital, and $5 million in fresh cash. The Series C round gave IgX about a year to secure dramatic results in the laboratory, and thus justify a next round of funding.

Synergy Takes Shape

On the basis of this new drug platform, Henry and Snape rebuilt IgX Corporation. A professional recruiter found Donald H. Picker, who joined in October 1998 as a member of the IgX board. After the IPO was withdrawn, Picker became president and CEO. Picker had a Ph.D. in chemistry and brought wide executive experience from such biopharmaceuticals firms as LXR Biotechnology, Corvas, Genta and Johnson Matthey, where he developed Paraplatin and other leading anticancer drugs. "There's really a gold mine of drugs that could come out of this compound," effused Picker about the iminosugars. "This platform by itself is a whole company."[18]

Gary S. Jacob had a Ph.D. in biochemistry, was a tenured Monsanto Fellow, and had previously led Monsanto's glycobiology research. He arrived as senior vice president and chief scientific officer. IgX headquarters moved into bigger offices in nearby Edison, New Jersey, and the company was renamed Synergy Pharmaceuticals.

Synergy renamed NNDNJ, its lead iminosugar compound, to SP104. It targeted the enzyme alpha-glucosidase, needed for the proper folding of the envelope proteins of viruses that assemble and bud from the cellular endoplasmic reticulum, notably the viruses that cause both hepatitis B and C. The two viruses have entirely different life cycles, but they share in common this budding from the endoplasmic reticulum. Thus, SP104 could be a single therapy for both types of hepatitis. Significantly, SP104 inhibits folding without viral resistance. Without an envelope, the virus stays locked inside the host cell so it does not replicate and thus can not mutate into a resistant form. Even after fifteen passages of the virus through a mouse model, no increased resistance to the drug appeared. (With other hepatitis treatments, resistance appeared after only three passages.) In addition, the simple iminosugar had a different toxicity profile than the nucleoside drugs then used to treat hepatitis, meaning the iminosugar was ideal for combination chemotherapy. Furthermore, the compound had virtually no effect on the normal folding of host cellular glycoproteins. The host cell seemed to compensate when glycoprocessing was impaired, but viruses which cooperate closely with their hosts to replicate could not compensate. Synergy also discovered that closely related galactose compounds, N-nonyl-deoxygalactojirimycin, were specifically lethal for the hepatitis C virus, with no effect on the liver.

Hepatitis B and C were both billion dollar markets. More than 140 million people worldwide were infected with hepatitis C, and twice that many were infected with hepatitis B. Four times more people worldwide were infected with hepatitis than with HIV. Most of those infected with hepatitis B and C did not even know they were, since they could remain asymptomatic for years. There were six major genotypes of the hepatitis C virus, and countless mutations, which clustered geographically. Three-quarters of all those infected with hepatitis B reside in the Asia-Pacific region. In the United States, 1.25 million people had chronic hepatitis B, of which 300,000 had the disease in an active state. These formed the treatable population. Of the 3.9 million Americans with chronic hepatitis C, mostly of genotype-1, 900,000 had active disease. Each year in the United States, about 5,000 people died from liver disease caused by hepatitis B, and about 10,000 died from hepatitis C. In addition, twenty to forty percent of those with chronic hepatitis B developed either liver cancer or cirrhosis. Hepatitis-induced cirrhosis is the most common reason for liver transplants, which cost more than $250,000 each. Without a viable prophylaxis, the transplanted liver is almost always reinfected. The rate of new hepatitis infections in the United States was dropping — from 230,000 annually in the 1980s to 36,000 in 1996 — because a diagnostic antibody kit devised by Chiron in 1990 eliminated the virus from the transfusible blood supply. However, the Centers for Disease Control predicted that the death toll from hepatitis would triple by 2010 as those infected decades ago succumbed to liver failure.

The FDA had licensed alpha interferon, beginning in 1996, to treat acute hepatitis. Schering, Amgen, and Roche Laboratories each sold an alpha interferon drug, and Schering also sold theirs in combination with the antiviral ribavirin. (Ribavirin alone did nothing.) Yet less than twenty percent of Americans responded to interferon monotherapy, and less than forty percent responded to interferon combination therapy. Interferon had serious flu-like side effects, and combining it with ribavirin added anemia as a side effect. While interferon did a good job of ridding the body of the hepatitis viral load and the debilitating liver enzymes it produced, four out of five patients ultimately relapsed. Patients had to inject themselves with the interferon three times a week, and a course lasted two years. Plus, it was expensive. A course of interferon monotherapy cost about $10,000; combination therapy cost $17,000.

In the late 1990s, a number of biotech companies pitted themselves against hepatitis B and C. A variety of antivirals, many developed during research on HIV therapies, were in pre-clinical trials. All of these targeted viral proteins and so had high dose-limiting toxicity. Only one non-interferon therapy, a nucleotide inhibitor made by Vertex Pharmaceuticals, had progressed beyond Phase IIa trials but it was being watched very closely for suppressing immunity. Furthermore, because of the genetic variation in the hepatitis virus, developing a vaccine was proving very difficult.[19] As with IgX-CPL3, Synergy had a chance to develop a direct-acting drug without direct competition.

Lehman's Vetting

In April 1999, Lehman Bros. completed a four month review of Synergy's management and technology and accepted Synergy as an investment banking client. Henry opened the door for a new investment banking relationship by formally withdrawing the IgX S-1 in May 1999, and he engaged Lehman to find Synergy a merger partner or, if the IPO market in biotech returned, to take Synergy public. Frederick Frank was Lehman vice chairman and was one of the most influential investment bankers for health care and biotech in the United States. He had earlier represented IMED and Block Medical in the sales of both companies. Frank personally lead a team of four professionals at Lehman working on Synergy. Being vetted by Lehman put Synergy in a very good position for attracting merger partners.

One obvious merger partner was Glaxo Wellcome. Glaxo sold lamivudine, a nucleoside analogue reverse transcriptase inhibitor, as a hepatitis B treatment in Asia. Lamivudine was discovered by BioChem Pharma, licensed to Glaxo Wellcome for worldwide sales, approved by the FDA in 1995 and, under the tradename Epivir in the United States, became the most widely used antiviral agent against AIDS. Asian regulators licensed lamivudine as a treatment against hepatitis B, though the virus quickly mutated resistance to the drug at a rate of one-third of treated patients per year. *In vitro* data suggested lamivudine would be more potent in combination with SP104. Synergy presented their story in July 1999 at the Stevenage headquarters, and the Glaxo scientific antiviral group responded enthusiastically. To get approval for collaboration from Glaxo's internal therapeutic management team, though, Synergy needed to provide specific data on SP104's toxicity. This was especially important since it attacked a non-viral target. Glaxo offered to run toxicity screens against its own stem cell assays if Synergy provided SP104 under cover of a material transfer agreement. Throughout that summer, Glaxo continued to explore the prospects of a strategic partnership but moved very slowly. Partners more accustomed to the pace of biotech operations, Synergy concluded, might be found among pure biotech companies.

The option of keeping Synergy independent through a public offering, however, remained closed. Throughout 1999 no major biotech companies did an IPO. Merging with a public company arose as the best way to give Synergy shareholders liquidity. Henry already had extended the nominal ten-year life of HV II until 2002 largely to capture the returns from Synergy. Synergy shareholders expected that with the favorable announcements in the Synergy pipeline, the stock price of the public company would surge after the merger announcement. Thus, by July

1999, Lehman had started looking at midsize, publicly traded biotechnology firms with which Synergy might merge.

Synergy prepared itself for the merger by tightening operations. By June 1999, Synergy had $2 million left from the $5 million Series C placement and a burn rate of $500,000 per month. By August 1999, Synergy reduced its burn rate to $200,000 per month. That made it self-financing through April 2000. Still, Synergy needed about $7 million in new funding to complete the Phase I/II trials of its hepatitis compounds.

Question 9

Review the Domain financing offer [Attachments, Question 10, page 292] What are Domain's goals in creating this structure for the investment? From Synergy's point of view, is this a workable offer? Why or why not?

Domain Associates LLC was a leading venture fund in biotechnology — located in Princeton — and investors would notice its seal of approval on Synergy. Domain did not seek an equity stake in Synergy, as it stood, but only a deal that would finance future Phase I/II clinical trials for hepatitis. Domain agreed to provide an $8 million bridge loan for the Phase I/II clinical trials of the Synergy hepatitis C compound. Before giving this loan, however, Synergy had to get a big pharma licensing partner to commit to repaying Domain, with a 35 percent internal rate of return, upon successful completion of the trial.[20] In addition, Domain wanted twenty percent of future revenues from the drug, and the big pharma licensing partner had to take the product at the end of Phase II at a value agreed upon today. Synergy would get financed at a $50 million pre-money valuation and share in future profitability; Domain would take the clinical risk but get a predetermined exit, and the pharma partner would a candidate ready for Phase III trials at a predefined price and no early stage risk. Yet no big pharma partner would agree to such terms, so Synergy sidestepped the deal. In the meantime, Synergy needed cash.

Synergy also prepared itself for merger by bringing along other drug candidates to definable stages of the research and approval pipeline. If IgX inherited a good compound from Monsanto, research sponsored by Synergy superbly boosted its intellectual property estate. Synergy had in-licensed from Monsanto four major American patents or patent applications (and would later in-license 66 other more minor patents). Within a year Synergy had applied for six key patents originating from its own work. Synergy developed another glucosidase inhibitor, labeled SP116, to inhibit viral envelope folding.

Synergy-sponsored research also led to the discovery of a second mechanistic class of compounds, called the DGJ series or galactose series. These compounds work by altering the composition of the viral protein coat (rather than its folding within a host cell) rendering the viral particle non-infective. Unlike the DNJ compounds, which showed a broad range of activity against other flaviviruses, the DGJ compounds showed activity only against the hepatitis virus. As with the DNJ compounds, with the DGJ compounds no drug resistance developed.

Another Synergy compound blocked the neuron discharges that cause seizures in an epilepsy mouse model, even two weeks beyond the removal of the drug. Epilepsy was the most prevalent neurological disorder, after cerebrovascular disease and migraines. It affected 2.5 million people in the United States, making for a one billion dollar market. One million of those patients either got inadequate therapy from the available drugs or suffered severe side effects from the barbiturates usually prescribed. A Synergy iminosugar also dramatically retarded the growth of brain tumors in a mouse model. Synergy also discovered that their iminosugar drugs resulted in a thirty percent decrease in weight gain over sixty days in the mouse model. Thus, Synergy entered the merger talks with seven disease indications for its iminosugar candidates: hepatitis B, hepatitis C, epilepsy, brain cancer tumors, multiple drug resistant cancers and obesity. Plus, the University of Arizona group continued, with Synergy funding, to use polyclonal avian technology to treat herpes simplex keratitis eye infections. Herpes simplex keratitis was one of the leading causes of blindness in the western world, with an estimated market of $600 million annually. A drug candidate returned good initial data in rabbit studies. For a company its size, Synergy had a superb intellectual property estate and growth potential. All these indications were preclinal, though, and generally resulted from tests with in vitro laboratory assays. Synergy did not have the capital to proceed with in vivo tests with animals. Lack of capital was restraining the development of the platform technology.

Merger Partners

By September 1999, following three months of effort, Lehman had contacted more than 25 biotech companies of varying size. Synergy management then presented their science. All showed interest in the potential products, but thought Synergy was still too early to acquire. They wanted to see human clinical data on Synergy's new lead compound. So Henry, Snape, and Picker went to work identifying less obvious merger candidates from among smaller public and private biotech companies.

GLYCODesign quickened Synergy's pace. GLYCODesign was introduced to Synergy through a business acquaintance of Snape's, and they liked what they saw. GLYCODesign first reached a general agreement with Synergy, followed by the first firm offer, set to expire on 19 November 1999. Henry and Snape slowed down negotiations with GLYCODesign, then moved quickly to develop other bidders. Henry and Snape got six promising candidates into general merger discussions. Over the last half of 1999, with deadlines constantly looming, Henry and Snape negotiated complex deals with these six companies, each company and each deal unique. The interplay between these competing deals, moving to a close simultaneously, kept corporate options open and provided insurance should one or more of the deals fall through.

It was fairly easy to find interested partners, though not all of them had the capital available to fund Synergy drug development. In September and October, Synergy management met with 21 companies to present the Synergy story. Synergy started with a scientific review of its intellectual property, and serious candidates would then discuss management issues and merger terms. Some companies — like XTL and ViroPharma — executed material transfer agreements so they could spend two to four weeks testing Synergy compounds in their own assays. (Infectious hepatitis C virus has never been cultured for laboratory studies; thus researchers have devised a variety of surrogates to test candidates in the laboratory.) Most companies grew so excited about the science that Synergy had to spend some effort making it clear they wanted to be acquired rather than enter into a strategic partnership. Shire Pharmaceuticals especially liked the Synergy science presentation, but could not see further than a strategic alliance.

Question 10

Why was the Synergy board not interested in a strategic partnership?
Why did they think it more important to be acquired?

GLYCODesign, Inc., a private firm in Toronto with fifty employees, hoped a merger with Synergy would create a pure play in glycotherapeutics. GLYCO's drug platform was built on carbohydrate processing inhibitors (CPIs) which modify the cell-surface carbohydrates implicated in diseases. Its lead drug candidate, a swainsonine hydrochloride named GD0039 which inhibited the Golgi enzyme alpha-mannosidase, was in Canadian Phase II clinical trials for renal cell carcinoma and colorectal cancer. In July 1999, for a $10 million stock swap, GLYCO acquired Vascular Therapeutics, Inc., a Silicon Valley company developing antithrombotics for cardiovascular diseases caused by blood clots.[21] Soon after, GLYCO signed a confidentiality agreement to begin talks with Synergy. GLYCO had a broad base of Canadian venture capital partners, and had engaged KPMG to seek additional private financing to fund further acquisitions to build critical mass in glycotherapeutics. GLYCODesign wanted to build a $200 million market value to get the attention of investors prior to an IPO. As part of that plan, in November 1999, GLYCODesign entered into a $56 million deal with Seikagaku of Tokyo to develop a new class of anti-inflammatory compounds.

Synergy agreed in principle to a merger with GLYCODesign. GLYCO proposed acquiring all the shares in Synergy for 6.5 million common shares in GLYCO, representing twenty percent of the post-merger entity. Synergy shareholders would get an additional 4.65 million shares if they submitted an investigational new drug application for NNDNJ for hepatitis C by the end of 2000, bringing Synergy's ownership in the merged entity to 33.8 percent. To fund operations of the merged entity, GLYCODesign would raise an additional $12 million financing, at an $80 million combined valuation, half of which would fund trials for NNDNJ. Closing of this merger depended upon first raising $8 million of this financing for the merged entity. Synergy's New Jersey operation would be shut down, though Picker would become COO of GLYCODesign and Jacob a vice president. Subsequently, Lehman would plan a public offering to raise $40 million, at a pre-money valuation in excess of $100 million.

There were a number of slow-down points open to discussion. Synergy wanted the deal contingent upon $20 million in financing being available to the merged company, but no less than $12 million, and a commitment of at least $5 million to fund NNDNJ development for one year. Until GLYCO could deliver financing on that level, Synergy would not agree to exclusivity in negotiations. Another point of contention was GLYCO's conditions on Synergy's balance sheet. GLYCO wanted Synergy to have, on closing, a net cash position of at least $0.5 million, with current liabilities paid off including any termination costs and outstanding payments to Monsanto.

XTL Biopharmaceuticals Ltd. was another private firm, located in Israel. XTL had a mouse model for human antibody screening and a monoclonal antibody platform, dubbed Trimera(XTL), which they were using to develop treatments for hepatitis. XTL asked to first test SP104 on its mouse model and were impressed. XTL also had a monoclonal antibody for hepatitis in Phase III trials, and the combination of the XTL antibody with Synergy's compounds would create the only pure hepatitis play in the stock market. XTL's mouse model to test human antigens already gave them a strong source of cash flow. Furthermore, XTL had an excellent team of venture backers. XTL agreed that Synergy shareholders would own 25 percent of the merged entity. Henry and Snape structured this deal much like the proposed deal with GLYCO, with Synergy earning additional ownership of the merged company through its success in clinical trials. In Synergy's opinion, though, XTL was a much stronger story than GLYCO.

ViroPharma Inc. also tested Synergy's hepatitis C compound with its own assays and found that SP104 worked better than their own compound, with no resistance. ViroPharma was public and, because the product lines of the two companies were so close, Lehman let them know Synergy would consider an outright acquisition. ViroPharma spent four months evaluating Synergy's intellectual property, then abandoned their merger quest. Soon after breaking off talks, Synergy later learned, ViroPharma licensed its own compound to another firm.

Regardless, both Henry and Snape preferred a merger with an undervalued, midsize, public biotech company, with an earnout over six to twelve months based on performance milestones. Eventual news of

Synergy's success with its hepatitis C treatment, post-merger, would drive explosive growth in the common stock price of any public company.

Nabi offered that better fit. Nabi complemented both of Synergy's drug platforms in that Civacir, its lead product then in chimpanzee studies, was a human polyclonal antibody for the treatment of hepatitis C. Nabi HB was an immunoglobulin for treating hepatitis B. Nabi was a fully-integrated, public, biopharmaceutical firm based in Boca Raton, with $225 million in annual revenues, net income of $2.5 million, and a market capitalization fluctuating around $160 million. Lehman Bros. proposed that Nabi acquire 19.9 percent of Synergy for $6 million in Nabi common stock By acquiring 19.9 percent, Nabi would not be required to consolidate Synergy financials with its own. If Nabi had to deduct Synergy's considerable research expense from its P&L statement, Nabi's earnings would be depressed or eliminated. After acquiring 19.9 percent of Synergy for Nabi stock, Nabi would then get a non-exclusive option to acquire the rest of Synergy over 18 to 24 months at prices escalating at thirty percent, compounded per annum, over the original price to reach a total Synergy valuation of $42 million. This deal would be similar to the deal Fred Frank had recently structured for Roche and Genentech, which gave Roche the option to acquire Genentech. If another company made an offer to acquire the rest of Synergy, Nabi got right of first refusal to match it.

Henry and Snape also discussed a deal with Zonagen structured much like the approach taken with Nabi. Zonagen was a public company with $40 million cash on its balance sheet. Zonagen had a drug development culture like Synergy, and its CEO shared similar views. It had a technology platform based on phenthalomine and was developing a class of products for erectile dysfunction and fertility. Zonagen offered to acquire fifteen percent of Synergy for $4.5 million — $1.5 million in cash and $3.0 million Zonagen common stock — for a pre-money valuation of $30 million for Synergy. Henry and Snape hoped Zonagen would commit $15 million to fund trials of SP104 through Phase III, and make milestone performance payments to Synergy. However, the Zonagen board decided it could not add this additional load to its burn rate, even though Zonagen had $40 million in cash.

Zonagen would get the option to acquire the remaining 85 percent of Synergy at values rising to $40 million over eight months. Based on Lehman's experience, the infusion of Synergy technology on Zonagen stock would, over eighteen months, lead to a tripling of each Synergy share to $15 (for a $150 million acquisition valuation). Any increase in Zonagen's market capitalization over $40 million would mean the Synergy acquisition paid for itself. Frank let Zonagen know that Lehman would be available to do a secondary offering, if needed, after the stock doubled.

By January 2000, Synergy had five active potential partners — three were public companies and two were private. The Synergy board had set 15 January as the decision date. XTL and GLYCO emerged as better candidates because the IPO market for biotech grew white hot. Fred Frank and Lehman had just brought Tularik public on 12 December, raising $97 million with a $400 million premoney valuation. The stock came out above its offering range, quickly doubled to $40 per share, then doubled again. This was for a company with only one drug out of Phase I trials. Maxygen went public that same month, also with triple digit gains. Throughout 1999, only fourteen biotech firms had gone public, raising $4.3 billion, meaning they were pretty well established firms. As 2000 opened, smaller biotech companies rushed into IPOs. Throughout that year, 75 biotech companies raised $7 billion in the public markets (though, notably, by the close of the year half were trading below their IPO prices.) Because it was preclinical, Synergy could not itself do an IPO. Still, with the sector plump with new cash, springtime of 2000 was a good time to close a deal.

Zonagen was not the best match strategically with Synergy, but they made an offer that met many of the Synergy conditions. On 15 February Synergy prepared a press release announcing the deal with Zonagen. Yet after the preliminary agreement was in place, Zonagen imposed a condition Synergy shareholders could not accept. Zonagen insisted its ownership of Synergy increase quarterly if Synergy did not complete a private financing of $5 million on its own. Synergy shareholders refused to let an acquirer gain greater ownership through a financing contingency. If Synergy was required to complete a financing to close the acquisition on acceptable terms, it could just as easily complete the financing and stay independent. Furthermore, Zonagen was hardly in any position to make new demands. The FDA had placed a clinical hold on all phenthalomine-containing products, Zonagen's entire pipeline, to explore possible carcinogenicity. Though Vasomax, Zonagen's lead product, had passed Phase III trials for treating erectile dysfunction, Zonagen could not bring it to market. The November before Zonagen had hopes that the FDA might lift its hold, but as the days passed its story and cash position weakened. (In July 2000, Zonagen cut its staff to thirteen people and put itself up for sale — where it remains.) Then another candidate for Synergy flashed into sight.

United Therapeutics

United Therapeutics (UT) was one of the many companies Synergy had approached before November 1999. UT was a good candidate. They had two drug candidates in Phase III trials for chronic disease states — BeraProst for peripheral vascular disease and UniProst for pulmonary hypertension. Both compounds had been discovered by Glaxo, then abandoned during its mergers. United Therapeutics licensed the compounds in 1995 then got UniProst through FDA reviews. UT came to see themselves as experts in late-stage drug development — especially with candidates abandoned by big pharma. SP104 fit their story. Plus, UT had only one technology platform and to thrive as a discovery-free biotechnology company they needed to show they could add new platforms to their pipeline, especially one for a large market disease. Furthermore, UT had learned the value of secondary offerings for young biotech companies, and they had about $100 million on their balance sheet.

On 15 February 2000, UT called Synergy and asked about the status of other merger candidates. Upon hearing that a Synergy merger was imminent, UT made an offer which met all of the needs of the Synergy board.

In March 2000, United Therapeutics made a $5 million equity investment in Series D preferred stock to acquire a fifteen percent share in Synergy.[22] This included $3 million in cash (half of which went to pay off a bridge loan secured in November 1999) and 21,978 shares of UT common shares valued at $2 million (less than one percent of outstanding UT shares). UT shares had been trading on NASDAQ since 17 June 1999, and in March 2000 they had a market value of $91. UT also agreed to performance-based milestone payments of $22.2 million each for hepatitis B and C therapies, based upon success in subsequent clinical trials. The combination of these payments equated to a valuation of Synergy between $75 and $100 million, or $8 per share. To generate this valuation,

Klynveld Peat Marwick Goerdeler (KPMG) prepared a net present value study of Synergy's license with UT, which projected royalty and milestone payments of $1.4 billion for two products, one for hepatitis B and one for hepatitis C.

UT also committed to fund Synergy operations for the next two years through $15.2 million in non-dilutive funds to pay all expenses leading to the Phase I/IIa clinical studies for the hepatitis B and C candidates. By the fall of 2000, UT was spending at a rate of $400,000 a month to get Synergy products through laboratory research and into early human trials. As result, Synergy's burn rate dropped to about $75,000 annually — the cost of some salaries for administrative overhead.

The royalty agreement was as attractive to Synergy as the equity investment. UT agreed to pay Synergy net royalties of up to six percent on all eventual sales of Synergy products, but no less than $12.8 million per year for each disease indication with a qualified drug. The markets for Synergy's two hepatitis compounds by year three, if estimates were accurate, could generate $230 million in royalties.

The UT license had the effect of funding Synergy for two years so it could find a better merger partner. Synergy had a product portfolio of enormous potential, protected by 83 worldwide patents, consistent with the $100 million already invested by Monsanto. Scientists were working on two multibillion dollar disease indications. Synergy's ultimate success, though, now went through UT. Synergy had become dependent upon UT both for its financing and for achieving key milestones in its research and development.

Question 11

Review the pro forma model of Synergy cash flows and the KPMG valuation study dated July 2000 [Attachments, Question 12, page 297]. How can you use this information to structure various, perhaps competing, merger deals? Why would Synergy continue to seek a merger partner after the lucrative license with UT?

Soon into this Synergy/UT partnership, the science hit a glitch. Synergy's two lead DNJ compounds, SP104 against hepatitis B and SP116 against hepatitis C, showed some unexpected toxicity in rat studies. So did SP226 and SP234 from the DGJ series. These compounds could not advance to the clinic as scheduled.

To compensate for the delay caused by the failed toxicity studies, Synergy and UT amended their license agreement to cover the development of analog compounds. Synergy agreed to cut in half the milestone and royalty payments for any approved products resulting from the new analogs. Synergy also gave UT warrants to purchase an additional ten percent of Synergy's outstanding stock, though Synergy tied these warrants to $3.3 million of additional UT funding for analogs research.

The analog program was expensive, though successful. Synergy developed a DNJ analog, named SP150A, that during in vitro tests against hepatitis B showed efficacy equivalent to SP104 but with ten times less toxicity in a rodent stem cell assay. As insurance, Synergy also developed three additional analogs of SP150A for in vitro toxicity studies. Synergy also developed new cell-based assays to speed up toxicity screening of future analogs. And Synergy demonstrated that its DNJ analogs worked synergistically in combination with alpha-interferon and ribavirin against the hepatitis virus.

Synergy's first candidate into trials, though, would be a DGJ compound named SP231, part of its galactose series, against hepatitis C. SP231 showed no toxicity in the two-week tests on dogs or rats. Synergy then manufactured 300 grams of SP231 to begin single dose safety and pharmokinetic studies in humans once the application was approved by the FDA.

Synergy's CEO, Donald Picker, brought great experience in drug development. Picker himself designed the DNJ analog program and the individual compounds. The University of Iowa synthesized the SP231 drug substance for UT. Hoyle Consulting used the substance for the toxicology studies in dogs and rats. Hoyle drafted the investigational new drug application for clinical trials in humans, and contracted with PharmaResearch to conduct the trials. Picker also lined up contract manufacturers to make the eventual clinical trial materials (CMT) according to FDA good manufacturing practices (GMP). A separate set of relationships with contractors and universities paced the milestones leading to approval of SP150. And each of these scientific milestones, in turn, paced Henry's and Snape's efforts to negotiate a better merger arrangement for Synergy.

New Merger Partners

In December 2000, a month after amending its agreement with UT, Synergy started looking for an acquirer. Dain Rauscher Wessels (DRW), led by biotechnology expert Ed Lagerstrom, prepared a book on Synergy for a wide mailing. Lehman Brothers, as before, contacted a more focused set of companies through Fred Frank's personal networks. DRW honed a short list of eighteen candidates, seven of which began due diligence. All had a position in antivirals; most were developing hepatitis drugs. Three of the seven were large biotech companies with market capitalizations in the range of $1.5 to $2.5 billion, with revenues exceeding $500 million, and with net income exceeding $20 million. Three of the others were mid-sized biotechnology companies with market capitalizations in the $200 million to $500 million range. One smaller company had a market capitalization in the range of $125 to $200 million.

Only companies that were already public, the Synergy board decided, would be candidates. From Synergy's perspective, merger with a public company would create the opportunity for the larger financings needed to develop Synergy's platform to disease indications beyond hepatitis B and C. Synergy was now a year older than when it sought merger candidates leading to the UT deal. Synergy had spent $6 million more on its science, and had two compounds ready for the clinic.

Synergy also had developed exciting new intellectual property. Kunwar Shalubhai, former head of the cancer prevention group at Monsanto, began working with Synergy funding at Thomas Jefferson University. There Shalubhai devised a uroguanylin-based formulation to treat colon cancer. Uroguanylin is a peptide hormone produced in the gastrointestinal tract that binds to a unique receptor which activates ion and fluid transport. The body's production of uroguanylin declines with aging, and its absence is linked to colon cancer and gastrointestinal inflammation. Metastatic colorectal cancer was the second largest cause of cancer deaths in the United States, with 134,000 cases occurring every year. In preclinical mice studies, oral administration of uroguanylin inhibited polyp formation and the subsequent progression to colon cancer. Synergy filed a patent application for using this peptide to treat cancer and needed cash to develop the product.

DRW, Lehman Brothers, and the Synergy shareholders charted a course to find the best long-term merger partner for Synergy. It was decided that the current value of Synergy was $35 million, which was a discount to the $53 million Synergy valuation established by the UT investment in line with the stock market sell off in biotech stocks. Yet as 2001 aged into 2002, Synergy increasingly needed cash to fund development of products for three indications: multiple myeloma and bone resorbtion, colon cancer and ulcerative colitis, and for hepatitis B. United Therapeutics was now funding development of Synergy's hepatitis C compounds.

Synergy entered into lengthy discussions with three potential merger partners: ICN Pharmaceuticals, Inc., Oxford Glyco Sciences (OGS), and Callisto Pharmaceuticals, Inc. ICN was the biggest of these. It was listed on the New York Stock exchange, had $600 million in revenues, $40 million in after tax earnings, and a market capitalization of $2 billion. OGS was listed on the London Stock Exchange, had $50 million in revenues, break-even operations, and $350 million in cash. Callisto was listed over-the counter, had an estimated market value of $45 million, cash of $3.5 million, and was a development stage company.

Discussions with ICN started first. ICN had prepared a letter of intent to buy Synergy at a $35 million valuation, payable 19 percent at closing. Four milestone payments over eighteen months were linked to success in Synergy's clinical trials, which ICN would fund. The Synergy board saw ICN as a mature, cash-rich pharmaceutical company. Its product pipeline was good, but needed the boost from Synergy. ICN offered stability for Synergy's scientific staff, as well as the freedom to continue managing their own work.

Synergy's enthusiasm was muted only by their concern that they were selling their upside. Though the deal put an attractive valuation on Synergy, Synergy shareholders would own less than two percent of ICN. Synergy's success in clinical trials would do little to move a stock as big as ICN. Furthermore, ICN's upside was limited because it had licensed the major driver of its stock, a hepatitis C treatment to Schering-Plough. Plus, the ICN stock story was tainted by a controversial chairman and CEO who had just survived a proxy initiative to oust him.

Then the ICN deal quickly unraveled. Milan Panic, the ICN chairman, had founded ICN thirty years ago with his own funds and had built it up to its $2 billion valuation. Panic had previously been cited by the SEC for insider trading in ICN stock, and institutional investors felt that the controversy swirling around Panic caused ICN to persistently trade at a discount to the price/earnings multiple standard in the pharmaceutical industry. One attempt to oust Panic in 2001 failed. A new proxy fight to oust Panic was launched in 2002, as Synergy was deep in discussions. The deal looked very attractive, but as the letter of intent was being circulated among the interested parties, Panic lost this proxy fight and was abruptly terminated by the restructured ICN board of directors. The new management terminated discussions with Synergy in July 2002. Synergy turned its attention to its backup options.

OGS had raised $500 million through various security offerings, several through Lehman Brothers, but had failed to build a viable technology platform. OGS had a single product, and needed Synergy to fill its pipeline of potential drugs. Its CEO of many years had just departed, and was succeeded by the former head of North American operations for Bayer AG. OGS stock was depressed, having fallen from UK£15 to UK£2.50. OGS market capitalization was $350 million, equal to its cash on hand. This was enough cash, though, to acquire Synergy if they did not want to use stock.

OGS began its due diligence on Synergy in the fall of 2002 and in January offered a term sheet that the Synergy board considered an insult. OGS offered Synergy a valuation of $12 million, with only $2 million up front, followed by six small milestone payments of about $1 million each for what Synergy scientists considered to be major clinical accomplishments. Henry and Snape figured that if Synergy achieved these clinical goals on its own its valuation would exceed $100 million. Synergy officially declined the OGS proposal in November 2002. Six months later, in April 2003, OGS announced that it would itself be acquired by Celltech Group plc.

Callisto Merger

Discussion with Callisto heated up as the discussions with OGS first stalled. Callisto had developed a diagnostic kit for Obsessive Compulsive Disorder, which was the first biological test to diagnose a psychiatric illness. But it had only one continuing drug development program, a medical countermeasures program on a platform of super antigen antagonist technology. It was indicated for toxic shock syndrome and sepsis, and it could also protect against staphylococcal and strepto-coccal bioweapons. Callisto hoped to first sell the product to the new fed-eral Project Bioshield project. The Bioshield office, launched in the aftermath of the September 2001 terror attacks on the United States, would spend $6 billion over the coming decade to buy and stockpile medicines against terrorism. To qualify drugs for sale to Project Bioshield, the FDA issued special requirements—safety in animal models, which Callisto had already demonstrated, and safety in humans, which Callisto expected to demonstrate within a year. If Callisto began selling tens of millions of dollars of drugs to the government within three years, its val-uation could rise by $100 to $200 million. Synergy's products would add to that.

After a long period of due diligence on Synergy, Callisto offered its letter of intent in November 2002. Callisto started by suggesting an own-ership split of the merged company as 75 percent Callisto shareholders and 25 percent Synergy shareholders. Synergy countered with 55 percent Callisto and 45 percent Synergy. After three months, Callisto agreed to a sixty-forty split. Synergy shareholders would be subject to a one-year lockup before selling their shares.

Henry and Snape liked Callisto's small size. Starting with a low total valuation of the merged company at $80 million—far less than with ICN—the upside could be a multiple of five to eight times should Synergy prove successful in its Phase II trials. The deal valued Synergy at $32 million pre-merger, which was comparable to the ICN deal. Callisto did not have the cash flow or stability of ICN, but Synergy share-holders would own forty percent of the company.

The experience of Millennium Pharmaceuticals demonstrated that Synergy might earn this valuation. Millennium had successful results in early 2002 in a Phase II trial of VELCADE, its multiple myeloma drug, and its valuation shot up by hundreds of millions of dollars. The FDA granted Priority Review of VELCADE in March 2003, and two months later it was in the market. Though Millennium's compound proved suc-cessful in only twenty percent of myeloma patients, it was the first new drug in more than a decade to be approved for multiple myeloma, and the stock market anticipated a $500 million market.

Likewise, Genta Incorporated was a year or two ahead of Synergy in trial experience. Five years previously Genta, Inc. had a total market capitalization of $10 million and a single candidate, Genasense, for follicular lymphoma. Picker had been COO of Genta, and invented its drug candidate. When Genta successfully completed its Phase II trial for lymphoma, its market capitalization rose to $200 million. Genta then completed Phase II trials in lung cancer, chronic lymphocytic leukemia, and multiple myeloma, then signed a licensing deal with Aventis. Its market capitalization soared to $1.1 billion in 2002, then settled to $600 million in the depressed biotechnology market of early 2003.

Based on the valuation models of Millennium and Genta, Henry and Snape figured that forty percent ownership of a possible $400 million dollar boost in market valuation for the merged Callisto/Synergy would be a great return for their funds. They signed the letter of intent.

Callisto would focus on developing drugs to treat multiple myeloma— a cancer of the blood which causes the bone marrow to overproduce malignant plasma cells. It is especially deadly, and there are few available treatments. It represents one percent of all cancers, and two percent of all cancer deaths. Each year 15,000 new cases are diagnosed, and only thirty percent of patients survive more than five years.

Synergy's lead compound was now Atiprimod, a macrophage-targeting cytokine inhibitor that was both antiproliferate and antiangiogenic. As a small molecule, it was orally-available. Callisto would fund the Phase I/IIa clinical trails against multiple myeloma and osteolytic bone disease from its small but sufficient cash reserves of $2.5 million. The trial would begin immediately after the merger, and would take nine to twelve months to show any efficacy (about the time the lockup on stock sales by Synergy shareholders would end). The trial would cost only $1.5 million because the compound had already been in a Phase I trial for rheumatoid arthritis conducted by GlaxoSmithKline. No safety or toxicity issues had appeared in a hundred patients at different dosing levels. Atiprimod had also been invented by Picker at a company he worked for previously, then in-licensed to Synergy. Product manufactured to GMP standards was already available for trials. And Atiprimod continued to be developed by AnorMED Inc. for use in rheumatoid arthritis and other autoimmune diseases.

Synergy continued to develop its analog of uroguanylin, the human intestinal hormone, to treat colon cancer. And Synergy would also bring into the merged company its hepatitis C trial and its rich license with United Therapeutics.

Henry, Snape and the Synergy board were very enthusiastic about the merger, and presented it to the Synergy shareholders for approval. Only United Therapeutics balked. UT owned about 26 percent of Synergy, and 75 percent of shares had to vote for the merger. Synergy believed UT wanted to reduce the size of its required milestone payments. Synergy had just successfully completed its Phase I trials for hepatitis C. UT knew that Synergy was running out of cash, and Synergy had to bargain. Snape came up with a quid pro quo solution to UT's threatened no vote. Synergy would return the hepatitis C compound license to UT, and UT would relinquish its ownership in Synergy. UT also paid Synergy $750,000 in cash, which Synergy used to pay off vendors and $350,000 of maturing bridge debt. With UT's shares no longer outstanding, each Synergy share-holder's ownership thus increased by approximately 26 percent.

Simply put, Snape and Henry thought Synergy's multiple myeloma compound was more valuable than its hepatitis C compound. The FDA had approved Millennium's myeloma compound for sale after just a suc-cessful Phase II trial. If Synergy's compound got similar fast-track treat-ment, Atiprimod could be an approved drug in only eighteen months. Synergy's hepatitis C compound would not get NDA approval for three to four years. Furthermore, the Atiprimod Phase II trial could be com-pleted for $2.5 million, while NDA approval of the hepatitis C compound could cost up to $15 million. Finally, the stock market would react much more quickly to a success with multiple myeloma than with hepatitis C.

When Henry and Snape returned to Callisto free to close the merger, they were stunned by Callisto's proposal that the ownership split in the merger be revised to an eighty to twenty percent split Callisto had attrib-uted half of Synergy's value to its license with UT, and that license was no longer part of Synergy's assets. Thus, the eighty-twenty split now put the pre-merger value of Synergy at $16 million, half of what it had been. Common shareholders were most drastically affected by accepting the $16 million valuation. The total investment in Synergy through issues of four series of preferred stock was $22 million. The $22 million liquida-tion preference of these shareholders was $6 million more than Callisto's valuation of Synergy. Since the preferred shareholders lost $6 million of their investment at close of the transaction, the common shareholders have no equity in the merger proceeds, and were wiped out at the closing of the merger transaction.

Synergy accepted the terms, and on 30 April 2003 the merger closed. HVF II owned seven percent of Callisto common equivalent shares, which were locked up through April 2004.

Two months later Callisto announced several management changes.[23] Henry and Snape joined the Callisto board. Synergy's management would run the merged company, and its scientists would direct drug development. Jacobs was named acting CEO. Picker was named vice president for drug development. Good news also arrived. That June the National Cancer Institute announced that it had found Atiprimod highly potent in NCI screening assays. NCI offered a screening agreement, in which it would fund studies of Atiprimod in animal models of colorectal metastasis and other solid tumors.

Callisto's venture backers, with help from Henry and Snape, now set about raising new funds for the merged company. Henry and Snape remained optimistic. Shareholders of the old Synergy owned twenty percent of a potential $400 million valuation with Phase II myeloma trial success in 2004, which would give Synergy shareholders an $80 million gain. HVF II with original investments of $8 million would own 36 percent of that gain, or $28 million. New England Growth Fund with $4 million of original investment would own fifteen percent, or $12 million. Both funds could still make good returns, and they would know if they would within a year. More clinical trials would come after the Phase II trial, but the success of Phase II would give the venture capitalists and Synergy shareholders huge potential up side in Callisto, which is run by Synergy's former management with Snape and Henry *still* influential at the board level. Post merger, Callisto raised $10 million in institutional equity at a $70 million valuation wich reflected financial market enthusiam for the new Callisto technology platform. Calendar 2004 could be a very big year for all Callisto shareholders with impressive science and adequate company financing in place, and a major Phase II multiple myeloma clinical trial underway at two of the most prestigeous cancer clinics in the U.S., M.D. Anderson and Dana-Farber Institute, Harvard Medical School.

Question 12

Assuming the final terms of each of the three deals — ICN, OGS, and Callisto — were each available at the same time, which would you recommend that the Synergy board accept? Compare the advantages and disadvantages of each deal. Which deal would serve the old Synergy shareholders the best — given the availability of funding for the post-merger company, the stock market upside, ease of liquidity, and the ability of Synergy management to control its scientific development?

Citations to Published Sources

1 St. Mary's Hospital in Chicago, Humana-Michael Reese Hospital in Chicago, University of Illinois at Chicago, University of Arizona in Tuscon, Wistar Institute of Anatomy and Biology in Philadelphia, the Department of Pharmacology of the Ohio State University in Columbus, and the Medical Center of the University of California at San Diego.

2 Charles R. Sterling and Vitaliano A. Cama, U.S Patent No. 5,753,228: *Antiparasite therapy by means of enteral administration of hyperimmune hen egg yolk antibodies.* Filed 25 August 1992; issued 19 May 1998. See also Vitaliano A. Cama and Charles R. Sterling, "Hyperimmune hens as a novel source of anti-*Cryptosporidium* antibodies suitable for passive immune transfer," *Journal of Protozoology* 38/6 (November-December 1991) 435-436.

3 Luis A. Guarda, Stanley A. Stein, Karen A. Cleary, and Nelson G. Ordonez, "Human cryptosporidiosis in the Acquired Immune Deficiency Syndrome," *Archives of Pathology and Laboratory Medicine* 107 (November 1983) 562-566.

4 Deirdre L. Church and Chris E. Forsmark, "Dealing with diarrhea in HIV disease," *Patient Care* (30 September 1993) 49-74.

5 H.L. Dupont, C.L. Chappell, C.R. Sterling, P.C. Okhuysen, J.B. Rose and W. Jakubowski, "Infectivity of *Cryptosporidium parvum* in healthy volunteers," *New England Journal of Medicine* 332 (1995) 855-859.

6 William R. MacKenzie, et al., "A massive outbreak in Milwaukee of Cryptosporidium infection transmitted through the public water supply," *New England Journal of Medicine* 331 (1994) 161-167; J.B. Rose, C.P. Gerba, and W. Jakubowski, "Survey of potable water supplies for *Cryptosporidium* and *Giardia*," *Environmental Science and Technology* 25/8 (1991) 1393-1400; Denise Grady, "Turbid tap water may be source of unexplained intestinal ailments: Ills blamed on food poisoning may be caused by water," *New York Times* (4 November 1997) D1.

7 Daniel C. Okun, Chair, *Report of the Expert Panel on New York City's Water Supply*, prepared for the Environmental Protection Agency (24 March 1993).

8 Robert G. McNeil, "Why tech VCs have left biotech," *Venture Capital Journal* (August 1999) 42-45.

9 For background on how Soave structured her trials and the debate on quantitation as an end point measure, see "Statement of Rosemary Soave, Cornell University Medical College," in *Public Hearing: NDA 20-871/Nitrazoxanide* (U.S. Food and Drug Administration, Center for Drug Evaluation and Research, Antiviral Drug Advisory Committee, 6 May 1998) 18-43.

10 For a scientific review of these preliminary trials, see David J. Ritchie and Evelyn S. Becker, "Update on the management of intestinal cryptosporidiosis in AIDS," *Annals of Pharmacotherapy* 28 (June 1994) 767-777.

11 On clinical studies in different countries using protease inhibitors to resolve acute cryptosporidiosis, see Andrew Carr, Deborah Marriot, Andrew Field, Eva Vasak, and David A. Cooper, "Treatment of HIV-1 associated microspridiosis and cryptosporidiosis with combination antiretroviral therapy," *The Lancet* 351 (24 January 1998) 256-261; Norbert A. Foudraine, et al., "Improvement of chronic diarrhoea in patients with advanced HIV-1 infection during potent antiretroviral therapy," *AIDS* 12/1 (1998) 35-41; Edmund J. Bini and Jonathon Cohen, "Impact of protease inhibitors on the outcome of HIV-infected patients with chronic diarrhea," *American Journal of Gastroenterology* 94/12 (December 1999) 3553-9; and P. Maggi, et al., "Effect of antiretroviral therapy on cryptosporidiosis and microsporidiosis in patients infected with human immunodeficiency virus type 1," *European Journal of Clinical Microbiology and Infectious Diseases* 19/3 (March 2000) 213-217. Some laboratory studies described the role of protease in the replication cycle of *C. parvum* and suggested that, rather than acting indirectly against it through bolstered CD4 counts, the protease inhibitors acted directly against the parasite; see, for example, J.R. Forney, S. Yang and M.C. Healey, "Protease activity associated with excystation of *C. parvum* oocysts," *Journal of Parasitology* 82/6 (December 1996) 889-92.

[12] For population studies of the decline in cryptosporidiosis, see Klaus E. Monkenmuller, et al., "Declining prevalence of opportunistic gastrointestinal disease in the era of combination antiviral therapy," *American Journal of Gastroenterology* 95/2 (February 2000) 457-462. Most articles on the decline of opportunistic infections in AIDS patients following combination therapy don't even include discussion of cryptosporidiosis.

[13] Robert Perciasepe, James R. Elder, Stig E. Regli, and Paul Berger, *Assessing the Public Health Threat Associated with Waterborne Cryptosporidiosis: Report of Workshop* (National Center for Infectious Diseases in collaboration with the Environmental Protection Agency, June 1995); Daniel G. Colley, *Waterborne cryptosporidiosis* threat addressed National Center for Infectious Diseases and Centers for Disease Control and Prevention, EID/Online edition1/2 (April-June 1995); Lawrence O. Gostin, Zita Lazzarini, Verla S. Neslund, and Michael T. Osterholm, "Water quality laws and waterborne diseases: *Cryptosporidium* and other emerging pathogens," *American Journal of Public Health* 90/6 (June 2000) 847-853.

[14] For a report on how the spread of combination therapy disrupted a clinical trial in France in 1997 for paromycim against cryptosporidiosis, see V. LeMoing et al., "Decreased prevalence of intestinal cryptosporidiosis in HIV-infected patients concomitant to the widespread use of protease inhibitors," *AIDS* 12/11 (1998) 1395-97.

[15] The IgX S-1 registration statement is available at Edgar Online, the web-accessible database of the Securities and Exchange Commission, as 0000889812-98-002382.rtf. The registration withdrawal is available as 0000936392-99-000643.rtf.

[16] "Statement of Robert Dudley, Senior Vice President, Clinical Research and Development, Unimed Corporation," in *Public Hearing: NDA 20-871/Nitrazoxanide* (U.S. Food and Drug Administration, Center for Drug Evaluation and Research, Antiviral Drug Advisory Committee, 6 May 1998) 15.

[17] The process patents are James R. Behling, et al., U.S. Patent No. 5,151,519: *Process for the preparation of 1,5-(alylimine)-1,5-dideoxy-D-glucitol and derivatives thereof*. Filed 7 May 1990; issued 29 September 1992; and James R. Behling, et al., U.S. Patent No. 5,281,724: *Process for the preparation of 6-(n-butylamine)-6-deoxy-1,2-0-(imeihylethylidine)-a-L-Sorbofuranose and derivatives thereof*. Filed 25 June 1991; issued 15 January 1994.

[18] John George, "Lab spin-off pursues billion-dollar drug," *Philadelphia Business Journal*/Online Edition (19 February 1999); see also "New company developing promising new hepatitis drug," *Jeff News Online* (March 1999).

[19] John Henkel, "Hepatitis C: New treatment helps some, but cure remains elusive," *FDA Consumer Magazine*/Online 33/2 (March-April 1999); Jennifer Van Brunt, "Drug-makers hustle to halt HCV," *Signals Magazine*/Online (14 December 1999).

[20] Vidhan K. Goyal, Neela Gollapudi, and Joseph P. Ogden, "A corporate bond innovation of the 90s: The clawback provision in high-yield debt," *Journal of Corporate Finance* 4/4 (December 1998) 301-20.

[21] Mary Welch, "GlycoDesign, VTI Merge In Stock Deal Worth $10M," *BioWorld Today* (12 August 1999) 1, 5.

[22] "United Therapeutics inlicenses anti-viral compounds developed at University of Oxford and Searle/Monsanto," *PR Newswire* (31 March 2000); "Unither developing glucosidase inhibitor hepatitis B & C drugs from Synergy," *Antiviral Agents Bulletin* (June 2000); Mary Welch, "United Therapeutics buys stake in Synergy, Rights to Antivirals," *BioWorld Today* 11/63 (3 April 2000) 1; "Synergy Pharmaceuticals Signs Agreement," *Genetic Engineering News* (15 April 2000) 73.

[23] "Callisto Pharmaceuticals announces appointment of new members of the board of directors: Certain management changes in connection with merger agreement with Synergy Pharmaceuticals," *BusinessWire* (30 June 2003).

Index to Attachments

Question 5

Letter: New England Partners.

"IgX Corporation: Proposed terms of investment."

"Memorandum of terms for Series B preferred stock of IgX Corp."

Question 7

"IgX Corporation: Descriptive Memorandum," Vector Securities International Inc. (April 1998).

Consolidated financial statement, pp. F-1 to F-6; from IgX Corp. Form S-1 Registration Statement (30 September 1998).

"Stercamacim Licensee NPV IRR: AIDS Market/ Europe and US," from *Stercamacim Business Review* (IgX Limited, September 1997).

Rosemary Soave, "Treatment of AIDS-related cryptosporidial diarrhea with IGX-CP, a compound prepared from egg yolks of hyperimmunized hens." (Draft)

Question 8

Timothy M. Block, et al., "Treatment of Chronic Hepadnavirus infection in a woodchuck animal model with an inhibitor of protein folding and trafficking," *Nature Medicine* 4/5 (May 1998) 610.

Question 9

Jesse I. Treau to Donald H. Picker, 21 September 1999.

Domain Associates LLC, "Synergy-Domain Research Partners: Agreement Outline June 28, 1999."

Question 11

KPMG Life Sciences, "Proforma Model of Synergy Pharmaceuticals' Hepatitis B and Hepatitis C Product," (2 June 2000).

Synergy Audit, March 2002, KPMG Auditors.

Attachments: Question 5

1) New England Partners Letter, Terms Sheet & IRR Valuation Schedule

2) Memorandum of Terms for Series B Preferred Stock of IgX Corp.

NEW ENGLAND PARTNERS

NEW ENGLAND GROWTH FUND L.L.P.
BCP VENTURES, INC.
NEW ENGLAND PARTERNS L.L.P.

NEGF II, L.P.
NEGF ADVISORY COMPANY, INC.
NEW ENGLAND PARTNERS II, L.P.

November 7, 1997

Al Henry
IgX Limited
4370 La Jolla Village Drive
Suite 400
San Diego, CA 92122-1251

Dear Al:

Bob, Chris and John agreed with me that you have done a great job with IgX and we are definitely interested in leading this round and in helping IgX realize its full potential.

I look forward to receiving the private placement memo from Ambient Capital. Following up on our discussion, I am attaching a scenario that should overcome investors' concerns about market volatility and the cyclical nature of the biotechnology sector. Basically, the approach I am suggesting protects the investor on the downside and at the same time provides unlimited upside. At the same time the company has complete flexibility with respect to the timing and terms of an IPO and avoids a protracted discussion on the valuation of this round. The scenarios provide for reasonable IPO valuations and up to 20% decrease in these valuations without an adjustment to the investors' conversion price.

The mechanics of handling such adjustments could be through conversion price, escrowed stock or warrants-whatever works best for the company and the investors.

For the reason I mentioned, the maximum amount New England Partners would be able to invest in IgX is $3 million. Once I have had a chance to read the private placement memo, perhaps we could talk next week about specific investor targets and the fundraising strategy. I would also like to hear your reaction to the valuation proposal.

Thank you again for coming to Boston. It would be great to work with you again.

Best Regards,

Edwin Snape
Principal

Assumptions

IGX Pre Money Valuation	35,000,000
New Equity	8,000,000
Total Post Valuation	43,000,000
Desired IRR:	75%

Return Analysis			
Year 0	Year 1	Year 2	Year 3
(43,000,000)	75,250,000	131,687,500	230,453,125 75% IRR
(43,000,000)	60,200,000	105,350,000	184,362,500 20% Below
(43,000,000)	52,675,000	92,181,250	161,317,188 30% Below

IF IPO Valuation is 20% below expectations, then a ratchet kicks in to add more shares:

In Year 1 the Formula is:	$14,000,000
Divided by	IPO Share Price
Minus	Initial NEGF II Shares
Equals	Additional New NEGF II Shares
In Year 2 the Formula is:	$24,500,000
Divided by	IPO Share Price
Minus	Initial NEGF II Shares
Equals	Additional New NEGF II Shares
In Year 3 the Formula is:	$42,875,000
Divided by	IPO Share Price
Minus	Initial NEGF II Shares
Equals	Additional New NEGF II Shares

Note: This assumes a one-to-one conversion preferred to common

IgX Corporation
Proposed Terms of Investment

Series B Financing

Issuer:

IgX Corporation, a Delaware corporation ("IgX").

Purchaser:

Institutional private equity and venture investors.

A total of $6.45 million has been committed to date for this round. IgX completed a first closing in late December 1997 for $4.45 million and is planning a second closing for April, 1998.

New England Partners has committed $3 million to this round; Ed Snape, one of the principals of this fund, has joined IgX's Board of Directors. Dr. Snape is also the Managing Partner of Vista Group, a $400 million family of venture capital funds. Henry Venture II has invested $2 million in this Series B round.

Amount:

$10 million total investment. The Company may elect to accept additional commitments beyond the $10 million.

Security:

Series B Convertible Preferred stock of IgX issued at $6.41 per share.

Ownership Interests:	On a post investment basis, the Series B Convertible Preferred Stock holders will own 22% of IgX equity interest at the $10 million total investment level.
	Pre-money valuation is $35 million.
Valuation Protection:	All investors in this round will have the benefit of a potential valuation adjustment in the event a merger with a public company or an IPO does not yield investors in this round an IRR of 75%. If the valuation event does not yield a value of at least 80% of that required to provide a 75% IRR, then investors will be issued additional shares sufficient for investors to achieve the minimum 75% IRR. Examples of the mechanics of this valuation protection feature are shown on the attachment.
Liquidation Preference:	In the event of a liquidation of the Company, the holders of the Series B Convertible Preferred stock shall be entitled to receive, in preference to the holders of the common stock and in parity with the holders of the currently issued and outstanding Series A Convertible Preferred Stock, an amount equal to (a) $6.41 per share of Series B Convertible Preferred Stock (the "Base amount") and (b) an amount equal to a 10% simple interest annual return on the Base Amount from the date of issuance to the date of distribution. A consolidation or merger of the Company (except a merger in which the Company is the surviving corporation) or the sale of all or substantially all of the assets of the Company shall be deemed a liquidation of the Company.

**Redemption:**	Neither the issued and outstanding Series A Convertible Preferred nor the Series B Convertible Preferred Stock is redeemable by the Company.
**Dividend:**	Dividends on both the Series A and the Series B Convertible Preferred Stock will accrue at a 6% compound annual rate. This dividend may accrue or be paid in cash at the option of the Company.
**Conversion Rights:**	Subject to anti-dilution adjustment, each share of Series B Convertible Preferred Stock is convertible into common stock on a share for share basis at the option of the holder. Series B Convertible Preferred Stock is automatically converted into common stock at the then applicable conversion rate, upon the closing of an underwritten public offering of common stock.
**Anti-Dilution Adjustments:**	There will be standard full ratchet anti-dilution rights for Series A and Series B Convertible Preferred for two years from date of closing.
**Voting Rights:**	Series B Convertible Preferred will have voting rights equal to 22% equity ownership interest.
**Board of Directors:**	In addition to the existing board of directors, one representative from the Series B investor group (i.e. lead institutional investor).

Expected Closing Date:	A second closing is planned for April, 1998.
Registration Rights:	After the Company has completed an IPO, the investor group shall have two S-1 "demand" registration rights and unlimited "piggyback" registration rights, at the Company's expense.
Information Rights:	The Company will provide the investor group with monthly, quarterly and year-to-date financial statements which measure results versus budget. The Company will also provide to investor group an annual budget before the beginning of each fiscal year. The Company's financial statements will be audited annually by a "Big Six" accounting firm. Other information will be made available as investors may reasonably request.
Other Terms:	Standard affirmative and negative covenants.
Expenses:	IgX shall reimburse the investor group for normal and reasonable legal and other expenses related to this investment.

Merger with Public Company/
Initial Public Offering: The Company is actively pursuing a merger with a public company to provide a public quote for IgX shareholders, post-merger, and to achieve the target 75% IRR described earlier. Investment bankers are assisting the Company in merger discussions. If a public company merger is for some reason not accomplished, then an alternative liquidity event will be sought in the form of an IPO after the Company completes its Phase III clinical trial which is estimated to be in Q1, 1999. The Company favors merging with a public biotech company which has a substantial cash position to fund further IgX clinical trials and new product development.

Attachments: Question 7

1) Vector Securities

2) Stercamacim Business Review

3) New York Hospital —
Cornell Medical Center
R. Soave, M.D.
Phase I/II Clinical Trial

CONFIDENTIAL

SUMMARY FACT SHEET

TABLE OF CONTENTS

IgX Corporation, IgX Limited, the IgX logo and Stercamacim are trademarks and trade names of IgX Corporation.

SUMMARY FACT SHEET

Company   IgX Corporation

Ownership Private. Henry Venture II Limited owns 61% of IgX; New England Partners owns 10%; and management, directors and founding shareholders own the remainder.

Locations

Headquarters	Summit, New Jersey
Production facilities	Granard, Ireland; Tucson, Arizona
Operations office	High Wycombe, Englad
Research & development	University of Arizona, Tucson, Arizona

Business development office SanDiego, California

Employees 35

Business IgX is an international bioscience company which develops pathogen-specific treatments for infectious diseases of the human gastrointestinal (GI) tract. The Company is presently focusing its efforts on *Clostridiurn difficile-*, *Cryptosporidium parvum* and *Helicobacter pylori*-induced infections. IgX developed its proprietary technology using polyclonal antibodies derived from hyperimmune egg yolks of hens that have been hyperimmunized with specific and purified antigens. IgX believes its platform technology can be applied to develop separate drug treatments for as many as sixteen infections of the GI tract, including rotavirus, astrovirus, *Salmonella typhimurium, Shigella, F. Coli* (ETEC), *F. Coli* (ETEC), *E. Coli* (H7:0157), *Campylobacter jejuni, Cryptosporidium parvum, Giardia, Clostridiurn difficile, Helicobacter pylori, Cyclospora, Isospora,* cytomegalovirus, *Mycobacterium avium* complex, and *Vibrio cholerae.*

SUMMARY FACT SHEET

Development Products

IgX's present four products in development include:

Stercamacim (IGX-CPL3): The Company's lead product in development, Stercamacim, is a ployclonal antibody treatment for *Cryptosporidium parvum*. Stercamacim is in Phase III clinical trials for the treatment of cryptosporidial diarrhea in patients with advanced HIV disease. The trial is a double-blind, placebo-controlled, randomized study of the efficacy of lyophilized, low lipid content IGX-CPL3, given orally for four weeks, The study is being conducted at 26 sites in South Africa and Mexico and is expected to be completed in the first quarter of 1999. Stercamacim is addressing a market in which no effective treatment currently exists.

IGX-CDL3: IgX's second product, IGX-CDL3, is a polyclonal antibody treatment for *Clostridium difficile* infection. IGX-CDL3 is currently undergoing animal studies, and a Phase I/II clinical trial is planned to commence in early 1999 in Europe or the US. Initial results in hamsters are positive.

IGX-HPL3: IgX has a third product based on polyclonal antibodies which is for the treatment of *Helicobacter pylori* infection. IGX-HPL3 is in the preclinical testing phase. Antigen development is underway, and animal studies are planned for 1998.

IGX-M: IGX-M, IgX's fourth product, is a vasoactive peptide targeted at cerebral malaria infections caused by *Plasmodium falciparum*. IGX-M does not involve polyclonal antibodies and is therefore distinct from the Company's core technology. IGX-M is currently undergoing animal studies.

Technology The core technology of IgX derives multiple polyclonal antibody products from hyperimmune egg yolks. Such poly-

SUMMARY FACT SHEET

clonal antibody products can deliver high concentrations of pathogen-specific antibodies to the site of infection and have a rapid onset of actions, while active vaccine immunization may take weeks or months to provide adequate immune protection. Accordingly, IgX has focused on a passive antibody-based immunologic approach toward the prevention and control of infection.

For bacterial pathogens, the polyclonal antibodies will be directed to either binding sites on the surface of the bacteria or to bacterial products, such as toxins or enzymes. When binding to the bacterial surface, the antibodies interfere with bacterial adhesion and attachment, not allowing the bacteria to colonize tissues in the host polyclonal antibodies bind to toxins or enzymes, interfering with their receptors and can also neutralize those molecules. Antibodies directed against bacterial surface sites or products are intended to interfere with the bacterial colonization and damaging of host tissues and to eliminate the disease.

For *C. difficile*, the polyclonal antibodies will be directed to binding sites on the surface of the bacteria, interfering with bacterial adhesion and attachment to the host's tissues. This binding of antibodies blocks the colonization of *C.difficile* in the intestinal tract of patients. Also, polyclonal antibodies will bind to *C. difficile* toxins, interfering with their receptors and neutralizing those molecules, interfering with the bacterial colonization and toxin damage to the host tissues eliminates the presentation of disease.

Regarding parasitic infections, IgX's polyclonal antibodies have been shown to bind effectively to parasites when in transit from cell to cell in the gastrointestinal tract. These antibodies recognize multiple binding sites on the target

SUMMARY FACT SHEET

pathogen and have multiple potential mechanisms of action including the neutralization of toxins. If the parasite cannot invade a cell, it dies and is swept from the intestine. The reproductive cycle is thus interrupted, and the infection will terminate over time.

Manufacturing

IgX intends to maintain control of its proprietary manufacturing processes by maintaining rights to the manufacture of bulk materials required for the commercialization of its products. Material for the current Phase III clinical trial for Stercamacim is manufactured in IgX's pilot facility in Granard, Ireland. The Company has a second pilot manufacturing plant in Tucson, Arizona to provide product for US clinical trials and animal studies at the University of Arizona. Upon the successful completion of Phase III clinical trials, anticipated to take place in the fist quarter of 1999, IgX will begin construction of a full production facility in Ireland. The facility is expected to be operational by the end of 1999.

SALIENT FEATURES

Salient

Features   The following key features represent the strengths of IgX that could be further developed and leveraged within another organization.

- Strong platform technology
- Expansive market opportunity
- Patented intellectual property
- Advanced negotiations underway for the development of a strategic alliance network
- Favorable tax treatment and government grant
- Experienced management team and Board of Directors

Proposed

Transaction The Board of Directors of IgX has determined that the Company's business potential is best achieved if IgX is combined with (a) a more mature pharmaceutical company that can leverage its sales and marketing capabilities for Stercamacim as well as its clinical trial expertise and resources for the progression of IGX-CDL3, IGX-HPL3 and IGX-M, or (b) a public company seeking to expand its product portfolio and markets and with sufficient cash resources to accelerate the development of the IgX products. For these reasons, the Board of Directors has elected to seek a merger partner for the Company. Vector Securities International, Inc., is acting as IgX's exclusive financial advisor for the purpose of assisting the Company in conducting discussions and negotiations leading to the consummation of a merger of the business, assets or stock of the Company. Although the preferred form of consideration is stock, the Board of Directors is inviting bids consisting of a number of other forms of consideration, including cash, debt, contingent value rights and earnout agreements.

SALIENT FEATURES

Strong platform technology

IgX's platform technology creates polyclonal antibodies with a number of beneficial characteristic: (i) clinically well-tolerated, (ii) rapid and specific, and (iii) do not promote the development of resistant strains.

Well-tolerated egg yolk-derived antibodies. Orally delivered egg yolk-derived polyclonal antibodies have been administered in a Phase I/II clinical study which demonstrated a lock of toxicity associated with these products, except in those patients with an intolerant reaction to eggs. The results of the IgX Phase I/II clinical trial at Cornell Medical Center in New York demonstrate an excellent safety profile for the Company's lead products, Stercamacim, in the treatment of cryptospordial diarrhea in AIDS patients.

Rapid onset of specific action. IgX's polyclonal antibody products deliver high concentrations of pathogen-specific antibodies to the site of the infection and have a rapid onset of action, unlike active vaccinations that may take several weeks to provide adequate immune protection and cannot be administered to immunocompromised patients, such as those with AIDS. IgX's technology provides passive immune protection which is immediate and organism-specific.

Do not promote the development of resistant strains. With appropriate immunization regimens, IgX's polyclonal antibodies can be produced that recognize different strains of the same pathogen and affect, even those strains that may be resistant to antibiotics. In contrast, other classes of anti-infective, including antibiotics and monoclonal antibodies, work by interrupting a single mechanism or by binding to a single site and are therefore more likely to be overcome by bacterial adaptation. Unlike broad-spectrum antibiotics, IgX's polyclonal antibody products are selective for specific pathogens and do not disrupt the gastrointestinal tract's normal bacterial flora that ordinarily prevent the overgrowth of certain disease-causing pathogens. The comparative selectivity of polyclonal antibodies should permit their use for prolonged periods to prevent infections without promoting the development of resistant strains. Experts are concerned about vancomycin-resistant bacteria which may result from over-prescription of vancomycin, a drug which is also widely used as a treatment for *C. difficile*. The IgX hyperimmune product, therefore, offers an alternative to antibiotic drug therapy.

Stability and Ease of Use. All of IgX's hyperimmune products are currently in the form of stable powder concentrates with a shelf life exceeding eighteen months. These products can be formulated into a number of different formats, including tablet, capsules and sterile liquids. The standard dosage form is a dry powder which, when reconstituted with water and sucrose, has a sweetened taste.

Expansive market opportunity

IgX's lead product, Stercamacim, is for the treatment of cryptosporidial diarrhea, and has worldwide annual market potential estimated at over $2 billion. Currently, no effective treatment for cryptosporidial diarrhea exists. The Company's second product, IGX-CDL3, is a proposed treatment for *Clostridium difficile* infection which has an estimated total potential worldwide annual market of $25 billion. *C. difficile* is prevalent in the developed economies of the US, Europe and Japan as well as in developing countries. IgX's third product, IGX-HPL3, also has an expansive potential market for the treatment of *Helicobacter pylori*. A recent study has shown that *H. pylori* eradication therapy could save nearly $1 million per year per million inhabitants in Western Europe compared to maintenance or episodic therapy. IgX also has proprietary rights to a novel vasoactive peptide treatment for cerbral malaria which is known to infect 200 to 800 million new patients annually.

Patented intellectual property

IgX has recently been issued a patent covering its core technology as related to cryptosporidiosis. In addition, the Company has one allowed

SALIENT FEATURES

patient and three additional patent applications for its products, core technology and manufacturing processes:

- IgX filed its first patent application in December 1994 covering a method of treating an intestinal parasitosis caused by *Cryptosporidium parvum* using an effective parasite-reducing amount of hen egg yolk antibodies. This patent was allowed by the US Patent & Trademark Office on October 28, 1997.

- An application was filed in June 1997 covering the reduced lipid formulation of the original anti-*C. parvum* treatment used in Phase I/II clinical trials and additional antibody preparations in egg yolk for any other antigen. This patent application covers products prepared from eggs of domestic hen and other avian systems.

- A patent application was filed March 1997 covering the use of a monoclonal antibody as an anti-*C. parvum* preparation.

- In July 1997 IgX filed a patent application for IGX-CDL3, which is a lyophilized hyperimmune hen egg yolk preparation with a low-lipid content, having had the bulk of its native lipid content removed. This preparation contains polyclonal antibodies targeted against *C. difficile* infections.

In-depth negotiations underway for the development of a strategic alliance network

IgX has been negotiating strategic alliances with pharmaceutical companies whereby IgX would grant a license to sell and, in certain individual international markets, manufacture IgX products for payment of an upfront fee and continuing royalties based on sales. IgX is also discussing joint ventures with certain foreign governments, whereby IgX proprietary technology would be used to manufacture IgX products for certain foreign national markets. IgX will also consider developing its own product distribution network for certain markets, where it is appropriate and cost-effective.

BUSINESS STRATEGY

Favorable tax treatment and government grant

IgX has created a tax-favorable legal structure which will limit its corporate tax rate to 10% for a period of ten years for profits derived from Irish manufacture of IgX products through the Irish incorporation of its subsidiary. In addition, the Irish government has granted IgX $2.2 million for the establishment of its full-scale manufacturing facility in Ireland, pending successful completion of Phase III clinical trials.

Experienced management team and Board of Directors

IgX's executive management ream and Board of Directors have extensive experience in the areas of pharmaceuticals, biotechnology, life sciences research, medical technology, finance and other relevant areas. See Management section.

CLINICAL RESULTS

IgX's objective is to develop and rapidly commercialize new orally available pharmaceutical products that use the Company's proprietary hyperimmune egg yolk-based technology to treat and prevent infections of the human gastrointestinal tract. The Company is pursuing this objective using the following strategies:

Target life-threatening diseases initially. IgX is initially targeting life-threatening infections in immunocompromised patients, specifically AIDS patients. If treatment of AIDS patients with Stercamacim is successful, then the product is expected to be particularly efficacious with the broad immune-competent population which is many times larger than the AIDS population for IgX target diseases, Since Stercamacim is for the treatment of life-threatening disease, the product is expected to receive an expedited regulatory review.

Leverage proprietary technology. IgX is leveraging its proprietary core technology based on hyperimmune egg yolk immunoglobulin to develop a portfolio of orally delivered polyclonal antibody products that would treat other diseases of the gastrointestinal tract and that are based on similar manufacturing processes. The technology employed in the development of Stercamacim is similar to that which IgX is using to treat diseases caused by *C. difficile* and *H. pylori*. Although outside of the core technology platform of polyclonal antibodies, the Company's fourth product IGX-M is a vasoactive peptide targeted a cerebral malaria which uses similar mechanisms of action and is expected to follow a similar developmental course. IgX believes that individual drug treatments could be developed for as many as sixteen separate infections of the GI tract.

Develop manufacturing capability to seek regulatory approval in both the European Union and the US. IgX intends to maintain control of its proprietary manufacturing processes by maintaining rights to the manufacture of bulk materials required for the commercialization of its products. The Company has built a GMP pilot production

CLINICAL RESULTS

facility in Granard, County Longford, Ireland to support the Phase III clinical trials in South Africa and Mexico using IGX-CPL3. A second pilot plant in Tucson, Arizona serves to provide product for US clinical trials and animal studies at the University of Arizona. If the Phase III clinical trial is successful, IgX plans to build a full-scale manufacturing facility in Ireland to meet its long term production needs. Pending successful completion of Phase III clinical trials, IgX will receive a $2.2 million grant from the Irish government to build a manufacturing facility in Ireland.

IgX has advanced the clinical regulatory process for Stercamacim through Phase I/II and is currently conducting multinational Phase III trials. The Phase I/II trials were conducted with IGX-CP, a high lipid, liquid formulation of the product. Phase III trials are being conducted with IGX-CPL3, an improved, lyophilized, low lipid formulation.

Phase I/II

A Phase I/II, open label, pilot trial evaluating the safety and efficacy of an earlier, higher fat, liquid formulation (IGX-CP) in the treatment of cryptosporidiosis in 24 AIDS patients was completed in November 1995. All 24 patients were males in the late stage AIDS with a mean CD4 count of 32 cells per mm^3 and a duration of 3 to 9 months of cryptosporidial illness. AIDS patients were chosen for the IgX Phase I/II trial because they represent the most severely ill group of patients available. The IgX theory was that if the drug worked with this group of patients, it would certainly be efficacious with other patient groups in both the immune-compromised patient (chemotherapy, geriatric, pediatric) and the immune-competent patient, thereby providing useful proof of concept.

Sixteen of the 24 patients completed at least 2 weeks of treatment; eight patients discontinued with the first week. Mean compliance during the 6-week study was 95% at the low dose level and 60% at the high dose level. Six patients received extended treatment on a compassionate basis;

CLINICAL RESULTS

only one patient was assigned to the high does level. Duration of compassionate extension ranged from 2 to 30 weeks.

Primary efficacy endpoints included daily frequency of bowel movements, stool consistency, and stool oocyst quantitation. Body weight and the patient's global assessment of treatment were secondary parameters. The evaluable patient population comprised 16 patients who were treated for a least 2 weeks; 11 at the low dose and five at the high dose. Although patients were assigned to two dose levels, the high dose twofold higher than the low-dose, due to poor compliance at the high dose, two clear dose levels did not exist and a comparison of the two doses was not undertaken.

Among the 11 evaluable patients receiving low dose IGX-CP, six patients (54.5%) demonstrated a decrease in the daily frequency of bowel movements relative to baseline after 5 weeks of treatment; at 6 weeks, six of eight patients (75%) who were still in the study demonstrated a decrease. Daily frequency of liquid stools improved in eight of the 11 evaluable low does patients (73%) after 3 weeks relative to baseline; and after 6 weeks, in six of the eight (75%) patients who were still in the study. Among patients who were receiving the high dose, the frequency of daily bowel movements relative to baseline decreased in three of four evaluable patients (75%) after 3 weeks; after 6 weeks of treatment, two of five evaluable high dose patients (40%) demonstrated a decrease. The daily frequency of liquid stools after 3 weeks on the high dose decreased in three of four (75%) patients relative to baseline; only one of five (20%) high dose patients still demonstrated a decrease after 6 weeks. (The clinician believes this was because of a lipid buildup in the high dose patients which induced some diarrhea. Subsequently, IgX lowered the lipid content of CPL3 by approximately 50%.)

Phase III

A Phase III double-blind, placebo-controlled, randomized multi-center study has been designed to evaluate the safety and efficacy of oral, lyophilized, low lipid content IGX-CPL3 in the treatment of cryp-tosporidial diarrhea in patients with advanced HIV disease over a four-week period. Once again, IgX has chosen to treat the most severely inpatient group available, believing that when successful, the product will prove efficacious for any patients suffering from cryptosporidial diarrhea. One hundred and thirty-two HIV-positive inpatients or outpa-tients with CD4 counts lower than 180mm3 and proven cryptosporidial diarrhea, are being included in this study to ensure a minimum of 90 evaluable patients at completion. The study is being conducted in 26 study sites in South Africa and Mexico.

Patients who meet all specified screening criteria are informed in writing about the proposed study and, if they decide to participate, sign an informed consent form. The screening visit is followed by the screening period (duration between 0 and 7 days). This period is as short as possible but is flexible to allow sufficient time to collect all the data and perform all the screening examinations necessary to complete the inclusion and exclu-sion criteria. By the end of the study, 185 eligible patients will have been included and randomized to receive one of two treatments: 4.12 x 106 AU IGX-CPL3 per day, or matching placebo, for four weeks. It is expected that at least 90 patients will complete the four-week, double-blind treatment.

During this four-week double-blind treatment period, patients have been designated to receive five oral doses of 824.000 AU IGX-CPL3 or placebo every 4 hours while awake (i.e., 5 times a day from 7:00 a.m. to 11:00 p.m.). On the evening before inclusion, and on every subsequent treatment day in the morning, patients will receive omeprazole 20 mg p.o. Omeprazole (Losec) is prescribed to inhibit the secretion of gastric acid, which may affect antibodies during passage through the stomach.

Patients whose stool frequency has not decreased during this four week double-blind treatment period will then be treated with open-label active IGX-CPL3 and omeprazole orally, or active IGX-CPL3 alone by naso-duodenal tube or percutaneous gastrostomy (if already fashioned),

CLINICAL RESULTS

for a further four weeks (until the week 8 visit). Patients whose stool frequency has decreased during the four week double-blind treatment period will not be treated further, but will be followed up for four weeks (until the week 8 visit).

IGX-CDL3 for *Clostridium difficile* is currently being tested in hamster models and these animal studies are expected to be successfully completed by Q2 1998, with an IND filed and Phase III clinical trial beginning in the US in Q1 1999. This product is currently being manufactured in Granard, Ireland, for use as the placebo in the Phase III trial to treat cryptosporidial diarrhea.

IGX-HPL3 is intended for the treatment of ulcerogenic complications due to *Helicobacter pylori*. This gram-negative bacteria has been associated with 80% gastric and 90% of duodenal ulcers in humans. These initial efforts are focused on the identification of the antigens and subsequent antibody generation under IgX's core technology. In-vitro testing for this product is scheduled for late 1998. In-vivo studies in already identified mouse models will commence following the completion of successful in-vitro studies. IgX intends to file an application for a Phase I/II clinical trial evaluation within months of completion of in-vivo studies.

FINANCING HISTORY

IgX Corp. was founded 1992 by Henry Venture II Limited, a $60 million venture fund. The fund currently owns 61% of IgX; New England Partners owns 10%; and management, directors and various individual founding shareholders own the remainder.

IgX Limited was formed in September 1995. In December 1995, IgX Corp. became a wholly owned subsidiary of IgX Limited. Operations were conducted through IgX Corp. in the US prior to 1996. During 1996, IgX Limited began operating in the Republic of Ireland. In December 1997 IgX Limited became a wholly owned subsidiary of IgX Corp., a Delaware corporation.

In December 1997, IgX raised $5 million in a private offering of Series B Convertible Preferred stock ("Series B") to New England Partners, an investment company, and certain other existing shareholders, including Henry Venture II Limited. The per-share price of the Series B offering was $6.41. Currently, 6.2 million common shares and common share equivalents are outstanding, excluding options and warrants. IgX is continuing to raise additional funds through the Series B private placement.

Currently, 1.1 million options are outstanding, with an average exercise price of $3.00.

FINANCING HISTORY

Fully-Diluted Capitalization Table
(Assumes 1:1 Conversion of Preferred Stock)

Stockholder	Number of Shares	Percentage
Common stock		
Henry Venture	350,030	5.2%
IX Limited	360,000	5.3%
Stock Options	1,048,357	15.6%
New England Growth Fund (NEGF) II LP Warrants	370,000	5.5%
Series A Preferred Stock		
Henry Venture II Limited	3,500,001	52.0%
IX Limited	200,000	3.0%
Series B Preferred Stock		
NEGF II, L.P.	311,910	4.6%
English and Scottish PLC	155,955	2.3%
Henry Venture II Limited	311,910	4.6%
Other Investors	24,762	1.9%
Total	67,732,925	100%

SUMMARY HISTORICAL AND PROJECTED FINANCIAL DATA

(dollars in thousands)

	Historical 1997	1998	1999	2000	Projected 2001	2002	2003	2004
Selected Income Statement Data:								
Revenues								
Royalty	$ —	$ —	$ —	$ 24,888	$ 32,982	$ 107,792	$ 138,403	$ 165,642
Licensee Research Payments	—	4,500	9,000	9,600	9,600	9,600	—	—
Total Revenue —	—	4,500	9,000	34,488	42,582	117,392	138,403	165,642
Corporate Costs:								
Research & Development Costs	572	2,300	3,098	4,260	6,060	6,060	6,060	6,060
Admin. & Bus. Development	2,066	2,720	2,684	3,200	3,200	3,200	3,200	3,200
Non-allocated Production Costs	216	218	218	240	240	240	240	240
Total Corporate Costs	2,854	5,238	6,000	7,700	9,500	9,500	9,500	9,500
EBITDA	(2,854)	(738)	3,000	26,788	33,082	107,892	128,903	156,142
Depreciation	176	176	176	400	400	400	400	400
Operating Income	(3,030)	(914)	2,824	26,388	32,682	107,492	128,503	155,742
Income Taxes (1)	—	—	—	7,319	13,073	42,997	51,401	62,297
Net Income	$ (3,030)	$ (914)	$ 2,824	$ 19,069	$ 19,609	$ 64,495	$ 77,102	$ 93,445
Selected Cash Flow Statement Data								
Depreciation and Amortization	$ 176	$ 176	$ 176	$ 400	$ 400	$ 400	$ 400	$ 400
Increases in Working Capital	4,000	1,000	1,000	1,000	1,600	2,000	2,000	2,000
Capital Expenditures	—	3,200	2,400	500	500	500	500	500
Selected Balance Sheet Statement Data:								
Cash and Cash Equivalents	3,000							
Interest-Bearing Debt	1,500							
Shareholders' Equity	(3,000)							
Growth Rates:								
Total Revenue	NA	NM	100.0%	283.2%	23.5%	175.7%	17.9%	19.7%
EBITDA	NA	NM	NM	792.9%	23.5%	226.1%	19.5%	21.1%
Operating Income	NA	NM	NM	834.4%	28.9%	228.9%	19.5%	21.2%
Net Income	NA	NM	NM	575.2%	2.8%	228.9%	19.5%	21.2%
As Percentage of Total Revenue:								
Research & Development Costs	NM	51.1%	34.4%	12.4%	14.2%	5.2%	4.4%	3.7%
Admin. & Bus. Development	NM	60.4%	29.8%	9.3%	7.5%	2.7%	2.3%	1.9%
Non-allocated Production Costs	NM	4.8%	2.4%	0.7%	0.6%	0.2%	0.2%	0.1%
EBITDA	NM	-16.4%	33.3%	77.7%	77.7%	91.9%	93.1%	94.3%
Net Income	NM	-20.3%	31.4%	55.3%	46.1%	54.9%	55.7%	56.4%
Tax Rate	0.0%	0.0%	0.0%	27.7%	40.0%	40.0%	40.0%	40.0%

(1) Income Taxes assume utilization of net operating losses.

MANAGEMENT

Member of Management

Albert J. Henry	Chairman
Edwin Snape, Ph.D.	Director, Chairman, Executive Committee for Corporate Development
Carroll "Bo" Allen	Executive Vice President of Market and Business Development
Robert L. Renfroe	Vice President, Operations
Vitaliano A. Cama, DVM	Vice President, Research and Development
Charles R. Sterling, Ph.D.	Director of Research, Chairman Scientific Advisory Board
Tony Geoghegan	Controller
Annette Fernandez, Ph.D.	Director, Global Market and Business Development
Randolph C. Steer, MD, Ph.D.	Director
Kenneth D. Polin	Director

Albert J. Henry has served as Chairman of the Company since its inception and was CEO until April 1997. Mr. Henry has been Chairman and CEO of Henry & Co. and of Henry Venture Funds I and II Limited since 1983. He was formerly Vice Chairman of IVAC Medical Systems, Inc., Director, Chief Financial Officer and Chairman, Executive Committee, IMED, and was previously Chairman of Henry & Associates, New York, a Wall Street securities research and 'venture capital firm. Previously, he held various officer positions with First National City Bank (now Citicorp) in New York.

MANAGEMENT

Edwin Snape, Ph.D. is IgX Director and Chairman, Executive Committee for Corporate Development, Dr. Snape is a managing partner of the Vista Group, a $400 million family of venture capital funds, Dr. Snape is also one of four principals of New England Partners, the venture capital firm that led the Series B investment round. Dr. Snape has founded and served as a lead/first round investor in many medical device biotechnology companies. These companies have achieved a combined market capitalization in excess of $4 billion.

Carroll "Bo" Allen is the Company's Executive Vice President of Market and Business Development and has been a director of the Company since 1996. Mr. Allen has served as Vice President of Business Development and Marketing for Kimeragen and CoCensys. He has 19 years industry experience in pharmaceutical sales, marketing and business development with Sandoz, Boehringer-Ingelheim GmbH and Ciba-Geigy.

Robert L. Renfroe has served as Vice President Operations of the Company since 1995. Mr. Renfroe was formerly the Genral Mangaer of Ireland and VP-Operations for IMED Corp. from 1980 to 1987. Previously, Mr. Renfroe managed the building of the Oxford Laboratories (division of G.D. Searle) medical solutions and device production plant in Athy, County Kildare, in 1971, and an Oxford Labs medical disposable production plan in Spiddal, County Galway in 1974.

Vitaliano A. Cama, DVM, has served as Vice President Research and Development of the Company since 1995. He has been a research associate in the Department of Veterinary Science at the University of Arizona since 1988. With Dr. Sterling, he is the co-inventor of hyperimmune egg yolk treatment for C. Parvum. From 1982 to 1987 he was supervisor of AVI-VET' poultry farmers in Lima, Peru. At the same time from 1983-1985 he was teaching assistant in the Department of Animal Production, School of Veterinary Medicine, Universidad Nacional Mayor de San Marcos, Lima.

MANAGEMENT

Charles R. Sterling, Ph.D., has been Director of Research and Chairman of the Scientific Advisory Board of the Company since 1992. He heads the Department of Veterinary Science, University of Arizona Dr. Sterling and Dr. Cama are the co-inventors of the hyperimmune egg yolk treatment for C. parvum. Dr. Sterling's laboratory at University of Arizona has conducted basic research relating to enteric protozoan parasites and C. parvum in particular, which has been funded by the national Institute of Health (NIH), Environmental Protection Agency (EPA), United States Department of Agriculture USDA), American Water Works Association Research Foundation (AWWARF), private foundations, state and local agencies and private industry.

Tony Geoghegan, is IgX Corporation Controller and Manager of corporate cash flow. He has a fourteen-year background with Coopers & Lybrand and has been associated with IgX founders for 12 years in an audit capacity.

Annette Fernandez, Ph.D. has been Director, Global Market and Business Development of the Company since 1997. Dr. Fernandez was previously the co-director of Technology Assessment & PharmacoEconomic Services (TAPES) Institute of Excellence at the Jefferson Health System in Philadelphia, Pennsylvania. At the Thomas Jefferson University Hospital, Dr. Fernandez was Assistant Project Director and consulted to major pharmaceutical companies on product development and economic research.

Randolph C. Steer, MD, Ph.D. has been an IgX director since 1996 and a member of the Scientific Advisory Board since 1993, Dr. Steer is an independent regulatory consultant with a broad background in the commercial development of drugs, biologicals and medical devices. He was previously the Medical Director at Ciba-Geigy Pharmaceuticals following a position in the R&D division of Man-Marion Laboratories. Dr. Steer is a member of the board of directors of Techne Corporation, a manufacturer of cellular biologic reagents, BioCryst Pharmaceuticals, a drug design and development company, Kimeragen, Inc., a gene repair company and Maret, Inc., a wound healing company.

MANAGEMENT

Kenneth D. Polin has been a director of the company since 1992. Mr. Polin is currently a partner of Zevnik, Horton, Guibord, McGovern, Palmer and Fognani, LLP and was formerly a corporate partner at Brobeck, Phleger & Harrison.

REPORT OF INDEPENDENT ACCOUNTANTS

To the Board of Directors and Stockholders of IgX Corp.

In our opinion, the accompanying consolidated balance sheet and the related consolidated statements of operations, of capital deficiency and of cash flows present fairly, in all material respects, the financial position of IgX Corp. and subsidiary (the "Company") (a development stage company) at December 31, 1996 and 1997, and the results of their operations and their cash flows for each of the three years in the period ended December 31, 1997 and for the period from inception (February 11, 1992) through December 31, 1997, in conformity with generally accepted accounting principles. These financial statements are the responsibility of the Company's management; our responsibility is to express an opinion on these financial statements based on our audits. We conducted our audits of these statements in accordance with generally accepted auditing standards which require that we plan and perform the audit to obtain reasonable assurance about whether the financial statements are free of material misstatement. An audit includes examining, on a test basis, evidence supporting the amounts and disclosures in the financial statements, assessing the accounting principles used and significant estimates made by management, and evaluating the overall financial statement presentation. We believe that our audits provide a reasonable basis for the opinion expressed above.

The accompanying financial statements have been prepared assuming that the Company will continue as a going concern. As discussed in Note 2 to the financial statements, the Company is a development stage enterprise and has suffered recurring losses and net cash outflows from operations since inception that raise substantial doubt about its ability to continue as a going concern. As such, the Company is dependent upon capital infusions from existing and/or new investors to fund operations. Management's plans with regard to these matters are also described in Note 2. The accompanying financial statements do no include any adjustments that might result from the outcome of this uncertainty.

PRICEWATERHOUSECOOPERS LLP

Stamford, Connecticut
September 14, 1998

IgX, Limited

STERCAMACIM
Business Review

IGX-CPL3 Sales Forecast

for AIDS Related Cryptospidial Diarrhea
in North America and Western Europe
(September 1997)

License Year	1	2	3	4	5
Total Patients	1,103,008	1,105,766	1,108,530	1,111,301	1,114,080
Treatable Patients	33.173	33,256	33,339	33,422	33,506
Penetration Rate	50 %	55 %	60 %	65 %	70 %
Treated Patients	16,586	18,291	20,003	21,725	23,454
Average Number of Treatments	28	28	28	28	28
Cost per Treatment	$100.00	$103.00	$106.90	$109.27	$112.65
Average Cost per Patient	$2,800.00	$2,856.00	$2,913.12	$2,971.38	$3,030.81
Total Sales	$46,442,152	$52,238,365	$58,272,371	$64,551,947	$71,085,101

License Year	6	7	8	9	10
Total Patients	1,116,865	1,119,657	1,122,456	1,125,262	1,128,075
Treatable Patients	33,590	33,674	33,758	33,842	33,842
Penetration Rate	70 %	70 %	65 %	60 %	55 %
Treated Patients	23,513	23,572	21,943	20,305	18,613
Average Number of Treatments	28	28	28	28	28
Cost per Treatment	$115.93	$119.41	$112.99	126.68	$130.48
Average Cost per Patient	$3,091.43	3,153.25	$3,216.32	$3,280.65	$3,346.26
Total Sales	$72,688,070	$74,327,186	$70,574,459	$66,614,689	$62,284,734

"Total Patients" includes patients with AIDS or HIV, based on conservative projections of rates of infection.
"Treatable Patients" is calculated as 3 percent of total patients, the lowest reported incidence rate of IADS/HIV patients infected with cryptosporidiosis.
"Penetration Rate" is the number of treatable patients who go on therapy.
"Average Number of Treatments:" five doses per day, for 28 days is the minumum course for an acute infection.

Stercamacim Licensee
NPV IRR
AIDS Market
Europe and the U.S.

STERCAMACIM LICENSEE YEARS	1	2	3	4	5	6	7	8	9	0
INPUTS-DOMESTIC COSTS (E.U.)										
CAPITAL COSTS										
USE OF EXISTING PLANT & EQUIPMENT	$ 64	$ 66	$ 68	$ 70	$ 72	$ 74	$ 76	$ 79	$ 81	$ 84
NEW PLANT, PROPERTY & EQUIPMENT	$ 1,968	$ -	$ -	$ -	$ -	$ -	$ -	$ 500	$ -	$ -
EXPANSION PP&E	$ 226	$ 233	$ 240	$ 247	$ 254	$ 262	$ 270	$ 278	$ 286	$ 295
PROCESS CAPITAL	$ 50	$ 52	$ 53	$ 55	$ 56	$ 58	$ 60	$ 61	$ 63	$ 65
TOTAL CAPITAL	$ 2,308	$ 351	$ 361	$ 372	$ 382	$ 394	$ 406	$ 918	$ 430	$ 444
EXPENSES										
COST OF GOODS SOLD										
RAW MATERIALS	$ 4,604	$ 9,396	$ 9,866	$ 10,359	$ 10,877	$ 11,421	$ 11,992	$ 11,421	$ 10,877	$ 10,359
ENERGY & POWER	$ 90	$ 95	$ 101	$ 107	$ 114	$ 120	$ 128	$ 135	$ 143	$ 152
TRANSFER PRICING	$ 11	$ 12	$ 12	$ 13	$ 14	$ 15	$ 16	$ 17	$ 18	$ 19
COST OF COMPONENTS	$ 22	$ 23	$ 25	$ 26	$ 28	$ 29	$ 31	$ 33	$ 35	$ 37
PRODUCTION LABOR	$ 1,229	$ 1,303	$ 1,381	$ 1,464	$ 1,552	$ 1,645	$ 1,743	$ 1,848	$ 1,959	$ 2,076
ENGINEERING MODIFICATIONS	$ 14	$ 15	$ 16	$ 17	$ 18	$ 19	$ 20	$ 21	$ 22	$ 24
OPERATING MANUALS	$ 12	$ 12	$ 13	$ 13	$ 14	$ 14	$ 14	$ 15	$ 15	$ 16
DEPRECIATION	$ 231	$ 266	$ 302	$ 339	$ 377	$ 417	$ 457	$ 549	$ 592	$ 637
SUBTOTAL-COST OF GOODS SOLD	$ 6,213	$ 11,122	$ 11,716	$ 12,338	$ 12,994	$ 13,680	$ 14,401	$ 14,039	$ 13,661	$ 13,320

Stercamacim Licensee
NPV IRR
AIDS Market
Europe and the U.S.

CONFIDENTIAL

STERCAMACIM LICENSEE YEARS	1	2	3	4	5	6	7	8	9	0
INPUTS-DOMESTIC COSTS										
EXPENSES										
COST OF SALES										
DIRECT SALES	$ 5,000	$ 5,050	$ 5,101	$ 5,152	$ 5,203	$ 5,255	$ 5,308	$ 5,361	$ 5,414	$ 5,468
COST TO HALT CURRENT SALES	$ -	$ -	$ -	$ -	$ -	$ -	$ -	$ -	$ -	-
DISTRIBUTOR COMMISSIONS	$ 464	$ 522	$ 582	$ 645	$ 710	$ 726	$ 742	$ 705	$ 666	628
ADVERTISING	$ 2,500	$ 2,000	$ 500	$ 515	$ 530	$ 546	$ 563	$ 580	$ 597	615
MARKET RESEARCH	$ 500	$ 250	$ 263	$ 276	$ 289	$ 304	$ 319	$ 335	$ 352	369
PRODUCT LIABILITY INSURANCE	$ 250	$ 260	$ 280	$ 290	$ 299	$ 308	$ 317	$ 326	$ 336	346
WARRANTIES & GUARANTEES	$ 35	$ 40	$ 45	$ 50	$ 55	$ 60	$ 65	$ 70	$ 80	90
PRODUCT SERVICE	$ 12	$ 13	$ 14	$ 14	$ 14	$ 15	$ 15	$ 16	$ 16	17
SUBTOTAL-COST OF SALES	$ 8,761	8135	6785	6942	7100	7214	7329	7393	7461	7533
RESEARCH & DEVELOPMENT EXPENSES										
R&D EXPENSES										
PRODUCT DEVELOPMENT	$ 500	$ 100	$ -	$ -	$ -	$ -	$ -	$ -	$ -	-
PRODUCT IMPROVEMENTS	$ 10	$ 10	$ 9	$ 9	$ 9	$ 9	$ 8	$ 8	$ 8	8
TECHNICAL ASSISTANCE FEES	$ 50	$ 50	$ 50	$ 40	$ 40	$ 40	$ 20	$ 10	$ 10	10
PRODUCTION RESEARCH	$ 100	$ 100	$ 100	$ 90	$ 80	$ 70	$ 60	$ 50	$ 40	30
SUBTOTAL-R&D EXPENSES	$ 660	$ 260	$ 159	$ 139	$ 129	$ 119	$ 88	$ 68	$ 58	$ 48

Stercamacim Licensee
NPV IRR
AIDS Market
Europe and the U.S.

STERCAMACIM LICENSEE YEARS	1	2	3	4	5	6	7	8	9	0
INPUTS-DOMESTIC COSTS										
EXPENSES										
ADMINISTRATION										
GENERAL & ADMINISTRATIVE	$ 710	$ 746	$ 783	$ 822	$ 863	$ 906	$ 951	$ 999	$ 1,049	$ 1,101
ADMINISTRATIVE REPORTING	30	30	30	30	30	30	30	30	30	30
TRAINING EXPENSES	1,000	750	500	500	500	500	500	500	500	500
MANAGEMENT FEES	350	300	250	250	250	250	250	250	250	250
TRAVEL EXPENSES	450	425	400	400	300	300	300	300	250	200
AUDITING EXPENSES	32	32	31	30	33	36	39	42	42	42
INSPECTION COSTS	150	50	25	20	24	28	32	36	40	40
EXPEDITING COSTS	40	40	30	30	20	20	20	15	15	10
REBATES TO GOVERNMENTS	1,644	2,223	2,187	2,455	3,108	3,180	3,432	3,190	2,678	2,456
SUBTOTAL-ADMINISTRATION	$ 4,406	$ 4,596	$ 4,236	$ 4,537	$ 5,128	$ 5,250	$ 5,554	$ 5,362	$ 4,854	$ 4,629
REGULATORY COMPLIANCE										
REGULATORY	$ 3,000	$ -	$ -	$ -	$ -	$ -	$ -	$ -	$ -	$ -
PRE-CLINICAL TRIALS	1,000	-	-	-	-	-	-	-	-	-
PHASE 1 CLINICAL TRIALS	1,000	-	-	-	-	-	-	-	-	-
PHASE 2 CLINICAL TRIALS		1,000	-	-	-	-	-	-	-	-
PHASE 3 CLINICAL TRIALS	7,000									
SUBTOTAL-REGULATORY	$ 12,000	$ 1,000	$ -	$ -	$ -	$ -	$ -	$ -	$ -	$ -

Stercamacim Licensee
NPV IRR
AIDS Market
Europe and the U.S.

CONFIDENTIAL

Synergy Pharmaceuticals, Inc.   257

STERCAMACIM LICENSEE YEARS	1	2	3	4	5	6	7	8	9	0
INPUTS-DOMESTIC COSTS										
EXPENSES										
LEGAL										
LEGAL EXPENSES	$ 300	$ 300	$ 275	$ 275	$ 250	$ 250	$ 250	$ 250	$ 250	$ 250
PATENT & TRADEMARK FILINGS	$ 50	$ 50	$ 50	$ 50	$ 50	$ 50	$ 50	$ 25	$ 25	$ 25
ADDED REGISTRATION FEES	$ 88	$ 88	$ 44	$ 44	$ 44	$ 44	$ 44	$ 12	$ 12	$ 12
ATTORNEY FEES	$ 400	$ 350	$ 300	$ 300	$ 300	$ 300	$ 300	$ 200	$ 200	$ 200
SUBTOTAL-LEGAL	$ 838	$ 788	$ 669	$ 669	$ 644	$ 644	$ 644	$ 487	$ 487	$ 487
LICENSING										
LUMP-SUM PAYMENTS	$ 5,000	$ -	$ -	$ -	$ -	$ -	$ -	$ -	$ -	$ -
MINIMUM GUARANTEED ROYALTY	$ -	$ -	$ -	$ -	$ -	$ -	$ -	$ -	$ -	$ -
ROYALTY RATE (%)	$ -	$ -	$ -	$ -	$ -	$ -	$ -	$ -	$ -	$ -
RUNNING ROYALTY PAYMENTS	$ 11,610	$ 13,059	$ 14,568	$ 16,137	$ 17,771	$ 18,172	$ 18,581	$ 17,643	$ 16,653	$ 15,571
SUB-LICENSING	$ 348	$ 391	$ 437	$ 484	$ 533	$ 545	$ 557	$ 529	$ 499	$ 467
COST OF TECHNOLOGY SEARCH	$ 33	$ 33	$ 33	$ 33	$ 33	$ 33	$ 33	$ 33	$ 33	$ 33
AGREEMENT TERMINATION COSTS	$ -	$ -	$ -	$ -	$ -	$ -	$ -	$ -	$ -	$ -
SUBTOTAL-LICENSING	$ 16,991	$ 13,483	$ 15,038	$ 16,654	$ 18,337	$ 18,750	$ 19,171	$ 18,205	$ 17,185	$ 16,071

Stercamacim Licensee
NPV IRR
AIDS Market
Europe and the U.S.

STERCAMACIM LICENSEE YEARS	1	2	3	4	5	6	7	8	9	0
INPUTS-DOMESTIC COSTS										
EXPENSES										
TAXES										
FEDERAL TAX RATE (%)	10%	10%	10%	10%	10%	10%	10%	10%	10%	10%
STATE TAX RATE (%)	3%	3%	3%	3%	3%	3%	3%	3%	3%	3%
FEDERAL TAXES ($)	$ (559.4)	$ 1,020.3	$ 1,669.3	$ 2,011.4	$ 2,341.6	$ 2,360.9	$ 2,363.3	$ 1,761.5	$ 1,644.9	$ 1,469.8
STATE TAXES ($)	$ (173.0)	$ 315.6	$ 516.3	$ 622.1	$ 724.2	$ 730.2	$ 730.9	$ 544.8	$ 508.7	$ 454.6
TAX CREDITS ($)										
SUBTOTAL-TAXES	$ (732.4)	$ 1,335.8	$ 2,185.5	$ 2,633.5	$ 3,065.8	$ 3,091.0	$ 3,094.2	$ 2,306.3	$ 2,153.6	$ 1,924.4

Stercamacim Licensee
NPV IRR
AIDS Market
Europe and the U.S.

CONFIDENTIAL

STERCAMACIM LICENSEE YEARS	1	2	3	4	5	6	7	8	9	0
INPUTS-INTERNATIONAL COSTS										
CAPITAL COSTS										
ADDED PLANT PROPERTY & EQUIPMENT	$ 3,000	$ 750	$ 250	$ 250	$ 250	$ 250	$ 200	$ 100	$ 50	$ 25
EXPENSES										
CURRENCY (GAINS)/SHORTFALLS	$ 50	$ 54	$ 57	$ 61	$ 66	$ 70	$ 75	$ 80	$ 86	$ 92
COUNTRY TAXES	$ 961	$ 990	$ 1,020	$ 1,050	$ 1,082	$ 1,114	$ 1,147	$ 1,182	$ 1,217	$ 1,254
FOREIGN WITHHOLDING TAXES	$ 1,238	$ 1,275	$ 1,313	$ 1,353	$ 1,393	$ 1,435	$ 1,478	$ 1,523	$ 1,568	$ 1,615
DUTIES	$ 50	$ 52	$ 53	$ 55	$ 56	$ 58	$ 60	$ 61	$ 63	$ 65
RESERVE FUND	$ 200	$ 210	$ 221	$ 232	$ 243	$ 255	$ 268	$ 281	$ 295	$ 310
LICENSOR SPECIAL SERVICES	$ 20	$ 21	$ 22	$ 24	$ 25	$ 27	$ 28	$ 30	$ 32	$ 34
ADDED INSURANCE	$ 50	$ 53	$ 55	$ 58	$ 61	$ 64	$ 67	$ 70	$ 74	$ 78
ADDED DEPRECIATION	$ 751	$ 766	$ 781	$ 797	$ 813	$ 829	$ 846	$ 863	$ 880	$ 898
SUBTOTAL-INTERNATIONAL COSTS	$ 3,320	$ 3,366	$ 3,523	$ 3,629	$ 3,739	$ 3,852	$ 3,970	$ 4,091	$ 4,216	$ 4,345

Stercamacim Licensee
NPV IRR
AIDS Market
Europe and the U.S.

STERCAMACIM LICENSEE YEARS	1	2	3	4	5	6	7	8	9	0
INPUTS-REVENUES & SAVINGS										
PRODUCT SALES										
LICENSED PRODUCT SALES	$ 46,422	$ 52,238	$ 58,272	$ 64,551	$ 71,085	$ 72,688	$ 74,327	$ 70,574	$ 66,614	$ 62,281
CONVEYED SALES	$ -	$ -	$ -	$ -	$ -	$ -	$ -	$ -	$ -	$ -
INCREMENTAL SALES-OTHER PRODUCTS	$ 1,000	$ 1,030	$ 1,061	$ 1,093	$ 1,126	$ 1,159	$ 1,194	$ 1,230	$ 1,267	$ 1,305
INGREDIENTS	$ -	$ -	$ -	$ -	$ -	$ -	$ -	$ -	$ -	$ -
DISTRIBUTION AGREEMENTS	$ -	$ -	$ -	$ -	$ -	$ -	$ -	$ -	$ -	$ -
SUBTOTAL-PRODUCT SALES	$ 47,422	$ 53,268	$ 59,333	$ 65,644	$ 72,211	$ 73,847	$ 75,521	$ 71,804	$ 67,881	$ 63,586
OTHER REVENUES										
SUB-LICENSING FEES	$0	$0	$0	$0	$0	$0	$0	$0	$0	$0
TECHNOLOGY ADVANCE BACK SALES	0	0	0	0	0	0	0	0	0	0
CROSS-LICENSING VALUE	0	0	0	0	0	0	0	0	0	0
SUBTOTAL-OTHER REVENUES	$0	$0	$0	$0	$0	$0	$0	$0	$0	$0
SAVINGS										
INFRINGEMENT SUIT	$0	$0	$0	$0	$0	$0	$0	$0	$0	$0
MANUFACTURING EFFICIENCIES	0	0	0	0	0	0	0	0	0	0
SUBTOTAL-SAVINGS	$0	$0	$0	$0	$0	$0	$0	$0	$0	$0

Stercamacim Licensee
NPV IRR
AIDS Market

CONFIDENTIAL

Europe and the U.S.

STERCAMACIM LICENSEE YEARS	1	2	3	4	5	6	7	8	9	0
INPUTS–MISCELLANEOUS										
VALUE										
VALUE OF EQUITY SHARES	0	0	0	0	0	0	0	0	0	0
VALUE OF KNOW-HOW	250	300	350	400	450	500	550	500	450	400
WORKING CAPITAL AS % OF SALES	25%	25%	25%	25%	25%	25%	25%	25%	25%	25%
GUESS FOR IRR	35%									
DISCOUNT RATE	25%									

Stercamacim Licensee
NPV IRR
AIDS Market
Europe and the U.S.

STERCAMACIM LICENSEE YEARS	1	2	3	4	5	6	7	8	9	0
OUTPUT SUMMARY FOR LICENSEE										
REVENUES										
PRODUCT SALES	$ 47,422	$ 53,268	$ 59,333	$ 65,644	$ 72,211	$ 73,847	$ 75,521	$ 71,804	$ 67,881	$ 63,586
OTHER REVENUES	0	0	0	0	0	0	0	0	0	0
SAVINGS	0	0	0	0	0	0	0	0	0	0
TOTAL REVENUES	$ 47,422	$ 53,268	$ 59,333	$ 65,644	$ 72,211	$ 73,847	$ 75,521	$ 71,804	$ 67,881	$ 63,586
EXPENSES										
COST OF GOODS SOLD	$ 6,213	$ 11,122	$ 11,715	$ 12,338	$ 12,992	$ 13,680	$ 14,401	$ 14,039	$ 13,662	$ 13,319
COST OF SALES	$ 8,761	$ 8,135	$ 6,784	$ 6,941	$ 7,101	$ 7,214	$ 7,329	$ 7,392	$ 7,462	$ 7,534
RESEARCH EXPENSES	$ 660	$ 260	$ 159	$ 139	$ 129	$ 119	$ 88	$ 68	$ 58	$ 48
ADMINISTRATIVE	$ 4,406	$ 4,596	$ 4,236	$ 4,537	$ 5,128	$ 5,250	$ 5,554	$ 5,362	$ 4,854	$ 4,629
REGULATORY	$ 12,000	$ 1,000	$ -	$ -	$ -	$ -	$ -	$ 4,000	$ 3,000	$ 2,000
LEGAL	$ 838	$ 788	$ 669	$ 669	$ 644	$ 644	$ 644	$ 487	$ 487	$ 487
LICENSING COSTS	$ 16,991	$ 13,483	$ 15,038	$ 16,654	$ 18,337	$ 18,750	$ 19,171	$ 18,205	$ 17,185	$ 16,071
INTERNATIONAL	$ 3,320	$ 3,366	$ 3,523	$ 3,629	$ 3,739	$ 3,852	$ 3,970	$ 4,091	$ 4,216	$ 4,345
TOTAL EXPENSES	$ 53,189	$ 42,750	$ 42,124	$ 44,907	$ 48,070	$ 49,508	$ 51,157	$ 53,644	$ 50,923	$ 48,433
PROFIT BEFORE TAX	$ (5,767)	$ 10,518	$ 17,209	$ 20,736	$ 24,140	$ 24,339	24364	18160	$ 16,958	15152
TAXES	$ (732)	$ 1,336	$ 2,186	$ 2,634	$ 3,066	$ 3,091	$ 3,094	$ 2,306	$ 2,154	$ 1,924
PROFIT AFTER TAX	$ (5,034)	$ 9,183	$ 15,023	$ 18,103	$ 21,075	$ 21,248	$ 21,270	$ 15,853	$ 14,804	$ 13,228

CONFIDENTIAL

Stercamacim Licensee
NPV IRR
AIDS Market
Europe and the U.S.

STERCAMACIM LICENSEE YEARS	1	2	3	4	5	6	7	8	9	0
OUTPUT SUMMARY FOR LICENSEE										
CASH FLOWS										
PROFIT BEFORE TAX	$ (5,767)	$ 10,518	$ 17,209	$ 20,736	$ 24,140	$ 24,339	$ 24,364	$ 18,160	$ 16,958	$ 15,152
DEPRECIATION	$ 982	$ 1,032	$ 1,083	$ 1,136	$ 1,190	$ 1,246	$ 1,303	$ 1,412	$ 1,472	$ 1,534
CHANGE IN WORKING CAPITAL	$ (11,856)	$ (1,462)	$ (1,516)	$ (1,578)	$ (1,642)	$ (409)	$ (418)	$ 929	$ 981	$ 1,074
CAPITAL EXPENDITURES	$ (5,308)	$ (1,100)	$ (611)	$ (622)	$ (633)	$ (644)	$ (606)	$ (1,018)	$ (481)	$ (469)
VALUE OF EQUITY SHARES	$ -	$ -	$ -	$ -	$ -	$ -	$ -	$ -	$ -	$ -
VALUE OF KNOW-HOW	$ 250	$ 300	$ 350	$ 400	$ 450	$ 400	$ 400	$ 350	$ 350	$ 300
BEFORE TAX CASH FLOWS	$ (21,699)	$ 9,289	$ 16,515	$ 20,073	$ 23,506	$ 24,931	$ 25,042	$ 19,833	$ 19,280	$ 17,592
PROFIT AFTER TAX	$ (5,034)	$ 9,183	$ 15,023	$ 18,103	$ 21,075	$ 21,248	$ 21,270	$ 15,853	$ 14,804	$ 13,228
DEPRECIATION	$ 982	$ 1,032	$ 1,083	$ 1,136	$ 1,190	$ 1,246	$ 1,303	$ 1,412	$ 1,472	$ 1,534
CHANGE IN WORKING CAPITAL	$ (11,856)	$ (1,462)	$ (1,516)	$ (1,578)	$ (1,642)	$ (409)	$ (418)	$ 929	$ 981	$ 1,074
CAPITAL EXPENDITURES	$ (5,308)	$ (1,100)	$ (611)	$ (622)	$ (633)	$ (644)	$ (606)	$ (1,018)	$ (481)	$ (469)
VALUE OF EQUITY SHARES	$ -	$ -	$ -	$ -	$ -	$ -	$ -	$ -	$ -	$ -
VALUE OF KNOW-HOW	$ 250	$ 300	$ 350	$ 400	$ 450	$ 400	$ 400	$ 350	$ 350	$ 300
AFTER TAX CASH FLOWS	$ (20,966)	$ 7,953	$ 14,330	$ 17,440	$ 20,440	$ 21,840	$ 21,948	$ 17,526	$ 17,126	$ 15,667

BEFORE TAX IRR	70.20%
BEFORE TAX NPV	$ 32,557
AFTER TAX IRR	64.00%
AFTER TAX NPV	$ 26,744

Treatment of AIDS-Related Cryptosporidial Diarrhea with IGX-CP, a Compound Prepared from Egg Yolks of Hyperimmunized Hens

Rosemary Soave, M.D.

New York Hospital-Cornell Medical Center

New York, New York

ABSTRACT

Background. Cryptosporidiosis is a major cause of diarrhea in AIDS patients. We evaluated a new compound (IgX-CP), prepared from egg yolks of hyperimmunized hens and containing anti-*Cryptosporidium* antibodies, as treatment for cryptosporidial diarrhea in patients with AIDS.

Methods. We conducted an open-label study in 24 patient with AIDS and cryptosporidiosis who were free of enteropathogens. Patients received either a low dose (2.06×10^6 AU/day) or a high dose (4.12×10^6 AU/day) IgX-CP and famotidine 40 mg/day for up to 6 weeks.

Results. Of the 11 evaluable patients receiving low dose IGX-CP, six had a decrease in daily frequency of bowel movements at Week 3; at Week 6, six of eight patients demonstrated a decrease. In the high dose group, three of four evaluable patients had a decrease at Week 3, and one of five had a decrease at Week 6. The daily frequency of liquid stools also decreased in both dose groups. Four of 16 evaluable patients were classified as clinical responders after at least 6 weeks of treatment. Complete parasitologic response (oocyst eradication) occurred in only one patient receiving low dose IGX-CP. Treatment with IGX-CP was relatively safe but was poorly tolerated in some patients because of a feeling of satiety.

Conclusions. IGX-CP in combination with famotidine is safe for use in this patient population. We observed an overall favorable effect of IGX-CP on diarrhea and a lesser effect on oocyst eradication. The high lipid content of the drug may limit tolerability of higher doses. The results indicate that IGX-CP is a promising treatment for cryptosporidiosis in patients with AIDS and should be studied in larger, placebo-controlled trials.

INTRODUCTION

Cryptosporidium parvum is an important cause of enterocolitis and diarrhea in humans and significantly contributes to morbidity and mortality in AIDS patients. In immunocompetent hosts, cryptosporidiosis lasts an average of 10 to 14 days, with stool oocyst shedding persisting for approximately 2 weeks following clinical resolution. In AIDS patients, the infection escalates in severity, with frequent, voluminous, and watery bowel movements (up to 25 stools per day in a volume of up to 20 liters per day). Profound weight loss can occur, and associated symptoms include cramping upper abdominal pain, nausea, and headaches. The typical course of the infection in AIDS patients is persistence of symptoms, with death occurring within months, typically due to other opportunistic infections or neoplasms.

The prevalence of cryptosporidiosis in AIDS patients in the United States has been reported to be as high as 10 to 20 percent (Laughon 1988, Johanson 1990, Juranek 1995). Similar prevalence rates have been recorded in Britain (Connolly 1988, Blanshard 1992). Cryptospordidiosis prevalence is also high in developing countries, especially in children (Das 1996). In Africa and Haiti, *Cryptosporidium* is considered the most important cause of diarrhea (Wittner 1993).

Presently, no chemotherapeutic agent has been demonstrated to have reliable preventive or treatment efficacy against cryptospordiosis. Preliminary data suggest that passive immune transfer may be effective in treating this condition. Several recent preclinical studies have provided evidence that both polyclonal and monoclonal *C.parvum*-neutralizing antibodies may significantly reduce the severity of disease caused by this parasite (Tzipori 1986, Tzipori 1987, Fayer 1989a, 1989b, Arrowood 1989, Riggs 1989, Unger 1990, Nord 1990). Treatment of cryptosporidiosis with hyperimmune bovine colostrums (HBC), evaluated in compassionate trials in AIDS patients (Ungar 1990, Nord 1990), has been demonstrated to resolve diarrhea within a few days.

The use of eggs from hyperimmunized hens (i.e., hens hyperimmunized with *C.parvum* oocyst antigens) is an alternative to the production of HBC suitable for passive transfer. Eggs laid by hens hyperimmunized with *C.parvum* oocyst antigens have high anti-*C.parvum* activity (similar to HBC) and have been shown to produce significant parasite reduction when administered to *C.parvum*-infected-neonatal mice (Cama 1991). Egg production is constant, and large-scale production and storage are feasible, even under conditions likely to exist in developing countries where cryptosporidiosis is prevalent. IGX-CP, which is prepared from yolks of eggs laid by hyperimmunized hens, contains anti-*Cryptosporidium* antibodies and is being developed for the treatment of cryptosporidial enteritis in patients with AIDS. (*should we limit this to AIDS patients?*) We conducted a small clinical trial aimed at obtaining preliminary data on the safety, tolerance, and efficacy of two dose levels of IGX-CP (2.06 x 10^6 AU/day or 4.12 x 10^6 AU/day) in the treatment of cryptospordial diarrhea in patients with AIDS.

METHODS

The study was conducted at the New York Hospital-Cornell Medical Center in New York City. Patients eligible for study participation met the Center for Disease Control and Prevention criteria for AIDS and had a diagnosis of cryptosporidiosis (as defined by chronic diarrhea, i.e., an average of three or more liquid/semi-formed bowel movements per day for a minimum of 2 weeks, and the presence of *Cryptosporidium* oocytes in stool within 7 days of study entry). Patients were not to have any enteropathogens other than *Cryptosporidium*. Eligible patients also had a CD4+ count of <150/mm3 and were not receiving any other medication for treatment of cryptosporidiosis (antiretroviral and antidiarrheal regimens were to be stable).

Patients were excluded if they had, among other factors, a history of intestinal Kaposi's sarcoma, intestinal hycobacterium avium-intracellulare infection, or cytomegalovirus colitis; had used within the 30 day prior to study entry any investigational drug or other therapy with potential activity against cryptosporidiosis (e.g., arithromycin, spiramycin, paromomycin); had a known hypersensitivity to eggs or to famotidine, or had an active opportunistic infection requiring systemic antimicrobial therapy.

The protocol and statement of informed consent and subsequent amendments to these were reviewed and approved by the New York Hospital-Cornell Medical Center Committee on Human Rights

Research. In addition, approval was given to extend treatment beyond 6 weeks on a individual patient basis. All patients gave written informed consent.

As amended, the protocol allowed 15 patients to receive a low dose (2.06 x 10^6 AU/day) of IGX-CP, and because this dose was adequately tolerated, 15 patients were to be enrolled to receive a higher dose (4.12 x 10^6 AU/day). Patients also received 20-mg famotidine tablets (Pepcid®) twice a day. The duration of treatment was to be a maximum of 6 weeks (the protocol initially proposed 3 weeks of treatment with IGX-CP). At the end of 3 weeks of treatment, patients who successfully tolerated IGX-CP without any toxicity, had not changed clinically, or had shown improvement and wished to stay on the product, were eligible for continuation on IGX-CP for up to a total of four weeks, or in the case of patients treated compassionately, for longer.

IGX-CP is a frozen (20°C) solution composed of hyperimmune egg yolk (50%), purified water (45%), and sucrose (5%). A 7-day supply of IGX-CP was provided at each weekly visit. Individual doses were provided frozen in patient bags, containing IGX-CP equivalent to 412,000 AU each. Patients were to self-administer IGX-CP, 412,000 AU (one bag or approximately 75g or 70 to 100 mL) or 824,000 AU (two bags or approximately 150g or 140 to 200mL), orally every 4 hours while awake (from 6 a.m. to 10 p.m.) five times daily, for a total of 2.06 x 10^6 AU/day or 4.12 x 10^6 AU/day. Each day, patients were to thaw the following day's medication by placing the bags containing frozen IGX-CP in the refrigerator (4°C) for 8 to 24 hours prior to use. Pepcid 20 mg was provided in manufacturer blister packs to be taken orally twice a day. Pepcid dosing was to begin 1 week prior to initiation of IGX-CP.

Patients were seen weekly during the study and at 2 weeks after treatment for evaluations of safety, tolerability, and efficacy. Patients underwent physical examinations and evaluation for adverse events, and they responded to an Associated Symptoms Questionnaire, which evaluated nausea, vomiting, abdominal pain, urgency, incontinence, and night-time bowel movements. Patients also maintained a daily diary to record the frequency of bowel movements and stool consistency beginning 1 week prior to treatment and throughout the study.

Patients who received study medication are included in the analysis of safety. Safety was evaluated on the frequency and types of adverse events, results of the Associated Symptoms Questionnaire, and clinically significant laboratory results. Efficacy analysis was performed on all patients who were treated for at least 2 weeks during the trial. Subsets of patients who were treated for 3 and 6 weeks were analyzed separately. An intent-to-treat analysis was also performed, using all patients who met the entry criteria and received any test medication. [*The New England Journal will probably want to know the statistical tests used, but I did not have this information. Is it available? Or should we just say, "Because the sample size was so small, no formal statistical testing was performed"?*]

The primary efficacy parameters are stool cryptosporidial oocyst grade (quantified on a scale from 0-4, based upon numbers of acid fast cryptosporidial oocysts seen with microscopy) and frequency of daily bowel movements and bowel consistency based upon physician review of patient diaries. Patients were classified as responders based on parasitologic and/or clinical response.

Parasitologic response was evaluated by comparing stool oocyst quantitation on the last day of treatment to baseline. Parasitologic response is defined as follows: *eradication*-two consecutive stool examinations, obtained at least one week apart, negative for *Cryptosporidium* oocysts; *substantial reduction*-decrease in oocyst quantity by at least p grades ("many" to "few" or "rare"; "moderate" to "rare"); *persistence*-no substantial reduction or an increase in *Cryptosporidium* oocysts.

Clinical response was evaluated by comparing the average number of daily bowel movements over the week prior to start of IGX-CP to the average number over the week prior to the last day of treatment. Clinical response is defined as follows: *complete response*-clinical resolution of diarrhea to one to three (predominantly formed) bowel movements per day; *partial response*-50% or more reduction in average number of daily bowel movements but still over three bowel movements per day, or change in stool consistency to predominantly (>75%) formed; *No response*-50% or less decrease in average daily bowel movement frequency.

Secondary efficacy parameters were the patient's global assessment of treatment score (on a 7-item scale of movement) and body weight at the end of treatment.

RESULTS

Sixty-two patients were screened and 24 patients were enrolled into the study. All patients met the inclusion and exclusion criteria, with the exception of five patients who had laboratory abnormalities at screening that were outside the range specified in the original protocol. These patients were enrolled at our discretion with study monitor approval. The first 15 patients were assigned to receive the low dose treatment (2.06 x 10^6 AU/day); nine patients then were assigned to receive the high dose treatment (4.12 x 10^6 AU/day).

Twenty-four of the patients were male. Twenty of the 24 patients (83%) were Caucasian and four (17%) were Hispanic. The mean age was 38.1 years, ranging from 30 to 49 years. Mean body weight was 64.1 kg (range, 49.1 to 84.1 kg), and the mean height was 176.2 cm (range, 161 to 185 cm).

All patients were HIV-seropositive, with a mean CD4+ count of 32.3/mm^3, ranging from 0 to 124/mm^3. Mean Kamofsky Performance Status score at baseline was 74.6 (range, 60 to 90). Mean duration of cryptosporidiosis at study entry was 8.6 months (range, 1 to 35.3 months). According to interviews, patients were averaging 7.5 stools/day in the 2 weeks prior to study (range, 3 to 24 stools/day). Patients were in a late stage of disease as evidenced by a history of numerous other opportunistic infections other than cryptosporidiosis.

Ten patients discontinued study participation prior to completion of the protocol. Eight patients (4 at the low-dose level and 4 at the high-dose level) discontinued during the first week of treatment. Reasons for discontinuation within the first week of treatment were intercurrent or concurrent illness (one patient); adverse experience (one request/refusal (two patients). In addition, two patients discontinued from the study because of treatment failure after at least 3 full weeks of therapy but before completing 6 weeks of therapy. The drop out rate in the high dose group (six of nine patients) was higher than that in the low dose group (four of 15 patients).

Compliance with the treatment was based on the number of doses reported to be taken (from the patients' study medication record). In the low dose group, the overall mean dose consumed during the 6-week study was 33.4 bags (95.4 percent compliance). In the high dose group, the overall mean dose consumed during the 6-week study was 41.9 bags (59.9 percent compliance). Four patients received extended treatment on a compassionate basis beyond the 6-week period; only one of these patients received the high dose level. The duration of extended compassionate treatment ranged from 2 to 30 weeks.

Among the 11 evaluable patients who received low dose IGX-CP, six patients (54.5 percent) had a decrease in their frequency of daily bowel movements relative to baseline after 3 weeks of treatment (the decrease ranged from 13 to 61.8 percent) (Table 1). After 6 weeks of low-dose treatment, six of the eight patients (75 percent) who were still in the study demonstrated a decrease (range, 1 to 60 percent). The daily frequency of liquid stools decreased from baseline in eight of the 11 low dose patients (73 percent) after 3 weeks of treatment and in six of eight (75 percent) after 6 weeks.

Among the patients receiving high dose IGX-CP for whom data were available, the frequency of daily bowel movements decreased from baseline in three of four patients (75 percent) after 3 weeks of treatment (the decrease ranged from 5 to 38 percent) (Table 1). Following 6 weeks of treatment, two of five (40 percent) high dose patients demonstrated a decrease in the frequency of daily bowel movements (the decrease was 17 and 48 percent respectively). The daily frequency of liquid stools after 3 weeks on the high dose decreased in three of four patients (75 percent) relative to baseline; only one of five high dose patients (20 percent) still demonstrated a decrease after 6 weeks.

Four of the 16 evaluable patients (25 percent) were classified as clinical responders; three were in the low dose group and one was in the high dose group. Clinical response occurred after at least 6 weeks of treatment and was noted even after 1 month of treatment for one patient and after 2 weeks of treatment for another.

Parasitologic response was evaluated by comparing oocyst grade on the last day of treatment to baseline. Eradication occurred in one patient after 1 week on low dose IGX-CP. Two patients experienced substantial reductions at the end of treatment, one in the low dose group after 36 weeks of treatment and one in the high dose group after 12 weeks of treatment. Stool oocyst grade decreased by 1 point in five of 11 (45 percent) patients receiving low dose IGX-CP after 3 weeks of treatment. After 6 weeks, a decrease of 1 point was observed in only two of the eight (25 percent) low dose patients who were still in the study.

Body weight gain of at least 1 kg occurred in only one of the 10 patients (10 percent) receiving low dose IGX-CP at Week 3. At Week 6, four of the seven patients (57 percent) still in the study had a weight gain of at least 1 kg relative to baseline. Among the patients receiving the high dose, two of four (50 percent) gained at least 1 kg after 3 weeks of treatment; after 6 weeks, two of five patients (40 percent) had a weight gain of at least 1 kg relative to baseline.

After 3 weeks of treatment, four of the 11 evaluable low dose patients (36 percent) indicated that they had felt either slightly or moderately improved in the past week. After 6 weeks of treatment, three of seven patients receiving low dose IGX-CP (43 percent) indicated that they had felt either slightly or markedly improved in the past week. Among patients receiving high dose IGX-CP, two of five evaluable patients (40 percent) indicated that they felt either slightly or moderately improved during Week 3; after 6 weeks of treatment three patients (60 percent) indicated that they had felt either slightly or moderately improved in the past week.

Results of the intent-to-treat analysis of efficacy were similar to those obtained for the evaluable patient population.

Thirteen of the patients reported 16 adverse events, nine of which occurred during treatment with IGX-CP. One of the events, acute pancreatitis in a patient receiving low-dose IGX-CP, was considered possibly related to treatment. Pancreas divisum was the likely cause of this event; however, the possibility that IGX-CP exacerbated continuation of treatment. There were no laboratory abnormalities that lead to a reduction in dosage and no patient discontinued from the study because of an adverse laboratory event.

No deaths were reported during the study; however, seven patients died following termination of treatment (4.5 to 8 weeks after the last dose). None of the deaths were considered to be treatment related, and all were a result of aggressive end-stage AIDS.

Four patients discontinued from the study because of adverse events, although adverse event was given as the primary reason for discontinuation in only one patient. Adverse events contributing to patient discontinuation included preclusion of oral intake because of pneumonia and severe cough, initiation of total parenteral nutrition, and inadequate response to study drug with initiation of alternative anticryptosporidial therapy.

Several patients were unable to tolerate IGX-CP, especially in the high dose group. They reported satiety, inability to continue ingesting IGX-CP, "fullness" and "bloating." We did not consider these symptoms to represent adverse tolerance of all foods. Overall, it was estimated that the maximal tolerated dose of IGX-CP was six to seven bags (412,000 AU each) per day, equivalent to 2.88×10^6 AU per day.

Patients completed an Associated Symptoms Questionnaire on a weekly basis. Table 2 presents the questionnaire results.

DISCUSSION

Cryptosporidiosis in patients with AIDS is a severe, debilitating, and life-threatening gastrointestinal disease. The mainstay of therapy remains hydration and nutritional support. Many pharmacologic agents have been used with variable success (Ritchie 1994). Nonspecific antidiarrheal treatment has included loperamide and opiates, nonsteroidal anti-inflammatory therapy with indomethacin, and peptidomimetic therapy with somatostatin analogs such as octreotide and vapreotide. Numerous antiportozoal and antibiotic agents have been used either because of their success in treating other opportunistic infections or because they have shown activity against Cryptosporidium in-vitro. The macrolide antibiotics spiramycin, erythromycin, and azithromycin and the aminoglycoside antibiotic arithromycin have shown limited effectiveness in decreasing symptoms or fecal oocyte excretion in AIDS patients with cryptosporidiosis. Treatment of HIV infection with zidovudine therapy has resulted in improvement in intestinal cryptosporidiosis in some patients with AIDS (Greenberg 1989, Connolly 1988).

Passive immune transfer using hyperimmune bovine colostrums (HBC) and a related therapeutic modality of oral bovine transfer factor (an extract of lymphocytes from calves inoculated with *Cryptosporidium*) have been studied in small numbers of AIDS patients with intestinal cryptosporidiosis (Louie 1987, McMeeking 1990, Ungar 1990, Nord 1990). These therapies appear to benefit some patients. The difficulty in producing such agents on a large scale and of standardizing their potency will make it difficult to perform large-scale controlled clinical trials and activity than HBC. Faster and larger scale production should be possible, and there may be higher uniformity in antibody activity. Significant parasite reduction has been demonstrated with hyperimmune yolks in neonatal mice infected with *C.parvum* (Cama 1991.)

IGX-CP is prepared from yolks of eggs laid by hyperimmunized hens and contains anti-*Cryptosporidium* antibodies. This is the first study evaluating the potential of IGX-CP as a treatment of cryptosporidial enteritis in patients with AIDS. The study was an open-label, ascending dose, pilot study of two dose levels of IgX-CP given for 6 weeks in patients with AIDS and cryptosporidial diarrhea. Patients were evaluated weekly to assess the safety, tolerance and efficacy of the treatment.

Twenty-four male patients were enrolled in the study. The first 15 patients received a low dose of IGX-CP (2.06 x 10⁶ AU/day), and the next nine patients received a high dose (4.12 x 10⁶ AU/day). Sixteen of the 24 patients completed at least 2 weeks of treatment; eight patients discontinued within the first week. Mean compliance during the 6-week study was 95 percent at the low dose level and 60 percent at the high dose level. Satiety, which occurred only at the high dose, was the only reported cause of intolerance and was significant factor in both the dropout rate and the low compliance rate of that group. We believe that the feeling of satiety in these patients was due to the high lipid content of the original formulation of IGX-CP. Reducing the lipid content would enable a higher dose of antibodies or Aus to be delivered to the patient each day. Future studies of this IGX-CP will employ a new formulation with a lower lipid content, and patients will be administered 8.24×10^6 AU/day, which is double the antibody level of the compound used in this study.

Sixteen patients completed at least 3 weeks of therapy and were therefore considered evaluable for efficacy. Of those, four (25 percent) met the study criteria for a clinical and/or parasitologic response.

Patients receiving either 3 weeks or 6 weeks of therapy: bowel movement frequency was reduced in 60 percent of patients completing 3 weeks of therapy and in 67 percent of patients completing 6 weeks of therapy. Although the small sample size limits the analysis, there was no evident additional benefit to increasing the dose of IGX-CP beyond 2.06×10^6 AU/day.

Although the study results were promising, three aspects of the study design limit their interpretability, especially with regard to evaluating efficacy: there was no placebo control group, the study was not blinded, and few patients were studies. Cryptosporidiosis has a variable course in patients with AIDS and can resolve spontaneously in 20 percent or more of patients (McGowan 1993, Flanigan 1992, Blanshard 1992). The clinical course tends to be more severe in patients with lower CD4+ counts, and in patients with CD4+ counts as low as those in this study, spontaneous remission would be rare. Most patients in this study were also on antiretroviral therapy, which can also be associated with resolution of intestinal cryptosporidiosis in patients with AIDS (Flanigan 1992, Greenberg

1989). Including antiretroviral and antimicrobial therapy) and severity of disease (including CD4+ counts and concomitant opportunistic infections), and large enough to demonstrate a drug effect in a disease which has a greatly variable natural history.

CONCLUSIONS

In conclusion, IGX-CP in combination with famotidine is safe for use in this patient population. The high lipid content may limit tolerability of doses greater than 2.88×10^6 AU/day. For the doses and duration of IGX-CP used in this trial, we observed an overall favorable effect on diarrhea and a lesser effect on oocyst eradication. These results indicate that the maximum tolerated dosing regimen of 2.88×10^6 AU/day should be studied in larger, placebo-controlled trials to evaluate its efficacy for the treatment of intestinal cryptosporidiosis in patients with AIDS.

REFERENCES

Orowood MJ, Mead JR, Mahrt JL, Sterling CR. Effects of immune colostrums and orally administered ....porozoite monoclonal antibodies on the outcome of *Cryptosporidium parvum* infections in neonatal mice. Immun 1989;57:2283-8.

Manshard C, Jackson AM, Shanson DC, Grancis N, Gazzard BG. Cryptosporidiosis in HIV-seropositive patients. NE J Med 1992; 116:840-2.

Cama VA, Sterling CR. Hyperimmune hens as a novel source of anti-*Cryptosporidium* antibodies suitable for passive immune transfer . J Protozol 1991;38:42s-43s.

Connolly GM, Dryden MS, Shanson DC, Gazzard BG. *Cryptosporidial* diarrhea in AIDS and its treatment. Gut 19988;29:593-7.

Das P. *Cryptosporidium* related diarrhea. Indian J Med Res 1996;104:86-95.

Thayer R, Perryman LE, Riggs MW. Hyperimmune bovine colostrums neutralizes *Cryptosporidium* sporozoites and protects mice against oocyst challenge. J Parasitol 1989a;75:151-3.

Thayer R, Andrews C, Ungar BLP, et al. Efficacy of hyperimmune colostrums for prophylaxis of cryptosporidiosis in hyperimmune calves. J Parasitol 1989b;75:393-7.

Flanigan T, Whalen C, Turner J, et al. Cryptosporidium infection and CD4 counts. Ann Intern Med 1992;116:840-2.

Greenberg RE, Mir R, Bank S, Siegal FP. Resolution of intestinal cryptosporidiosis after treatment of AIDS with AT. Gastroenterology 1989:97:1327-30.0

Johanson JF, Sonnenberg A. Efficient management of diarrhea in the acquired immunodeficiency syndrome (AIDS). A medical decision analysis. Ann Intern Med 1990;112:942-8.

Juranek DD. Cryptosporidiosis: sources of infection and guidelines for prevention. Clin Infect Dis 1995;21(Suppl 1):S57-61.

Laughon BE, Druckman DA, Vernon A, et al. Prevalence of enteric pathogens in homosexual men with and without acquired immunodeficiency syndrome. Gastroenterology 1988;94:984-93.

Riggs MW, Perryman LE. Infectivity and neutralization of *Cryptosporidium pavrum* sporozoites. Infect Immun 1987;55:2081-7.

Riggs MW, McGuire TC, Mason PH, Perryman LE. Neutrlization sensitive epitopes are exposed on the surface of infectious Cryptosporidium parvum sporozoites. J Immunol 1989;143:1340-5.

Ritchie DJ, Becker ES. Update on the management of intestinal cryptosporidiosis in AIDS. Ann Pharmacother 1994;28:767-78.

Tzipori S, Roberton D, Cooper DA, White L. Chronic cryptosporidial diarrhea and hyperimmune cow colostrums [letter]. Lancet 1987;ii:344-5.

Ungar BLP, Ward DJ, Fayer R, Quinn CA. Cessation of *Cryptosporidium*-associated diarrhea in an acquired immunodeficiency syndrome patient after treatment with hyperimmune bovine colostrums. Gastroenterology 1990;98:486-9.

Wittner M, Tanowitz HB, Weiss LM. Parasitic infections in AIDS patients. Infect Dis Clin North Am 1993;7:569-86.

Table 1

Change in Total Number of Bowel Movements Relative to Baseline After Treatment with IGX-CP.

Total Number of Bowel Movements per Week and Percent Change from Baseline

Patientnt No.	Baseline	Week 3		Week 6*		2 Week Follow-Up	
Low dose group (2.06 x 10⁶ AU/day)							
01	83	68	-18.1	n/a†	n/a	57	-31.3
02	33	34	+3.0	29	-12.1	14	-57.6
04	51	61	-19.6	50	-2.0	n/a	n/a
06	37	44	+19.0	n/a	n/a	52	+40.5
08	42	23	-45.2	26	-38.1	n/a	n/a
010‡	75	48	-36.0	30	-60	34	-54.7
011§	34	29	-14.7	n/a	n/a	13	-61.8
012	46	40	-13.0	25	-45.7	40	-13.0
013	25	29	+16.0	54	+116.0	53	+112.0
014	47	38	-19.2	43	-8.5	n/a	n/a
015	26	62	+138.5	38	+46.2	n/a	n/a
High dose group (4.12 x 10⁶ AU/day)							
018	38	36	-5.3	50	+31.6	45	+18.4
019	78	48	-38.5	95	+21.8	133	+70.5
021	34	n/a	n/a	28	-17.7	n/a	n/a
023	37	27	-27.0	19	-48.7	n/a	n/a
024	63	64	+1.6	72	+14.3	64	+1.6

* Or end of treatment if that occurred before Week 6 (but after Week 3)

† n/a, data not available.

‡ At the 1-month follow-up evaluation, Patient 010 reported 46 total bowel movements per week (-38.7 percent change from baseline).

§ At the 1-month follow-up evaluation, Patient 011 reported 27 total bowel movements per week (-20.6 percent change from baseline).

Table 2

Number of Patients with a Change in Daily Frequency of Associated Symptoms from Baseline to End of Treatment.

Symptom	Decrease	No Change	Increase	Data not available
Nausea	4	10	7	3
Vomiting	2	10	9	3
Abdominal pain	10	7	4	3
Urgency	5	11	5	3
Incontinence	3	11	7	3
Night time bowel movements	4	13	4	3

Attachments: Question 8

Treatment of chronic hepadnavirus infection in a woodchuck animal model
with an inhibitor of protein folding and trafficking

Reprinted with permission from
Nature Medicine, Volume 4, Number 5,   May 1998

Treatment of chronic hepadnavirus infection in a woodchuck animal model with an inhibitor of protein folding and trafficking

Timothy M. Block[1], Xuanyong Lu[1], Anand S. Mehta[2], Baruch S. Blumberg[2,3], Bud Tennant[4], Mathew Ebling[1], Brent Korba[5], David M. Lansky[6], Gary S. Jacob[6] & Raymond A. Dwek[2]

[1]Viral Hepatitis Group, Kimmel Cancer Center, Jefferson Medical College, Philadelphia, Pennsylvania, 19107, USA
[2]The Glycobiology Institute, Department of Biochemistry, Oxford University, Oxford, OX13QU, UK
[3]Fox Chase Cancer Center, Philadelphia, Pennsylvania 19111, USA
[4]Department of Clinical Sciences, College of Veterinary Medicine, Cornell University, Ithaca, New York 14853, USA
[5]Division of Virology, Georgetown University College of Medicine, Rockville, Maryland, USA
[6]Monsanto Company, 800 N. Lindberg Boulevard, St. Louis, Missouri, 63167, USA
Correspondence should be addressed to T.M.B., A.S.M. or R.A.D.

A novel strategy for anti-viral intervention of hepatitis B virus (HBV) through the disruption of the proper folding[1] and transport[2] of the hepadnavirus glycoproteins is described. Laboratory reared woodchucks chronically infected with woodchuck hepatitis virus (WHV) were treated with N-nonyl-deoxynojirimycin (N-nonyl-DNJ), an inhibitor of the endoplasmic reticulum (ER) α-glucosidases. The woodchucks experienced significant dose dependent decreases in enveloped WHV, resulting in undetectable amounts in some cases. The reduction in viremia correlated with the levels of hyperglucosylated glycan in the serum of treated animals. This correlation supports the mechanism of action associated with the drug and highlights the extreme sensitivity of the virus to this type of glycan inhibitor[1,2]. At N-nonyl-DNJ concentrations that prevented WHV secretion, the glycosylation of most serum glycoproteins appeared unaffected, suggesting great selectivity for this class of therapeutics. Indeed, this may account for the low toxicity of the compound over the treatment period. We provide the first evidence that glucosidase inhibitors can be used *in vivo* to alter specific steps in the N-linked glycosylation pathway and that this inhibition has anti-viral effects.

More than 350 million people worldwide are chronically infected with hepatitis B virus (HBV) and as many as 150 million may die from liver disease in the absence of intervention[3]. Promising nucleoside therapies are under development, but virus resistant mutants are frequent[4] and alternatives are needed. Our studies of HBV glycobiology suggested a novel approach in which the inhibition of the initial steps in glycan processing results in the misfolding and aberrant intracellular trafficking of the HBV M protein[1,2], thereby preventing the formation of infectious enveloped virus. The exquisite sensitivity of HBV to alterations in the envelope proteins induced by α-glucosidase inhibitors might allow antiviral activity at doses that do not affect host glycosylation. Here we report proof of this concept in a woodchuck animal model of HBV infection.

Woodchuck hepatitis virus (WHV) is a naturally occurring hepadnavirus pathogen of woodchucks[5]. WHV shares biochemical properties with human HBV such as glycosylated envelope proteins; sensitivity to glucosidase inhibitors *in vitro* (unpublished data); and the capacity to establish chronic infections in woodchucks that resemble the human HBV infection in so far as they cause chronic hepatitis and hepatocellular carcinoma[5]. Woodchucks with chronic WHV infection are recognized as good animal models in which to test HBV anti-viral agents. Nucleoside analogues, for example, displaying efficacy against WHV in woodchucks have been shown to be effective against human HBV in clinical settings[6]. In these studies, drug efficacy is the ability to reduce WHV viremia. We now demonstrate that inhibitors of ER glucosidases can also be used to reduce the amount of WHV viremia in chronically infected woodchucks.

Twenty, one-year-old woodchucks, inoculated with WHV at birth[7] were shown to be chronically infected with WHV by the finding of serum viral DNA[5]. The 20 animals were divided into five treatment groups. Placebo or the α-glucosidase inhibitor N-nonyl-DNJ was administered orally in aqueous suspension by dose syringe twice daily for four weeks. N-nonyl-DNJ is the 9-carbon alkyl derivative of deoxynojirimycin (DNJ) and has been shown to be 100–200 times more potent than N-butyl deoxynojirimycin (NB-DNJ) in inhibiting HBV in cell based assays (manuscript in preparation). There was no clinical, biochemical or hematological evidence of drug toxicity and the body weights of N-nonyl-DNJ treated woodchucks were similar to placebo treated controls (see methods). Serum WHV DNA was measured weekly by dot-blot hybridization during the four week treatment period. No significant differences in the serum levels of total WHV DNA were observed between drug treated and control groups. The α-glucosidase inhibitor NB-DNJ has previously been shown to prevent virion morphogenesis and secretion, but in contrast to other hepadnaviral inhibitors, not viral DNA synthesis[1]. Since only enveloped viral DNA is infectious, the amount of viral DNA contained within viral envelopes in the presence of drug was determined by polymerase chain reaction (PCR) amplification of viral DNA following immunoprecipitation (IP) with rabbit antiserum hyperimmune against the WHV surface antigen. The IP-PCR method is routinely used in the analysis of enveloped HBV secretion from cells treated with imino sugars[8].

All animals in groups 1 & 2 (placebo and 6.25 mg/kg N-noyl-DNJ twice a day respectively) experienced an upward trend in the amount of WHV enveloped DNA in their serum. However, groups 3, 4 and 5 (12.5, 25 and 50 mg/kg twice a day respectively) showed a sharp reduction in virus, with the exception of animal F271. These reductions were statistically significant (P = 0.0136 for all treatment doses) with a pronounced dose-dependent response. The difference between placebo and group 5 was greatest (p = 0.001). Two of the four animals (designated with an asterisk) in groups 3, 4 and 5 contained no PCR detectable enveloped WHV DNA by the fourth week of treatment (animals F392, M404, F393, M414, M363 and F402) (Fig. 1a). Although all of the animals in the higher dose groups displayed reductions in viremia, responsiveness varied, as has been found to some degree with other drug studies using the woodchuck model[9]. As these are outbred animals, this variation may be the result of genetic heterogeneity within the woodchuck population. It is interesting to note that the reductions in viremia seen here are similar to that seen with the nucleoside analogue lamivudine in humans after 28 days of therapy[10]. Consistent with other inhibitors of hepadnaviruses[9,10], after treatment ceased viral titers in the majority of animals returned to pre-treatment levels (data not shown).

The physical state of the viral DNA, which is undetectable by the immuno-PCR assay (but is seen by dot blot hybridization), was determined by ultracentrifugation through a discontinuous sucrose density gradient. Briefly, serum from animal M286 before and after treatment was resolved by sedimentation through sucrose gradients—shown to resolve infectious, enveloped virions from nucleo-

---

Fig. 1 Enveloped WHV DNA serum levels during and after N-nonyl-DNJ treatment. Woodchucks chronically infected with WHV received placebo 6.25, 12.5, 25 or 50 mg/kg of pure N-nonyl-DNJ twice daily for four weeks. **a,** Change in enveloped WHV levels. Animals in which no enveloped WHV DNA was detected are indicated by the asterisk. **b,** Change in enveloped WHV levels as a function of serum N-nonyl-DNJ concentration. Each animal, represented by a number (representing dose group) and a letter (individual animal), is plotted along the X-axis based on its four week average level of serum N-nonyl-DNJ, and on the Y-axis based on relative change in serum enveloped WHV. Animals in which no enveloped WHV DNA was detected are indicated by the asterisk. Animal identities: Placebo (group 1): 1a (F343), 1b (F301), 1c (F304), 1d (M364); 6.25 mg (group 2): 2 (F283), 3 (M285), 2c (M305), 2d (F391); 12.5 mg (group 3): 3a (M256), 3b (F271), 3c (F392), 3d (M404); 25 mg (group 4): 4a (M322), 4b (F163), 4c (F393), 4d (M414); 50 mg (group 5): 5a (F231), 5b (M286), 5c (F363), 5d (F402).

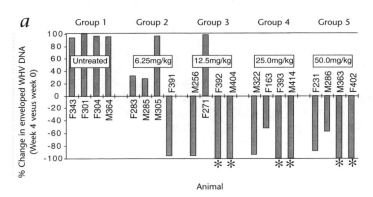

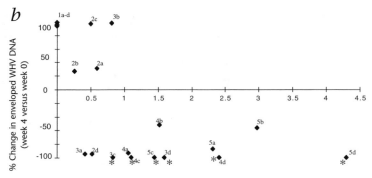

capsids[2]. The viral DNA remaining in the serum of animal M286 after treatment with the glucosidase inhibitor did not appear to be contained within intact virions, but rather was present predominantly within non-enveloped nucleocapsids (manuscript in preparation). Since previous tissue culture work has shown that glucosidase inhibitors cause a build up of viral DNA within the infected cell[1], it is possible that intracellular viral DNA, lacking envelopes, which has accumulated in the hepatocytes of treated animals is discharged into the serum[11-13]. This discharge may occur more easily in woodchucks due to the core particles' cytoplasmic location, as opposed to the nuclear location found in human hepatitis B virus[14]. Also, as an infected hepatocyte contains many more core particles than it secretes fully enveloped viral particles (unpublished data), the lysis of only a few infected cells could produce this background of non-enveloped viral DNA.

Some of the animal to animal variability observed may be attributable to variability in the amount of serum N-nonyl-DNJ in each animal. The change in enveloped WHV DNA in each animal, after four weeks of treatment with either placebo or increasing amounts of N-nonyl-DNJ, as a function of serum drug concentration, shows that animals with little or no serum N-nonyl-DNJ experienced an increase in enveloped WHV DNA, whereas those with more than 1 µg/ml usually experienced a 10–100 fold decrease, with some animals having no detectable enveloped WHV (asterisk) as determined by IP-PCR. Drug dosage did not always correlate with drug serum levels, as was the case for animal 5c (M363) which is from the highest dose group but with only a mid-level serum concentration (compare Fig. 1a & b). This is indicative of animal to animal variability in drug bioavailability.

One result of inhibiting glycosylation processing at the ER glucosidase step is that secreted glycoproteins may contain hyperglucosylated structures. This is demonstrated (Fig. 2, inset) for untreated and treated HepG2 cells in which the secreted glycoproteins from glucosidase inhibited cells contain a small amount of hyperglucosylated glycans. Oligosaccharide sequence analysis confirms the highlighted peak (Fig. 2 inset, arrow) as the $Glc_3Man_7GlcNAc_2$ structure. This structure represents approximately 10% of the total glycan pool from the culture medium of HepG2 cells that had been subjected to glucosidase inhibition. Oligosaccharide sequencing also reveals that the other structures associated with the profile are complex type glycans, thought to arise from the use of a non glucosidase mediated pathway (the endomannosidase) in the Golgi apparatus[15]. The glycan profiles from the serum of animal M404 pre-treatment and post-treatment (Fig. 2) show that the $Glc_3Man_7GlcNAc_2$ structure also appears in the glycan profile of serum from N-nonyl-DNJ treated animals. The drug has very little effect on the total glycosylation of serum glycoprotein (Fig. 2). However, the effect on virus secretion was dramatic (Fig. 1a), highlighting the extreme sensitivity of HBV to these types of inhibitors and indicating that only minor changes in glycosylation are required to prevent HBV secretion. Note that the very minor change in glycosylation seen in treated animals also implies that the inability to immunoprecipitate virus in Fig. 1a is not the result of changes in the glycosylation of the WHV S protein. Consistent with this, and our finding that the HBV S protein secreted from glucosidase inhibited cells contain complex glycan[1], is the observation that the WHV S protein from untreated and treated animals migrates with the same mobility on SDS PAGE gels, indicating that its glycosylation is unchanged.

The relationship between the amount of hyperglucosylated glycan and the change in viremia for the nine animals examined after three weeks of N-nonyl-DNJ treatment is shown in Fig. 3. As no four-week woodchuck serum was available, glycan analysis was performed on three-week serum. The three week change in

Fig. 2 Serum HPLC glycan profiles from woodchuck M404 prior to treatment (top) and three weeks post-treatment (bottom). X-axis shows the retention time of the glycans on the HPLC column. Note that whereas after 115 minutes, there are no peaks in the untreated animal, the treated animal has a small peak at approximately 116.5 minutes. This peak has been shown by oligosaccharide sequencing to be the $Glc_3Man_7GlcNAc_2$ structure. As a control, the top inset shows the total glycan profile from the secreted glycoproteins from HepG2 cells which have been either untreated (top) or treated with $1000\mu g/ml$ of the glucosidase inhibitor NB-DNJ (bottom). The $Glc_3Man_7GlcNAc_2$ peak is indicated. Glucosidase inhibition does not lead to 100% production of the $Glc_3Man_7GlcNAc_2$ structure due to the presence of a shunt pathway[11].

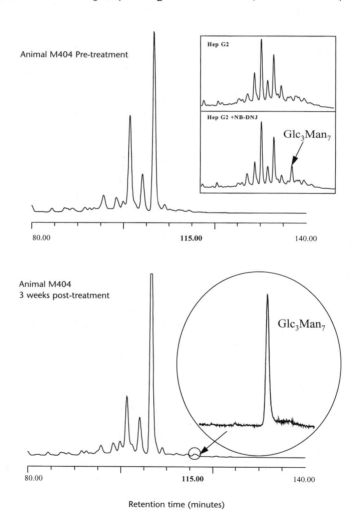

viremia for those animals tested (Fig. 3a) are plotted against the amount of serum hyperglucosylated glycan (Fig. 3b). Clearly, animals with the greatest amount of hyperglucosylated glycan experienced the greatest reduction in viremia. The varied response within dose groups seen in Fig. 1a,b can be attributed to the differences in hyperglucosylated glycan (Fig. 3b). For example, animals F271 and M256, while in the same dose group, had markedly different responses to the drug. The glycan analysis revealed that animal M256 had more than 25 times the amount of hyperglucosylated glycan in the serum than animal F271, and several animals from different dose groups (M305, M404 and F402a) showed the same drop in virus and the same percentage of hyperglucosylated glycan. Therefore, the hyper-glucosylated glycan seen in treated animals represents a biochemical marker, which can be used as a measure of drug efficacy. The amounts of hyperglucosy-lated glycan, as a fraction of total serum glycan, seen in treated animals was quite low, consistent with the idea that the alteration of only a minority of WHV gly-coprotein molecules is sufficient to disrupt the envelopment process and hence the secretion of virus[1,2].

Glucosidase inhibition *in vitro* leads to a decline in the amount of HBsAg secret-ed from HBV infected cells and a marked reduction in sub-viral particles con-taining the HBV M glycoprotein[1,2]. Indeed, it is believed that the inhibition of the α-glucosidases prevents the interaction of the M protein with chaperones like calnexin and causes the misfolding of the M protein[16]. This misfolding inhibits the envelopment process and prevents the formation and secretion of HBV. Consistent with this, preliminary evidence suggests that woodchucks responding to drug treatment experience a disappearance of a polypeptide shown by N-ter-minal sequence analysis to be the WHV M protein (manuscript in preparation).

We have previously shown that glucosidase inhibition prevents the secretion of enveloped HBV particles and causes the accumulation of immature "naked" core particles within the cell[1]. Further work has shown that these particles are slowly sent to lysosomes for destruction and hence their accumulation does not continue to increase but rather remains at a slightly elevated level[1,2,8]. In situa-tions where core particles are produced independently of the envelope proteins (therefore no enveloped virus can be produced) there appear to be mechanisms that limit the over-accumulation of core particles[11]. This mechanism of regula-tion may be the same as that seen during glucosidase inhibition.

The use of glycosylation processing inhibitors for treating human disease has been attempted in the past[17]. For example, NB-DNJ was tolerated in people and possessed anti-HIV properties *in vitro*[18]. However, problems achieving therapeutic serum concentrations may have limited the usefulness of the drug. The use of a derivative, such as N-nonyl-DNJ, with enhanced anti-HBV activity (as compared with NB-DNJ) allows glycosylation processing to be a therapeutic target for HBV.

Perhaps the most attractive feature of glucosidase inhibition as a treatment for chronic HBV is the possibility of synergy and complementation with drugs that target specific viral functions. For example, it seems likely that glucosidase inhibitors would be effective against HBV mutants that have become resistant to nucleoside analogues[19]. Moreover, since N-linked glycosylation of the envelope glycoproteins is a host mediated event, and is itself essential for virion secre-tion[1,2,8], selection of viral mutations resulting in drug-resistant escape mutants are unlikely. Because nucleoside analogue resistant mutants are a serious clinical prob-lem in HIV and HBV infection, drugs that retain activity against these viruses will be of great value. To this end combinatorial therapy with N-nonyl-DNJ and a nucleoside analogue like lamivudine (which targets the viral polymerase) may provide mutation resistant treatment. Indeed, synergy studies *in vitro* with N-nonyl-DNJ and lamivudine have shown promise, with greater than 100-fold increases in potency as compared with each drug individually (manuscript in preparation).

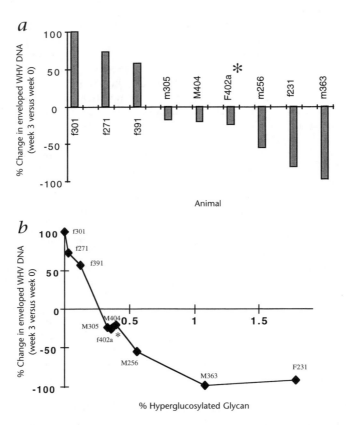

Fig. 3 $Glc_3Man_7GlcNAc_2$ structure acts as a surrogate marker for drug efficacy. ***a***, Change in serum enveloped WHV after three weeks of drug treatment as determined by IP-PCR for those animals on which glycan analysis was performed. Animal F402a, marked with an asterisk, is from two weeks post treatment. ***b***, Relationship between the amount of hyperglucosylated glycan (X-axis) and the change in viremia (Y-axis) at three weeks. Animals with a greater amount of hyperglucosylated glycan have the greatest reduction in viremia, and animals from different dose groups that have the same change in viremia, have the same degree of hyperglucosylated glycan in their serum.

Although initial toxicity tests in rats and these woodchuck studies indicate that this drug is well tolerated (glucosidase inhibitors have also been used and tolerated in human clinical trials[17]), extended treatment protocols in woodchucks are needed to better determine the therapeutic value and possible toxicity of this compound.

Because the mechanism of action of α-glucosidase inhibitors appears to be induction of misfolded or otherwise defective viral proteins, glucosidase inhibitors may be useful therapeutics for other viruses that bud from the endoplasmic reticulum. Preliminary evidence has shown that Bovine diarrhea virus (BVDV), a pestivirus akin to hepatitis C virus, is extremely sensitive to glucosidase inhibitors.

Methods

Glucosidase inhibitors and woodchucks. Glucosidase inhibitors N-butyldeoxynojirimycin (NB-DNJ) and N-nonyl-deoxynojirimycin (N-nonyl-DNJ) were provided by Monsanto Searle, Inc. Twenty, one-year-old laboratory reared woodchucks (age, sex and weight matched), chronically infected with WHV by inoculation with 10^7 genomes of WHV at birth, were separated into five age, weight and sex matched groups. All animals were treated in compliance with the National Research Council's criteria. Groups of five animals received twice daily, by syringe, either aqueous suspensions of placebo, or 6.25 mg/kg, 12.5 mg/kg ; 25 mg/kg or 50 mg/kg of pure N-nonyl-DNJ. Each week, animals were anesthetized (50 mg/kg Ketamine, 5 mg/kg xylazine) and body weights and serum samples were taken. Tests for toxicity included the measurement of serum γ-glutamyl transferase, aspartate transaminase, alanine transaminase, alkaline phosphatase and total serum bilirubin levels[20]. Routine hematological tests, feeding patterns, and stool samples were comparable within all dose groups[20]. The serum N-nonyl-DNJ level was determined by HPLC. WHV was determined by dot blot analysis (see text) or IP-PCR.

Detection of WHV DNA by IP-PCR. IP-PCR was performed and quantified using conditions previously described[8] using a WHV specific antibody (which recognizes the "a" epitope on the WHV S envelope protein[21]) and substituting WHV specific primers XY3 and XY4 which have the 5'–3' sequences 2418– AGA CCT CCT AAT GCA CCC ATT–2440 and 2968–TTC CCA AGA ATA TGG TTT ACC–2947, respectively, where the numbers refer to the nucleotide sequence along the WHV genome, using the *Eco*R1 cleavage site as nucleotide 1.

Statistical Analysis. Because of the large variability in viral load from animal to animal, data were first subjected to logarithmic transformation before analysis. The difference in the viral loads before and after four weeks of treatment, at each dose level, was regarded as the effect of the treatment; and its logarithmic transformation (to the base e) was the random variable under study. Alternative statistical tests such as the Likelihood Ratio Chi-Square test and the Mantel-Haenszel Chi-Square test also were used to confirm the statistical significance between the placebo and treatment doses.

Glycan Analysis. Samples taken for oligosaccharide analysis were based on sample availability. As no four week woodchuck serum was available for oligosaccharide analysis, the glycans associated with the serum of several three week treated animals were analyzed. 300µl of clarified woodchuck serum from animals treated with either placebo or N-nonyl-DNJ were treated with hydrazine using a Glycoprep 1000 machine (Oxford Glycosciences, Abingdon, Oxfordshire, UK) to release their glycans, which were fluorescently labeled at their reducing end with 2-aminobenzamide (using the Signal Labeling Kit, Oxford Glycosciences). Glycans were subsequently analyzed by normal phase HPLC[22]. Glycan structures were identified using sequential exoglycosidase digestion as described[23].

Acknowledgments

This work was supported by the Hepatitis B Foundation, through a gift from the Blanche and Irving Laurie Foundation; NATO and Monsanto-Searle, Inc. We thank Bill Mason (Fox Chase Cancer Center), Fran Platt, Nicole Zitzmann, Taj Mattu, Terry Butters and Pauline Rudd (Glycobiology Institute, University of Oxford) for their comments. We thank Anthony Willis (Department of Biochemistry, University of Oxford) for performing N-terminal sequence analysis on several samples and Shanti Mehta for help with the statistical analysis.

RECEIVED 15 JANUARY; ACCEPTED 26 MARCH 1998

1. Mehta, A., Lu, X., Block, T.M., Blumberg, B.S. & Dwek, R.A. Hepatitis B virus envelope proteins vary dras-
    tically in their sensitivity to glycan processing. *Proc. Natl. Acad. Sci. USA* **94**, 1822–1827 (1997).
2. Lu, X. *et al*. Aberrant trafficking of hepatitis B virus glycoproteins in cells in which N-glycan processing is
    inhibited. *Proc. Natl. Acad. Sci USA* **94**, 2380–2385 (1997).
3. Sherker, A. & Marion, P. Hepadnaviruses and hepatocellular carcinoma. *Ann Revs. Microb.* **45**, 475–508
    (1991).
4. Tipples, G.A. *et al*. Mutations in the HBV RNA-dependent DNA polymerase confers resistance to lamivu-
    dine in vivo. *Hepatology* **24**, 714–717 (1996).
5. Tennant, B.C. & Gerin, J.L. The woodchuck model of hepatitis B virus infection. In: The Liver: Biology and
    pathobiology. 3rd edition. Eds. Aries, I.M. *et al*. *Raven press*, Publisher (NY, NY) pp. 1455–1466 (1994).
6. Hoofnagle, J.H. & DiBisceglie, A.M. Drug Therapy: The treatment of chronic viral hepatitis. *New Engl. J.
    Med.* **336**, 347–356 (1997).
7. Wong, D.C., Shi, J.W.K., Purcell, R.H., Gerin, J.L. & London, W.T. Natural and experimental infection of
    woodchucks with woodchuck hepatitis virus, as measured by new, specific assays for woodchuck hepati-
    tis surface antigen and antibody. *J. Clin. Microb.* **15**, 484–490 (1982).
8. Lu, X., Mehta, A., Butters, T., Dwek, R. & Block, T. Evidence that N-linked glycosylation is necessary for
    hepatitis B virus secretion. *Virol.* **213**, 660–665 (1995).
9. Cullen, J.M. *et al*. In vivo antiviral activity and pharmacokinetics of (-)-cis-5-fluoro-1-[2-(hydroxymethly)-
    1,3-oxathiolan-5-yl] cytosine in woodchuck hepatitis virus-infected woodchucks. *Antimicro. Agents Chemo.*
    41, 2076–2082 (1997).
10. Nowak, M.A. *et al*. Viral dynamics in hepatitis B virus infection. *Proc. Natl. Acad. Sci. USA* **93**, 4398–4402
    (1996).
11. Ueda, K., Tsurimoto, T. & Matsubara, K., Three Envelope Proteins of Hepatitis B virus: Large S, Middle S,
    and Major S needed for the formation of Dane particles *J. Virol.* **65**, 3521–3529 (1991).
12. Seifer, M., Heermann, K.H. & Gerlich, W.J. Replication of hepatitis B virus in transfected nonhepatic cells.
    Virol. **179**, 300–311 (1990).
13. Wei, Y., Tavis, J.E. & Ganem, D. Relationship between viral DNA synthesis and virion envelopment in hep-
    atitis B virus. *J. Virol.* **70**, 6455–6458 (1997).
14. Abe, K., Kurata, T. & Shikata, T. Localization of woodchuck hepatitis virus in the liver. *Hepatology* **8**, 88–92
    (1988).
15. Moore, S.E. & Spiro, R.G. Demonstration that Golgi endo——D-mannosidase provides a glucosidase inde-
    pendent pathway for the formation of complex N-linked oligosaccharides of glycoproteins. *J. Biol. Chem.*
    265, 13104–13112 (1990).
16. Werr, M. & Prange, R. Role for calnexin and N-linked glycosylation in the assembly and secretion of hep-
    atitis B virus middle envelope protein particles. *J. Virol.* **7**, 778–782
17. Jacob, G.S. Glycosylation inhibitors in biology and medicine. *Curr. Opin Struct. Biol.* **5**, 605–611(1995).
18. Karpas, A. *et al*. Amino sugar derivatives as potential anti-HIV agents. *Proc. Natl. Acad. Sci. USA* **85**,
    9229–9233 (1988).
19. Fontana, R.J. & Lok, A.S.F. Combination therapy for chronic hepatitis B. *Hepatology* **26**, 234–236 (1997).
20. Korba, A.B. *et al*. Liver-targeted antiviral nucleosides: Enhanced antiviral activity of phosphatidyl-
    dideoxyguanosine versus dideoxyguanosine in woodchuck hepatitis virus infection *in vivo. Hepatology* **23**,
    No. 6, 958–963 (1996).
21. Lee, W.M. *et al*. Antibodies to polymerized albumin in woodchuck hepatitis virus infection. *Viral Immuno.*
    6, 13–19 (1993).
22. Guile, G.R., Rudd, P., Wing, D., Prime, S.B. & Dwek, R.A. A rapid high-resolution high-performance liquid
    chromatographic method for separating glycan mixtures and analyzing oligosaccharide profiles. *Anal.
    Biochem.* **240**, 210–226 (1996).
23. Rudd, P.M. *et al*. Oligosaccharide Sequence Technology. *Nature* **388**,205–208 (1997).

Attachments: Question 9

1) Domain Associates Commitment Letter for $15 Million Financing

DOMAIN ASSOCIATES, L.L.C.
PRINCETON • LAGUNA NIGUEL

James C. Blair
Brian H. Dovey
Arthur J. Klausner
Richard S. Schneider
Kathleen K. Schoemaker
Jesse I. Treu

Olav B. Bergheim
Rober J. More
Nicole Vitullo
Jason S. Holden
Lisa A. Kracutler

September 21, 1999

Mr. Donald H. Picker
President and Chief Executive Officer
Synergy Pharmaceuticals, Inc.
980 Amboy Avenue, 2nd Floor
Edison, NJ 08837

Dear Don:

Domain Associates, L.L.C. would like to assist Synergy Pharmaceuticals in its efforts to secure funding for the development of SP-104 (or a second generation compound) as a treatment for Hepatitis B and/or Hepatitis C.

As we discussed, Domain would consider investing in this project, with the goal of moving SP-104 through Phase I and/or Phase II clinical trials. The way we would proceed would be as follows:

Synergy Pharmaceuticals would present the development plan to a number of potential pharmaceutical company or biotechnology company partners to which Synergy would offer marketing rights to SP-104. Domain would assist Synergy in these efforts by suggesting several suitable companies to approach, and by allowing Synergy to say that Domain is considering a funding participation.

Naturally, the terms of a licensing agreement with a marketing partner are not known at this time; however, it is Domain's intention that the venture capital funds invested in the project earn a preferred return of at least 30% per year, and that the return to Domain be predicated solely on the success of the project. That is, Domain's return would be made promptly upon successful reaching of the project milestone goals in either cash or possibly stock in the marketing partner's company. The milestones would be negotiated by mutual consent of Synergy. Domain and the marketing partner company.

Sincerely,

Jesse I. Treu

JIT/KAR
Cc: B. Boveroux

One Palmer Square • Princeton, NJ 08542 • (609) 683-5656 • FAX (609) 683-9789

SYNERGY — DOMAIN RESEARCH PARTNERS
Agreement Outline June 28, 1999

Synergy Pharmaceuticals Inc. (Synergy) and Domain Associates (Domain), together, the Partners, agree to develop and finance the development of a pharmaceutical product for the treatment of hepatitis B and hepatitis C.

Capitalization:

Synergy will own 100% of the Common Stock of a new subsidiary (Hepatitis Corp. or HepCorp).

Domain Associates (Domain) on its own behalf or on behalf of a syndicate of investors of its choosing will own Preferred Stock of HepCorp.

Contributions of the Partners:

Synergy will contribute the necessary rights and patent licenses for the development, manufacture and marketing of N-Nonyl DNJ (Product) for the use as a treatment for hepatitis B and/or hepatitis C (Fields). The Territory (Territory) granted to HepCorp shall be the maximum possible to be granted by Synergy, i.e., worldwide except for certain Asian countries (including Japan and China).

Domain will contribute $XX million of capital for the development of Product in the Fields. Contributions shall be made according to a schedule agreeable to the Partners.

Operations:

Conduct of Research: HepCorp will contract with Synergy for the development of Product in the Fields according to an agreed-upon Development Budget (Budget).

Development Program: The objective of the Development Program shall be to complete Phase II human clinical studies in one or both Fields and to then sell/license Product to Pharma for further development and commercial marketing. HepCorp shall conduct the Development Program in an expeditious and efficient manner with due regard to the requirements of the FDA and other domestic and international regulatory agencies and the balancing of development risks and costs. The Developmnent Program for a particular Field may be terminated upon the direction of the Board should Product fail to demonstrate efficacy or shall exhibit commercially or ethically unacceptable toxicities.

Board of Directors: The Board shall consist of four Directors-two from Synergy and two from Domain. The Directors shall approve the Budget (which shall be proposed by Synergy) and, in general, shall oversee the operations of HepCorp.

Preferred Stock:

YYY million shares, par value $.001 per share.

Dividends: 30% annual rate. Dividends are cumulative. Dividends, shall not be required to be declared or paid prior to the delivery, pursuant to a sale or licensing agreement, of a Product to Pharma.

Voting: Non voting

Redemption: Mandatory redemption: Immediately following the consummation of a sale/licensing of a Product to Pharma, Synergy shall call for redemption 100% of the then outstanding Preferred Stock at a price of 100% plus all accrued and unpaid dividends.

Failure to deliver an acceptable product for sale/license: Should Development Program fail to deliver a Product in any Field to Pharma, the Partners may seek to find alternative licensees or otherwise to obtain economic value. Following such efforts, should HepCorp be dissolved or otherwise effectively cease operations, any remaining assets shall be utilized to redeem 100% of the Preferred Stock at its then value. Preferred stockholders shall have no other recourse to the assets or equity of Synergy.

Sale/Licensing of Products:

Prior to the sale of Preferred Stock to Domain, the parties shall have obtained a commitment from a third party (presumably a pharmaceutical of biotechnology company) (Pharma) to purchase or license a Product from HepCorp following the completion of Phase II clinical studies, i.e., proof of efficacy in main. The Partners shall use their best efforts to enable HepCorp to identify and negotiate with Pharma to obtain such licenese. This shall include participation in key meetings and provision of appropriate documentation showing the commitment of Domain and its syndicate of investors. The economic terms of any such sale/license shall be approved by the Partners.

1. The basic economics of the deal would be driven by a Liquidation Preference accruing a base return to the Preferred Investors after which there is a split of the Buyout amount between the Common (Synergy) and the Preferred's. I'd suggest an 80:20 sharing, with 80% of the share going to Synergy.

2. The budget and milestones for the Buyout would be determined in negotiations with the buyout partner ("Pharma"). The workscope of the project would, of course, be determined in this negotiation process.

3. Dividends would be reinvested in the Preferred Stock, giving the effect of compounding.

4. Preferred Stock would have a Liquidation Preference equal to the purchase price of the Preferred plus all accrued and unpaid dividends.

5. Buyout Value would be negotiated with Pharma, payable in Pharma stock at the average stock price of, eg, 10 days prior to the buyout announcement date. This Pharma stock would be registered stock.

6. Preferred Investors in Hepcorp would also receive warrant coverage of Pharma stock, at 100% of the Preferred Stock determined using current Pharma stock price, with an exercise price of 100% of current Pharma stock price. Exercise window would start at the buyout target date and be open for two years from that date. It might be convenient if Hepcorp owned the warrants and these were added to the Liquidation Preferences of the Preferred investors.

7. The Preferred Stock in Hepcorp might be purchased in several take-downs or closings.

8. Pharma might desire a BOD seat on Hepcorp Board. This would be OK, but ought to disappear upon failure to execute the buyout.

9. Why would the Preferred Stock be non-voting? If the project fails to meet objectives, Preferred's would need to have a full voice in what happens next.

Attachments: Question 11

KPMG Study

Proforma Model of Synergy Pharmaceuticals' Hepatitis B and Hepatitis C Product

June 2, 2000

KPMG Life Sciences

The KPMG Life Sciences Group was engaged by Synergy Pharmaceuticals to create a proforma model of their product for Hepatitis B and C. In order to perform its work, KPMG met with Company Executives, examined market literature and interviewed experts in the field of hepatitis therapy. In addition, KPMG was given a copy of a financial analysis previously performed by Synergy.

The reader should note the following:

- the model is solely based on the development of product(s) for Hepatitis B and Hepatitis C infections, within the context of Synergy's interpretation of the terms of the United Therapeutics agreement. The company indicated that their technology could be lead to products for other diseases, each with their own associated expenses and revenues. The model does not evaluate the impact of varying the interpretation of the United Therapeutics agreement, as well as that of Synergy developing other products/indications, nor was KPMG asked to do such an evaluation.

- This model is not an in-depth analysis of the issues that can affect the outputs and should not be construed as such. The Company supplied all technical information and claims concerning the product(s). KPMG was not asked to and did not perform technical due diligence to verify or refute such claims. The Company has sole responsibility concerning the validity of the claims about its products and technologies. In addition, the Company supplied the market penetration rates based on their understanding of the market and their assumption of the product's utility as a 'first-line' therapeutic with highly desirable characteristics. No primary market research was performed to validate or invalidate assumptions used in the models.

The report is structured as follows
• Review of data as to the epidemiology of Hepatitis B and C, ultimately to arrive at an assumption as to the potential number of

treatable patients.
- Analysis of the present cost for the standard of care for Hepatitis B and Hepatitis C.
- List of assumptions, used in the model.
- Sensitivity analysis on the impact of varying key assumptions.

Because of the special nature of this report, it is not intended for purposes other than to assist Synergy Pharmaceuticals in the evaluation of their product for Hepatitis B & C. This report is confidential to Synergy Pharmaceuticals and is for internal use only by management and employees of the Company. This report may not be copied, quoted or referred to, whole or in part, for use external to the Company without prior written consent from KPMG.

This report is not intended for use by Synergy to promote the Company or its products as well as to solicit investment in the Company.

Epidemiology

The following Tables contain information on the calculation of potential Hepatitis B and C populations in the United States, France, Germany, Italy, Spain and the United Kingdom.

HEPATITIS B EPIDEMIOLOGY				
		YEAR		
		2000	2005	2010
United States	Total Population[1]	274,900,000	286,300,000	298,000,000
	Prevalence of Chronic HBV[2]	1,250,000	1,302,000	1,355,000
France	Total Population	59,100,000	59,600,000	59,700,000
	Prevalence of Chronic HBV	218,000	220,000	223,000
Germany	Total Population	82,1000,000	81,900,000	81,000,000
	Prevalence of Chronic HBV	365,000	370,000	375,000
Italy	Total Population	56,700,000	56,300,000	55,300,000
	Prevalence of Chronic HBV	2,075,000	2,110,000	2,140,000
Spain	Total Population	39,210,000	39,330,000	39,180,000
	Prevalence of Chronic HBV[3]	145,000	145,100	145,000
United Kingdom	Total Population	59,250,000	59,710,000	60,000,000
	Prevalence of Chronic HBV	230,000	235,000	240,000
	Total Prevalence	4,283,000	4,382,000	4,478,000

[1] Source: Census Statistics
[2] Source: Calculated from prevalence rate data supplied by Timely Data Resources and cross-checked against figures supplied by Decision Resources Cognos Report
[3] No figures are available for prevalence in Spain, the rate was assumed to be similar to that of France

HEPATITIS B EPIDEMIOLOGY				
		YEAR		
		2000	**2005**	**2010**
United States	Total Population[4]	274,900,000	286,300,000	298,000,000
	Prevalence of Chronic HBV[5]	4,950,000	5,150,000	5,364,000
France	Total Population	59,100,000	59,600,000	59,700,000
	Prevalence of Chronic HBV	340,000	345,000	345,000
Germany	Total Population	82,1000,0000	81,900,000	81,000,000
	Prevalence of Chronic HBV	400,000	395,000	392,000
Italy	Total Population	56,700,000	56,300,000	55,300,000
	Prevalence of Chronic HBV	535,000	530,000	525,000
Spain	Total Population	39,210,000	39,330,000	39,180,000
	Prevalence of Chronic HBV	575,000	580,000	580,000
United Kingdom	Total Population	59,250,000	59,710,000	60,000,000
	Prevalence of Chronic HBV	360,000	360,000	360,000
	Total Prevalence	7,060,000	7,360,000	7,566,000

[4] Source: Census Statistics
[5] Source: Calculated from prevalence rate data supplied by Timely Data Resources and cross-checked against figures supplied by Decision Resources Cognos Report

Estimate of Potential Patient Populations

Hepatitis B Virus
- In acute infections, the vast majority of infected individuals (65-90%) have silent infections or simply display flu-like symptoms. The remaining 10-35% of the acutely infected individuals has the 'classical' symptoms associated with hepatitis such as, jaundice, dark urine or light colored stools. In symptomatic patients, the present standard of care is non-disease specific and consists mainly of supportive care.
- Infected individuals who fail to clear viral particles from their circulation after six months are classified as chronic carriers. The CDC estimates 6-10% of infections become chronic.
- The prevalent population, characterized in epidemiological studies, constitutes the chronic population. Chronically infected patients have a high risk of developing cirrhosis and other chronic liver ailments. It is estimated that 1/3 to 1/2 of chronic HBV carriers display overt symptoms at some point during the course of their infection (Timely data Resources, Decision Resources and CDC estimates)
- Based on these data the Table below presents our estimates of symptomatic chronic HBV population[6].

ESTIMATED CHRONIC SYMPTOMATIC HBV POPULATIONS			
	YEAR		
	2000	2005	2010
United States	500,000	521,000	542,000
Europe (F, G, I, S, UK)	1,213,000	1,232,000	1,249,000

Hepatitis C Virus
- Acute infection is clinically silent in up to 95% of infected individuals. In the remaining 5% the prevalent symptom is jaundice.
- In approximately 80% of the infected individuals, the disease becomes chronic whereby six months post-infection they are unable

---

[6] Assumes a 40% symptomatic rate amongst chronic population

to clear the viral particles (Timely Data Resources and CDC).

- It is estimated that 70% of the chronic carriers would become symptomatic at some point during their lifetime (Timely Data Resources and Decision Resources).

Based on these data, the Table below presents our estimates of the symptomatic chronic HCV population[7].

ESTIMATED CHRONIC SYMPTOMATIC HCV POPULATIONS			
	YEAR		
	2000	2005	2010
United States	1,785,000	1,858,000	1,934,000
Europe (F, G, I, S, UK)	1,255,000	1,315,000	1,310,000

Estimated Cost of Therapy for Chronic Hepatitis

HBV

- The standard of care today is Epivir–HBV (lamuvidine) available from Glaxo Wellcome.

Based on Epivir-HBV (lamivudine dosing schedule from Physicians Desk Reference (PDR) – 2000: *"The recommended oral dose of Epivir-HBV for treatment of chronic hepatitis B in adults is 100 mg once daily."*)	
100	mgs/day (Source: PDR)
270	days/year (Assumes ~ 75% compliance)
$272.59	Epivir-HBV AWP – Tab, PO, 100 mg, 60s ea (Source: Red Book)
$4.54	price/100 mg tablet (calculated)
$1,226.66	cost per patient/year ($4.54/day * 270 days)
$1,250	**rounded cost per patient/year AWP**
$1,000	**Estimated cost per patient ex-manufacturer**

---

[7] Assumes 70% of chronic carrier are symptomatic at any one time.

- This is the cost in the United States. Typically, European prices for pharmaceutical products are, in most cases, at least 20% lower due to their pricing system.
- Therapy with Epivir is chronic throughout the lifetime of the patient.
- It is now known that HBV mutants resistant to Epivir can occur in large numbers of patients. Because of this, there is market resistance to using the product.

HCV
- The present standard of therapy is Rebetron (interferon alfa-2b plus ribavirin) from Schering Plough.
- The estimate cost of Therapy with Rebetron is as follows;

$700 AWP for two week therapy pack
Course of therapy 24 – 48 weeks
$8,400 to $16,800 AWP for a full course
$6,720 to $1,3440 ex-manufacturer for a full course

- This is the cost in the United States. Typically, European prices for pharmaceutical products are, in most cases, at least 20% lower due to their pricing system.
- Typical patient goes through one course of therapy.

Proforma Assumptions

1. Potential patient populations as noted above for Hepatitis B and C. These consist of the symptomatic chronic carrier populations. Only the United States and the five major European markets are evaluated.
2. Product is assumed to launch in early 2005, as stated by Synergy.
3. Product is assumed to be front-line therapy with an excellent efficacy and safety profile, as well as no resistance develops. Product is also assumed to be chronic, lifetime therapy. (THIS IS THE CRITICAL ASSUMPTION.) Assumption as stated by Synergy.
4. Penetration rates are as supplied by Synergy.

---

5. Price for per treatment is based on chronic therapy with lamivudine as the benchmark. The United States price reflects a 50% premium over the lamivudine price due to the overall product profile. The same pricing is used for HBV and HCV since available information indicates they will have the same dosing regimens. European pricing is at a 20% discount from the Untied States price.
6. Royalty rates, milestone payments and R&D/operating expenses are as supplied by Synergy Pharmaceuticals. Our understanding is that all expenses related to HBV/HCV are reimbursed by United Therapeutics.
7. Tax rate is 40% and taxes are paid starting in 2004 after the NOL is exhausted.
8. Number of shares was supplied by Synergy.
9. Market cap based on EPS for the third year of sales (2007) with a 40% discount and 30 multiple.
10. NPV analysis based on 2010 with a 3x terminal value.

Sensitivity Analysis

As part of the exercise we performed a series of sensitivity analyses to identify key assumptions that could affect the valuation. We observed the following:

- A 10% increase in the price of the product (2000 basis) increases the market cap by 10% and the NPV by 8-10%.
- A 10% increase in the potential HBV patient population leads to a 3% increase in market cap and a 2-3% increase in the NPV.
- A 10% increase in the potential HCV patient population leads to a 6.6% increase in market cap and a 5.5 to 6.4% increase in the NPV.
- A one-year delay in the European launch leads to a 14% decrease in market cap and 10-11% decrease in NPV.
- A one year delay for launch in both the United States and Europe leads to a 27% decrease in market cap and 20 to 25% decrease in NPV.
- A ten-point decrease in market share leads to a 20% decrease in market cap and 20-25% decrease in NPV.

Proforma Valuation of N-Nonyl DNJ (Synergy Pharmaceuticals)

All monetary values are $US MM (except Price per Treatment)

Hepatitis B

		2000	2001	2002	2003	2004	2005	2006	2007	2008	2009	2010
No. Chronic Symptomatic Hep B Sufferers (US)	1%	500,000	504,250	508,536	512,859	517,218	521,614	526,048	530,519	535,029	539,577	544,163
Penetration (%)							25%	35%	50%	60%	60%	60%
Treated Patients							130,404	184,117	265,260	321,017	323,746	326,498
Price Per Treatment, w/ ann. increase of	2%	$1,500	$1,530	$1,561	$1,592	$1,624	$1,656	$1,689	$1,723	$1,757	$1,793	$1,828
Hepatitis B Sales (US)		$0	$0	$0	$0	$0	$216.0	$311.0	$457.1	$564.2	$580.4	$597.0
No. Chronic Symptomatic Hep B Sufferers (EU)	0.4%	1,213,000	1,217,246	1,221,506	1,225,781	1,230,071	1,234,377	1,238,697	1,243,032	1,247,383	1,251,749	1,256,130
Penetration (%)							25%	35%	50%	60%	60%	60%
Treated Patients							308,594	433,544	621,516	748,430	751,049	753,678
Price Per Treatment, w/ ann. increase of	2%	$1,200	$1,224	$1,248	$1,273	$1,299	$1,325	$1,351	$1,378	$1,406	$1,434	$1,463
Hepatitis B Sales (Europe)		$0	$0	$0	$0	$0	$408.9	$585.9	$856.7	$1,052.3	$1,077.1	$1,102.5
Hepatitis B Sales (US & Europe)		$0.0	$0.0	$0.0	$0.0	$0.0	$624.8	$896.9	$1,313.8	$1,616.5	$1,657.4	$1,699.5
Synergy Revenues												
Net Royalty	6%	$0	$0	$0	$0	$0	$37.5	$53.8	$78.8	$97.0	$99.4	$102.0
License Milestones		$0.2	$1.2	$1.6	$6.4	$12.8						
Total Hep B Revenues		$0.2	$1.2	$1.6	$6.4	$12.8	$37.5	$53.8	$78.8	$97.0	$99.4	$102.0
Expenses (borne by Synergy Partner)		$0	$0	$0	$0	$0	$0	$0	$0	$0	$0	$0
EBITDA		$0.2	$1.2	$1.6	$6.4	$12.8	$37.5	$53.8	$78.8	$97.0	$99.4	$102.0
NOL Balance	($15)	($14.8)	($13.6)	($12.0)	($5.6)	$0.0	$0.0	$0.0	$0.0	$0.0	$0.0	$0.0
EBITDA after NOL		$0.0	$0.0	$0.0	$0.0	$7.2	$37.5	$53.8	$78.8	$97.0	$99.4	$102.0
Tax	40%	$0.0	$0.0	$0.0	$0.0	$2.9	$15.0	$21.5	$31.5	$38.8	$39.8	$40.8
After Tax Net		$0.0	$0.0	$0.0	$0.0	$4.3	$22.5	$32.3	$47.3	$58.2	$59.7	$61.2

Hepatitis C

		2000	2001	2002	2003	2004	2005	2006	2007	2008	2009	2010
No. Chronic Symptomatic Hep C Sufferers (US)	1%	1,785,000	1,799,280	1,813,674	1,828,184	1,842,809	1,857,552	1,872,412	1,887,391	1,902,490	1,917,710	1,933,052
Penetration (%)							25%	35%	50%	60%	60%	60%
Treated Patients							464,388	655,344	943,696	1,141,494	1,150,626	1,159,831
Price Per Treatment, w/ ann. increase of	2%	$1,500	$1,530	$1,561	$1,592	$1,624	$1,656	$1,689	$1,723	$1,757	$1,793	$1,828
Hepatitis C Sales (US)		$0	$0	$0	$0	$0	$769.1	$1,107.0	$1,626.0	$2,006.2	$2,062.7	$2,120.7

		1	2	3	4	5	6	7	8	9	10	11
No. Chronic Symptomatic Hep C Sufferers (EU)	1%	1,255,000	1,266,923	1,278,958	1,291,108	1,303,374	1,315,756	1,328,256	1,340,874	1,353,612	1,366,472	1,379,453
Penetration (%)							25%	35%	50%	60%	60%	60%
Treated Patients							328,939	464,889	670,437	812,167	819,883	827,672
Price Per Treatment, w/ ann. increase of	2%	$1,200	$1,224	$1,248	$1,273	$1,299	$1,325	$1,351	$1,378	$1,406	$1,434	$1,463
Hepatitis C Sales (Europe)		$0	$0	$0	$0	$0	$435.8	$628.2	$924.1	$1,141.9	$1,175.8	$1,210.7
Hepatitis C Sales (US & Europe)		$0.0	$0.0	$0.0	$0.0	$0.0	$1,204.9	$1,735.3	$2,550.2	$3,148.1	$3,238.5	$3,331.5
Synergy Revenues	6%											
Net Royalty		$0	$0	$0	$0	$0	$72.3	$104.1	$153.0	$188.9	$194.3	$199.9
License Milestones		**$0.2**	**$1.2**	**$1.6**	**$6.4**	**$12.8**	$0	$0	$0	$0	$0	$0
Total Hep C Revenues		$0.2	$1.2	$1.6	$6.4	$12.8	$72.3	$104.1	$153.0	$188.9	$194.3	$199.9
Expenses (borne by Synergy Partner)		$0	$0	$0	$0	$0	$0	$0	$0	$0	$0	$0
EBITDA		$0.2	$1.2	$1.6	$6.4	$12.8	$72.3	$104.1	$153.0	$188.9	$194.3	$199.9
NOL Balance	($15)	($14.8)	($13.6)	($12.0)	($5.6)	$0.0	$0.0	$0.0	$0.0	$0.0	$0.0	$0.0
EBITDA after NOL		$0.0	$0.0	$0.0	$0.0	$7.2	$72.3	$104.1	$153.0	$188.9	$194.3	$199.9
Tax	40%	$0.0	$0.0	$0.0	$0.0	$2.9	$28.9	$41.6	$61.2	$75.6	$77.7	$80.0
After Tax Net		$0.0	$0.0	$0.0	$0.0	$4.3	$43.4	$62.5	$91.8	$113.3	$116.6	$119.9
Total N-Nonyl DNJ Sales		$0	$0	$0	$0	$0	$1,829.7	$2,632.2	$3,863.9	$4,764.5	$4,895.9	$5,030.9

9/12/03

Product

Proforma Valuation of Synergy Pharmaceuticals — EPS Model

All monetary values are $US MM (except Earnings Per Share data)

		2000	2001	2002	2003	2004	2005	2006	2007	2008	2009	2010
Total N-Nonyl DNJ Sales		$0.0	$0.0	$0.0	$0.0	$0.0	$1,829.7	$2,632.2	$3,863.9	$4,764.5	$4,895.9	$5,030.9
Revenue												
Hep B License Milestones		$0.2	$1.2	$1.6	$6.4	$12.8	$0.0	$0.0	$0.0	$0.0	$0.0	$0.0
Hep C License Milestones		$0.2	$1.2	$1.6	$6.4	$12.8	$0.0	$0.0	$0.0	$0.0	$0.0	$0.0
Hep B Royalties	6%	$0.0	$0.0	$0.0	$0.0	$0.0	$37.5	$53.8	$78.8	$97.0	$99.4	$102.0
Hep C Royalties	6%	$0.0	$0.0	$0.0	$0.0	$0.0	$72.3	$104.1	$153.0	$188.9	$194.3	$199.9
Total Revenues		$0.4	$2.4	$3.2	$12.8	$25.6	$109.8	$157.9	$231.8	$285.9	$293.8	$301.9
Royalty Paid to Tech Source		$0	$0	$0	$0	$0	$0	$0	$0	$0	$0	$0
Synergy's share of COGS		$0	$0	$0	$0	$0	$0	$0	$0	$0	$0	$0
Gross Profit		$0.4	$2.4	$3.2	$12.8	$25.6	$109.8	$157.9	$231.8	$285.9	$293.8	$301.9
Operating Expenses												
Research & Development		$0	$0	$0	$0	$0	$0	$0	$0	$0	$0	$0
Marketing & Sales		$0	$0	$0	$0	$0	$0	$0	$0	$0	$0	$0
Administrative Costs		$0	$0	$0	$0	$0	$0	$0	$0	$0	$0	$0
Misc.		$0	$0	$0	$0	$0	$0	$0	$0	$0	$0	$0
Total Expenses		$0	$0	$0	$0	$0	$0	$0	$0	$0	$0	$0
Income (Loss) from Operations		$0.4	$2.4	$3.2	$12.8	$25.6	$109.8	$157.9	$231.8	$285.9	$293.8	$301.9

Line item	Assm.											
NOL Balance		($30)	($29.6)	($27.2)	($24.0)	($11.2)	$0.0	$0.0	$0.0	$0.0	$0.0	$0.0
Income (Loss) from Ops. after NOL		$0.0	$0.0	$0.0	$0.0	$14.4	$109.8	$157.9	$231.8	$285.9	$293.8	$301.9
Income Tax	40%	$0.0	$0.0	$0.0	$0.0	$5.8	$43.9	$63.2	$92.7	$114.3	$117.5	$120.7
Net Income (Loss) / Net Cash Flow		$0.4	$2.4	$3.2	$12.8	$8.6	$65.9	$94.8	$139.1	$171.5	$176.3	$181.1
Terminal Value	3											$543.3
Adjusted Cash Flow	$0	$0.4	$2.4	$3.2	$12.8	$8.6	$65.9	$94.8	$139.1	$171.5	$176.3	$724.5
Shares Outstanding (millions)		12.30	12.30	12.30	12.30	12.30	12.30	12.30	12.30	12.30	12.30	12.30
Diluted Shares Outstanding (millions)		12.30	12.30	12.30	12.30	12.30	12.30	12.30	12.30	12.30	12.30	12.30
E.P.S. (Net Income)		$0.03	$0.20	$0.26	$1.04	$0.70	$5.36	$7.70	$11.31	$13.94	$14.33	$14.72
Diluted E.P.S. (Net Income)		$0.03	$0.20	$0.26	$1.04	$0.70	$5.36	$7.70	$11.31	$13.94	$14.33	$14.72

Discounted at **40%**

Multiple of **30**

NPV of Adjusted Cash Flow (2010 BASIS)

Market Cap (2007 BASIS) **$396**

Rate	NPV
25%	$220
35%	$123
45%	$73

$1.07 $32.18   EPS

Synergy Case Solution

Imagine you are the CEO of a biotech company that has some interesting in vitro and animal data for a compound derived from a broad technology platform you own and against a specific disease indication. How much capital do you seek in your first round of funding? What issues guide your estimation to that amount? How does the stage of a biotech company's development influence its ability to attract funding?

Answer:

1. A startup biotech company with little or no laboratory research performed has a much more difficult task in raising capital than a company with *in vitro* or *in vivo* data. (The research and people of a start-up company are largely untested.) Later stage research efforts attract capital based upon efficacy of trials.

2. It is necessary to have preliminary efficacy data, preferably in vivo, for treating a disease target in order to attract corporate or institutional capital to a biotech research effort or company.

3. To begin the process of raising capital you must create a Business Plan which identifies:
    A. Research Expenditures sufficient to provide *in vitro* and *in vivo* efficacy data in the established animal model for the target disease state. (Is the time period 2 years or more?)
    B. Include personnel and facility costs for the estimated time period to produce efficacy data.
    C. Estimate market size in patients and dollars for the projected therapy. Institutional and corporate investors are sensitive to projected size or market (Big Pharma has minimum size or market levels for investment).
    D. Research and describe competitive therapies in the plan. Investors will assess if your new technology will be successful based upon their own due diligence.
    E. Make the plan for as many years as estimated to show efficacy data, preferable *in vivo* in the accepted standard animal model.

Question 2, page 169

1. HV II had invested $1.2 million as seed money in IgX and was seeking to establish a $15 million valuation for the Series A round of funding. What multiple returns was HV II seeking over its own cost?

Answer:

A. The $15 million of the pre-money value of the Series A financing is 12.5 times the $1.2 million cash already invested in Synergy from inception in February 1992 to September 1994.

Question 2, page 169

2. Is it usual for founding or seed investors to seek a multiple return at the Series A round of funding? Why or why not? Give examples.

Answer:

A. IgX has been in existence for approximately 30 months, as a seed-financed biotech company and has developed laboratory data in vivo to support efficacy claims for its first compound, IGX-CP (Cryptosporidium parvum)

B. Also, the IgX technology platform has been validated because IgX showed that polyclonal antibodies could be developed to be disease-specific, that is, to treat infections other than cryptosporidiosis.

C. Valuation of IgX is further enhanced because the first Phase I/II human clinical trial was imminent. Biotech companies about to enter Phase I/II trials are typically valued in current markets in a range of $7 million to $15 million because it is assumed that in vitro and/or in vivo laboratory data are good enough to warrant FDA approval for a Phase I/II trial.

D. IgX valuation is also positively affected by the forecasted size of the North American and European markets for cryptosporidiosis which was estimated at the time to be approximately $500 million annually. This size market is attractive to Big Pharma and warrants an initial company valuation of approximately $15 million.

E. IgX had done laboratory work on other disease indications which could be treatable by disease-specific polyclonal antibodies developed from the IgX technology platform. E. coli and H. pylori were two additional disease indications which had large markets in North America and Europe and further enhanced the IgX projected valuation. Based upon the above several factors a $15 million premoney valuation for the IgX series A financing was reasonable.

Question 3, page 171

How would you evaluate the results of the Phase I/II clinical trial at Cornell? What do you do next based upon your assessment of the Phase I/II results?

Answer:

Cryptosporidial infection was usually fatal to AIDS patients.

1) The Phase I/II clinical trial was successful because bowel movement frequency was reduced 60 percent in patients with three weeks of treatment and 67 percent in patients with 6 weeks of therapy.

2) The above results convinced the investors, scientists and clinicians that a Phase III double-blind trial should be undertaken to further demonstrate efficacy.

Question 4, page 172

1. At this point, what value do you place on IgX to raise the Series B round of funding?

Answer:

A. IgX has completed a successful Phase I/II human trial at a prestigious hospital, Cornell Medical Center, with the leading US clinician in its first disease indication, cryptosporidiosis.

B. Discounted cash flow valuation of the markets for IGX-CP, *E. coli* and *H. pylori* with appropriate probability factors showed an IgX present value of $35 million at the time the Series B financing was undertaken.

Question 4, page 172

2. What are the major factors to consider in estimating a pre-money value for IgX?

Answer:

A. Size of target markets for the disease indications encompassed by the IgX technology platform.

B. Evaluation of appropriate discount rate and penetration rates for the chosen disease indications.

C. Pro forma P&L development using estimated market prices for therapy and estimated cost of goods sold to develop pre- and post-tax net income estimates forecasted for 10 years.

Question 4, page 172

3. What amount of funding should you seek?

Answer:

A. Sufficient financing to cover two and preferably three years of forecast IgX burn rate based upon the cost of R&D and human clinical trial development.

Question 4, page 172

4. Can any form of debt be used in the financing and at what mix of debt to equity?

Answer:

A. Start-up biotech companies have never been able to access debt markets because they are accumulating large cash flow deficits.

Question 5, page 180

Review the Series B term sheets. From the company's point of view, is this an attractive financing? Why or why not? From the investors' point of view is this an attractive financing? Why or why not? From both points of view, which terms would you recommend be changed?

Answer:

IgX's Point of View

1) For IgX all the positives of this financing are about pre money valuations. This is very attractive financing because it establishes a $35 million pre money valuation for IgX in what is essentially the company's first "outside" led financing.

2) Series B financings are always priced off the Series A, and potential "B" investors could question the "A" pre money valuation.

The series A financing was insider led by Henry Venture II, and might be questioned at Series B time as to whether the outside "market" had valued IgX, or whether insiders "propped up" the Series A valuation at $15 million pre money.

3) The $35 million Series B valuation was possible because IgX was in its Phase III trial. Its Irish plant had been built and was financed. Further, GMP approval was received to manufacture human clinical trial material.

Answer:

Investors Point of View

1) For the investors many positives reside in the protection of the 75 percent IRR ratchet. However, there are many fundamental positives in the IgX stage of company development.

2) Investors are getting a Phase III company with a novel technology platform which allows for additional therapies for multiple disease indications. This means more potential drug candidates.

3) The IgX burn rate is modest, and a $10 million financing should carry IgX for 24 months. (Ideally, young biotech companies should seek to have a minimum of 24 months operating cash in the bank.)

4) A reasonable pre money valuation for a Phase III biotech company which is in Phase III double blind, human clinical trials is generally in a range of $30 million to $50 million, depending upon market conditions and disease indications treated.

5) If investors are wrong about granting IgX a $35 million pre money valuation for the Series B financing, they have the protection of the 75 percent IRR ratchet which guarantees that subsequent financings validate the Series B valuation or else anti-dilution protection kicks in. This 75 percent ratchet is generous anti-dilution protection against a flat or down financing in a Series C round.

Question 6, page 182

How important is going public to the corporate development of a young biotech firm? What are the major considerations in selecting an investment banker for your company's IPO?

Answer:

Going public is important because of the amount of capital that can be raised in an IPO as compared to a private placement. Biotech companies are huge consumers of capital. It has been said that they drink money. Most biotech companies go public too early, but are very pleased to have a three, four or five year cash war chest. Also, publicly traded stock can be used to acquire technology or companies. Access to capital later is also facilitated by being public in the first place.

The best investment banker is often the one that will do the IPO the biotech company wants done, i.e. size and terms. Stature is always important in an investment banker, and ability to place the stock, while supporting the company with research and aftermarket activities including M&A.

Question 7, Page 184

How important is going public to the corporate development of a young biotech firm? What are the major considerations in selecting an investment banker for your company's IPO?

Answer:

1) Next to having successful science, access to significant amounts of equity capital is the most pressing need of a young biotech company.

2) Going public accesses the greatest amount of equity capital in a single transaction as compared to any other form of equity financing.

3) Most importantly, being public affords the young biotech company follow-on access to further capital if sufficient progress is made on the fundamental scientific development. Generally, follow-on financings are achievable if a company's science makes achievements according to plan. Follow-on financings are almost routine for a successful biotech company, given acceptable market conditions.

4) Becoming public is a very important business milestone for a biotech company.

Question 7, Page 184

As IgX CEO, what are the qualitative issues in favor of an IPO. Justify a valuation for the IgX IPO.

Answer:

1) Good and experienced management.

2) IgX is an institutionally financed bitech company with astute, professional shareholders, which is a selling point for the IPO.

3) IgX is a later stage biotech company already in Phase III human trials.

4) IgX has begun to create licenses for its potential products, and its in licensing of Monsanto/Searle technology gives it a second technology platform in the very large hepatitis market.

5) With the Monsanto/Searle license, IgX gained ownership of a substantial intellectual property (IP) portfolio in addition to its own IP portfolio.

Question 7, Page 184

Show how you justify a valuation for the IPO.

Answer:

1) The IgX Series B financing was at a pre money valuation of $35 million, and raised $7 million, for a post money valuation of $42 million.

2) Phase III biotech companies commanded pre money valuations in excess of $50 million in 1998 by comparative company analysis of the IPO market.

3) The after tax NPV of IgX-CPL3 is calculated at $26 million for one IgX product. IgX treatment for C. difficile and H. pylori were similar size markets for each, but were at an earlier stage development. Additionally, the Monsanto/Searle technology platform would support a $10 million to $20 million valuation. The incremental buildup of IgX valuation was in an approximate range of $65 million to $45 million.

4) Another check on the IPO pre money valuation is that the $65 million is an approximate 55 percent to 60 percent premium to the Series B financing. This is a reasonable premium to the last private financing according to prevailing market conditions.

Question 8, Page 187

What information in the *Nature Medicine* article supports the development of a drug candidate?

Answer:

1) As stated early in the case, positive in vivo animal data for a drug candidate compound is essential for further expenditure to continue toward a potential clinical trial.

2) The woodchuck animal study including four treatment groups of four animals each, showed eradication of the hepatitis B virus in some animals (particularly at 12, 25, and 50 mg/Kg dosing) and 10 to 100 times decrease in some other animals.

3) The limited study produced excellent results and could be used as the basis to conduct toxicology and further, expanded efficacy studies in the animal model.

4) With ever improving data from expanded animal experiments for hepatitis B, and moving to hepatitis C, the value of the new IgX (Synergy) technology platform for imino-sugar compounds, the value of IgX/Synergy would increase.

5) Expanded and positive experiments and data from imino-sugar compound experiments might attract a new corporate partner for IgX/Synergy for the new

technology platform. (In fact Synergy found United Therapeutics (UT) a new corporate partner based upon UT's interest in the Monsanto/Searle based imino-sugar technology platform.)

Question 9, Page 192

What are Domain's goals in creating this structure for the debt? Is this a workable offer?

Answer:

1) Domain offers to fund Synergy research through Phase I/II trial for up to $15 million in return for which they want a guaranteed take-out up front from "Big Pharma" which gives a minimum 30 percent IRR to Domain. Domain also wants other returns after Phase II clinical trial success.

2) Domain seeks to lock in a 30 percent IRR for a $15 million investment, but Domain does take the scientific development and clinical trial risk.

3) The proposal was not workable because no big pharma company would take the clinical trial risk and give Domain the 30 percent return at the same time.

Question 9, Page 192

From Synergy's point of view is this a workable offer?

Answer:

1) It would seem to be very attractive to provide much needed funding. Also Domain has a fine reputation in biotech financing and their indication of interest in Synergy's science and people is a good vote of confidence.

2) The concept was not workable because every "Big Pharma" that Synergy approached would not involve time performing due diligence on Synergy's science realizing they were required to five up a 30 percent IRR, and more if the trial succeeded. "Big Pharma" has capital to risk itself regarding new science developed by biotech companies, and does not want to give a generous return to a financial intermediary.

3) To Synergy the Domain proposal looked promising because it gave the small biotech company a way to finance its Phase I and II clinical trials. Regarding industry practice there were no takers.

Question 10, Page 195

Why was the Synergy board not interested in a strategic partnership? Why did they think it more important to be acquired?

Answer:

1) In September 1999, the Synergy shareholders had been investors for up to seven years. (HVII invested originally in 1992.) Synergy was a venture capital backed company and these money pools need a liquidity point within preferably 5 years.

2) Also, biotech public markets were still closed to a Synergy IPO and the company needed to align itself with a financially strong partner through a merger.

3) A strategic alliance generally provides funding and milestone payments for a specific compound targeted at a specific disease indication through one or two clinical trials. Funding usually covers scientific development, IND, regulatory, and trial expense and not corporate overheads separate from the trial in question.

4) Synergy would still have to raise financing for expanding its science to other disease targets for expanding its science to other disease targets and to support its management infrastructure.

5) An outright acquisition of Synergy by a well-funded, public pharma company cures all the issues described in (1) through (4). With an acquisition of Synergy, any success of Synergy clinical trials would be reflected in the stock price of the acquirer and Synergy shareholders could benefit in a share for share merger transaction.

Question 11, Page 200

How can you use the KPMG valuation study to structure various, perhaps competing, merger deals? Why would Synergy continue to seek a merger partner after the lucrative license with UT?

Answer:

1) The KPMG valuation study is important to Synergy because it establishes an NPV value for both hepatitis B and C performed by a respected outside third party and using a range of variables. The KPMG valuation gives dollar ranges which can be used in discussions with potential acquirers.

2) As Synergy nears its clinical trials, the KPMG study assumes greater significance, particularly as toxicity and animal efficacy studies indicate greater possibility of success in the clinic.

3) The Synergy valuation ranges use conservative assumptions regarding KPMG valuation range is $76 million to $125 million, which is a very acceptable level compared to the $53 million approximate valuation post the million invested funds, and add $15.2 million of non-dilutive UT funds committed to Synergy's R & D. Total $53 million post license Synergy valuation.)

Question 11, Page 200

Why would Synergy continue to seek a merger partner after the lucrative license with UT?

Answer:

1) Same reasons as before. An acquisition of Synergy by a well-financed, public pharma company gives Synergy shareholders what they want:

   a) A liquidity opportunity, even though shares received would be subject to at least a one year lockup.

   b) The acquisition removes financing issues forever for Synergy because the pharma parent will decide what disease indications to pursue, and how to finance them.

   c) Synergy can accept a valuation on acquisition which is lower than the KPMG range because Synergy would not sell the stock received in the merger, but rather would hope to see the parent company stock price rise with Synergy success in the clinic.

2) The UT license finances the Phase I/II trials for hepatitis B and C, but does not leave Synergy financed to pursue the other disease indications available as targets for the rich imino-sugar technology platform (i.e. epilepsy, arthritis, other viral indications).

Question 12, Page 209

Assuming the final terms of each of the three deals — ICN, OGS, and Callisto — were each available at the same time, which would you recommend that the Synergy board accept? Compare the advantages and disadvantages of each deal. Which deal would serve the old Synergy shareholders the best — given the availability of funding for the post-merger company, the stock market upside, ease of liquidity, and the ability of Synergy management to control its scientific development?

Answer:

Each deal had its appeal to Synergy. The major attributes of each are summarized below.

1. ICN was the largest company with the greatest cash, the greatest market capitalization and the most extensive corporate infrastructure to conduct research, clinical trials and manage the product development of Synergy's technology platforms. ICN was valuing Synergy at $35 million which was attractive at this point in Synergy's development. ICN's $2.8 billion market cap was considerable, but Synergy would contribute a small fraction of total value. There would be limited upside in ICN's stock from any Synergy success.

2. OGS had an extensive cash hoard to use in the development of Synergy's technology platforms. Its public stock was severely depressed, which meant that Synergy could be the beneficiary of upticks in the OGS stock price, which had room to move without becoming overvalued. OGS management was not as deep or broad in numbers of disciplines, such that Synergy would have become the Research department in a merged company — not a bad thing for Synergy scientists would be in charge of the drug development process.

3. Callisto was the cleanest sheet of paper of the three. Synergy would manage the entire merged company, direct the scientific development of the technology platforms and Synergy would own 20 percent of the merged public company, which was a $4 stock with substantial upside based upon success in clinical trials. Callisto also brought $3 million in cash to the merger, which was sufficient to complete the pivotal Phase II clinical trial for Synergy's Atiprimod, and thereby potentially create $80 million of value for Synergy shareholders with trial success. The venture capitalists of the Synergy board especially liked the potential upside in the Callisto stock, which had a market cap post merger of $100 million including Synergy. Success in the Atiprimod Phase II trial could add $300 million to $400 million to the market cap for a potential quadruple in the stock.

The **Bad**

The IVonyx business was restarted within two years after the company lost the entire $6 million of equity raised in its first financing due to a flawed business model, which did not work. The company then changed from a franchiser of infusion therapy pharmacies to become owner of direct offices dispensing home infusion therapy. IVonyx had three changes of management, endured a severe down financing and had problems of accounts receivable collection as its revenues grew to $40 million over eight years. It was then acquired by a public company for $20 million of cash, stock and earnout. Five months later, the acquiring company went bankrupt and all was lost.

IVonyx Group Services, Inc.

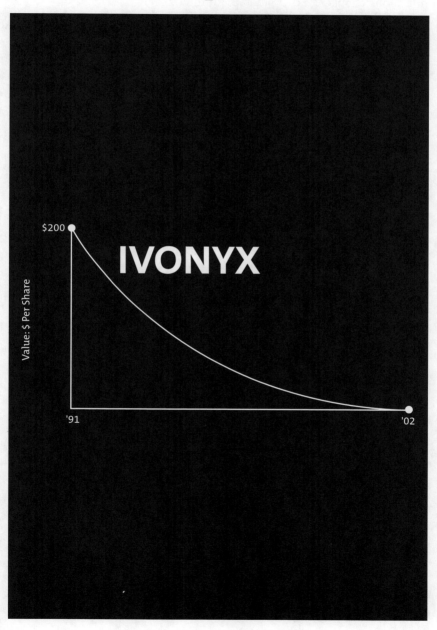

T here are two ways to get therapeutic drug treatment into humans — one is through oral medication and the other is through the vein, namely intravenous infusion. The concept of electronic infusion pumps controlling intravenous infusions produced numerous changes in drug therapy in the U.S.

The advent of electronic infusion pumps spawned the home infusion market. The home infusion services industry boomed in the 1980s as insurers sought cheaper ways of treating their insured, as infusion technology improved, and as patients on long-term therapy sought a better quality of life. While the home infusion industry portended enormous growth, it was not for the faint-hearted. Nor was it for those unable to nimbly reshape their companies to satisfy constantly shifting markets and regulations.

Al Henry entered the infusion services industry in 1988 through a small investment in an equipment distributorship named IVonyx. After the investment was made, the company struggled to reach profitability, and constantly re-authored its strategy and restructured its financing. It would be a long and wild ride.

Home Infusions: A New Industry

Medicare first allowed limited reimbursement of non-hospital services in 1977, but Medicare limited home infusion to patients who lacked a working digestive system and required TPN (total parenteral nutrition, with parenteral meaning around the stomach). TPN therapy had emerged in the late 1960s to feed patients a complete, predigested fluid of amino acids, dextrose, electrolytes, trace minerals, vitamins, and fat emulsions.[1] TPN fluid was too viscous to drip through the standard intravenous tubes used for saline solution. Delivered into the bloodstream by syringe, TPN had limited success.

The IMED volumetric pump revolutionized TPN therapy — much as it had revolutionized cancer chemotherapy — and was the technological key underlying what became the $20 billion solutions industry. With the advent of volumetric pumps in the 1970s, TPN fluid could be infused through a central line catheter — a plastic port protruding from the chest leading to a tube implanted directly into the vein upstream of the heart. The volumetric pump pushed the viscous fluid through a filter and into the catheter, from which it circulated more naturally through the body. Most illnesses that destroy the digestive tract — cancer, AIDS, acute pancreatitis — were chronic, so most TPN patients were lifers.

Similarly, enteral nutrition feeds patients who cannot eat orally because of an obstruction in the upper digestive system. They are victims of head, neck or esophageal cancer, gastrointestinal obstructions, or neurological disorders like strokes. A slightly less digested fluid is pumped through a naso-gastric tube running through the nose into the intestines. Like TPN, enteral nutrition often continues over a lifetime. Parenteral and enteral nutrition — in technology, patient mix, and Medicare funding — drove the early home infusion industry.

The HCFA (Health Care Financing Administration) was the agency that administered Medicare, the Federal government's $90 billion insurance program for the elderly and long-term disabled. On the issue of home infusion services, HCFA initially decided to fund only drugs and hardware — infusion pumps and catheters — on the premise they were prosthetic devices for patients lacking a digestive tract. HCFA did not pay for home nursing services. Infusion firms had to roll service costs into the $100 average price they charged HCFA for a bag of TPN fluid. As a result, the first home infusion services emerged from big equipment and solution suppliers and not from visiting nurses associations. Moreover, HCFA authorized home TPN to improve the quality of life for patients who would spend the rest of their lives hooked to this pump. HCFA did not expect infusions in the home to cost less than hospital infusions.

Home Health Care of America, founded in 1979 with venture backing from Kleiner, Perkins, Caufield & Byers, was the first pure-play in the home infusion market. HHCA built mixing pharmacies, trained IV nurses, and sought referrals from physician groups in major cities. With a business plan focused on the growth in Medicare TPN business, by 1982 it had revenues of $2 million and 18 percent pre-tax margins. HHCA stock debuted in March 1982, and investors awarded it a multiple of one hundred times earnings through the incredible biotechnology bull market of 1982-1983.[2]

By 1984, though, the home infusion market had shown preliminary signs of maturing. First, HCFA had seen the numbers of patients on home TPN swell, and wanted to be sure that private firms were not inducing them into the treatment. For the first time in what would be years of continuing struggle, home infusion firms like HHCA suffered from slow HCFA reimbursement. Second, new competitors emerged around hospital care. Medical costs had risen three times the rate of inflation during 1982, threatening to bankrupt the Medicare system. Late in 1982, Congress instituted a prospective payment system for Medicare. Prospective payment meant that HCFA categorized all treatments into 467 DRGs (for diagnosis related groups) and reimbursed hospitals only the amount specified for each patient with that diagnosis. Though not done through some comprehensive medical payments legislation, and despite a Reagan administration promise for general deregulation, the DRGs promulgated a standard classification of health services and thus insinuated the HCFA into all issues of health care pricing.

DRGs reshaped the home care industry. Hospitals now got one payment per diagnosis, regardless of how long the patient stayed in the hospital. Hospitals claimed their competitive advantage in the health care system came in the first few days of a visit, as they ran tests and performed procedures, rather than at the end when they monitored infections and observed the patient's recovery. DRGs did not apply to services provided in the home, even if by a hospital unit. Thus, hospitals had a financial incentive to move patients home as quickly as possible. "Quicker and sicker" discharges, Senator John Heinz called the practice.[3] The high point for hospital admissions and occupancy rates was 1981 and, perhaps under the pressure of DRGs, both rates have fallen continuously since. Others called this "high-tech home care" since it was not old-fashioned custodial care. It was enabled by new ambulatory medical devices — pumps, respirators, hemodialysis machines, and uterine, newborn, and heart monitors — that made care just as consistent at home as in the hospital. Most hospitals turned to their usual networks of providers beyond their walls — physician offices, pharmacies, visiting nurses associations. The few hospitals that expanded into home services mostly did so through joint ventures with their medical equipment suppliers — like Baxter Travenol or the American ContinueCare division of American Hospital Supply. The market expanded to welcome these firms, with a tripling in Medicare home care reimbursements between

1980 and 1985 from $662 million to $2,233 million. Within five years the total number of Medicare-certified home health agencies had doubled, led by for-profit rather than non-profit firms.

Pump manufacturers geared up development on the assumption that, as all home care grew, Medicare would expand its home infusion benefits to therapies other than TPN. While IMED locked up the market on high-end, multi-purpose pumps optimized for hospital use, other companies began building specialized pumps. A decade of heavy use taught pump designers that they could relax some reliability features to make pumps more portable and more user-friendly. Pharmacia Deltec of Sweden introduced a very popular CADD pump dedicated to home TPN infusions, with the whole system transportable in a backpack. Other companies, like Ivion Corp. made pumps optimized for specific thera-pies, and priced from $2,500 to $4,000 each. Many pumps eliminated the air-in-line alarms, always difficult to calibrate, as it became clear that the body could absorb more air than previously thought. Simultaneously, hospital supply companies introduced new catheters (or "venous-access devices") that could be left in the vein for days rather than hours, and kept sterile by the patient rather than a registered nurse. Nurses could supervise four home infusions per day, depending upon the time to drive between homes.

Medicare moved very slowly, however, in expanding its list of home infusion benefits. HCFA also grew more insistent on denying reim-bursement claims for home infusions already administered. By 1986 it became clear that early home infusion companies had undergone a prof-itless expansion, with revenues growing but earnings nonexistent. Stocks nose-dived. Companies actively sought to replace Medicare with cus-tomers like HMOs, and they began diversifying away from TPN, using the new technology to offer a wider range of therapies.

For example, Houston's HMSS, one of the first infusion companies, shifted into antibiotic infusions. Antibiotic drips treat a variety of dis-eases, including infections of the bone (osteomyelitis), of the heart lining (bacterial endocarditis), wounds, the kidney or urinary tracts, or various infections relating to AIDS. Antibiotics continued several times a day for the weeks following release from a hospital. Antibiotics could be infused with a less complex peripheral catheter — a thin plastic tube inserted by the nurse into a vein in the hand or forearm — and left there for days. "It was attractive that antibiotic patients were a younger population," said HMSS president Dale Ross, "more paid by private insurance."[4] By 1989, HMSS would have only seven percent Medicare patients, compared with twenty percent for its competitors.

Other home infusion companies signed agreements with pharmaceutical companies that made them part of the delivery system for new drugs that could not be packaged in pills or bolus injections. Sandoz Pharmaceuticals, for example, in 1989 made Caremark the exclusive home distributor of Clozaril, a drug used to treat schizophrenia. Private insurers also encouraged physicians to move chemotherapy, hydration, and pain management out of the hospital and into patients' homes. (Economists claimed, however, that the only cost advantages came from replacing the skilled labor in hospitals with unpaid family caretakers at home.) By 1987, all private insurers covered home drug infusions, as did the Veterans Administration hospitals. Over the next decade, roughly half of total home infusion sales would be paid by private insurers and the other half by Medicare, since most long-term disabled needing TPN were covered by Medicare.

When Home Health Care of America stock tumbled in 1984, due to its rapid entry into the low-margin enteral nutrition business, it was acquired by Pfizer and, in 1987, passed to Baxter Travenol's Caremark unit — at the still generous price of $586 million or forty times earnings. Baxter had entered the home care market in the late 1970s, when it introduced home kidney dialysis, and was a leader in supplying saline and dextrose solutions for infusions. Caremark was destined to become a diversified home health care company, with $500 million in revenues in 1989 and 40 percent of market share (not counting Baxter's sales of infusion products, which accounted for ten percent of its business.) Yet the Justice Department cleared the Baxter-Home Health Care merger on the reasoning that there were so few barriers to entry into the home health care business.

Small, personable local providers competed easily with large, national firms. A 1987 report by Hambrecht & Quist verified this impression of ease of entry. The home infusion market, they projected, would grow from $870 million annually in 1986 to $2.8 billion by 1991. They predicted profitable futures for the National Medical Care unit of W.R. Grace and the big independent public companies like Healthdyne of Georgia, New England Critical Care in Massachusetts, T2 Medical of Atlanta, Care Plus of Fort Lauderdale, Continental Health Affiliates of Englewood Cliffs, and HMSS in Houston. But overwhelmingly, Hambrecht & Quist concluded, this growth would be driven by small, local entrepreneurs.

Most remarkable about the home infusion industry was the many sources of start-up companies. Home infusion companies were started by hospitals seeking to monitot their own patients as they went home; sometimes hospitals set up outpatient clinics where patients came for catheter changes and to get supplies to take home. Yet hospitals tended to be bureaucratic and lacking in the entrepreneurial skills needed to run home infusion as a business. Likewise, the larger physician groups, especially those who had already built stand-alone outpatient clinics to treat cancers or persistent infectious diseases like Lyme disease, started home infusion agencies to provide continuity of care. Visiting nurses agencies, traditionally service-oriented philanthropic ventures run by retired nurses with less administrative experience, had the service infrastructure to provide home infusions.[5] However, HCFA's decision to reimburse equipment charges rather than nurse service charges initially kept nursing agencies out of the home infusion industry. Gradually nursing agencies invested in the necessary pumps and catheters and entered the industry. Sometimes makers of durable medical equipment established home infusion companies as an outlet for their pumps, monitors and catheters. Also, local pharmacists, those with an entrepreneurial small-business bent and the license needed to mix infusion solutions, bought infusion equipment and hired a nurse to deliver these solutions. The home infusion industry was growing rapidly, with various embedded sources of patient referrals, differing levels of clinical or business experience, and many competing business models.

Self-regulation came to the industry, as it usually did in health care, through the Joint Commission on Accreditation of Healthcare Organizations. The JCAHO issued standards for accrediting home care agencies for the first time in 1988.[6] Previously a mish-mash of professional societies had accredited home health agencies, though only JCAHO accreditation garnered the "deemed status" necessary to qualify for reimbursement from Medicare and most insurers. Firms paid JCAHO $3,000 to $10,000 to inspect their facilities, adding a small barrier to entry. Yet JCAHO certification, a standard measure of quality, largely obviated the need for brand building. Not only did JCAHO certification enable small firms to compete with large firms, but the way JCAHO structured the certification influenced the kind of business models they should pursue. JCAHO previously had only accredited hospitals and clinics, and they kept their focus on physical facilities. Agencies could be accredited for delivering health care in the home, or in a clinic, regardless of what kind of clinical therapies they provided. Thus, a home infusion firm would find it easier to merge with a home nursing firm — since they both worked in the home — than with a firm that provided infusions in an outpatient clinic.

The late 1980s into the early 1990s were flush times for the home infusion business. That would all change once private insurers turned to capitated contracts and the Clinton administration decried rising health care costs. But for now, private insurers made ever greater use of the proliferating base of infusion providers to deliver a wider variety of drugs, and cared only that they charged less than hospitals. And the HCFA — perhaps because Republican administrations catered to older voters, perhaps because of the lack of government oversight in the name of deregulation — expanded their coverage to more patients and loosened reimbursements. TPN was seen as a high margin business; every part of the industry was strong.

Question 1

Assume you are a partner in a venture fund. Review the summary of the Hambrecht & Quist January, 1987 Home Drug Delivery Industry Report. (Attachment #1, page 387) Do you find the home infusion industry attractive for investment? Why or why not? Which competitive approach to the industry shows the greatest potential?

The IVonyx Distributorship: 1987

Selling was in Alan Jordan's blood. Jordan began selling medical equipment with Baxter Laboratories in 1965, rising to become Baxter's top sales performer. In 1969 Richard Cramer lured him to IVAC, a pioneer in infusion control devices, and then to IMED to sell more modern volumetric infusion pumps. Jordan rose to IMED vice president of sales in a company filled with star salesmen. He helped draft IMED's strategy of selling directly to hospitals and replacing IMED's network of distributors with a direct sales force. After Warner-Lambert acquired IMED in 1983 Jordan left with his millions in IMED stock options. He joined the Winfield Corporation, which made systems to collect and dispose of infectious hospital wastes. He took some time off, then kept on selling.

Jordan founded IVonyx, Inc. in October 1986 as a distributorship of high-tech infusion equipment to alternative-site health care firms — clinics, physician groups and home health agencies not physically attached to a hospital. Jordan financed the firm with $500,000, personally secured a bank credit line of $373,000, and found $120,000 in a minority equity investment. He built a warehouse in near San Diego, and built an experienced sales network along the West coast. By December 1987, IVonyx had 23 employees and annualized sales of $3 million. "The hospital in the home:" that slogan was adopted by Curaflex, a leading home care firm. Indeed, one reason patients wanted home care was their belief that high-tech equipment enabled care at home to be as good as care in the hospital. Revenues from sales of all home infusion pumps were projected to grow from $18 million in 1986 to $133 million by 1990, and profits on durable medical equipment enjoyed the highest margins in the healthcare industry.[7]

As Jordan profited from the tremendous boom in home infusion start-ups, he saw first hand the inexperience of people entering the business. As his customers became more dependent on his expertise in home infusion technology, he hatched a plan to capture profits from his expertise.

In late 1987, Jordan restructured his distributorship into three interrelated companies. TPEN Systems, Inc. continued the distribution of products in the western states and expanded with sales into hospitals. IVonyx, Inc. sold "memberships," partnership agreements with local pharmacists, durable medical equipment firms, and any others who wished to enter the home infusion business. Members paid a $16,000 initiation fee and $3,000 in annual dues (raising to a $25,000 initiation fee and $5,000 annual dues by 1990). Members also bought a starter kit of $25,000 worth of equipment, and agreed to buy all supplies from an IVonyx purchasing pool over a five year period, for which they got a discount off the price. IVonyx provided its members with week-long training seminars — in compounding, patient education, billing, and marketing — so that they had a timely, turnkey and cost-effective entry into the home infusion market. IVonyx sold its members on-site service as a further revenue item.

IVonyx Financial Services, Inc. would help finance the members. It would also build a computerized billing system to link to third-party payers so members could collect receivables in under thirty days. Jordan expected that this billing service might become a stand-alone operation serving the entire home care industry. Jordan also expected to later establish five "beta sites" — model regional offices where IVonyx could hone home infusion procedures and incidentally generate revenues of $1 million annually. Using a sales staff of only three people working trade shows, IVonyx sold 32 memberships in five months. Jordan anticipated $7 million in sales for 1988, and 120 more signings in calendar 1989.

Jordan had kept in constant touch with his former IMED colleague, Al Henry. When Henry saw Jordan's easy success in generating membership revenue, in June 1988 the Henry Venture Fund made a small equity investment of $500,000 in IVonyx. Henry and Dave Hare, a vice president in Henry & Co., joined the board and laid plans for further developing its infusion services business.

Henry convinced Jordan to close out the TPEN Inc. equipment distributorship. Jordan originally started his membership program to boost equipment sales and did quite well. But by mid-1988 it was clear the supply network for infusion devices had matured and that supplying services promised better margins and bigger growth. Then in July 1988 San Diego-based Pancretec Inc., suddenly and without explanation, cancelled an agreement making IVonyx its sole distributor of a new line of portable infusion pumps on the west coast.[8] IVonyx had been Pancretec's top seller and had prepared for this new agreement by spending half a year and $1 million buying inventory and hiring and training staff. While the lawyers sorted out blame, IVonyx sought an advantage. IVonyx brochures were rewritten to claim that TPEN had been part of a master plan; that the distributorship had been "used as a holding company to recruit and train a staff of fourteen highly qualified salesmen while IVonyx transitioned to a home infusion company."

Franchising: 1988

Jordan and Henry planned to focus on local pharmacists. There were 58,000 independent pharmacists in the United States, about 3,000 of which had sufficient community stature and financial substance to provide a good base for a home infusions franchise. Community pharmacists who owned and operated their own stores understood business better than many physicians and nurses, plus they understood the importance of personalized care better than equipment companies and massive hospitals. Most community pharmacists had a natural entrepreneurial bent, and had already invested in various types of durable medical equipment — wheelchairs, prosthetics, monitors — to serve their customers. They already knew referring physicians and could give them constant feedback on patient progress. "The most personalized care comes from local caregivers," proclaimed an IVonyx brochure. Pharmacy professional societies offered whole-hearted support to companies like IVonyx that opened up home infusions to their members.[9] Some states licensed pharmacists as infusion-technicians, able to administer the infusions themselves. Plus, pharmacists had a monopoly on the most important component of a home infusion agency — the license to compound the perishable solutions.

If pharmacists were to provide personalized care and clinical excellence, though, they needed help elsewhere. Jordan and Henry decided to drop the membership-purchase plan, and instead drafted a contract specifying a franchise relationship between IVonyx and pharmacists. That way, IVonyx could help the franchisees build their businesses and charge a service fee as a percentage of collections. IVonyx could sell a franchise for $25,000, and then collect fourteen percent of gross revenues over the ten year period of agreement. IVonyx had already sold seventy memberships to local pharmacists and offered them franchise-like support — so long as IVonyx received twelve percent of any patient referral revenues directly attributed to IVonyx sales staff and eight percent of any revenues collected through headquarters action. IVonyx began converting memberships to franchises on the promise of even greater support.

IVonyx, for example, guided its franchisees to certifications. Jordan hired away Caremark's leading pharmacists to help IVonyx franchisees build and certify a required IVonyx Home Therapy Center, the core of which was a clean room for compounding the pharmaceuticals. Franchisees also agreed to buy a range of infusion equipment, and IVonyx forged purchasing agreements so franchisees could buy at a discount. In return, the center must assure staffing on-call around the clock, seven days a week. IVonyx quality assurance staff regularly audited solution samples, reviewed nurse charting, and did annual on-site visits to assure all franchises met IVonyx clinical standards. Each center submitted monthly patient care data to headquarters in a format useful in tracking therapy trends.

IVonyx helped with training. Franchisees had to attend a series of training classes, included as part of the license. IVonyx hosted a week-long National Training Session every month, to which franchisees sent staff to learn the latest in clinical procedures or administrative techniques. IVonyx provided regular on-site quality assurance reviews and helped franchisees stay abreast of ever-changing standards for home health care. IVonyx encouraged its franchisees to offer the widest possible range of home infusion therapies, including chemotherapy, antibiotic therapy, TPN, and pain management. They provided a curriculum for educating patients at home on how to care for their catheter, change dressings, and apply antibiotics. If drugs were used that required blood level monitoring, the nurses were trained to draw blood for the necessary laboratory tests. Nurses also selected the right equipment to minimize the impact on the patient's lifestyle. Nurses could place catheters for central, peripheral, subcutaneous, or intra-spinal routes. Everything they did was written down and sent to a physician for review.[10]

IVonyx helped with marketing. Franchises used the IVonyx name. IVonyx advertised nationally, attended trade shows, set up a regional system of salesmen, and built brand recognition. IVonyx prepared a fifteen-minute videotape, sent nationwide to 500 members of the Physicians Computer Network, in which two prominent Harvard physicians discussed the advantages of home infusions of TPN. In addition IVonyx training taught every employee to act as an indirect sales force.

Most importantly, IVonyx helped its franchises with billing. The only other firm franchising nationwide to pharmacists, OptionCare, was run by pharmacists who offered clinical training, but no help in marketing or billing. In eleven years, OptionCare had signed 184 franchises nationwide. OptionCare 1989 gross billings for all franchisees was $71 million (compared with $42 million in 1988), of which OptionCare itself received about $9 million gross revenues.[11] IVonyx did even better. In less than two years IVonyx signed fifty franchises in a better-educated market and was on track to sign up 250 the next year.

Question 2

At this stage in its evolution, what value would you place on IVonyx? What methodology and comparisons would you use for arriving at that value? Do you need to raise capital for the company to continue to grow? If so, how much and with what type of financing? Review the term sheet for the Series A round of financing [Attachment #2, page 395] Would you suggest that any terms be changed? Why or why not?

In December 1988 after six months of effort in showing IVonyx to other venture capitalists and institutional money pools, Henry closed IVonyx's first major equity funding, totaling $5.1 million, of which 28 percent came from the Henry Venture Fund and Henry Venture II. The rest came from Seaport Ventures Inc. of San Diego, S.G. Warburg of London and several British investment funds and insurance companies.[12] This Series A preferred stock was done on a company pre-money valuation of $2.5 million, or $8 per share. That December, the IVonyx board also approved a four-for-one split in its common stock, which made the Series A cost $2 per share. They also reserved a second option pool of 68,750 shares, all with five year vesting, for future issuance to franchisees who pioneer new operations, employees who boost revenues, and physicians who offered consultation on how to improve services.

Of this $5.1 million, $2.7 million went to pay off debt and $2.4 million funded operations, now moving at a brisk pace. It was an exuberant move into franchising. IVonyx's first major problem, in fact, was that growth came too fast.

Cash Flow Shortfall: 1989

In February 1989, new signings vanished. Jordan called together IVonyx management and outlined "Mission 100" — the plan to reach a hundred franchises by the end of the year. Henry became involved in implementing the plan and gradually began working four days a week on-site. Senior officers spent four weeks preparing a hundred page description of the company, which they submitted to the state of New York to obtain a franchisor license. It formed the basis for a nationwide licensing effort, which concluded six months and $200,000 later, when IVonyx announced it had licenses to sell franchises in all fifty states.

IVonyx management plotted new ways to get new franchises operational quicker. Potential signers had heard that IVonyx often failed to get franchises in operation ninety days after signature, as promised, and IVonyx understood that franchises could not return their fourteen percent of gross revenues until they were certified to serve patients. IVonyx had been especially slow in certifying members to receive patients because of the complexities of building clean rooms to Class 10,000 specifications. Once the pharmacists and nurses completed training they often waited 120 to 150 days for their clean room certifications. IVonyx made a breakthrough in May, by offering a proprietary, modular clean room in four configurations. It was also a new revenue item that franchisees had to buy, at prices ranging from $14,000 to $24,000 and returning a forty percent gross profit margin to IVonyx. As the first company to offer a modular room, signings accelerated to fourteen in May alone. (That fall IVonyx certified a franchise in only four weeks after the contract signing.) But, IVonyx burned capital in setting up the franchises already signed. Its headcount had swollen to 45, and it needed a new injection of capital well before 1990 as planned.

In the summer of 1989, IVonyx tried a second round Series B institutional financing with money pools and insurance firms. HMSS had just been acquired at good multiples, which should have made it easier to place IVonyx shares. IVoynx proposed a pre-money valuation of $11.3 million on the IVonyx Series B convertible preferred shares, or $10.64 per IVonyx common equivalent share (CES) as compared to $8 per CES for the Series A, a modest 33 percent increase in valuation over the Series A financing of the previous year. IVonyx forecast $4 million revenue for calendar 1989 compared with $900,000 on a comparable basis for the previous year. However, English and US financial institutions showed little interest in a company burning cash so quickly. After four months of effort the Series B financing was withdrawn.

After the failed financing was withdrawn, IVonyx constantly revised downward its forecast 1989 revenues. In December 1988 IVonyx had forecast $10 million in 1989 revenues. Revenues dropped $908,825 when IVonyx dissolved its equipment distributorship, partly offset by a $736,502 jump in franchise sales. At year end, though, IVonyx reported its revenues had dropped 7.1 percent between fiscal 1988 to 1989 from $3.0 million to $2.8 million. Perhaps a more telling number was that selling, general and administrative expenses as a percentage of revenue jumped from 109.3 percent in fiscal 1988 to 162.2 percent in 1989. This was understandable during the year of a major restructuring; what was worrisome was the inability to project when IVonyx would recover.

The timing of company growth was thrown out of kilter by a year of easy sales of franchises, followed by harder sales. It looked like IVonyx could never plug the lead-lag in financing — the lag between when IVonyx spent money to set up a franchise and the time when the franchise returned fees. It was possible that IVonyx's fourteen percent fee would not entirely cover IVonyx's expenditures on behalf of franchisees for nationwide marketing, collections and sales efforts to generate patient referrals regionally. What was more clear was that IVonyx received its fee more than fourteen months after a franchisee was identified. It took four to six months to take a prospect to the sale of a franchise. Then, another three to four months passed before patient referrals were generated. Subsequently, it took four to five months for franchisees to collect payment for patient therapy. The IVonyx business model forecast a DSO (days' sales outstanding) of 60 days; in fact, franchisee accounts receivable had a DSO of 140 days. IVonyx actually collected recurring cash flow some fourteen months after it first expended money throughout the sales cycle — which was defined by the venture capitalists as the elapsed time from initial expenditure to solicit prospects to the collection of a recurring revenue stream from franchisees.

Question 3

IVonyx faced a severe cash flow crisis because expenditures to support new franchisees were greater than revenues derived from franchisees, and because franchisee accounts receivable were much slower than the forecast DSO of sixty days. Detail your solution to the IVonyx cash flow crisis.

In August 1989, IVonyx tried to control the burn rate, develop a new strategy, and turn around the company. The headcount in headquarters was reduced from 42 to 28. As part of Mission 100, management authored a plan to get patient referrals from large insurers and regional HMOs which would benefit all IVonyx offices nationwide. Direct relationships with insurers and HMOs might further improve DSO for accounts receivable. IVonyx also hired the leading sales manager of HMSS, who brought to IVonyx much needed experience.

As then structured, though, it was difficult for IVonyx to sign national contracts. IVonyx had to rewrite its franchise agreement so that headquarters could enter into national contracts on behalf of the franchises, and that bound the franchises to contracted pricing. Headquarters circulated a list of pricing for HMO contracts for prior consent from each franchise. HMOs, they discovered, strongly preferred per diem, all-inclusive pricing. Franchises found the pricing shockingly low, but headquarters assured them that the prices allowed them a return of forty percent, even after they paid their fourteen percent fee to IVonyx. IVonyx had to get information from each franchisee — furnishing numbers and certifications — so that headquarters could coordinate the details of a nationwide contract. IVonyx renamed its director of patient referral the "Vice President of Member Happiness," and he led a major effort of training seminars to bring the franchisees in tune with the new national contracting strategy.

Fortunately, the IVonyx contract already specified that headquarters could bill on behalf of the franchisees. Competitor OptionCare had never established a national billing service for its 190 franchises. When OptionCare started seeking out managed care contracts they had to sell their franchises a separate service, called OptionNet, that allowed headquarters to sign contracts referring patients to franchises. However, all contacts still had to be billed locally, which scared off quite a few national payers.

IVonyx had bigger control problems with the branches that had joined as members and not yet converted to a franchise. Their annual dues covered only a fraction of their drain on corporate resources, and they added nothing to the strategy of national contracting. In late 1989 IVonyx began a final push to convert members to franchises. As incentive to convert, IVonyx lowered its fees from fourteen percent to nine percent. By March 1990, 38 members had converted to franchise agreements. Those that still failed to convert were weeded out. Private insurers began requiring JCAHO accreditation, an expensive process which few members could complete without IVonyx help. Otherwise, IVonyx canceled membership agreements based on accounts receivable they owed to headquarters.

With a big increase in referrals for the final quarter, IVonyx franchises expected to report gross patient billings for 1989 of $4.5 million. This returned fees of $500,000 to IVonyx, up from $80,000 in 1989, but this was a pittance compared with IVonyx's rate of expenses. IVonyx had simply become addicted to a constant infusion of initial fees from new franchise signings. During 1989 IVonyx had signed sixty new franchises, and expected to sign five more monthly from then on. Each new franchise brought IVonyx $50,000 in gross revenues ($25,000 franchise fee, $15,000 for modular clean room, and $15,000 for instruments and disposables) so that during 1990, they could expect $2.5 million from new signings.

However, some economic forecasters saw clear signs of a recession beginning in 1990. If the general economy turned sour and net new business formation declined, regardless of what the sales force promised, IVonyx would sell far fewer new franchise licenses. Yet IVonyx was still committed to supporting new franchisees that only slowly returned recurring revenues. Existing franchisees already voiced considerable discontent and frustration over how slow it took to generate revenues despite their investment of considerable time and money. Franchisees unable to build a referral base constantly threatened lawsuit against IVonyx for failure to support them as promised. IVonyx could not cut back services to franchisees. IVonyx faced another clear cash crisis as it entered 1990.

Restart: 1990

In October 1989 IVonyx planned to open a company-owned and operated branch. It would open in Chicago, home of IVonyx's recently hired director of regional sales, who predicted the branch could generate $1 million annual revenues within six months. "This move toward direct company-owned business," wrote Henry to an investment banker in October 1989, "is analogous to Holiday Inn having both company-owned and franchised facilities....This balance of direct and franchise revenue sources will make IVonyx a very powerful story when it comes time to go public." The goal was to improve agency problems as IVonyx pursued national contracts, and to serve as a model facility at which franchisees could train. It quickly became clear, however, that no one in IVonyx had the experience to operate a branch generating that level of revenues.

So in December 1989, IVonyx started looking hard for acquisition candidates with help from consultants and investment bankers. IVonyx sought a regional home infusion company doing about $3 million annually in direct revenue, with twenty percent pre-tax profit margins and, above all, very strong leadership. Such an acquisition addressed two broad trends, both affecting the flow of capital, that had been identified in the home infusion industry of the late 1980s: the proliferation of managed care and problems with getting paid.

Ever more patients were switching from private health insurance to managed care programs, like regional HMOs, managed care affiliates of major insurers, or company-run insurance programs. Because most managed care firms had rationalized their own health care costs, they were very good at dictating prices to subcontract suppliers like the home infusion firms. Because many managed care agencies owned hospitals and clinics, they had less incentive to shift costs to patient homes. Some providers willingly played by HMO rules. New England Critical Care, which was positioning itself for an IPO, was notorious for cutting prices to post managed care contracts on its books. Other home health care firms had real trouble protecting their niches under the profusion of managed care. CarePlus, which had started in 1983 as a comprehensive home health company, could not compete with the HMOs and sold off all but its infusion services. "You end up with a group of businesses that are medically-related," said CarePlus president Bob Wood, "but the reimbursement systems aren't the same, the management techniques aren't the same."[13]

The private insurers that early had led the move to home infusions, because it halved the costs of hospital infusions, remained reliable customers. Indeed, between 1986 and 1990 the number of home infusion patients covered by private insurance grew six fold. However, insurers got ever better at dictating prices and scrutinizing bills from home health firms.[14] Furthermore, more hospitals opened their own home infusion offices and were willing to low-ball prices to get a second charge on treating a patient. Hospital case managers referred fewer patients with private insurance to outside firms.

In less than a decade, home infusion had gone from being perceived as a solution to cost containment to being perceived as a part of the problem. In the early 1980s countless economic studies calculated substantial savings per patient over hospital infusions — a median placed the savings at sixty percent. By the early 1990s, economic analyses showed instead that costs were substantially less than prices.[15] In 1984, the HCFA released a report showing that one-third of Medicare reimbursements to home health agencies were for services that should have been denied. By 1987, the HCFA's actual denial rate rose to seven percent. The HCFA tried to impose cost containment on home care but, rather that setting a total package rate as with the DRGs, they set limits on a line item basis which left little flexibility for firms to find economies.[16] In 1988 the Medicare Catastrophic Coverage Act expanded the variety of home infusion benefits to 900 types (from thirty in 1980). This broader coverage gave the HCFA reason enough for full-scale regulation of the industry. When this broadened Medicare coverage was repealed the following year, the funds for home infusions disappeared but its prescriptive pricing and regulatory apparatus for home infusions remained.

Furthermore, the Medicare system was notoriously bad at paying bills. The National Association for Home Care charged that the HCFA intended to dismantle its home care benefit with disastrous paperwork requirements and unbearable denial rates. Like most home infusion firms, Healthdyne served Medicare TPN patients. Healthdyne grew from $7 million sales in 1983 to $65 million in 1988 when the HCFA cracked down on payments for durable medical equipment. The HCFA found patients paying thousands of dollars to lease equipment they could have bought for a few hundred. HCFA's retroactive rule changes cost the Healthdyne equipment division and other firms about $400 million in cancelled payments. As a result, most companies doubted Medicare patients could ever be a viable market. While IVonyx sought a larger percentage of private payer customers, they were required by law to accept Medicare patients and did so, without hesitation, so that they never had to tell a physician they had a problem accepting any patient.

To sort through these broad market trends, IVonyx sought help from franchises. An IVonyx Member Advisory Board, was convened made up of the most successful franchisees to recommend improvements in operating policy for all members. A Patient Referral Marketing Committee consisted of top management, leaders of health care firms, and physicians. They recommended ways of building a more diversified patient base, and helped plot the pursuit of national contracts. Gradually, the membership of the advisory committee shifted solely to physicians, who then focused on improving IVonyx clinical practice. Unfortunately, government agencies had made compensating these experts for their time like stepping on eggs.

In November 1989 Congress passed a budget bill that contained a section titled "Physical Ownership of, and Referral to, Health Care Entities," otherwise known as the Stark Amendments. California congressman Fortney "Pete" Stark, chairman of the health subcommittee of the House Ways and Means Committee, wrote the amendments as a condition for adding a home infusion benefit to the short-lived 1988 Medicare Catastrophic Coverage Act. The Stark amendments required that every bill a health care facility submitted to Medicare indicate whether the referring physician had an investment in the facility. The law sent tremors through the home infusion industry, especially companies like T^2 Medical that claimed physician-ownership of most of its branches assured clinical quality control. The U.S. Department of Health and Human Services only slowly developed safe harbor regulations implementing the Stark amendments, which finally appeared in 1991.

Every infusion services firm lived under threat of being overwhelmed by shifting regulations. The home infusion industry was generally poorly regulated, which presented both opportunity and risk. Medicare required that infusion firms be accredited by the JCAHO, but many niche firms were able to operate without accreditation. Each branch needed registration with the FDA and the Drug Enforcement Agency to dispense controlled substances. OSHA monitored employee safety at each firm. Each branch also had to abide by state laws regulating pharmacies, home labor, nursing licensing, health planning, and professional ethics. IVonyx protected itself only by making its franchisees scrupulously adhere to the various state laws restricting business relationships between physicians and pharmacists, even though the laws were often vague and still uninterpreted by the courts.

Direct patient care, IVonyx concluded, was the best solution to these industry trends. Company-owned flagship branches could invest time in following changes in regulation and clinical care and help its franchises stay current. If IVonyx were going to spend more effort on collections, it should be collecting those for its own P&L statement rather than its franchisees. Sales volume and quality assurance were important if IVonyx were to attract and profit from national contracts.

On New Year's Day 1990, after some months of preparation, Al Jordan resigned as CEO and president of IVoynx.

In March 1990, IVonyx completed acquisition of Total Infusion Care, Inc. which operated facilities in Sacramento and Detroit under the name Complete Infusion Care. CIC had revenues of $1.3 million in fiscal 1989, and gave IVonyx direct operations in infusion services.

CIC expected to get preferred provider contracts from each of the big three auto makers and from the UAW. CIC had assembled a seasoned management team from National Medical Care and had recruited some excellent salespeople from the largest home health care firms — like Caremark and Homedco — who were inclined to seek bigger, nationwide contracts. That was exactly the sort of business plotted for IVonyx's restart.

Question 4
What do you think of IVonyx's acquisition of CIC in concept? Was the acquisition good, bad or unimportant?

Adding Branches

The CIC Sacramento branch was on track to do $1.5 million gross revenues in 1990, while CIC Detroit projected $2.5 million in direct business. These branches would serve as flagship operations that displayed to the franchisees IVonyx philosophies and good standards. Compared to San Diego, Detroit was more central to people travelling for training sessions and shared a time zone with the majority of franchisees.[17] IVoynx added slightly to the staff of 45 in Detroit, and eliminated 50 positions at IVonyx's former headquarters in Temecula, California.

Rather than boosting earnings throughout 1990, IVonyx instead boosted revenues by adding branches. In one year, by April 1991, IVonyx had grown from two direct branches to sixteen — four new branches from acquisitions and ten built from the ground up.

Two criteria determined where IVonyx would open shops: a good referral base and expected market penetration of five percent or $1 million within a few months. Company branches usually occupied 3500 square feet, leased in a suburban office park, and needed $50,000 for medical equipment and the clean room. IVonyx moved much quicker getting direct operations up and running, compared with franchises, but they still consumed $500,000 and posted three quarters of operating losses. Most were run by a general manager, a certified pharmacist, and at least one registered nurse. All branches underwent JCAHO certification, an intensive process finally completed in February 1992. In addition to rewarding the sales staff for generating referrals, branch managers were rewarded for keeping the patients. Options for mid-level managers were awarded on the basis of profitability so that they balanced the drive for new revenues with the desire to contain costs company-wide. As expertise shifted to the branches, IVonyx further tightened its headquarters staff.

The number of franchisees dropped from 75 to 29 as IVonyx weeded out the chronic complainers and low business outlets that fell below stipulated covenants. Mom-and-pop operations had increasing difficulty competing in an industry where barriers to entry remained so low — $100,000 was still the minimum most pharmacists needed for a clean room, equipment and some advertising. IVonyx could only enter the big leagues of the industry by competing for national contracts from HMOs, third party payers, and self-insured corporations. Competition for these contracts depended upon low capitated or per diem pricing and having high clinical standards of quality. IVonyx decided to add only high-quality franchises and keep the total number around fifty.

In 1990, the IVonyx board voted to attempt another Series B financing, to attract $3 million of new equity capital, but at a smaller valuation. The board decided that the market would set the valuation. Henry embarked upon another road show, visiting venture capitalists and later-stage money pools to see what valuation would attract $3 million of new investment. The IVonyx board and Series A shareholders were alarmed to learn from prospective institutional investors that they would be willing to make new investment only at a pre-money valuation of $3.5 million to $4 million. Thus, a $3 million investment from this new investor group would get them almost half of IVonyx ownership, making them the largest investor group.

Even at that valuation, it took six months of effort visiting potential investors before the Series B closed in September 1990 at a pre-money valuation of $3.5 million. IVonyx raised $2.98 million in new equity at an IVonyx common equivalent share value of $0.44, post-split. The Series A investors had paid $2 per IVonyx CES, post-split. IVonyx placed shares worth about $1 million with Jeffrey Picower of JMP Group and the remainder with Dr. David H. Smith and the Euro Canadian Specialist Investment Fund B — once his Henry Venture Fund and HVF II kept the largest exposure. The Series B round was expanded to issue 1.9 million more shares (bringing the total to 10.2 million) to acquire CIC.

This Series B closing boosted IVonyx cash to $3.4 million, giving IVonyx sufficient funds for operations through July 1991 when it was forecast IVonyx would surely turn cash positive. That December, IVonyx finally closed a loan agreement with Christiania Bank whereby IVonyx could borrow up to $1.25 million, secured by accounts receivable. The effort to secure Series B financing dramatically boosted Henry's stake in this one company. IVonyx had just burned $5.1 million in capital in less than a year, and he had just committed more to it.

Question 5

Review the failed Series B term sheet and the term sheet for the Series B shares which ultimately closed. [Attachments #3 and #4, page 403 and page 412] What are the proposed pre-money valuations of each term sheet? What are the major differences between the failed and the closed Series B financing? What is the effect of each "B" financing on the then existing IVonyx shareholders by class (i.e. the Series A shareholders, common shareholders, and the management option pool)? Show your calculations and discuss the effect in monetary terms and dilution. Did management suffer any ill effect as a result of the Series B financing? How so?

Henry's restart of IVonyx worked. By December 1990, total current assets had increased to $3.3 million, up from $1.6 million a year earlier, due to a $1.4 million increase in accounts receivable from the company-owned branches. Revenues increased 49.2 percent to $4.2 million in fiscal 1990, versus $2.8 million in 1989, largely due to $3.0 million in revenues from new company-owned branches. Net loss for 1990 was $800,000 versus $3.1 million for the previous year. Furthermore, patient therapies performed per franchise had been growing consistently over the year, so that service fee revenues from franchises increased 229 percent, from $97,635 in 1989 to $320,761 in 1990, offset only by decreases of 69 percent in medical product sales and of 78 percent in new membership revenues. Importantly, IVonyx's restructuring also laid a ground work for future explosive growth rates in net revenues: 173 percent in 1991, 68 percent in 1992, 40 percent in 1993, and 68 percent in 1994.

As part of its restructuring, IVonyx slowed creation of new branches and sped acquisition of well-run existing offices. In March 1991 they bought a Memphis office started by four pharmacists affiliated with the University of Tennessee medical campus. It came bundled with an excellent referral base at Tennessee's major teaching hospital, as well as a set of six franchises they had started with pharmacists throughout the state. IVonyx opened a round of Series C convertible preferred shares valued at $1.00. In exchange of 250,000 shares of IVonyx Series C stock plus an earn-out of 25 percent of pre-tax profits from the Memphis branch, the pharmacists signed a non-compete agreement and continued to serve as a referral base for the company. This acquisition generated $4 million in revenues for IVonyx in 1991.

In the first quarter of 1991, IVonyx turned a profit of $52,000 on $2.2 million quarterly revenues. In the second quarter, IVonyx had net income of $400,000 on $4.0 million revenues. In July 1991 the IVonyx board approved a $2 million line of credit with National Bank of Detroit (NBD).

IVonyx planned to accelerate the acquisition of new branches. While this might limit short-term earnings, it positioned IVonyx for aggressive growth through national contracts and made it a more attractive merger partner. During 1991, IVonyx had doubled its number of branches from 11 to 22. In early 1992 they studied each branch, but decided to divest of none. All were at least breaking even, except for Cincinnati which had just picked up almost $250,000 in monthly revenues from a group of fourteen physicians who had just ended their ties with T^2 Medical.

By December 1991, a little more than a year since the Series B down-financing, IVonyx and Lehman Bros. closed an oversubscribed $7 million placement of Series C convertible preferred shares. Purchasers were U.S. health care firms and insurance and pension funds. The placement valued the company at $32 million, or $1.00 per common share.

This was a valuation of 2.4 times revenues. During 1991 sales had jumped to $13.2 million from $4.2 million in 1990. December 1991 alone showed $2.3 million revenues. The loss for 1991 was $320,000, versus $2.9 million for 1990. After losing $8.4 million in its first four years of operations, IVonyx finally showed a profit. In December 1991, the National Bank of Detroit boosted IVonyx's line of credit from $2 million to $5 million, with an additional $1 million term loan facility.

IVonyx planned for an IPO sometime around March 1992.

Disclosure of a shortfall in collections during November 1991, however, sent a shock wave through the company. Collections had always been a problem. Several directors of reimbursement had come and gone as they failed to keep up with the pace in IVonyx revenue growth. One was fired in late 1990, when IVonyx still had $450,000 in accounts receivable dated over 120 days from the pre-acquisition business of CIC. IVonyx insisted that this be collected by the end of the year. Under generally accepted accounting principles, 120 days was the point at which, to keep a balance sheet conservative, accounts receivable had to be written off. IVonyx's review of outstanding accounts showed that DSO for franchise receivables was only 96 days, while DSO for direct accounts was 125 days. The director of billing explained that his staff, worn down by franchise complaints, had devoted more attention to franchise billing. He was reminded that collecting IVonyx direct accounts receivable contributed more to IVonyx cash flow.

Rather than disrupting corporate organization at a crucial time, in December 1991 the IVonyx board made plans to improve collections.

Missed IPO: Spring 1992

On 10 February 1992, Henry met with Fred Frank of Lehman Brothers to ask him to underwrite an IPO for IVonyx. Of six transactions in the health care industry valued over $1 billion during 1989, Frank led five. He had recently closed the $74 billion acquisition of Genentech by Hoffman LaRoche. The

IVonyx board had discussed a pre-offering valuation at $60 million to $75 million. This was a small deal for Lehman Brothers.

Lehman agreed that, if IVonyx could report $5.1 million in first quarter 1992 revenues and $700,000 pre-tax income, Lehman Bros. would agree to the higher $75 million valuation. Lehman calculated all the potential multiples and determined that IVonyx could go public based on a price/earnings multiple of twenty times 1992 estimated after-tax net income of $3.55 million. The Series C investors would double their investment in less than twelve months.

Question 6

Based on this progression in IVonyx valuation, from founding to the planned IPO, what internal rates of return would the earned by the Series A, B and C investors? Are these acceptable IRRs?

Frank's advice on preparing for the road shows was that IVonyx have ready answers about changing competitive and regulatory pressures: How did IVonyx policy on physician stock ownership differ from that of T², Total Care and Caremark? What about the forthcoming report on Home Infusion Therapy Under Medicare in which the U.S. Office of Technology Assessment questioned the real cost savings of infusions at home?[18] How did IVonyx intend to take market share from companies like Caremark that may have grown too big to be responsive to clients?

The key to the successful IPO, though, proved to be making first quarter forecasts to justify the $75 million valuation. IVonyx management put every branch on alert. The board circulated a memo reminding everyone that they would re-evaluate the employment and stock options of any manager that missed their numbers. IVonyx redesigned its corporate logo to be more identifiable to a general public. IVoynx also executed a letter of intent in a $14 million deal to acquire a Los Angeles-based company, once the IVonyx IPO had closed. The pressure was on.

A problem then arose with the audit. Ernst & Young had assigned IVonyx to accountants with limited experience in home infusion. Ernst & Young then demanded that IVonyx write off $500,000 more for contractual allowances than IVonyx thought realistic and restate its 1991 earnings. The IVonyx board felt they had spent much effort on the Ernst &

Young audit. The board approved this 1991 draft audit by Ernst & Young only so they could present a bound report at the March board meeting. They then hired a new auditor, but had to delay the IPO filing from May until the new auditors signed their work in June 1992.

Then the market for an IPO turned mixed. Most dramatically, Medical Care America, a surgical outpatient company which had recently acquired an infusion company, Critical Care America, declared a large and unexpected loss in its first quarter. The stock of the newly-merged company dropped from $55 to $15 in one week, and stocks in all other home infusion companies declined across the board. Recently offered stocks in Curaflex, TPC and HIC also declined that spring. On the upside, Rehab Clinics, Inc., a company run by John Foster, went public at $100 million, on trailing twelve months revenue of $45 million. Health services companies could still go public with good growth records and respected management.

By June IVonyx could report actual first quarter revenues of $4.9 million (against a forecast of $5.1 million) with pretax income of only $293,000 (against a forecast of $675,000). The board also increased contractual allowances by $100,000 to conform to Ernst & Young suggestions. The $200,000 shortfall in revenues came almost entirely from Puerto Rico. Collections failed to compensate for the shortfall. Having missed their numbers, the board decided not to go forward with the IPO. "We must see better tone in the price action of home infusion companies," Henry noted to his HVF II investors. "Patience will be exercised to maximize the IPO valuation and minimize the dilution from going public at too low a price. Meanwhile, the company is well-financed and continues to experience dramatic growth." In September 1992 some disgruntled Series C shareholders, thinking the restatement of 1991 earnings derailed the IPO, asked IVonyx to buy back $1.7 million of shares.

Question 7

Now that IVonyx delayed its IPO because of the battering of large infusion companies in the markets, how would you improve IVonyx operations to make it more attractive for the next IPO window? How would you improve IVonyx operations if your goal was to create a liquidity opportunity through a merger with a larger public health care company?

Collections and Credit Facilities

Collections had simply failed to keep up with the growth of the company. At the start of the year, IVonyx augmented its staff of seven billers with five new hires and collections jumped. Collections in February 1992 were up $1.076 million, a 58 percent increase over December 1991.

Reimbursement in home health care changed constantly — payers asked IVonyx to submit new forms or follow new procedures even as IVonyx offered new services at a mix of prices. In early 1992 IVonyx modified its intake form to more clearly separate approval of patient intake with insurance verification. Branches now sent delivery tickets to billing twice weekly rather than at month-end. They improved their tracking of reimbursement for individual patients, and they added an audit staff so that original bills were not returned for incomplete information. Once billing submitted the original bill, the collections department had greater authority to follow up.

IVonyx's biggest headache was Medicare in South Carolina. PEN South Carolina (the parenteral/enteral nutrition component of its Medicare program) had moved into new offices that January, which delayed payments to all home infusion companies. IVonyx collections dropped from $1.15 million to $900,000 in May 1992, largely from PEN South Carolina's delinquency. Across all its operations, Medicare accounted for 50 percent of IVonyx sales and 56 percent of its outstanding accounts. (Exhibit #7, page 385) DSO on Medicare accounts averaged 180 days, versus 100 days on commercial and Blue Cross billings. PEN South Carolina received gross billings of $900,000 monthly from IVonyx, one-third of IVonyx's total billings. In July IVonyx collected only $340,000. Breakie visited PEN South Carolina to personalize the importance of expedited payment and hired a trainer from PEN South Carolina to make sure IVonyx billers did the paperwork right. When that failed to move PEN South Carolina, IVonyx asked Michigan Senator Carl Levin to intervene. Slowly, receivables from PEN South Carolina rose. Still, by July 1992, PEN South Carolina owed IVonyx $3.7 million total, and 90 percent of the $1.4 million in accounts receivable was aged over 120 days — the point at which IVonyx should write it off.

A second headache was IVonyx's new computerized billing system. IVonyx had long before abandoned hopes of selling its billing system as a separate service. They were certainly no better at getting paid than most health care companies. In fact, after analyzing what sorts of accounts were aging past 90 days, IVonyx hired a New Mexico firm, Medical Reimbursements Systems, Inc., to re-bill its most languishing accounts. At a cost of $82,000, IVonyx expected MRS to collect $400,000 by third quarter 1992. IVonyx also invested in a new nationwide billing system designed by KSH Systems, Inc. It was a fairly new system, but promised to get bills out the door five days earlier and was already used by Critical Care America and recommended by Price Waterhouse. KSH did not get the system working as planned by June 1993, and as 1994 dragged on IVonyx had to rely on its old manual billing.

Despite basic problems its core operation, that fall IVonyx continued its expansion. The board issued shares of Series D convertible preferred stock, valued at $1.50 per share, for use in acquisitions. IVonyx tried to rationalize the process of evaluating acquisition candidates, since so much time was spent deciding which were worth pursuing. IVonyx acquired a facility in Cleveland which did $70,000 in monthly revenues. IVonyx considered a fifty percent share in a nursing agency that handled 75 patients for other infusion companies around New York City. The acquisition, though in itself complex, would allow IVonyx easy entrance into the New York market, since state law required that infusion companies have a home health agency license. This license would otherwise take eighteen months to get. IVonyx expected to take major market share from Caremark, which serviced New York from a compounding site fifty miles away in New Jersey. Because of Caremark's complicated delivery schedules, they often demanded patients take an eight day supply of materials. In a big breakthrough, in June 1992, the Catholic hospital system in New York named IVonyx its exclusive provider of home infusions.

Even as gross revenues grew, collections stagnated. Since first quarter 1992, IVonyx collections averaged $1.2 million per month. IVonyx's bank became nervous. As 1992 entered its fourth quarter, the board decided that a new CFO would focus not on headlong revenue growth and struggling collections, but on a new Profit Optimization Plan. Under the POP, IVonyx closed 7 of its 22 branches that were losing money in competitive markets. These 7 accounted for only twelve percent of IVonyx consolidated revenue, and by closing them IVonyx served notice that other under performing branches might also be closed.

This restructuring of operations required a $1.7 million charge against the 1992 income statement, and a restatement of 1991 results. IVonyx completed 1992 reporting $18.9 million in revenues, versus $12 million in 1991. Income from operations was $797,934 in 1992 versus a loss of $3 million in 1991. The net loss for 1992 after non-recurring charges due to restructuring was $1.3 million, compared to a 1991 net loss of $3.2 million, as restated. By the end of 1992, IVonyx was in notably better shape than when it had attempted its IPO. It had significant revenue growth, and operating earnings before restructuring changes.

Executing the Business Plan: 1993

IVonyx decided to wait out the deflated public market in infusion stocks and dedicate itself to sterling execution of its 1993 business plan. The plan called for revenues in excess of $30 million from the remaining fifteen branches, as compared to $18.9 million for the same branches in 1992. Income was forecast at $4 million versus $797,934 on a comparable basis. This would be seventy percent same-store revenue growth and a 400 percent increase in income for the year.

Increasingly, the NBD line became IVonyx's most crucial financial indicator in that NBD pegged the level of the loan to IVonyx cash flow. IVonyx was $3.9 million into the $5 million NBD line in October 1992, when NBD approved a $2 million increase in the accounts receivable line from $5 million to $7 million as well as a $2 million term loan facility for acquisitions, up from $1 million. When IVonyx planned to write off $3.8 million in accounts aged over 240 days so that their 1992 balance sheet was conservatively stated, they had to discuss it with NBD. The NBD loan had a tangible net worth requirement of $5 million. IVonyx current net worth was then $10.5 million, with $2.2 million in intangibles, so the write-off would have reduced tangible net worth to $4.5 million.

Based on promises of improved collections, in January 1993 NBD injected up to $900,000 into IVonyx by allowing it an advance of 25 percent of accounts aged 120 to 240 days. When IVonyx closed the seven branches and revenue dropped, they assured their bankers that total operating expenses also dropped — from $1.486 million in October 1992 before the POP was implemented to $1.3 million that January. The NBD forecast of incremental bank debt was to peak at $1.184 million in March 1993, when IVonyx was to have its collections in order. Rather, the peak came because NBD grew concerned about IVonyx viability. In June 1993, IVonyx agreed to a new loan agreement with NBD:

"IVonyx maximum line of credit will be reduced from $7.5 million to $6.5 million. The borrowing base will be increased to include 40% of accounts receivable over 120 days (formerly only 25% of A/R greater than 120 days were included). Our tangible net worth requirement has been reduced from $5 million to $3.6 million, and the total liability to tangible net worth ratio relaxed to 2.5 to one from 1.5 to one formerly."

Actual pretax income for second quarter 1993 showed a loss of $85,000 versus an NBD forecast pretax profit of $711,000. Capital expenditures and interest expenses surged as IVonyx drew down its line. IVonyx predicted third quarter revenue would be $300,000 below the NBD forecast, because it had become more difficult to write new business. With a renewed focus on sales, IVonyx expected to boost its $2 million monthly net revenue run rate to $2.6 million by September. Yet despite expectation of new referrals at these existing branches, the yearly forecasts looked well off. IVonyx also put emphasis on collections to stay within the NBD covenants. Over the course of 1993, IVonyx had dropped DSO from 160 days to 136 days. IVonyx modified its commission plan for regional vice presidents and branch managers so that commissions dropped almost to nothing if their DSO went over 150 days. IVonyx set its goal at further dropping DSO to 100 days. But as 1994 dragged on, monthly collections stagnated around $2 million per month, receivables aging grew beyond $8.5 million, and DSO stopped its decline.

One acquisition showed special promise to leapfrog IVonyx revenue to a higher level. After months of effort, by the end of 1993 IVonyx formed a joint venture with John Reyes et al (ITDS), a home infusion company in Puerto Rico. IVonyx already had a good sized branch on the island servicing an agreement with a 400 bed hospital to provide outpatient parenteral nutrition. IVonyx had been spending about $15,000 per month in mixing fees with the ITDS pharmacy. When the deal closed in April

1994, Reyes received $150,000 cash, payable immediately, and IVonyx Series D shares worth $150,000. The new IVonyx-Reyes joint venture pharmacy held one of only two licenses on the island for mixing TPN.

Positioning for Sale

IVonyx ended 1993 on an optimistic note. They hit their revenue and earning schedules, and continued driving down costs. At their level of operations in late 1993, one-half of every dollar increase in revenue contributed directly to pre-tax earnings. IVonyx looked like a very good acquisition candidate in an industry undergoing real growth and consolidation. The total number of home infusion firms or branches nationwide grew forty percent to 759 during 1993. Independent providers accounted for $2.5 billion of the 1993 total market, while national providers accounted for $2 billion.[20] IVonyx was well positioned as a good mix of both.

The investment community predicted an overwhelming urge to merge in the industry, though it was unclear what direction the mergers would take. The Clinton health care proposals exacerbated that uncertainty. In April 1993, W.R. Grace paid $112 million for an 85 percent stake in Home Intensive Care, then acquired Home Nutrition Services in a deal valued at $110 million. Four other acquisition then made the W.R. Grace National Medical Care subsidiary the third largest infusion provider by revenues — operating in a hundred markets — thinking bigness would help it compete for national managed care contracts.

Other mergers positioned infusion services as an outlet for devices or drugs. Abbey Healthcare Group, a large provider of durable medical equipment, entered the infusion therapy business in September 1993 with its $197 million acquisition of Total Pharmaceutical Care of Torrance, California. (TPC had gone public just three years earlier, at a total market value of $70 million.) TPC had reported 1992 of $64 million from its 35 pharmacy branches in 12 states.[21] "Our strategy," said an Abbey spokesperson, "is to offer a fully integrated home health care delivery system." Hoffman La Roche acquired McKinnon's, the largest local infusion provider in New Orleans, as part of the same vertical integration strategy in supplying drugs that was pursued by Merck in its earlier acquisition of Homedco. Homedco, likewise, was on the prowl for infusion providers it might acquire that could serve as an outlet for Merck products.

Late in 1993, Henry wrote to Frank justifying a $100 million offering price for IVonyx:

> "The annualized run rate of estimated Q4 1993 is revenues of $33 million with operating income before corporate overhead and taxes of $8.64 million. We focus on operating income before corporate overhead, because if Hoffman La Roche, Homedco, TPC or other home infusion companies acquired IVonyx they could eliminate corporate expense by merging our operation with their own. For example, there would be no need for two billing and reimbursement units, and clinical support, regional sales VPs and accounting functions could be consolidated."

IVonyx wanted cash rather than pooling and sought the same multiples Abbey Healthcare had established in acquiring TPC. Early in 1994, IVonyx wrote to Fred Frank of Lehman Bros. and listed a dozen potential acquirers — nursing agencies, pharmaceutical firms, drugstore chains, other infusion firms. IVonyx offered facilities in 47 cities, had successfully converted four franchisees into company branches, and offered immediate market share to any acquirer. IVonyx had in place sixty national and regional managed care contracts, including exclusive contracts with two Fortune 50 companies, a joint marketing effort with one of the largest nursing agency chains, and an agreement with one of the largest hospital chains for an early discharge program. Between 1991 to 1993, managed care revenues grew from 19.7 percent to 38 percent of total IVonyx revenues. Any acquirer could easily build on these managed-care relationships. Furthermore, IVonyx corporate overhead had stabilized at $5.3 million per year, which an acquirer could drive down by integrating IVonyx into its existing billing, sales and corporate functions. Likewise, the average operating income for the branch network increased to 23.4 percent of net revenue in 1993, up from 17.3 percent in 1992 and 8.1 percent in 1991. Most operating expenses of the IVonyx branch network were fixed and could easily support annual revenues of $50 million. Finally, IVonyx had a $13.8 million net operating loss carry forward for federal income tax purposes.

Then 1994 opened even better than expected: IVonyx revenue was up 38 percent and income from operations was up 1,800 percent over first quarter 1993. IVonyx believed it had the highest internal growth rate in revenues in the entire industry. The TPC valuation multiples were two times calendar year forecast revenues, and twenty times calendar year forecast after tax income. After eliminating overhead expense, that gave IVonyx a valuation a range of $90 million to $140 million (two times revised $45 million revenue and twenty times $7.2 million income.) Lehman Bros began showing IVonyx, and Abbey and Homedco visited Livonia. IVonyx management doubled its efforts at hitting its projections of $40 million in revenues and $6 million pretax income.

A Consolidating Industry Brings Regulation: 1994

Government action turned 1994 turbulent for the home infusion industry, in the aftermath of 1993 Congressional hearings on the home infusion industry. The hearings began with emotional testimony from Mrs. Marie Kostas-Weber of Cleveland Heights, Ohio. After an illness destroyed the gastrointestinal tract of her ten-year-old daughter Sarah, Mrs. Kostas moved her from Mt. Sinai Hospital back home so she could live a normal life. They bought TPN formula from Critical Care America, which charged them 2000 percent more for some drugs — on average $1000 more per day — than had the hospital. After Sarah burned through a $1 million private insurance policy and became dependent on Medicaid, CCA refused to supply her, claiming she suddenly showed an allergy to latex tubes. Kostas got a court order to keep the drugs coming, though CCA gave no training or service and simply dropped them off at the door stoop. When CCA once delivered the wrong drugs, it was Mrs. Kostas who checked the records and corrected a life-threatening mistake. CCA continued to bill her $95,000 per month, though Medicaid paid only a fraction of that. Chairman John Dingle characterized the home infusion industry as making multimillion dollar profits by targeting patients who "tend to be highly vulnerable and largely captive populations" with "potential for considerable abuse."[22] The hearings concluded in September 1993 with the HSS inspector general listing the great variety of new ways in which home infusion companies defraud the government — mostly disguised kickbacks and false billings — and vowing some unspecified crackdown. The press claimed the industry was out of control, but no government agency was willing to lay a clear path to rational regulation and standardized reporting of treatments or costs.

T² Medical of Alpharetta, Georgia started 1994 under visible scrutiny by the SEC and HHS inspector general. HHS accused T² of violating the Stark amendment rules against physicians referring patients to clinics they owned. T² became one of Wall Street's high-fliers in the late 1980s because of its physician management agreements whereby T² managed a home infusion center owned by a referring physician. To dodge Stark's regulatory bullet, T² exploited an exemption for stockholders, and bought out the physician owners in exchange for restricted T² stock. Those same physicians, now T² stockholders, kept referring patients to T² infusion centers. T² became synonymous with physician self-dealing. Even after it promised to end these agreements, T² could not assure Wall Street that HSS might not find further fault with physician involvement.

More damaging to the entire infusion industry, was T² 's investigation by the SEC. Earlier in 1993, an investment group led by T² CEO Joseph Allegra, M.D., made an $18 per share offer to acquire T². During the "fairness opinions" an anonymous letter tipped T² chairman to questionable accounting in writing off doubtful accounts. The chairman released an audit confirming the accounting errors and the buyout deal unraveled. Allegra resigned as CEO. T² stock tumbled from a high of $60 in early 1992 to a low of $5.25 in summer 1993, and stockholders sued. T² restated its first six months of fiscal 1993 earnings, down from $37 million to $24 million. It came on a continuing loss of market share. For fiscal 1993, T² net income dropped 36 percent to $41 million, or $1.02 per share, compared with 1992 net income of $65 million, or $1.60 per share. T² hoped to escape its reputation by looking for either a merger or an acquirer. Homedco and Abbey Healthcare reviewed T² books and declined to make an offer. W.R. Grace made a bid valued at $10.25 per share but T² directors, perhaps enticed by huge finder fees for putting together the deal, rejected it in favor of a merger bid valuing shares at $10.50.[23]

In February 1994 T² merged with three much smaller infusion providers — Curaflex Health Services, HealthInfusion, and Medisys — in a $550 million stock deal that created Coram Healthcare Corp. Interestingly, more than half of Coram's assets — $300 million — was goodwill, and both HealthInfusion and Curaflex also had to increased their provisions for bad debt, but without restating earnings in 1993.[24] Months later, most senior management was gone, and Coram adopted the Curaflex strategy of offering one-source home care to managed care providers. "To be a player at the managed-care table is going to require a massive scale that allows you to be a low-cost provider of service," claimed Coram CEO James Sweeney.[25] Coram then continued its acquisition strategy — primarily in both home infusions and home respiratory therapy — adding Homecare Management, which specialized in services to organ transplant patients, and HMSS, Inc., another strong regional provider of infusion services. The government ended its investigations in October 1994 after the successor of T^2 paid a $500,000 fine. With annual revenues of $500 million, Coram was finally able to establish its place as America's second largest infusion provider, behind Caremark International.

Caremark, likewise, was clouded in uncertainty. At the May 1990 annual shareholder meeting, the Baxter chairman called Caremark the jewel in its crown. Caremark's share price had doubled since it was spun off from Baxter International in November 1992, and it was on track to become America's most diversified provider of non-hospital health care products and services to outpatients, especially to national payers and on a capitated price. Caremark closed eleven branches in 1993, to consolidate its regional operations, though its revenues for all patient care services grew 7.8 percent to $1 billion for the year. Caremark bought Critical Care America, the struggling home infusion division of Medical Care America, for $175 million in cash in March 1994. This brought to 125 the number of Caremark infusion branches nationwide.

Then, in August 1994, a Federal grand jury indicted Caremark on 51 counts following an investigation by the HHS inspector general into $1.1 million in suspicious "research grants" that Caremark paid a Minneapolis physician for prescribing the growth hormone Protropin, a drug made by Genentech, distributed by Caremark and infused via its Home Health Care of America subsidiary. An AIDS victim in Atlanta alleged that Caremark gave kickbacks to his local doctor amounting to a quarter of his home health care bills. U.S. Attorney General Janet Reno proclaimed, "We have made health care fraud a major law enforcement priority, and we are going to pursue it as vigorously as we can." Government investigations focused on home health care companies where, compared with hospitals and other fixed facilities, the law was notably new and vague. Caremark claimed they would be entirely vindicated when allowed to present its case. Then, in September Caremark was indicted again for alleged kickbacks to an Ohio physician for referrals to the Caremark home infusion branch. In October 1994 Caremark failed to sell its entire infusion subsidiary to W.R. Grace and focus instead on physician practice management and prescription drug benefit services. Caremark finished 1994 with earnings of $80.4 million on sales of $2.43 billion. In January 1995, Caremark finally sold its home infusion unit to Coram for $300 million (about half of what Sweeney had sold Caremark to Baxter for in 1987). The combined Coram/Caremark operation held 23 percent of the home infusion services market. "Home infusion had become the least profitable business in our portfolio," noted Caremark chairman C.A. Piccolo.[26] Ultimately, Caremark was acquitted or settled favorably in each of these cases, yet by February 1995 short-sellers held 13 percent of its shares.[27]

In the summer of 1994 Abbey Healthcare Group finished cleaning out the senior executive ranks of TPC, the company on which IVonyx had based its multiples, for misrepresenting facts and inflating TPC's value during merger discussions. Abbey remained under criticism for rushing into the home infusion industry at all cost, criticisms which cleared when it announced plans to merge with Homedco Group. The two companies had headquarters less than a mile apart, south of Los Angeles near where IVonyx first started. The new company, named Apria Healthcare Group, became the largest in the home healthcare industry with combined revenues topping $1.6 billion in 1995.[28]

In this nebulous legal environment all home infusion firms suffered taint of suspected kickbacks and accounting fraud. IVonyx had followed both the spirit and the letter of the evolving regulations in home infusion services, was fully certified by the JCAHO, and had followed very conservative accounting principles. But the entire industry was depressed. Managed care buyers had taken advantage of the consolidation in the industry to force down prices. Prices for all home care services had dropped fifteen percent in 1994 and, while the decline leveled off, prices showed no sign of recovering in 1995.[29] Rather than sell the company for less than its full valuation, IVonyx delayed merger discussions.

IVonyx continued to grow its revenues and net income.

Then IVonyx, too, was besmirched by the widening government investigation of Medicare fraud. In March 1995, IVonyx was served with a subpoena in an FBI investigation of its Puerto Rico branch. The FBI brought charges against the branch manager, one employee, and one referring physician for billing the HCFA for patients who did not technically qualify for Medicare. IVonyx officers cooperated fully and were exonerated of any wrong-doing. IVonyx counsel tried to quickly negotiate a settlement by which IVonyx would pay $4 million to Medicare over five years. However, the settlement had to be approved by the HCFA and the U.S. Department of Justice, and the size of the settlement was not big enough to warrant priority treatment. Settlement would not be reached for two years.

The summer of 1995 marked the end of eighteen months of rapid consolidation in the industry. Indeed, the structure of the industry would not change substantially over the next five years. As merger and acquisition swirled around it, IVonyx had failed to find a liquidity partner.

IVonyx In Decline

Lingering uncertainty about the potential damage done by its Puerto Rico branch suffused all IVonyx merger discussions. Not until May 1997, two years after the initial subpoena, did IVonyx receive notification that the U.S. Department of Justice would approve its proposed settlement. This clarified the ultimate downside for IVonyx, so that IVonyx auditors could accrue the $4 million settlement, write off all goodwill, and generally clean up the balance sheet in advance of a sale. Yet the execution of the settlement dragged on. Without an executed agreement, IVonyx could not complete acquisition of two infusion providers that would have added $15 million to its revenues. Not until June 1998 did IVonyx execute the settlement with the U.S. Attorney for the District of Puerto Rico. IVonyx made an initial payment of $200,000 followed by monthly payments of principal and interest totalling $70,000 for sixty months, secured by the right of offset against the company's Medicare receivables. IVonyx and its management would suffer no further penalty, either corporate or personal.

Meanwhile, IVonyx itself began to unravel through a decline in revenues, perhaps because its competitors continued to force their market-share and price-pressure strategies. Net revenues dropped from $25.487 million in 1997 to $22.786 million in 1998. Revenues recovered, to $25.876 million in 1999, but it came at the cost of net income, which fell from $781,000 in 1997, to a loss of $493,000 in 1998, to a loss of $70,000 in 1999. In January 1997, IVonyx sold the assets of its Sacramento pharmacy to Pediatric Services of America.[30] Over the past seven years, revenues at that office never rose much above $1.2 million, and IVonyx sold it for only $105,000. In September 1998, the HV II investment in IVonyx was valued at only $600,000.

Because of revenue uncertainty, banks balked at extending lines of credit to IVonyx. In 1995, National Bank of Detroit reduced its $6.5 million line of credit to a $5 million line. After much effort to get that amount increased, in March 1997, IVonyx established a new $6 million revolving credit line with HCFP Funding, Inc. The HCFP facility bore interest of prime plus 2.4 percent, which saddled IVonyx in 1998 with $1 million in fees and interest. Furthermore, all cash collections were controlled by the lender and first applied to reduce outstanding borrowings. In the fall of 1998, IVonyx again looked for working capital. It did find better terms, that would shave $300,000 from interest payments over the coming year, but it was unable to increase the line of credit. Moreover, IVonyx was unable to borrow the full amount of the existing HCFP line. Because of the aging of IVonyx's $10 million in accounts receivable, IVonyx was able to draw down only $4.5 million.

As a result of legal uncertainty, declining revenues, and cash constrictions, IVonyx grew increasingly desperate to find a merger partner. Yet between 1995 and 2000, potential suitors approached IVonyx as though it had a revolving front door.

A Revolving Door of Suitors

In the summer of 1996, IVonyx retained the investment banking firm of Dabney/Resnick to find potential acquisition partners, expecting a $40 million total company valuation. In October 1996, IVonyx and HHCO, a publicly-owned home nursing agency, signed a letter of intent to merge. IVonyx called off the merger when they discovered operational weakness in HHCO during due diligence.

Soon after, in March 1997, Infu-Tech, Inc. announced that it had signed a letter of intent to merge with IVonyx. On the news, Infu-Tech stock shot up 24.1 percent to $4 11/32. Infu-Tech had home and outpatient operations in 27 states and a strong regional presence in New York and New Jersey. In 1992, Infu-Tech had spun off of Continental Health Affiliates, which ran assisted living and nursing homes, and Continental still owned 58 percent of the company. Infu-Tech had reported revenues for the fiscal year ended 30 June 1996 of $24.6 million and net income of $1.2 million after paying its parent company a $1.2 million management fee. Thus, Infu-Tech and IVonyx were about matched in size, with redundancy in some branch offices, as well as easily trimmed overhead in their headquarters.[31] Infu-Tech would be the surviving entity and the board would have equal representation from both companies. The deal assumed a pre-money valuation of IVonyx at $18.68 million. IVonyx shareholders would get 1,870,000 shares of freely-tradable common stock. After Infu-Tech assumed $7.2 million in debt and the $4 million Medicare settlement, IVonyx shareholders got about 37 percent of the merged company.

"There is continued consolidation in the home health care industry," stated Jack Rosen, Infu-Tech's president and CEO, "and this acquisition will allow us to achieve operating efficiencies by building critical mass, creating cost savings on overhead expenses, and provide for geographic expansion of our network." Concurrent with the merger talks, Infu-Tech set up a disease management division with the latest databases so they could work with managed care companies to better treat patients with chronic conditions. Pro formas for the combined companies showed revenues of $50 million and net income of $4 million. At a ten to twelve times price/earnings multiple, the combined entity would have a market capitalization of $40 million to $50 million.

As Infu-Tech performed its due-diligence — though not officially tied to the merger — IVonyx also planned to issue a Series E preferred stock. The Series E would convert into equity the $1,983,000 in subordinated debt maturing soon, at a valuation pegged to the merger price per share. The creation of the Series E would have a dilutive effect, but it was expected that all shareholders would purchase their pro-rata shares. Henry Venture II planned to convert its $1.25 million of subordinated debt into IVonyx equity, to give the fund an 18 percent ownership in the merged company. If the merged company achieved its goal of $100 million in market value within two years through acquisitions and internal growth, then Henry's investment and hard work in repositioning of IVonyx would create a very good return. By September 1997, though, IVonyx and Infu-Tech called off their merger talks. IVonyx languished over 1998, and the CEO resigned.

The Turnaround Begins: 1999

A turnaround began when a new CEO took over in early 1999. The CEO added or replaced 38 managers and sales staff, while reducing the overall number of positions. Some got increased responsibility in sales and in generating referrals. New information systems allowed IVonyx to identify unprofitable contracts, which they then could renegotiate. The strength of IVonyx's referral network was evident in that it did business in twenty states, while maintaining physical offices in only five. The first quarter of 1999 showed revenues at $9 million and EBITDA of $631,000, with March setting new highs for revenues, EBITDA and collections. IVonyx renegotiated a $7 million bank line with a new lender, DVI, which would save $300,000 in annual interest charges and allow more flexible borrowing against accounts receivable.

The pace of suitors remained high, though their quality improved as the new CEO bolstered the company. In May 1999 IVonyx signed a letter of intent to be acquired by In Home Health, Inc., a wholly-owned subsidiary of Manor Care. IHH would pay $2 million in cash to IVonyx shareholders and assume $17 million in IVonyx liabilities. Of that $17 million, IHH would pay $4.5 million in cash to various IVonyx debt holders, thus removing the threat of bankruptcy and possible residual claims against IVonyx shareholders. IVonyx still owed the federal government $3.3 million of its Puerto Rico settlement, and that claim would not be removed by bankruptcy. Then Infu-Tech returned and made an offer similar to the IHH offer. Infu-Tech offered to assume $17 million in IVonyx liabilities, of that paying $1.5 million to IVonyx debt holders on closing and an additional $1 million cash to debt holders over the year following closing. In addition, IVonyx shareholders would receive 800,000 shares of Infu-Tech common stock, then trading over the counter for $2.00 per share. The IVonyx board selected the better offer, clearly from IHH, though discussion with IHH fell apart in June 1999 before due diligence began. The

IVonyx board had negotiated a great deal for IVonyx with IHH, but the IVonyx turnaround was not yet well enough established.

To find a merger partner willing to close a deal, the IVonyx board selected First Healthcare Partners as its investment banker. FHP prepared a book, and in September 1999 began to contact potential partners. IVonyx ended 1999 on a high note. December month revenues were $3 million for the first time in the company's history, and EBITDA for the year exceeded $3.3 million. Operating expenses were $1 million less for 1999 than for 1998. As before, growth created cash flow problems as monthly disbursements for costs of good sold exceeded collections. IVonyx again made the top priority new billing and collection systems, which by May 2000 would boost average monthly collections from $1.75 million to $2 million. As a bridge to the point that collections improved, IVonyx needed about $1 million in cash. FHP was exploring the option of an up-front partial cash investment from potential partners to buy them exclusivity while they negotiate a final acquisition. They also looked for a high-yield lender that would accept an equity kicker as part of a collateralized loan. However, as FHP struggled to find the $1 million needed to bridge operations, IVonyx shaved costs and ramped up collections.

First Healthcare Partners found three interested partners. In addition, the CEO of In Home Health had recently resigned, and the IHH board renewed merger discussions with IVonyx. Their assumption was that the merged entity would have $110 million in annual revenues.

The first quarter of 2000 went well. EBITDA topped $1.3 million. Net income was $738,000, versus $113,000 year ago. Strong results allowed IVonyx to reopen negotiations on credit facilities. In addition, IVonyx aggressively wrote off $2.0 million of old receivables, which improved DSO as well as the overall quality of the balance sheet. Daiwa and Fleet Bank agreed to a $10 million line of credit — the $2 million boost over the DVI limits would greatly ease IVonyx cash flow — and as they began due diligence DVI agreed to boost its existing line to $8 million. Collections for second quarter 2000 exceeded revenues and July collections reached $2.7 million, well beyond projections. Still, the sales staff had lined up substantial new opportunities that IVonyx could not service because of its cash constraints.

Chartwell Diversified Services was the next to offer a letter of intent to acquire IVonyx. HVII would receive $2.25 million in cash at closing, plus 23 percent of an earnout estimated to total $8 million. The earnout was established as two percent of net revenue growth, not net profits, over the coming five years. Though that deal also fell through, Chartwell was actually a worthy merger partner. It was a privately held conglomerate of smaller infusion companies, with revenues of about $100 million. Chartwell had forgone the pursuit of national contracts in favor of a local, boutique approach to building its referral base. IVonyx now also stood as essentially a high-quality boutique provider. By 2000, that was the right place to be.[32]

The structure of the home health industry had not changed substantially since its reshaping in 1994. Half of the market belonged to nominally national providers; half in small regional firms. HMO giant CIGNA announced in 1996 that Olsten Staffing Services would be its national provider for home infusion services on a capitated contract, leading many to predict that the mom-and-pops would finally shake out of the industry. However Olsten, like every other national firm, need to subcontract extensively with regional specialists to service these contracts. IVonyx, for example, in June 1995 had allied with Homedco after it had won a national capitated contract with Ford Motor Company and the United Auto Workers union. Yet subcontracting trimmed already tight margins, for the subcontractor as well as for the national networks.

The performance of the big companies steadily degraded under price pressures and escalating government scrutiny. Coram in 1995, the year after its formation, lost $334 million on revenues of $603 million, driving its debt to $450 million, and causing its stock to plunge from $25 to $5. By 1999, Coram had almost trimmed its operations into profitability when it imploded. Coram sued Aetna US Healthcare, its largest source of revenues and one of the largest private payers in the United States, claiming Aetna had misled Coram into a capitated contract on which Coram lost money. Aetna pulled its business, and Coram ended 1999 with revenues of $521 million and a loss of $115 million. Its shares dropped to ¢11, giving it a market value of only $5.5 million.[33] With $252 million in debt coming due in May of 2001, Coram's board filed for bankruptcy.

Apria likewise slipped into bankruptcy as its board of directors — still divided into warring camps of Homedco and Abbey origins — failed to agree on an expansion strategy. Apria salespeople offered discounts to seal deals with managed care giants, and to service them they sometimes needed to subcontract at rates above what they had negotiated. By 2000 a new board had forced a restructuring and Apria was looking to spin off its infusion services.[34] Columbia/HCA Healthcare Corp., one of the largest private operators of hospitals, virtually abandoned its home health operations in 1998 following a government raid in July 1998 to uncover fraud. Other public infusion providers that had gone public in the early 1990s, like OptionCare and Infu-Tech, suffered essentially flat revenues through the decade, piling up debt during the years they could not squeeze out profits.

Meanwhile, HCFA had launched Operation Restore Trust in 1995 backed by 350 dedicated agents of the Federal Bureau of Investigation. While they did root out fraud and paperwork errors in Medicare billings, most of the billing they contested where over the medical necessity of specific visits or home care at all.[35] Twelve percent of all home care providers folded shop in 1998, largely because of problems with Medicare reimbursements. More planned to shut down as HCFA required a surety bond against overpayments, or because HCFA was moving toward a prospective payment scheme.

The only new entry into the industry was Gentiva, spun off in 1999 from Olsten Corp. The Swiss staffing firm Adecco S.A. bought Olsten in 1999 for its temporary staffing and information technology services.[36] Olsten quickly settled several lingering disputes with the federal government — including one fine of $61 million — arising from its home health care operations. Olsten had accumulated $750 million in debt across all its operations, yet spun off Gentiva with a remarkably clean balance sheet. Gentiva was born afresh — with revenues of $1.3 billion and the ability to borrow to enhance its information technology. Gentiva picked up Aetna's national contract, and established itself as the leader in the home health industry. The internet, though, changed everything.

drkoop.com Inc.

drkoop had a very loyal following. Two million registered users worldwide clicked onto drkoop to help them take charge of their healthcare choices. "Our vision," proclaimed the company's website, "is to accelerate the change of healthcare into a consumer-centric, market-driven industry." drkoop compiled information from various trusted sources, then tailored it to the interests of each user. More than 300 hospitals advised their patients to turn to drkoop for answers to basic questions. Better informed consumers would work in concert with physicians to more efficiently reach their health goals. While this was good for America, it proved a dubious business model. The cost of generating such information outstripped what drkoop could charge for advertising. drkoop's e-commerce efforts at selling healthcare products online also drained their cash. Revenue of $10 million in 2000 (barely higher than their 1999 revenues) came with a $22.8 million operating loss. The stock tumbled from a high of $36 in July 1999 soon after its IPO to less than ¢20 by March 2001. Shareholders filed a class action lawsuit, and management was thrown out.

The drkoop brand name was its greatest asset. No other health services company, on the internet or otherwise, had such widespread and positive brand recognition. WebMD garnered more hits than any internet health site, especially following its alliance with AOL, but the press questioned whether its commercial policies influenced its content. Some optometry firms advertised nationally, but from a position of price rather than quality. The Red Cross and Planned Parenthood had strong brand recognition, though they were non-profits. To leverage drkoop's strong brand, the new management forged a new strategy.

drkoop moved away from a business model based on advertising and e-commerce, and focused instead on acquisitions that would give it off-line revenues. $27.5 million in cash was raised in August 2000 to fund its repositioning.

drkoop forged a strategic alliance with Siemens/Shared Medical Systems to promote secure online communication between patients, their physicians, and local health care organizations. In March 2001, drkoop acquired StayfitUSA, a small firm which provided employers with employee wellness benefits like discounted fitness club memberships and smoking cessation programs. drkoop intended to move healthcare into the home and workplace, take a leadership role in the fragmented wellness marketplace, and execute multiple revenue models under the drkoop brand name. C. Everett Koop, who expanded his attachment with the firm, noted that bestowing knowledge is what the internet does best, but that's only part of a vibrant business. Right now, he said in an interview, "we're seeking to make a merger with a large company that understands what a benefit our kind of website would be to their business."[37]

IVonyx was that company. Introductions were made by Gene Terry, a member of the IVonyx board since 1991 and later also vice chairman of healthcare e-commerce firm Proxymed. In April 2001, IVonyx and drkoop signed a 162-page agreement outlining the deal.[38] The acquisition was structured as a sale of IVonyx assets, but not its accounts receivable nor its liabilities. drkoop acquired the going-concern assets of IVonyx — meaning contracts, branch office leases, operating systems, and inventories — for $3 million in cash, a $1 million earnout, and $4.1 million of newly issued drkoop common stock. IVonyx retained ownership of its liabilities as well as $13.3 million in net accounts receivable, which it continued to collect through a liquidating trust. Those receivables, plus the transaction cash were expected to pay-off IVonyx subordinated and secured debt. The deal was subject to the usual approvals, as well as the company entering into a $7 million working capital credit facility. The $1 million earnout was paid if IVonyx net income for the twelve months following the closing exceeded $3 million.

Following the acquisition, IVonyx's CEO became president of drkoop. He would work to improve cash flow with the goal of making the overall company EBITDA positive by mid-2002. IVonyx was then the largest privately held infusion company in the United States, and one of the most profitable. IVonyx earned $2.7 million on $28.4 million in 2000 revenues, with EBITDA margins on net sales exceeding twelve percent. It was JCAHO accredited (with commendation), enjoyed an excellent clinical reputation, and physicians appreciated IVonyx's ability to do almost every type of intravenous therapy. IVonyx now had a structure that could expand nationwide, with integrated information systems, and a coherent management philosophy. Another big advantage was that in January 2001 JCAHO standards for the infusion industry changed. JCAHO previously required separate certifications to provide infusion services in the home, or in long-term care facilities, or in ambulatory infusion centers. Now, certification were not based on where services were provided — a requirement that had long shaped the structure of the home health care industry. IVonyx could stay focused within its area of therapeutic excellence and — fitting the drkoop philosophy of educated consumers — expand that business to the home, the workplace, or outpatient clinics. And the price was right. drkoop paid about a quarter of IVonyx trailing revenues, less than three times its income.

Still, drkoop might run out of cash before closing the deal. After accumulating a deficit of $204.2 million at end of March 2001, drkoop had only $7 million in cash remaining. drkoop was struggling to drop the burn rate to $1 million a month in the second quarter of 2001, compared with $8 million a month the year earlier. Either company could walk away from the deal if not consummated by 11 August 2001.[39]

Yet the deal was also good for IVonyx shareholders. They finally got liquidity, though they lost about half of the cash they had invested in IVonyx since 1987. They also got an upside. The drkoop stock was distributed to IVonyx preferred shareholders, who then owned twelve percent of drkoop. The drkoop stock was registered with the SEC, was traded on the over-the-counter bulletin board after being delisted from NASDAQ, and subject to a one-year lock-up. It was far better than any previous deal IVonyx had pursued over the past few years. It held the potential to return substantial long-term gains if drkoop succeeded with its restructuring plan.

drkoop Bankruptcy

drkoop, however, had internal problems of its own. The company had raised $5 million from its shareholders to give it cash to operate both drkoop and IVonyx. The cash needs of drkoop were extreme, however, due to judgements against the company and prior debt obligations incurred after drkoop went public some years earlier. Koop stock was as high as $43 per share at one time and founding management had raised $125 million in its IPO, fueled by the mania for dot com stocks. By 2001, drkoop was down to $5 million in cash. It appeared to IVoynx that drkoop could raise perhaps $2 to $3 million more from its new group of investors post the IVonyx acquisition. This small amount of cash would fund working capital needs of IVonyx while IVonyx generated earnings for the merged company.

But, the cash drain at drkoop was dragging the merged company down. On December 16, 2001, drkoop filed for Chapter 7 Bankruptcy and voluntary liquidation. The drkoop stock was worthless and IVonyx was out of business overnight. All IVonyx employees, 240 of them, lost their jobs immediately. Legal actions continue to this day with numerous parties alleging wrong doing.

Notes to Published Sources

[1] On the invention of TPN, see S.J. Dudrick and J.E. Rhoads, "Total intra-venous feeding," *Scientific American* 226 (1972) 73. Stanley J. Dudrick first succeeded with TPN in beagle puppies while still a surgical resi-dent at the University of Pennsylvania in the early 1960s. See also *Surgery* 64 (1968) 134 and *Journal of the American Medical Association* 215 (1971) 939. On the early history of parenteral therapy as a business, see Paul de Haen, "Parenteral Drugs: Commerce and Science," *Journal of the Parenteral Drug Association* 32/1 (January 1978) 9-14.

[2] "Is home nutrition going hungry?" *In Vivo* (March 1985) 30-37.

[3] Senate Special Committee on Aging, *Staff Report: Impact of Medicare's prospective payment system on the quality of care received by Medicare benefici-aries* (26 September and 24 October, 1985).

[4] Thomas G. Donlan, "Medicare goes home: And could give infusion therapy a shot in the arm," *Barron's* (24 July 1989) 20.

[5] For a history of visiting nurses associations, see Karen Buhler-Wilkerson, *No Place Like Home: A History of Nursing and Home Care in the United States* (Baltimore: Johns Hopkins University Press, 2001).

[6] Joint Commission on Accreditation of Healthcare Organizations, *Standard for Accreditation of Home Care* (Chicago: JCAHO, 1988). On the history of regulation of home health care, see Allen D. Spiegel, "Regulation of high technology home care," in Maxwell J. Mehlman and Stuart J. Younger, eds., *Delivering High Technology Home Care* (New York: Springer Publishing Company, 1991) 67-83.

[7] Deborah Borfitz, "Infusion innovations," *Rx HomeCare* 10/4 (1988) 29-34.

[8] Mary Hardie, "Distributor names Pancretec in $2 million lawsuit," *San Diego Business Journal* 10 (21 August 1989) 3.

9   Kathi Gannon, "All pumped up," *Drug Topics* 138/18 (19 September 1994) 92; Patrick Catania and Martin A. Rosner, *Home Health Care Practice* (Health Markets Research, 1986).

10 On the state of the art in infusion therapy from a nursing perspective, see Sharon M. Weinstein, *Plumer's Principles and Practice of Intravenous Therapy: Sixth Edition* (Philadelphia: Lippincott, 1997); and Lynn Dianne Phillips, *Manual of I.V. Therapeutics* (Philadelphia: F.A. Davis Company, 1993).

11 Mary Wagner, "Despite gains in home infusion therapy, home care revenue growth remains flat," *Modern Healthcare* 20 (21 May 1990) 96-98; Al Henry, "Apples and Marshmallows," *San Diego Business Journal* (5 March 1990) 7.

12 Mary Hardie, "Health care startup captures $5.1 million in venture funds," *San Diego Business Journal* (27 March 1989) 12.

13 Thomas G. Donlan, "Medicare goes home: And could give infusion therapy a shot in the arm," *Barron's* (24 July 1989) 21.

14 Michael Selz, "Home health care companies learn painful lesson," *Wall Street Journal* (1 June 1990).

15 For reviews of various cost saving studies, see Warren Balinsky and S. Nesbitt, "Cost effectiveness of outpatient parenteral antibiotics: A review of the literature," *American Journal of Medicine* 87 (September 1989) 301-5; Warren Balinsky, *Home Care: Current Problems and Future Solutions* (San Francisco: Jossey-Bass Publishers, 1994) 126; and Allan D. Spiegel, "The economics of high technology home care: Doing right for the wrong reason," in Maxwell J. Mehlman and Stuart J. Younger, eds., *Delivering High Technology Home Care* (New York: Springer Publishing Company, 1991) 54. A health consumer perspective is presented in Steven Findlay, "There's no place like home," *U.S. News & World Report* 104 (25 January 1988) 68-70.

[16] U.S. General Accounting Office, *Need to Strengthen Home Health Care Payment Controls and Address Unmet Needs*; Publication No. HRD-87-9 (2 December 1987); F.R. Curtiss, "Recent developments in federal reimbursement for home health care," *American Journal of Hospital Pharmacy* 43/1 (1986) 132-139.

[17] Sandy Hook, "IVonyx pulls up stakes and moves to Michigan," *San Diego Business Journal* 11 (16 July 1990) 11.

[18] Office of Technology Assessment, *Home Drug Infusion Therapy Under Medicare*, OTA-H-509 (U.S. Government Printing Office, May 1992).

[19] Deborah Starr, "Refurbishing home care: employers are poised to benefit from a developing trend — integrated home health care," *Business & Health* (1 January 1994) 40.

[20] James A. Bennett, "Developing a successful home infusion practice," *Drug Topics* (7 June 1993) 62.

[21] Mary Chambers, "Home infusion partners with managed care," *Caring Magazine* (June 1993) 54-6.

[22] U.S. House of Representatives, Subcommittee on Oversight and Investigations, Committee on Energy and Commerce, *Hearings: Home Infusion Industry* (5 May and 8 September 1993).

[23] On the troubles of T², see Steven Sternberg, "How self-referrals can go sour: The travails of T² and its doctor investors," *Medical Economics* 71/11 (13 June 1994) 116-127; John Burns, "Homedco and Abbey among companies that have viewed T²'s books," *Modern Healthcare* (31 January 1994) 10; Andy Zipser, "Infuse-iasm: T² Medical spurns Grace for a merger and a new name," *Barron's* (4 July 1994) 13.

[24] John Burns, "Inside events unraveled T² buyout," *Modern Healthcare* (2 May 1994) 17-24.

[25] "Home health care gathers for growth," *Fortune* (June 1995) 25.

[26] Barnaby J. Feder, "Caremark will sell home infusion unit to Coram," *New York Times* (31 January 1995) C4.

[27] "Genentech executive and 3 from Caremark acquitted," *New York Times* (4 October 1995) C5; Barnaby J. Feder, "Caremark may soon be a big winner or a big loser. But which?" *New York Times* (10 March 1995) C4.

[28] James Sterngold, "$1 billion health pact is planned," *New York Times* (3 March 1995) C1.

[29] Milt Freudenheim, "Coram to merge with Lincare in a billion-dollar health venture," *New York Times* (19 April 1995) C1.

[30] "Pediatric Services of America Inc. acquires two California facilities and opens start-up locations in Texas and Connecticut," *Business Wire* (20 January 1997).

[31] "Infu-Tech CFO sees FY'97 earnings on track," *Dow Jones Newswires* (26 March 1997).

[32] Cori Vanchieri, "National Disasters," *Hospitals and Health Networks* 72/10 (20 May 1998) 50-52; Michele Bitoun Blecher, "Gloom and boom," *Hospitals and Health Networks* 72/23 (5 December 1998) 34. On the origins of capitated pricing and expectation of nationwide shakeouts see Michael Quint, "Health plans force changes in the way doctors are paid," *New York Times* (9 February 1995) A1; Christopher Palmeri, "Drip bags in the living room," *Forbes* (22 May 1995) 154-156.

[33] Richard Haugh, "Coram sets off a setback," *Hospitals and Health Networks* 73/11 (November 1999) 60-62.

[34] Rhonda L. Rundle, "Toxic Marriage: Health rivals try merger of equals, get merger from hell — At Apria, hostility flared, but board's even split left no way to quash it — both former chiefs lose out," *Wall Street Journal* (26 February 1998) A1.

[35] Milt Freudenheim, "An exam for home health care: A way to cut hospital costs, or a system out of control," *New York Times* (15 September 1995) C1; Thomas D. Roslewicz and John M. Hapchuk, "Where's the beef: How auditors helped reform payments for home health care," *The Journal of Government Financial Management* 50 (Spring 2001) 42-47.

[36] "Swiss temp firm shoots to No. 1 spot in US: Adecco agrees to acquire Olsten's staffing unit in a $840 million deal," *Wall Street Journal* (19 August 1999) A10.

[37] Ed Housewright, "Interview: C. Everett Koop," *The Dallas Morning News* (8 April 2001) 1J.

[38] "drkoop.com announces acquisition to expand its health and wellness offerings into home infusion market," *BW HealthWire: Press Release* (16 April 2001); "Drkoop grows beyond web in $7 million deal," *Wall Street Journal* (17 April 2001); Jeff Tieman, "Drkoop.com becomes a practitioner," *Modern Healthcare* 31/17 (23 April 2001) 20; Amanda Bronstad, "Ailing Drkoop acquires revenue stream, new president," *Los Angeles Business Journal* (14 May 2001) 7.

[39] "Drkoop.com may need more financing if acquisition of IVonyx is delayed," *Dow Jones Business News* (15 May 2001); "drkoop.com/IVonyx deal has August 11 walkaway date," *Dow Jones Corporate Filings Alert* (16 April 2001).

Exhibit #1

IVonyx Group Services, Inc.
Placements and Valuations

	June 1988	December 1988	December 1989
Investment Plan	Common	Series A	Series B
Total Company Valuation (pre-money)		$2.5 million	$3.5 m
Price per Share (split adjusted)	$9.25	$2.00 ($.825 common equivalent share value)	$0.443
Shares Placed	54054	2,555,500	14,233,680
Total Placement	$500,000	$5.1m	$2.98 m
New Cash	$500,000	$2.4 million	$2.98 m
Percentage of Company Purchased	7.7 %	%	44 %
Purchasers	HVF	HVF & HV II Seaport Ventures, Inc. S.G. Warburg	JMP Group Euro Canadian NVII
HV II Ltd. Ownership (post-money)	7.7 %	28.8 %	28 %
Ivonyx Revenues (trailing 12 months)	$	$900,000	

	December 1991	April 1992	1992	April 2001
Investment Plan	Series C	Aborted IPO	Series D	Acquisition
Total Company Valuation (pre-money)	$32 m	$70 m	$50 m	$21m
Price per Share (split adjusted)	$1.00	$2.00	$1.50	
Shares Placed	7,473,000	-0-	226,667	
Total Placement	$7 m	-0-	-0-	
New Cash		-0-	-0-	
Percentage of Company Purchased	20 %	50 %	For Acquisitions	100 %
Purchasers	Various	Lehman Bros.	-0-	drkoop.com
HV II Ltd. Ownership (post-money)	28 %		23 %	2.76 %
Ivonyx Revenues (trailing 12 months)	$4.7 m	$15 m	$20.0 m	25.76m

Exhibit #2-1

Statement of Operations:
IVonyx Group Services, Inc.

(years ended 31 December)
(dollars in thousands)

	1990	1991	1992	1993
Revenues:				
Patient Billings (net)	3,067	10,584	17,171	24,787
Franchise Operations	1,045	825	1,086	739
Other	147	200	15	68
Total Revenues	4,259	11,609	18,272	25,594
Expenses:				
Cost of Sales	1,1309	3,368	6,014	8,680
Operating Expenses	1,603	5,163	8,169	9,777
Bad Debt Expense	800	2,273	928	1,071
Total Expenses	3,712	10,804	15,111	14,528
Operating Profits	(547)	805	3,161	6,066
Corporate Expenses	3,120	4,191	5,133	5,290
	(2,575)	(3,386)	(1,970)	776
Minority Interest	0	0	0	74
Interest Expense	13	164	184	454
Pre-tax Income	(2,588)	(3,550)	(2,154)	248
Income Taxes	0	0	72	112
Net Income	$(2,588)	$(3,550)	$(2,226)	$136

Exhibit #2-2

Statement of Operations:
IVonyx Group Services, Inc.

(years ended 31 December)
(dollars in thousands)

	1993	1994	1995
Revenues:			
Patient services	24,687	33,129	32,146
Franchise operations	770	727	613
Other	37	123	123
Total Revenues	25,495	33,979	32,879
Expenses:			
Cost of supplies	8,680	12,736	14,215
Patient care, selling, G&A	14,773	16,128	18,290
Bad Debt Expense	1,071	1,648	2,260
Total Expenses	24,524	30,512	34,765
Income before other items	970	3,467	(1,886)
Other items			
Settlement with Medicare			4,000
Goodwill write-off			1,820
Facility closing costs	195		270
Change in estimated contractuals	1,700		
Interest expense	454	607	760
Minority interest	74	195	227
Total other items	2,422	801	7,076
Income before taxes	(1,452)	2,665	(8,962)
Income tax provision	112	163	173
Net income (loss)	($1,564)	$2,502	($9,135)

Exhibit #3-1

Balance Sheet
IVonyx Group Services, Inc.
(years ended 31 December)
(dollars in thousands)

Assets	1994	1995
Current assets		
Cash and cash equivalents	5	6
Accounts receivable	14,712	12,259
Inventories	763	624
Prepaid expenses	306	227
Total current assets	15,786	13,116
Note receivable	39	36
Property and equipment, net	1,184	1,227
Goodwill	1,988	0
Other assets	724	422
Total assets	$19,721	$14,801

Liabilities and Shareholders' Equity	1994	1995
Current liabilities		
Bank line of credit	5,825	4,575
Current portion of long-term debt	2,143	2,223
Accounts payable	4,041	5,258
Accrued compensation	634	655
Current portion of Medicare settlement	0	760
Total current liabilities	12,642	13,472
Long-term debt	196	321
Non-current portion of Medicare settlement	0	3,240
Total liabilities	12,838	17,033
Minority interest in consolidated subsidiary	101	110
Shareholders' equity		
Series A,B,C and D convertible preferred stock	61	61
Common stock	3	3
Paid-in capital	19,081	19,090
Accumulated deficit	(12,362)	(21,497)
Total shareholders' equity	6,783	(2,343)
Total liability and shareholders' equity	$19,721	$14,801

Exhibit #4-1

Cash Flow Statement
IVonyx Group Services, Inc.

(years ended 31 December)
(dollars in thousands)

	1993	1994	1995
Cash flows provided (used) by operating activities			
Net income (loss)	($1,564)	$2,502	($9,135)
Depreciation and amortization	436	472	531
Goodwill write-off			1,820
Loss on disposition of assets	19		450
Amort. of discount on sub. debt	19	24	21
Accrual of Medicare settlement			4,000
Change in minority interest	74	27	9
Provision for uncollectible receivables	1,071	1,648	2,260
Change in estimated contractuals	1,700		
Terminated acquisitions	195		
Changes in operating assets and liabilities			
Accounts receivable	(2,787)	(6,393)	193
Inventories	(119)	(24)	138
Prepaid expenses	(166)	43	79
Other assets	(123)	(73)	16
Accounts payable	436	1,534	1,218
Accrued compensation	128	(4)	21
Net cash provided by operating activities	(681)	(240)	1,622
Cash flows provided (used) by investing activities			
Purchases of property and equipment	(356)	(133)	(187)
Proceeds from sale of equipment	(100)	14	4
Acquisitions, net of cash acquired	(191)	(81)	
Collections of note receivable from related	—	4	3
Net cash flows used by investing activities	(647)	(197)	(181)
Cash flows provided (used) by financing activities			
Net decrease in bank line of credit	625	(300)	(1,250)
Payment on notes payable	(353)	(131)	
Net proceeds from bank note payable	470		
Issuance of preferred stock	115		
Repurchase of common stock		(10)	
Repurchase of stock options		(113)	
Exercise of common stock options	12	5	10
Payments on lease obligations	(254)	(281)	(200)
Proceeds from issuance of subordimnated debt	1,478	500	0
Net cash used by financing activities	2,094	(330)	(1,440)
Increase in cash and cash equivalents	765	(767)	1
Cash and cash equivalents, beginning of year	7	772	5
Cash and cash equivalents, end of year	$72	$5	$6

Exhibit #5

Location of IVonyx Direct Branches

Cities	Date Opened or Acquired	Date Closed
Traverse City, Michigan		
Lansing, Michigan		
New York	1992 April	
New Orleans, Louisiana	1991 November	
Jackson, Michigan	1991 November	
~~Little Rock, Arkansas~~	1991 October	
~~Dallas, Texas~~	1991 August	
~~Leesburg, Virginia~~	1991 August	
~~Wilmington, Delaware~~	1991 May	
Grand Rapids, Michigan	1991 May	
~~Boston, Massachusetts~~	1991 May	
~~Indianapolis, Indiana~~	1991 March	
Memphis, Tennessee	1991 January	
~~Port St. Lucie, Florida~~	1990 November	
Chicago, Illinois	1990 October	
~~Cincinnati, Ohio~~	1990 October	
~~San Juan, Puerto Rico~~	1990 September	
~~San Angelo, Texas~~	1990 August	
~~San Diego, California~~	1990 July	December 1998
~~Miami, Florida~~	1990 June	June 2000
~~Corpus Christi, Texas~~	1990 May	
~~McAllen, Texas~~	1990 May	
~~Sacramento, California~~	1989 March	
Livonia, Michigan	1988 September	

*Those struck through were closed by June 1993 following the POP,
or the 1996 business plan.*

IVonyx Franchises by State
June 1993

13 States	38 Franchises
Ohio	10
Pennsylvania	5
Indiana	2
New York	1
California	1
Kentucky	2
Maryland	1
New Jersey	4
Tennessee	8
Wisconsin	1
Georgia	1
North Carolina	1
Florida	1

Exhibit #6

Analysis of Cost of Collections
IVonyx Group Services, Inc.
1992 and 1993

	Billing Department Expense	Collections	% Cost of Collections
June 1992 YTD	443,100	6,038,067	7.3
July	99,522	893,554	11.1
August	109,866	1,379,387	7.9
September	118,511	1,117,282	10.6
October	108,302	1,284,692	8.4
November	109,757	1,436,511	7.6
December	114,381	1,285,277	8.9
Total 1992	1,102,639	13,434,770	8.2
January	106,674	1,471,779	7.2
February	100,929	1,743,091	5.8
March	117,809	1,743,091	5.5
April	128,533	1,695,453	7.6
May	110,029	1,931,525	5.7
June	101,686	1,953,045	5.2
July	100,238	1,566,261	6.4
August	111,398	1,587,522	7.0
September	103,753	1,578,528	6.6
October	111,899	2,279,205	4.9
November	109,000	1,962,570	5.6
1993 YTD Totals	1,201,943	19,908,939	6.0

Goal: Billing department expense should not exceed 5% of collections.

Exhibit #7

Summary of IVonyx Cash Collections
Trailing 12 Months through November 1992

	% of Actual Collections	% of Collections	Revenues
Medicare	327,284	1.6	2.7
Medicare -SC	4,699,781	23.6	26.9
Blue Cross/Shield	1,925,895	9.7	8.8
Medicaid	1,819,375	9.1	6.9
Commercial/Managed Care	11,136,741	55.9	54.7
Sub-Total	19,908,996	100.0	100.0
Franchise Income	925,501		
Income Tax Refunds	55,459		
Other	90,650		
Total Cash Collections	20,980,686		

Index to Attachments

Question 1

Bama B. Rucker, *The Home Drug Delivery Industry: An Outlook* (Hambrecht & Quist Incorporated, January 1987)

Question 2

"Memorandum of terms of sale of Series A preferred stock of IVonyx Group Services, Inc." (6 October 1988)

Question 5

"Memorandum of terms of sale of Series B preferred stock of IVonyx Group Services, Inc." (August 1989) [Failed placement].

"Memorandum of terms of sale of Series B preferred stock of IVonyx Group Services, Inc." (October 1989) [Successful placement].

Attachment #1

HAMBRECHT & QUIST
INCORPORATED

234 Montgomery Street
San Francisco, CA 94104
(415) 576-3300
Cable: HAMQUIST
Telex: 278392 HQ UR (RCA)

Institutional Research

277 Park Avenue
38th Floor
New York, NY 10172
(212) 207-1400
Telex: 237258 HQ UR (RCA)

The Home Drug Delivery Industry:
An Outlook

Industry Report

Bama B. Rucker
January 1987

Bama B. Rucker
Susan T. Witter
January 1987

THE HOME DRUG DELIVERY INDUSTRY: AN OUTLOOK

Summary and Conclusion

The health care service delivery market, traditionally dominated by hospitals, is undergoing even more radical changes than those being experienced throughout the health care industry. In particular, serious efforts to contain costs are moving patients out of hospitals and toward alternative methodologies for receiving care, a movement that is creating pockets of opportunity for providers of nontraditional delivery systems.

One such opportunity is the home drug delivery market, which we think could achieve a growth rate of 34% at least until 1990, with pretax margins in the 18-25% range. In 1986, this market captured approximately $850 million in revenues; by 1990 we expect revenues to reach at least $2.8 billion. We see no obstacles to continued long- term growth for the home drug delivery industry.

Today's home drug delivery industry originated in the early 1980s in the home infusion therapy market (see our March 1984 report, "The Home Infusion Therapy Industry," by Bama B. Rucker), which was developed by physicians and home health care providers who discovered that seriously ill patients could receive nutrient solutions by infusion at home at much lower cost than in the hospital. The success of the home infusion industry over the past six years legitimized this new approach to caring for critically ill patients. As they became educated about its technology and benefits, both insurers and physicians expanded the service beyond nutrients to drugs that could be infused intravenously in the home. Now a broader industry is being formed, the home drug delivery industry, to include pharmaceuticals administered intravenously or intramuscularly. This new market is taking shape at the same time that market forces are shifting the way patients are directed to health care delivery systems, from physicians and hospitals to insurance companies and self-insured corporations. This change in the direction of patient referrals could accelerate home drug delivery growth.

Because its size and growth potential is so enticing, we expect a rush of new competitors to attack the home drug delivery market. However, we believe that significant barriers to entry have been established by the current players that will insure industry profitability for at least several more years. Caremark and Travacare, a division of Baxter Travenol, clearly lead the market today. Four smaller players, similar only in the size of their revenues, follow: Home Nutritional Support, HMSS (Home Medical Support Systems), New England Critical Care, and Foster InfusionCare.

In order to identify the long-term winners in the home drug delivery industry, we measured the participants in the market using four fundamental criteria: (a) what is the structure of the payer mix or sources of reimbursement for services; (b) are operations decentralized and how long have they been so; (c) what is the product mix or revenue breakout by type of therapy; and (d) how is a player strategically positioned in terms of the current shift in patient referral sources from physicians/hospitals to insurers and self-insured. Our conclusion: Caremark is in a class by itself and, considering its superb research and development effort and elegant strategic plan, deservedly so. Meanwhile Travacare, whose presence in the marketplace cannot be ignored, is losing share but scrambling to regain its historic growth momentum. Travacare is poorly positioned for relationships with hospitals rather than insurers. Among the four smaller companies, our analysis highlights two: New England Critical Care and Home Medical Support Systems, a private company.

We continue to recommend the purchase of Caremark, a company that has emerged as the single strongest organization, one with strengthening skills and capabilities, in this exploding industry. Although at an earlier stage of development than Caremark, New England Critical Care is superbly positioned and we believe will be an increasingly powerful competitor over the new few years. New England Critical Care's stock is attractive at current prices.

Two Investment Candidates
in the Home Drug Delivery Market

($ in millions, except per share data)

	Price	Market Cap.	Calendar EPS			Calendar P/E		Trailing 12-mos. Rev.
			1986E	1987E	1988E	1987	1988	
Caremark	25¹/₄	396	0.75	1.00	1.35	25	19	149
New England Critical Care	16¹/₄	76	0.50	0.69	1.25	24	13	19

The Home Infusion Therapy Market

Although the home infusion therapy industry is almost nine years old, the explosion in both its medical acceptance and its revenue growth began in 1983. In that year, the industry generated an estimated $265 million in revenues; today, revenues have more than tripled to an estimated $868 million. Strong growth in the industry has been propelled by four significant factors: (a) changes in the economic environment for health care delivery, (b) more disease states becoming treatable by home infusion therapy, (c) growth in Medicare reimbursement revenues, and (d) the entrance of entrepreneurial companies into a former cottage industry. We discuss each of these factors briefly below.

First, changes in the economic structure of health care delivery have been instrumental in setting the stage for explosive revenue growth. The factor with probably the strongest impact on the economics of health care delivery was the implementation of Diagnostic-Related Groups, or DRGs, by the Medicare administration in the fall of 1983. This new federal prospective payment system, which preestablished reimbursement payments by individual procedure, collided with corporate America's response to rising health care costs in the form of higher deductions and copayments. As a result of the combined impact of these two forces, health care delivery changed from a system that seldom considered the cost of treatment to one that is tracking expenses carefully. New financial incentives-infusion therapy is 50-60% cheaper delivered in the home began to force patients out of the hospital sooner than they would have left in the past. This movement of patients away from the hospital has been crucial to the recent high revenue levels being experienced by almost all home infusion therapy providers

The second element contributing to the growth of the industry is the increasing number of disease states being treated with home infusion therapy, a list that is growing for two related reasons: financial incentives coupled with increased awareness amount physicians. The most conspicuous of the therapies now being delivered in the home are antibiotic treatments for nosocomial infections (infections acquired in the hospital) and total parenteral nutrition (TPN) for ovarian and breast cancers, but these are just the beginning. Over time, more and more patients will be identified as appropriate for home drug delivery treatment plans as the medical community increases its understanding of disease states. In particular, the for-profit home infusion therapy companies increasingly will work with academic medical hospitals to develop drug deliveries that reach untapped markets. Expanding indications for home drug delivery have been an important component of recent revenue growth for the industry, and will probably be an even stronger component in future revenue growth.

The third factor contributing to recent growth in the home infusion therapy market is the increase in Medicare revenues available for home treatments. In our 1984 report on the industry, we estimated that Medicare reimbursement contributed 50% of the total revenues generated by providers of parenteral nutrition and enteral nutrition (EN). Today, in spite of a decreased proportional contribution from Medicare to these therapies-an estimated 30% to the TPN revenue base and an estimated 40% to the EN increased from, 1984's $120 million to 1986's $220 million. This increase reflects mainly an increase in the number of patients receiving TPN and EN therapies; Medicare's reimbursement schedule has not changed over the past few years. We believe that the majority of these new patients are being serviced by the smaller home infusion companies, each of which generates $300,000-400,000 in revenues. Of the top for-profit market contenders, we believe Baxtor Travenol's Travacare services the largest number of Medicare patients.

Finally, over the past few years the home infusion therapy industry has been changing from a fragmented cottage industry to one serviced by small, aggressive entrepreneurial companies, the majority of which were funded by venture capitalist in the early 1980s. Before the advent of these ventures, only a few companies were actively pursuing the home infusion market, and most TPN patients were serviced either by hospitals' in-house pharmacies or by mom and pop operations. In 1986, entrepreneur-ial companies that generated $10 million-127 million claimed about 40 of the industrywide $868 million in estimated revenues. The other 60% of the industry's revenues came mainly from hospital-based programs and from mom and pop operations. However, these small concerns cannot provide care for critically ill patients that need more complex treatment plans, nor can they enjoy the economies of scale of a larger company.

Three years ago, we did not expect small, aggressive entrepreneurial companies to be as important to the home infusion therapy industry as they have become. In our 1984 report, we projected that the industry's most important competitors would be the larger supply companies, which have the products and the capital necessary to expand into the home infusion therapy market. However, the supply companies have not been able to make the psychological transition fro ma product orienta-tion to a service one. Travacare has been the only division of a large hos-pital supply company to survive, achieving an estimated $100 million in net revenues in 1986. In 1984, we also expected hospital chains to be major competitors in the home infusion market. Shackled with their own concerns about losing inpatient market share, however, hospital chains generally have not been able to compete effectively in the home drug delivery industry because they have too few patients in one loca-tion to benefit from the economies of scale that a freestanding center, which receive referrals from all surrounding hospitals, can enjoy. Overall, the smaller home infusion therapy companies have developed the service aspect of the home infusion business and have consistently created market share in an industry that has just begun to show its deli-cate infrastructure. Not only are these companies reshaping the industry, in their efforts to promote their services to hospital discharge planners and physicians they are stimulating unmet demand.

Attachment #2

This Series A financing was ultimately increased
to and closed at $5.1 million.

Memorandum of Terms for Sale of Series A Preferred Stock of IVonyx Group Services, Inc.

This memorandum summarizes the principal terms of the first-round venture capital financing of Ivonyx Group Services, Inc., a Delaware corporation (the "Company"):

Securities	Up to 481,250 shares of Series A Preferred Stock at $8.00 per share, for aggregate proceeds of up to $3,850,000. Minimum aggregate investment of $3,000,000 as a condition to closing.

Investors	The Henry Venture Fund Limited $900,000
	Henry Venture II Limited $850,000
	Mercury Asset Management $500,000
	Paribas Technologies $1,000,000
	CS Investment Ltd. $350,000
	Seaport Ventures $250,000

Terms of Series A Preferred Stock

Dividends	No established dividend rate — dividends are payable when and if declared by Board. Cash dividends may be declared and paid upon Common Stock only if cash dividends in the same amount per share have been declared and paid upon Series A Preferred Stock.

Liquidation Preference	In the event of a liquidation of the Company, the holders of the Series A Preferred Stock shall be entitled to receive, in preference to the holders of the Common Stocks, an amount equal to (a) $8.00 per share of Series A Preferred Stock (the "Base Amount") and (b) an amount equal to a 10% simple interest annual return on the Base Amount from the date of issuance to the date of distribution (collectively, the "Liquidation Preference"). After payment of the Liquidation Preference, holders of the Common Stock shall be entitled to receive the remaining assets of the Company. A consolidation or merger of the Company (except a merger in which the Company is the surviving corporation) or the sale of all or substantially all of the assets of the Company shall be deemed a liquidation of the Company.
Redemption	The Series A Preferred Stock is not redeemable by the Company.
Conversion Rights	Subject to antidilution adjustment, each share of Series A preferred Stock is convertible into one share of Common Stock at the option of holder. Series A Preferred Stock is automatically converted into Common Stock, at the then applicable conversion rate, upon the closing of an underwritten public offering of Common Stock at a public offering price of a least $40.00 (subject to adjustment for stock dividends, splits and similar transactions), with aggregate proceeds in excess of $7,500,000. Share

of converted Series A Preferred Stock shall be restored to the status of authorized but unissued shares.

Antidilution Adjustments	Conversion ratio adjusted on a full ratchet basis for the two-year period following closing; thereafter, on a standard weighted average basis, in the event of certain issuances of additional securities by the Company, other than the issuance of: (a) up to an aggregate of 160,323 shares of Common Stock (including options exercisable for Common Stock) to officers, directors, employees and consultants of the Company and other persons or parties with which the Company has a business relationship, (b) securities as dividends or distributions made on other Company securities, (c) securities upon the exercise, conversion or exchange of other Company securities, (d) securities in connection with business acquisitions and (e) securities issued in equity financings to persons with which the Company has business relationships (to the extent not in excess of 2% of the outstanding shares of Common Stock on a fully-converted, fully-diluted basis). Proportional adjustments for stock splits and stock dividends.
Voting Rights	Votes on an as-converted basis, as a single class with Common Stock except as otherwise required by law.
Protective Provisions	Consent of the holders of at least a majority of the Series A Preferred Stock shall be

required for the payment of cash dividends with respect to the Common Stock and the consent of holders of two-thirds of the Series A Preferred Stock shall be required for: (a) modification of the rights of the Series A Preferred Stock, (b) creation of any class or series of shares having preferences senior to the Series A Preferred Stock as to dividends or liquidation, or (c) merger, consolidation or sale or all or substantially all of the assets of the Company.

Election of Directors

Voting shall be on a cumulative basis. The number of directors shall be 5. Cumulative voting shall cease upon an underwritten public offering of the Company's Common Stock or by an amendment approved by 90% of all outstanding shares of capital stock of the Company, voting as a single class.

Indemnification

Maximum director and officer indemnification and limitations on liability.

Terms of Preferred Stock Purchase Agreement

Representations and
Warranties

Standard representations and warranties.

Registration Rights

(a) Beginning six months after the Company's initial public offering, two demand registrations upon initiation by holders of at least 20% of Common Stock owned by Alan E. Jordan ("Jordan") and Common Stock issued or issuable upon conversion of Series A

Preferred Stock (collectively, the "Registrable Securities"). Expenses paid by Company unless registration is withdrawn; in which case, initiating holders pay all expenses or forfeit right to one demand registration.

(b) Unlimited piggybacks subject to a cut-back at the underwriter's discretion. Cut-back pro rata among selling share-holders, provided that five shares of non-Jordan Registrable Securities shall be included for each one share of Jordan Registrable Securities included. Expenses paid by Company, except for underwriting discounts/commissions and selling shareholders' attorneys' fees.

(c) Unlimited S-3 registrations of at least $1,000,000, unless Company has effected two such registrations within last 12 months. Expenses paid by participating holders.

(d) Registration Rights terminate five years after the Company's initial public offering.

(e) Company may defer a demand registration or S-3 registration for up to 60 days upon a good faith determination by the Board of Directors that any such registration would be seriously detrimental to the Company and its shareholders.

(f) Standard indemnification by Company and selling shareholders. Assignment of rights only to holders of at least 20,000 shares of Registrable Securities (determined on a collective basis for distributes of partnerships). Amendment of registration rights, or grant of registration rights prior or superior to rights of holders of Registrable Securities, only with consent of company and holders of two-thirds of Registrable Securities.

(g) Investors agree to underwriter-imposed market stand-off arrangements in connection with initial public offering.

Financial Information

Standard rights to monthly unaudited and annual audited financial statements and annual budget and business plan. Standard inspection right for purchasers of at least 25,000 shares of Series A preferred Stock, with termination of certain information rights once Company becomes a reporting company.

Board of Directors

Initial members to be: Alan E. Jordan, Albert J. Henry, F. David Hare and Thomas McKinley, with one vacancy.

Expenses

Company to pay reasonable fees of Gibson, Dunn & Crutcher, special counsel to the Investors, not to exceed $20,000.

Right of First Offer

Holders of at least 5% of Series A Preferred Stock (or Common Stock issued upon conversion thereof) have a right of first offer to purchase securities to be issued in future by Company, subject to standard exclusions and subject to the loss of the right of first offer in the event of non-participation by an investor in two offerings.

Key-man Insurance	Company to initially purchase a $4,000,000 life insurance policy on Jordan plus appropriate disability insurance. First $2,000,000 in proceeds payable to Company, remaining $2,000,000 of proceeds to be used to repurchase Common Stock owned by Jordan at its then fair market value. Amount of coverage increased by Board of Directors from time to time.
Use of Proceeds	Used for general corporate purposes, including payment of certain Company indebtedness and deferred salaries.

Post-Closing
Capitalization:

	Share Outstanding	Fully-Diluted Capitalization
Series A Preferred Stock	481,250 (78.5%)	481,250 (59.9%)
Common Stock	131,655 (21.5%)	131,655 (16.4%)
Stock Options — granted or reserved for grant to officers, directors, employees, consultants and other persons or parties having a business relationship with the Company	—	160,323 (20.0%)
Warrants	—	30,000 (3.7%)
	612,905 (100%)	803,228 (100%)

Other Understandings and Agreements:

Covenant Regarding Stock Options

Under the terms of the Stock Purchase Agreement, the Company shall agree to grant non-qualified stock options (the "Jordan Options") pursuant to which Jordan shall have the rights, for the ten-year option period (unless sooner terminated as described below), to maintain no less than 15% ownership interest in the Company, assuming the exercise, conversion or exchange of all outstanding securities of the Company, with the payment of an exercise price of $6.40 per share of Common Stock. The Jordan Options shall terminate upon: (a) the Company's initial public offering of its Common Stock, (b) the termination of Jordan's employment for cause or as the result of his death, disability or voluntary resignation, or (c) the Board of Directors' decision to remove Jordan as Chairman and Chief Executive Officer or President of the Company in the event the Company fails to achieve 50% of gross revenues and 50% of pre-tax net income of the Company, as set forth in the Company's annual budget, as approved and as may be amended in good faith by the Company's Board of Directors.

Closing

On or before October 11, 1988

Nature of Memorandum

This Memorandum of Terms shall not constitute a binding contractual commitment on the part of the Company or the Investors.

Attachment #3

This was the failed Series B financing which was sought but not closed

Memorandum of Terms for Sale of Series B Preferred Stock of IVonyx Group Services, Inc.

This memorandum summarizes the principal terms of the Series B Preferred Stock financing of Ivonyx Group Services, Inc., a Delaware corporation (the "Company"):

Securities

Up to 375,940 shares of Series B Preferred stock at $10.64 per share, for aggregate proceeds of up to $4,000,000. The minimum aggregate investment required is $3,000,000.

**Major Series A Preferred
Stock Investors**

The Henry Venture Fund Limited	$1,250,000
Henry Venture II Limited	$ 850,000
Kolman & Co., as nominee for	
Mercury Asset Management	$850,000
Group Development Capital	
Trust PLC	$ 530,000
Seaport Ventures	$ 250,000
Euro Canadian Bank	$ 500,000
Sun Alliance and London Assurance	
Company Limited	$ 300,000
	$4,530,000

**Terms of Series B
Preferred Stock**

Dividends

No established dividend rate — dividends are payable when and if declared by Board. Cash dividends may be declared and paid upon Common Stock only if cash dividends in the same amount per share have been declared and paid upon Series A and Series B Preferred Stock.

Liquidation Preference

In the event of a liquidation of the Company, the holders of the Series B Preferred Stock shall be entitled to receive, in preference to the holders of the Common Stock and in parity with the holders of Series A Preferred stock, an amount equal to (a) $10.64 per share of Series B Preferred stock (the "Base Amount") and (b) an amount equal to a 10% simple interest annual return on the Base Amount from the date of issuance to the date of distribution. After payment of such liquidation preference and the liquidation preference of $8.00 per share applicable to the holders of Series A Preferred Stock, holders of the Common Stock shall be entitled to receive the remaining assets of the Company. A consolidation or merger of the Company (except a merger in which the Company is the surviving corporation) or the sale of all or substantially all of the assets of the Company shall be deemed a liquidation of the Company.

Redemption

The Series B Preferred Stock is not redeemable by the Company.

Conversion Rights

Subject to antidilution adjustment, each share of Series B Preferred Stock is convertible into one share of Common Stock at the option of holder. Series B Preferred Stock is automatically converted into Common Stock, at the then applicable conversion rate, upon the closing of an underwritten public offering of Common Stock at a public offering price of at least $40.00 (subject to adjustment for stock dividends, splits and similar transactions), with aggregate proceeds in excess of $7,500,000. Shares of converted Series B Preferred Stock shall be restored to the status of authorized but unissued shares.

Antidilution Adjustments

Conversion ratio adjusted on a full ratchet basis for the two-year period following closing; thereafter, on a standard weighted average basis, in the event of certain issuances of additional securities by the Company, other than the issuance of: (a) shares of Common Stock (including options exercisable for Common Stock) to officers, directors, employees and consultants of the Company and other persons or parties with which the Company has a business relationship, (b) securities as dividends or distributions made on other Company securities, (c) securities upon the exercise, conversion or exchange of other Company securities, (d) securities in connection issued in equity financing so persons with which the Company has business relationships (to the extent not in excess of 2% of the outstanding shares of Common Stock on a fully-converted, fully-diluted basis). Proportional adjustments for stock splits and stock dividends.

| Voting Rights | Voting on an as-converted basis, as a single class with Series A Preferred Stock and Common Stock except as otherwise required by law. |

Protective Provisions

Consent of the holders of at least a majority of the Series A and Series B Preferred stock shall be required for the payment of cash dividends with respect to the Common Stock and the consent of holders of two-thirds of the Series A and Series B Preferred Stock shall be required for: (a) modification of the rights of the Preferred Stock, (b) creation of any class or series of shares having preferences senior to the Preferred Stock as to dividends or liquidation, or (c) merger, consolidation or sale or all or substantially all of the assets of the Company.

Election of Directors

Voting shall be on a cumulative basis. The number of directors shall be 5. Cumulative voting shall cease upon an underwritten public offering or the Company's Common Stock or by an amendment approved by 90% of all outstanding shares of capital stock of the Company, voting as a single class.

Indemnification

Maximum director and officer indemnification and limitations on liability.

Terms of Preferred stock Purchase Agreement

Representations and Warranties

Standard representations and warranties.

Registration Rights

(a) Beginning six months after the Company's initial public offering, two demand registrations upon initiation by holders of at least 30% of Common Stock owned by Alan E. Jordan ("Jordan"), Common Stock issued or issuable upon conversion of Series A Preferred stock and Common Stock issued or issuable upon conversion of Series B Preferred stock (collectively, the "Registrable Securities"). Expenses paid by Company unless registration is withdrawn; in which case, initiating holders pay all expenses or forfeit right to one demand registration.

(b) Unlimited piggybacks subject to a cutback at the underwriter's discretion. Outback pro rata among selling shareholders, provided that five shares of non-Jordan Registrable Securities shall be included for each one share of Jordan Registrable Securities included. Expenses paid by Company, except for underwriting discounts, commissions and selling shareholders' attorneys' fees.

(c) Unlimited S-3 registrations of at least $1,000,000, unless Company has effected two such registrations within last 12 months. Expenses paid by participating holders.

(d) Registration Rights terminate five years after the Company's initial public offering.

(e) Company may defer a demand registration of S-3 registration for up to 60 days
upon a good faith determination by the
Board of Directors that any such registration would be seriously detrimental
to the Company and its shareholders.

(f) Standard indemnification by Company
and selling shareholders. Assignment
of rights only to holders of at least 20,000
shares of Registrable Securities (determined on a collective basis for distributes of partnerships). Amendment of
registration rights, or grant of registration rights prior or superior to rights of
holders of Registrable Securities, only
with consent of Company and holders
of two-thirds of Registrabel Securities.

(g) Investors agree to underwriter-imposed
market stand-off arrangements in connection with initial public offering.

Financial Information	Standard rights to monthly unaudited and annual audited financial statements and annual budget and business plan. Standard inspection right for holders of at least 5% of the outstanding shares of Series B Preferred stock (or Common Stock issued on conversion thereof), with termination of certain information rights once Company becomes a reporting company.
Board of Directors	Current members are: Alan E. Jordan, Albert J. Henry, and F. David Hare with two vacancies. Promptly after Closing, Richard

Fulford, Chairman of Citicorp-Scringeour Vickers ("CSV"), to be elected to the Board.

Right of First Offer

Holders of at least 5% of Series B Preferred Stock (or Common Stock issued upon conversion thereof), pari passu with Holders of at least 5% of Series A Preferred Stock (or Common Stock issued upon conversion thereof), have a right of first offer to purchase securities to be issued in future by Company, subject to standard exclusions and subject to the loss of the right of first offer in the event of non-participation by an Investor in two offerings.

Use of Proceeds

General corporate purposes.

Fees

CSV to receive a fee equal to 3% of the aggregate amount of the Series B Preferred Stock financing, payable in cash at Closing. CSV will also receive a five-year warrant to purchase 2,500 shares of the Company's Common Stock at an exercise price of $10.64 per share.

Post-Closing Capitalization:

	Shares Outstanding	Fully-Diluted Capitalization
Series B Preferred Stock	375,940 (32.5%)	375,940 (26.6%)
Series A Preferred Stock	636,375 (55.1%)	636,375 (45.0%)
Common Stock	143,675 (12.4%)	143,675 (10.2%)

Stock Options-granted or
reserved for grant to officers,
directors, employees, consultants
and other persons or parties having
a business relationship with the
Company   —   200,000 (14.1%)

Warrants-granted or   —   57,874 (4.1%)
reserved for grant

                                  1,155,990 (100.0%) 1,413,864 (100.0%)

Note: Foregoing assumes sale of 375,940 shares of Series B Preferred
        stock and adoption of the Company's 1989 Stock Option Plan.

**Other Understandings and
Agreements:**

Warrants   Richard Fulford to purchase, at fair market
                            value, five-year warrant to purchase 5,500
                            shares of the Company's Common Stock at
                            an exercise price of $10.64 per share. Henry
                            & Co. to purchase for cash, at full market
                            value, five-year warrant to purchase 17,000
                            shares of the Company's Common Stock at
                            an exercise price of $10.64 per share.

Closing   On or before August 15, 1989.

Stock Split   The Company may effectuate a four-for-
                            one stock split prior to or contemporane-
                            ously with the Closing.

Nature of Memorandum   This Memorandum of Terms shall not con-
                            stitute a binding contractual commitment
                            on the part of the Company or the
                            Investors.

Attachment #4

This is the Series B financing which was ultimately closed

Memorandum of Terms for Sale of Series B Preferred Stock of IVonyx Group Services, Inc.

This memorandum summarizes the principal terms of the Series B Preferred Stock financing of Ivonyx Group Services, Inc., a Delaware corporation (the "Company"):

Securities	Up to 6,772,009 shares of Series B Preferred Stock at $.443 per share for aggregate proceeds of up to $3,000,000; provided, however, that if the proposed financing becomes oversubscribed, the Company may raise up to $3,500,000 in the aggregate.*

Major Series A Preferred
Stock Investors

The Henry Venture Fund Limited	$1,250,000
Henry Venture II Limited	$ 850,000
Kolman & Co., as nominee for Mercury Asset Management	$ 850,000
Group Development Capital Trust PLC	$ 530,000
Seaport Ventures	$ 250,000
Euro Canadian Bank	$ 500,000
Sun Alliance and London Assurance Company Limited	$ 300,000

* *These numbers assume the effectiveness immediately prior to the closing of the Series B financing of a four-for-one stock split of the Common and Preferred Stock of the Company.*

Terms of Series B Preferred Stock

Dividends

No established dividend rate—dividends are payable when and if declared by Board. Cash dividends may be declared and paid upon Common Stock only if cash dividends in the same amount per share have been declared and paid upon Series A and Series B Preferred Stock.

Liquidation Preference*

In the event of a liquidation of the Company, the holders of the Series B Preferred Stock shall be entitled to receive, in preference to the holders of the Common Stock and in parity with the holders of Series A Preferred Stock, an amount equal to (a) $.443 per share of Series B Preferred Stock (the "Base Amount") and (b) an amount equal to a 10% simple interest annual return on the Base Amount from the date of issuance to the date of distribution. After payment of such liquidation preference and the liquidation preference of $2.00 per share applicable to the holders of Series A Preferred Stock, holders of the Common Stock shall be entitled to receive the remaining assets of the Company. A consolidation or merger of the Company (except a merger in which the Company is the surviving corporation) or the sale of all or substantially all of the assets of the Company shall be deemed a liquidation of the Company.

Redemption

The Series B Preferred Stock is not redeemable by the Company.

Conversion Rights

Subject to antidilution adjustment, each share of Series B Preferred Stock is convertible into one share of Common Stock at the option of holder. Series B Preferred Stock is automatically converted into Common Stock, at the then applicable conversion rate, upon the closing of an underwritten public offering of Common Stock at a public offering price of at least $2.00 (subject to adjustment for stock dividends, splits and similar transactions), with aggregate proceeds in excess of $5,000,000. Shares of converted Series B Preferred Stock shall be restored to the status of authorized but unissued shares.

Antidilution Adjustments

Conversion ratio adjusted on a full ratchet basis until October 11, 1990; thereafter, on a standard weighted average basis, in the event of certain issuances of additional securities by the Company, other than the issuance of: (a) shares of Common Stock (including options exercisable for Common Stock) to officers, directors, employees and consultants of the Company and other persons or parties with which the Company has a business relationship, (b) securities as dividends or distributions made on other Company securities, (c) securities upon the exercise, conversion or exchange of other Company securities, (d) securities in connection with business acquisitions and (e) securities issued in equity financings to persons with which the Company has business relationships. Proportional adjustments for stock splits and stock dividends.

Voting Rights	Votes on an as-converted basis, as a single class with Series A Preferred Stock and Common Stock except as otherwise required by law.
Protective Provisions	Consent of the holders of at least a majority of the Series A and Series B Preferred Stock shall be required for the payment of cash dividends with respect to the Common Stock and the consent of holders of two-thirds of the Series A and Series B Preferred Stock shall be required for: (a) modification of the rights of the Preferred Stock, (b) creation of any class or series of shares having preferences senior to the Preferred Stock as to dividends or liquidation, or (c) merger, consolidation or sale of all or substantially all of the assets of the Company.
Election of Directors	Voting shall be on a cumulative basis. The number of directors shall be 5. Cumulative voting cease upon an underwritten public offering of the Company's Common Stock or by an amendment approved by 90% of all outstanding shares of capital stock of the Company, voting as a single class.
Indemnification	Maximum director and officer indemnification and limitations on liability.
Amendment of Certain Rights of Series A Preferred Stock	Pursuant to the current Restated Certificate of Incorporation of the Company, upon the issuance of shares of Series B Preferred Stock, the conversion

price for each share of Series A Preferred Stock would be adjusted on a full-ratchet basis; that is, each share of Series A Preferred Stock would become convertible into 4.5147 shares of Common Stock of the Company. As a condition to the closing of the Series B Preferred Stock financing, the Company will obtain the written consent of the holders of Series A Preferred Stock to a restatement of the Certificate of Incorporation, whereby the Series A Preferred Stock conversion price will be adjusted so as to cause each share of Series A Preferred Stock to be convertible into 2,4242 shares of Common Stock (rather than 4.5157 shares of Common Stock as provided under the current Certificate of Incorporation).

Terms of Preferred Stock Purchase Agreement

Representations and Warranties

Registration Rights

Standard representations and warranties,

(a) Beginning six months after the Company's initial public offering, two demand registrations upon initiation by holders of at least 30% of Common Stock owned by Alan E. Jordan ("Jordan"), Common Stock issued or issuable upon conversion of Series A Preferred Stock and Common Stock issued or issuable upon conversion of Series B Preferred Stock (collectively, the "Registrable Securities"). Expenses paid by Company unless registration is withdrawn; in which case, initiating holders pay all expenses or forfeit right o one demand registration.

(b)   Unlimited piggybacks subject to a cut-back at the underwriter's discretion. Cut-back pro rata among selling shareholders, provided that five shares of non-Jordan Registrable Securities shall be included for each one share of Jordan Registrable Securities included. Expenses paid by Company, except for underwriting discounts/commissions and selling shareholders' attorney' fees.

(c)   Unlimited S-3 registrations of at least $1,000,000, unless Company has effected two such registrations within last 12 months. Expenses paid by participation holders.

(d)   Registration Rights terminate five years after the Company's initial public offering.

(e)   Company may defer a demand registration or S-3 registration for up to 60 days upon a good faith determination by the Board of Directors that any such registration would be seriously detrimental to the Company and its shareholders.

(f)   Standard indemnification by Company and selling shareholders.

Assignment of rights only to holders of at least 80,000 shares of Registrable Securities (determined on a collective basis for distributes of partnerships). Amendment of registration rights, or grant of registration rights prior or superior to rights of holders of Registrable Securities, only with consent of Company and holders of two-thirds of Registrable Securities.

(g) Investors agree to underwriter-imposed market stand-off arrangements in connection with initial public offering.

Financial Information

Standard rights to monthly unaudited and annual audited financial statements and annual budget and business plan. Standard inspection right for holders of at least 5% of the outstanding shares of Series B Preferred Stock (or Common Stock issued on conversion thereof), with termination of certain information rights once Company becomes a reporting company.

Board of Directors

Current members are: Alan E. Jordan, Albert J. Henry and F. David Hare with two vacancies.

Right of First Offer

Holders of at least 5% of Series B Preferred Stock (or Common Stock issued upon conversion thereof), pari passu with Holders of at least 5% of Series A Preferred Stock (or Common Stock issued upon conversion thereof), have a right of first offer to purchase securities to be issued in future by

Company, subject to standard exclusions and subject to the loss of the right of first offer in the event of non-participation by an Investor in two offerings.

Use of Proceeds   General corporate purposes.

**Post-Closing
Capitalization***

	Fully-Converted Shares	Fully-Diluted Capitalization**
Common	549,700 (4.1%)	549,700 (3.6%)
Series A Preferred Stock*	6,170,801 (45.7%)	6,170,801 (40.5%)
Series B Preferred Stock	6,772,009 (50.2%)	6,772,009 (44.5%)
Stock Options-granted or reserved for grant to officers, directors, employees, consultants and other persons or parties having a business relationship with the Company.	—	1,600,00 (10.5%)
Warrants – granted or reserved for grant	—	131,496 (.9%)
	13,492,510 (100.0%)	15,224,006 (100.0%)

Note: * Assumes the adjustment of conversion ration pursuant to amendment of Certificate of Incorporation.

** Assumes the sale of 6,772,009 shares of Series B Preferred Stock and the grant of all options under the Company's 1989

Stock Option Plan (which will be amended to authorize options to purchase
1,600,000 shares of Common Stock after
the closing of the proposed financing).

* *These numbers assume the effectiveness immediately prior to the closing of the
Series B financing of a four-for-one stock split of the Common and Preferred
Stock of the Company.*

**Other Understandings
and Agreements:**

Surrender of Certain Rights
by Alan Jordan

Alan Jordan, ("Jordan"), the Chief
Executive Officer of the Company, currently possesses the following rights pursuant
to the Series A Preferred Stock Purchase
Agreement as amended (the "Series A
Agreement"): (i) the right to maintain a
15% interest in the fully-diluted capitalization of the Company through the grant of
additional stock options to Jordan; (ii) the
right to approve the issuance of Preferred
Stock possessing rights on par with or
superior to those of the Series A Preferred
Stock; and (iii) the right to a seat on the
Board. As a condition to the closing of the
Series B Preferred Stock financing, Jordan
will surrender the foregoing rights.

Closing

On or before October 31, 1989.

Stock Split

The Company may effectuate a four-for-
one stock split prior to or contemporane-
ously with the Closing.

Nature of Memorandum   This Memorandum of Terms shall not constitute a binding contractual commitment
on the part of the Company or the Investors.

IVonyx Case Solution

Question 1, page 332

Assume you are a partner in a venture fund. Review the summary of the Hambrecht & Quist January, 1987 Home Drug Delivery Industry Report. Do you find the home infusion industry attractive for investment? Why or why not? Which competitive approach to the industry shows the greatest potential?

The industry is attractive for investment for the following major reasons:

1. Overall industry growth is forecast to be well above average when compared to other health care sectors of the economy, so a venture fund investing in health care would take a close look at home infusion.

2. Industry growth is forecast by Hambrecht & Quist and others. (H&Q says five year industry growth could be from $870 million in 1986 to $2.8 billion by 1991, for a forecast 26% CGR.)

3. There are approximately six public companies that comprise the industry along with many smaller local companies performing home infusion. The public companies are largely regional. The local companies are ripe for a roll-up strategy to achieve critical mass.

4. A good approach to the home infusion industry as a venture capitalist would be to acquire and roll up several regional infusion companies to achieve critical mass and then consider an IPO.

Question 2, page 337

At this stage in its evolution, what value would you place on IVonyx? What methodology and comparisons would you use for arriving at that value? Do you need to raise capital for the company to continue to grow? If so, how much and with what type of financing? Review the term sheet for the Series A round of financing [Attachment #1] Would you suggest that any terms be changed? Why or why not?

Question 3, page 339

Ivonyx has a severe cash flow problem in that expenditures required to support new franchisees for marketing, collections and other

services are greater than revenues derived from franchisees. Also, franchisee accounts receivable are much slower than the DSO of 60 days which was forecast, which delays IVonyx receiving the 14% of collections forecast. What is your solution to the cash flow crisis being faced by IVonyx?

Answer:
It is becoming obvious that the business model of selling franchises and performing critical business services for franchisees is not working. The venture capitalists must consider a restart and a new business model. Servicing patients directly through company-owned branches with pharmacies is necessary to accelerate revenues and cash flow.

The franchise-based business model has a sales cycle of 4-6 months to sell the franchise, 3-4 months to generate patient referrals and 4-5 months to collect franchisee receivables so that IVonyx could take its14% cut of collections. The total sales cycle before IVonyx collects any recurring cash and a franchisee begins to pay its way is 14 to 16 months. Original franchise business model is not working and is bleeding IVonyx of its cash war chest, which was $5.1 million from the Series A financing.

Minimizing the Cash Flow Burn
Equalize the expenses applicable to setting up new franchisees in business (i.e. Advertising, Marketing & Clinical Training expenses) with the pretax profit derived from sale of new franchises to create a neutral cash flow effect on IVonyx cash flow statement.

Equalizing burn rate with sales of new franchises would not create a neutral cash flow effect because of cost of goods sold payable related to equipment purchased by IVonyx and re-sold to the franchisee. These were 60-day payables.

Restructuring Issues & Solutions
1) Bring new franchise sale effort down to zero because sales dollars expended would show little result approaching recession. Don't spend on new franchise sales effort.

2) Minimize spending to support franchisees unless immediate revenue potential is indicated through patient referrals. Reduce or eliminate as possible general business development expenditures (Industry advertising, sales development brochures, patient handouts, glossy & printed, etc.)

3) Develop a more reliable revenue stream. It is easer for IVonyx to service and access patient than to have the franchisee do it supported by IVonyx business development expenditure. IVonyx should go direct and service patients directly. It will generate the patient referral and collect its cash return on business development expenditure quicker than through the franchise channel of generating revenue.

Question 4, page 345

What do you think of IVonyx's acquisition of CIC in concept? Was the acquisition good, bad or unimportant?

Answer:

The acquisition of CIC was most important because IVonyx achieved entry into the direct, Company owned branch structure of the home infusion industry immediately. The acquisition enabled IVonyx to de-emphasize its franchised operations immediately to concentrate on expansion of company-owned branches. IVonyx could now control its growth and use of capital by opening new company branches and not relying on the erratic performance of its franchise network. Also, the acquisition was accomplished for IVonyx stock, without conveying any precious cash to CIC shareholders.

Question 5, page 347

Review the failed Series B term sheet and the term sheet for the Series B shares which ultimately closed. [Attachments #3 and #4] What are the proposed pre-money valuations of each term sheet? What are the major differences between the failed and the closed Series B financing? What is the effect of each "B" financing on the then existing IVonyx shareholders by class (i.e. the Series A shareholders, common shareholders, and the management option pool)? Show your calculations and discuss the effect in monetary terms and dilution. Did management suffer any ill effect as a result of the Series B financing? How so?

Answer:

The Series A pre-money valuation was $2.5 million to raise $5.1 million for a post-money valuation of $7.6 million. The failed Series B financing proposed a pre-money valuation of $10.1 million or a 33% increase in valuation over the post-Series A valuation. Series A investors would have owned 55% of IVonyx and had a 33% gain on investment in approximately 18 months if the proposed Series B closed.

The Series B which did close was done at a $3.75 million pre-money valuation which wipes out 50% of the original shareholder investment value. The Series B raised approximately $2.98 million for a post-money valuation of $6.75 million. The Series B owns 44.5% post-financing as compared to 26.6% under the failed Series B, not closed. The Series A owns 40% post-B financing for a value of $2.6 million (0.4 x $6.73 million). The Series A has lost 50% of its original investment value. The Series B became the largest shareholder group by investing $2.98 million.

The common shareholders have been severely diluted by the failure of IVonyx to meet its forecasts and the resulting continuing need for subsequent financings. The common owned 21.5% of IVonyx post-Series A financing. They would have owned 10.2% under the proposed and failed Series B and ultimately common shareholders had 3.6% ownership under the closed Series B financing.

The option pool for mangement was 20% of the capitalization post-Series A financing, would have been 14.1% under the failed Series B, and ultimately wound up at 10.5% under the closed Series B. This decline in available ownership for management across the board was appropriate because it was the failure of management which required the additional, dilutive financings.

Moreover under the closed Series B, Al Jordan was forced to relinquish his right to 15% ownership of IVonyx through stock option grants in the future as well as his board seat. Management had failed to meet its business plan which necessitated a disastrous down-financing to save IVonyx. The Series B was closed at 44c per IVonyx common equivalent share (CES) post-split of 4.1. The Series A had been closed at $8 per share ($2 per CES, post-split). Management suffered financially with the failure of the business to perform, and Jordan resigned along with others.

The following table summarizes the effect of the "down financing" of the Series B.

Effect of Series B Financing

Class Ownership	Post Series A	Post Series B
Financing	$5.1 million	$3.75 million
Series A	59%	40.5%
Series B	0	44.5%
Common	16%	3.6%
Options	20%	10.5%

Series A, common and employee option pool diluted by Series B financing.

Question 6, page 350

What is the progression in IVonyx valuation since founding up to the intended IPO? Are the Series A, B and C investors projected to achieve acceptable IRRs with a successful IPO?

Answer:
The progression in valuation of IVonyx was from $8.5 million post-money Series A financing to projected $70 million pre-money valuation on the IPO.

The Series C IRR on the intended IPO was 100%. Series B IRR was 65% or 4.55 times return in three years. The Series A IRR was approximately 14% depending upon how many Series A share were received as anti-dilution protection from the Series C down-financing at $1.00 per share. Cap tables are not available in the case to compute the exact IRR, but it is in a range of 10% to 18% IRR.

Question 7, page 351

With the IVonyx IPO delayed by the battering of large infusion companies in the public stock markets, how would you improve IVonyx operations to make the company more attractive for the next IPO window or for a merger with a larger public healthcare company to give shareholders a liquidity opportunity?

Refocusing for Next IPO Opportunity

1. Implement the type of cost controls discussed and identified in the IMED case (detailed budgets, cost review by branch and corporate departments, head count assessment by department for productivity. Make biweekly or monthly review of actuals versus budget to identify reasons for variances).

2. Improve profitability and cash flow. The overall industry has cash flow issues so it demands management attention. IVonyx billing and collection activity needs vast improvement in both personnel and computerized billing systems.

   If necessary retain billing consultants to identify computerized system most applicable to IVonyx mix of business.

3. Add management depth in operations and to implement financial controls.

The **Living Dead**

Raytel began with invention of a revolutionary technology to digitize x-rays. It saw that technology stolen in a patent infringement by North American Phillips and AT&T, which crushed its products and market after initial Raytel successes. Subsequently, Raytel took its cash settlement, acquired another business, became a public company, and ultimately lost most of its equity value as that business reported losses over several years.

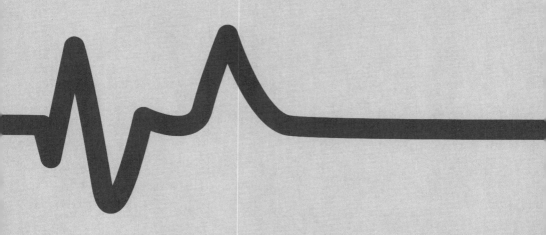

Raytel Medical Corporation

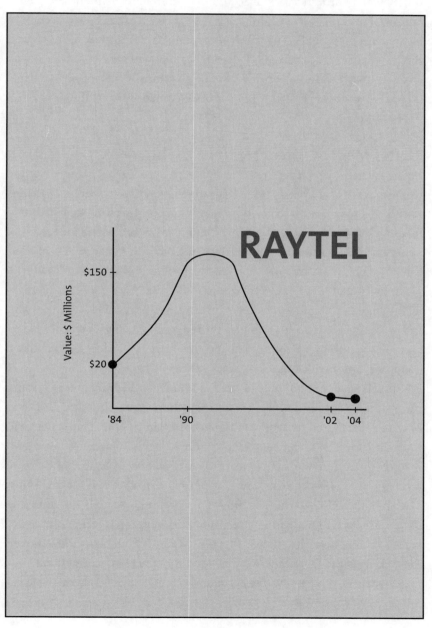

ometimes start-up companies linger too long or get hit with some unexpected problems. Then their venture investors are forced to assess how best to remix their cash and judgement. Raytel posed such challenges for the venture investors on its board. Al Henry joined the Raytel board in April 1984 after an initial investment by Henry Venture Fund (HVF), and continued on the board after Raytel went public in December 1995. The venture capitalists supported and advised Raytel chairman Richard Bader and his management team as Raytel faced a major lawsuit, and constant metamorphosis of its strategic direction, to create a $150 million public company from the ashes of a near-bankruptcy.

Raytel Medical Imaging, Inc.

Raytel started by making digital imaging systems. Raytel incorporated in October 1981 and commenced operations that December with funds raised through a research and development partnership that included mostly physicians. Clark M. Viehweg came up with the idea for Raytel, of applying a digital image compression technology to radiology images. But before he went far, Viewitt asked his former boss, Richard F. Bader, to serve as Raytel CEO. Bader had already started such successful high-technology companies as Eclectic Systems, Compression Labs, Inc., and Integrated Micro Systems. He had retired young and was teaching electrical engineering at Foothill College. But the Raytel idea seemed like a good one, and Bader was ready for a new challenge.

Raytel's goal was to build a system which could transmit, store, and receive radiological images — over a telephone line to remote locations, or over a local area network within a hospital or clinic. The system initially included four matched workstations — one station to send and receive (priced at the high end of $500,000), one to send only, one to receive only (priced at the low end of $100,000), and one for archiving. The stations acquired images either by scanning in x-ray film, or taking data captured digitally by computed radiological tomography (CRT scans) or magnetic resonance images (MRI). The stations then moved these images to where they were needed for expert interpretation.

Compared with x-rays over a light box, the Raytel system retrieved images quicker, sent them wherever needed, duplicated images flawlessly, stored them for years, and at a lower unit cost for most large hospitals. Silver prices were at historic highs in the early 1980s, and x-rays gelatins then held more silver than rare earth metals. Some large hospitals had millions of dollars in silver locked away in their x-ray vaults. And the Raytel images presented information no worse than x-rays. The Raytel images held 256 levels of gray, compared with thousands of grays in x-rays, but the human eye easily discerns only about 50 grays. Plus, the Raytel images could be magnified and manipulated to present the information as needed. Other companies sold systems for transmitting digitized images, but only Raytel offered the full range of features needed in an advanced cardiology practice.

If Raytel's technology became the standard method of transmitting digitized images, it might sell at least one station to all 3,000 hospitals in the United States. If one assumed a more reasonable penetration — amongst the larger, teaching and federal hospitals — then an estimated market of $1.4 billion settled to $500 million. Raytel might also expect to saturate some large hospitals with its stations — in the operating rooms, emergency rooms, intensive and critical care units, radiology departments, remote clinics, and offices of referring physicians. The average large hospital (more than 500 beds) produced 500,000 images a year. A capital investment in Raytel equipment could offset the heavy incremental costs of generating and using those images.

By the fall of 1983, Raytel had sold full systems to four flagship hospitals: University of California at San Francisco, Mallinckrodt Institute in St. Louis, Humana, and the Uniformed Armed Services Medical Center in Bethesda. Raytel stood without competition at its level of performance. Stanford University Hospital threw out their Digirad imaging system (which Henry had earlier refused to invest in) and in the fall of 1984 asked Raytel to replace it.

Raytel projected revenue at $6 million for fiscal 1984 (with fiscal years ending about 30 September), up from $1 million in fiscal 1983, with an after tax loss of $1 million. Bader had assembled an excellent team of top managers, with expertise in signal processing, data compression, semiconductors, and medical technology. Total headcount was 80 employees, with 45 in engineering and research, 19 in manufacturing, 10 in direct sales, and 6 in administration. Board chairman was D. James Bentley, founder of Bentley Laboratories, which was acquired by American Hospital Supply for $250 million. Cardiologist Thomas J. Fogarty was also an active member of the board. Bentley and Fogarty understood that Raytel could never grow as expected with funding from the R&D partnership. Bader wanted to look for bigger amounts of more sophisticated money from venture capitalists.

Question 1

You are a partner at HVF. Would you recommend an investment in Raytel? Describe your reasoning.

Lehman Brothers led the placement, but Bader already knew most of the investors — Hambrecht & Quist, Montgomery Ventures — from previous deals. Raytel was well positioned for a second round of funding from institutional investors, and Bader worked hard to close the deal.

Question 2

Review the "Summary of Terms" for the Raytel Series B shares dated February 1984, and the "Stock Purchase Agreement" as closed on May 3, 1984. (Please see Appendix, page 465). What significant changes were negotiated in the terms? What happened to the percent ownership of each class or Raytel's stock post financing Series B?

Series B

Raytel initially attempted to do the Series B private placement at $18.50 per share and to raise $8,000,000 through sale of 432,432 shares. The Series A had previously accounted for 417,000 shares outstanding, and Raytel had 951,000 common shares outstanding for a total outstanding common equivilant shares of 1.8 million post B financing. The total capitalized value would be $33.3 million if the contemplated Series B had closed.

Instead, Raytel closed on $8,000,000 of Series B equity at $8.75 per share which added 914,000 Series B shares, over twice the number of shares originally contemplated. The total capitalized value of Raytel post B financing became $19.97 million, and not $33.3 million as planned.

In April 1984, Henry Venture Fund closed on 228,571 shares of Raytel's series B convertible preferred stock, which equated to a 10% ownership.

Humana Inc., which expected to become a major customer of Raytel, also bought a 10% ownership. With the $8 million raised in the series B offering, Raytel could stay private for two more years and grow its business to solid profitability.

However, Raytel ended fiscal 1984 with revenues actually below the previous year ($1.0 million versus $1.1 million). Raytel's loss widened from $1.5 million to $3.2 million as it staffed up with sales people to camp outside meetings of hospital procurement committees — waiting for them to commit to buying the Raytel system.

Raytel technology was performing perfectly in a number of trials at leading hospitals nationwide. The problem was that falling occupancy rates nationwide also squeezed revenues at the big hospitals that invested on the cutting edge. More importantly, 40% of all reimbursements in cardiac diagnosis and therapy, and 25% of all reimbursements in diagnostic imaging, came via Medicare (as it would throughout the 1980s and 1990). And in October 1983 the Medicare system had imposed reimbursement via DRG (diagnostic-related groups.)

Biomedical devices firms quickly learned how DRGs affected their business. Under the DRG system, Medicare would only reimburse hospitals a fixed amount per patient rather than the actual costs incurred. Radiology departments quickly shifted from being a profit center in most hospitals to being a cost center. Every time a hospital sent a patient to the MRI, that reduced the amount the hospital made under DRGs. Hospitals now had a real incentive to cut costs and most did so by delaying capital expenditures. When hospitals did invest, they bought equipment that would generate new revenues.

In May 1985, Raytel had some breakthroughs. Culminating many months of trials and discussion, in four weeks Raytel signed six major orders totaling $1.3 million. When added to shipments totaling $2.0 million over the prior six months, it looked like Raytel might make its revenue projections of $6 million for fiscal 1985 — which it considered the critical mass needed to drive continued market acceptance.

Based on this optimism, in May 1985 Raytel completed a small equity financing of $2 million among existing shareholders. HVF invested $100,000. Raytel planned to use this financing to build its direct sales force, when it recived an unsolicited proposal from North American Philips (NAP).

North American Philips

NAP historically was a major presence in the radiological equipment business. Rumor was that NAP had tried for three years to develop a product like Raytel's, without success. General Electric, Seimens, and ATT were each trying to get into the medical imaging field, and NAP's alliance with Raytel would give it a huge leap. NAP wanted exclusive rights to market forthcoming Raytel products. NAP also offered to acquire 20% to 25% of Raytel for $8 million to $10 million in cash, at a per share price roughly double the $7 HVF had paid.

The marketing agreement with NAP did not immediately boost Raytel sales. NAP's 250-person sales force started touting Raytel's products to their contacts in radiological clinics, building excitement behind a joint display of NAP-Raytel at the November meeting of the Radiological Society of North America. NAP also bought engineering services from Raytel. Raytel finished fiscal 1985 with $4.1 million in revenues (much better than $1.0 million the year before) but still well below forecasts of $6 million.

After reviewing Raytel's results for fiscal 1985, on 19 October NAP acquired 19% of Raytel for $5 million at $6 per common share (with an option to boost its ownership to 35% at $9 per share). HVF had bought its preferred shares at $7 per share. NAP's shares were common stock, and represented a $5 million cash infusion for Raytel.

Raytel used the cash well, and in February 1986 launched a string of many consecutive months of profitability. Potential OEM partners started knocking on Raytel's door. ATT entered into an agreement to sell Raytel products for non-radiological uses to managers of information technology at hospitals. General Electric's nuclear power division sold Raytel imaging systems to analyze structural components of nuclear reactors. Raytel was able to increase its prices by one-third. NAP liked what it saw, and boosted its ownership in Raytel to 30%. The two NAP directors on Raytel's board suggested that Raytel delay further investment in a direct sales force to rely instead on NAP.

In June 1987 Raytel management starting preparing the company to go public in early 1988. Bader sought a valuation in the range of $100 million to $125 million, at multiples well in line with comparable offerings. The market for IPO's, however, was generally weak, and weakened even more with the market crash of October 1987.

The Raytel board would wait out a bear market, which would do little to derail Raytel's solid growth. For fiscal 1987, Raytel reported revenues
of $12.76 million, with good profitability. Hospitals continued to delay
capital expenditures, though Raytel had sufficient cash to wait them out.
NAP completed a detailed market study that very optimistically concluded that hospitals' pent-up demand for new equipment would make
the digital imaging market boom by 1989. Raytel technology still had no
competition. Then Raytel was blind-sided when it learned that NAP
wanted more of this market for itself.

NAP Treachery

Sometime in mid-1987, NAP had signed a joint venture agreement with
ATT to make and sell a high-end digitized tele-radiological device for
large hospitals. Raytel learned some facts about the relationship only
afterward. The essence of the story was that ATT approached NAP and
NAP accepted the terms eagerly. NAP knew plenty about radiology
departments, as the world's second largest supplier of radiological equipment. ATT, of course, knew plenty about telecommunication linkages.
Neither knew much about image compression, but both NAP and ATT
envied Raytel's lead. NAP then told Raytel that the deal was intended to
benefit Raytel. Raytel would supply all the workstations needed for the
ATT-NAP network.

Nevertheless, the first product catalog for the joint venture mentioned Raytel products only casually. It also showed that ATT planned to
produce its own workstations, which the catalog displayed prominently
even in applications where Raytel already had a machine on the shelf
that was far more appropriate.

The NAP-ATT joint venture first displayed their workstations at the
November 1987 convention of the Radiological Society of North America.
What Raytel representatives saw shocked them. ATT technology looked
a lot like Raytel technology. Notable even since the publication of the catalog, ATT products had converged rapidly toward Raytel's. Raytel got
confidentiality agreements from its NAP liaisons and directors, then
gave them complete access to Raytel technology. NAP had obviously fil-
tered this technology to ATT.

Meanwhile, Raytel started to hear reports from the field that NAP representatives actively bad-mouthed Raytel products. ATT salespeople actually got customers to send workstations back to Raytel and replace them with ATT workstations. All this fueled ever-wilder rumors in the marketplace about Raytel's products and Raytel's viability.

Raytel board meetings increasingly put the NAP members in the hot seat. By all outward appearances, though for some obscure motives, it looked like NAP was trying to kill Raytel. The NAP members continually asserted the other members were paranoid, and that the NAP relationship with ATT was meant to benefit Raytel. NAP insisted Raytel continue working, as a sign of their good faith and at their own expense, on technology to connect Raytel workstations to NAP equipment — work Raytel knew would be wasted if the relationship dissolved.

Despite all this, Raytel continued to give NAP the benefit of the doubt. Raytel depended upon NAP for half of its revenues. Raytel comforted their customers with the story that the ATT venture was aimed at multi-million dollar installations where Raytel does not compete. More importantly, NAP had invested $11 million in Raytel, at successively higher valuations, and received low-priority common stock. Furthermore, without the ability to go public, in early 1988 Raytel needed an infusion of cash. The two NAP members announced, in March 1988, that NAP would boost its ownership in Raytel by making a further investment of $3 million to $4 million. They also said NAP would contribute products from its German subsidiary for Raytel to upgrade for sale in the United States.

Then, on 15 May 1988, NAP abruptly announced it would make no further investment in Raytel — in either cash or product. NAP also placed into dispute its accounts payable to Raytel — which constituted most of Raytel's substantial accounts receivable. Soon after, NAP announced it would stop selling Raytel equipment and return unsold inventory sitting in their warehouses.

Raytel responded by immediately dropping headcount — from 65 to 25 people — to slow the cash burn rate. Raytel negotiated a one-year moratorium on all payments to its leasing company and landlord to save them several hundred thousand dollars. Raytel had $1.7 million in cash. With Raytel direct sales generating $300,000 to $450,000 per month (and NAP now selling none) Raytel would run out of cash that December.

Raytel estimated revenues for fiscal 1988 would fall to $7.8 million (versus $12.76 million for fiscal 1987), with a loss and inventory write-down totalling $5 million (versus $2 million in 1987).

The Raytel board responded by retaining Hambrecht & Quist, a Raytel investor, to find a buyer or strategic partner to replace NAP. Obvious partners would be two NAP competitors, General Electric or Picker. The Raytel board then held face-to-face discussions with increasingly senior officers at NAP, culminating with the president of Philips Medical Systems. These strung along for many weeks without satisfaction.

To measure the ultimate downside, investors like HVF had a considerable advantage in the capital structure of Raytel. NAP's $11 million investment in common stock was behind the HVF investment in convertible preferred stock. Raytel had no debt on its balance sheet, and a book value of about $11 million. Raytel had invested $22 million in developing its technology, which was still the envy of the marketplace. Raytel had 112 customers nationwide, all of whom were very happy. Thus, the value of the company would liquidate all preferred shareholders, leaving almost nothing for NAP or other common shareholders. However, liquidating now would return none of the value Raytel had built up over the years. The Raytel board decided to fight.

Alioto & Alioto

The board hired legal counsel to look into the extremely suspicious manner in which NAP and ATT dealt with Raytel. The law firm representing HVF thought Raytel had a very strong case against ATT for deliberate restraint of trade, against NAP and ATT for conspiracy to fix prices, and against NAP for breach of fiduciary responsibility in their role as directors and largest minority shareholders. Raytel's law firm agreed. They estimated damages on the order of $50 million, which in anti-trust cases would treble to $150 million. This anti-trust litigation would cost $500,000 to $1 million, and would take three to five years. Before taking this route, the board first decided to get a second opinion from a firm specializing in such litigation.

The second opinion came from Alioto & Alioto. Senior partner "Big Joe" Alioto was a former mayor of San Francisco. His firm had won three major anti-trust and unlawful competition suits against ATT in the past four years. Alioto took the case on a contingency basis: Raytel would pay them $100,000 and out of pocket expenses, and the firm received 30% of any settlement or judgment.

Alioto drafted a complaint, and served it to the NAP directors and their in-house counsel at a Raytel board meeting in September 1988. They expressed shock and dismay, and promised to tighten things up. Then they proceeded to stall, until it became apparent they intended to do nothing.

In October 1988, Alioto filed in the State of California its preliminary complaint against NAP, several of its subsidiaries, and its employees. Specifically, the NAP directors were charged with breach of fiduciary responsibility in their role as Raytel directors. It stipulated the breach of confidentiality and misrepresentations in marketing. The complaint also mentioned ATT as co-conspirator and, by conspiring in restraint of trade against Raytel, that ATT had violated federal anti-trust law.

Once Alioto proved that Raytel was prepared to square off on the courthouse steps, NAP and Raytel came to terms. Alioto figured that NAP would spend $3 million to fully litigate the issue, set that as a settlement floor, and negotiated upwards. On 26 December 1988, NAP agreed to an out-of-court settlement. NAP would pay Raytel $5.5 million in cash, and give back to Raytel all the stock they had acquired for $11 million. Raytel would then retire these common shares. In return, Raytel and its directors and principal shareholders would sign agreements preventing them from taking further action against NAP, ATT, and its employees. Now, Raytel directors had to decide whether to accept it.

Alioto thought Raytel had a very strong case on breach of fiduciary responsibility, and thought a jury would ultimately agree. Alioto would claim $50 million in damages, but experience led him to expect a jury to award about $10 million. The other issues were considered to be about 60/40 win situations. On the anti-trust issues, Alioto felt that available evidence indicated collusion and guilt. But because he also had to prove intent, which is almost never committed to paper, he estimated a 70/30 likelihood of losing that point. However, it was a big stake to win. At treble damages adding up to $150 million, that could be a substantial victory.

Furthermore, time was on NAP's side. Hambrecht & Quist did not find new OEM or acquisition candidates, so the Raytel board started their own discussions with Toshiba and Diasonics. Things got more dire as the cash started to run out. If they filed the case, it would take a year to determine jurisdiction — Raytel filed in California and NAP wanted jurisdiction in New York. Add another year to then get on the court calendar. The trial itself might take only a few months. Then add about two years for appeals. Thus, it might take four years for Raytel to see any money.

And the return might not be very great. If the fiduciary breach was proven, but not anti-trust violations, Raytel estimated a payment of $10 million. Since NAP owned 30% of Raytel, NAP would get $3 million of the damages. Alioto would also take his third. That would leave all other shareholders with $4 million, four years in the future. In the meantime, NAP lawyers could file enough discovery to make life miserable at Raytel, plus harassment countersuits to make life miserable for each individual Raytel investor and officer. The legal bills per individual suit could run $100,000 per year. With Raytel's present financial position, and with its name smeared in the marketplace, Raytel would run out of cash while the lawyers fought on. NAP or ATT could then buy Raytel out of bankruptcy, at auction, and kill the lawsuit.

Still, to get NAP to the negotiating table, Raytel investors had to prove they'd take the matter to court. Raytel investors made a verbal handshake around a conference table, to fund the lawsuit themselves by issuing a "super-preferred" stock that would give them first priority on any settlement. Alioto presented this as a statement of resolve to fight.

Question 3
___

If you held preferred shares in Raytel, would you settle or fight?

A New Strategy

In April 1989, the Raytel investors signed the settlement. The only change was that NAP would pay $5 million now and withhold the final $500,000 until April 1990, on the condition that Raytel was still in business then. NAP delayed this payment as a reservoir against lawsuits from smaller Raytel shareholders, who had not signed the release. If Raytel was liquidated in the short term, to the disadvantage of the smaller investors who held common shares, NAP would likely be sued. Raytel took this opportunity to finally buy-out the series A shareholders who had entered when Raytel was structured as an R&D partnership. Also, NAP paid Raytel $2 million to settle the disputed payments for workstations NAP had received but not yet paid for.

Alioto & Alioto took $1 million as their fee. Though entitled to 30% of the $5.5 million payment, they reduced their fee to encourage a quick close. After NAP's stock was retired, HVF ownership in Raytel rose to 9.2%.

Thus, by June 1989, Raytel found itself to be a very different company. The polish on Raytel's technology had tarnished, though it was still precious underneath. More time had passed, though, and the pent-up demand that industry observers placed just around the corner had still never appeared. Perhaps it never would. On the finance side, Raytel had an almost debt-free balance sheet, with $5.3 million in cash and $500,000 arriving in a year. Two research and development partnerships owed Raytel $1.5 million, represented by two full-recourse notes due in late 1989 and 1990. The Olicon service subsidiary generated $3 million in annual revenues, with comfortable profitability. Raytel's potentially most valuable asset, though, was a tax loss carryforward growing to $16 million. It was time to reconfigure Raytel's combination of cash and capabilities.

The Raytel board decided to start looking for acquisitions. Before the end of fiscal 1989, they hoped to acquire profitable businesses to create a synergistic critical mass that would be cash-positive. Raytel's tax loss carryforward gave it a big advantage over other leveraged buy-out groups that might want to do the same thing.

One idea was to construct a nationwide group of regional genetic testing laboratories. Raytel officers identified eight companies doing $2 to $11 million in annual revenues, with pretax profits well over 20%, strong regional followings, and owners reaching retirement age. If they bought several of these labs, and sheltered their pre-tax earnings into after-tax earnings, Raytel could quickly create a strongly cash-positive company. They then could drive greater margins by having each laboratory cooperate and specialize in tests with low volumes and high capital costs, such as the new DNA probes coming to market. But the leader of the key lab resisted Bader's efforts to arrive at a price.

Raytel would invest as little as possible in its imaging technology, but keep it vital. First, tax laws require the entity that generated the tax-loss to remain in business for two years after an acquisition. Second, the U.S. Army continued to study the Raytel workstations for outfitting its MASH units worldwide. The Surgeon General suggested he might order $100 million worth of equipment in the 1990 time frame, and asked Raytel to partner with Kodak's technical service force. Third, the key patents behind Raytel's data compression technology had applications in other areas, like document storage. EDS, for example, had invited Raytel to team on a bid to automate dental records for the employees of the State of California, a contract which might generate $1 million for Raytel.

The Raytel board fleshed out the details of its strategy of parallel downsizing and diversification. They downsized Raytel and its Olicon subsidiary to break even at a $5 million annual run rate. Raytel studied more than 75 acquisition candidates, over a nine-month period, before deciding that the perfect partner was CDI.

Raytel/CDI Medical Services, Inc.

By November 1989, Raytel signed a letter of intent to acquire CDI Medical Systems, Inc. and completed the deal on 28 February 1990.[1] It was a $22.2 million deal, cash, in a leveraged transaction — including a $2 million revolving credit line secured by accounts receivable, an $8 million bank term loan, $6 million in subordinated debt, and $6.5 million of equity in the form of series B convertible preferred shares. Of the equity, $4 million came from Raytel and $2.5 million from new investors like Merrill Lynch, Peregrine Ventures, the Anderson Group, and CDI management. Henry Venture II provided $300,000 in equity. HVF now owned 5% of Raytel/CDI, and Henry Venture II owned 3.6%.

The combination of CDI and Raytel made strategic sense. CDI had pioneered pacemaker monitoring in the 1970s, through a device that integrated electronic and telephone technology. By 1989, CDI had become the second largest pacemaker monitoring company in the United States. The largest was CardioCare, a subsidiary of Medtronics, America's largest manufacturer of implantable pacemakers. CDI had exclusive co-marketing agreements with the next four largest manufacturers, though it wasn't CardioCare that CDI competed against. Of the 500,000 pacemaker patients in the United States, about 250,000 had prescriptions for monitoring. Medtronics monitored 50,000, CDI monitored 25,000, smaller companies about 25,000, and physicians about 150,000. CDI hoped to give physicians a more reliable and cost effective alternative to doing the monitoring themselves.

CDI's strategy had been to grow by acquiring the patient lists of cardiology practices. CDI had a long history of stable earnings and steady, but slow, growth — between 5% and 10% each year. The entire pacemaker industry hardly grew any faster. The population of new pacemaker patients grew 15% each year, about 8% of them died, leaving a net gain of about 7% each year. By 1989, CDI did $16 million in revenues at a 27% pretax profit margin.

Because of this moderate growth, CDI's owners were willing to part with it. CDI was a wholly-owned subsidiary of the Andersen Group, a medium-sized, publicly-held conglomerate. Andersen had already been milking off profits from CDI to diversify into quicker-growth areas.

As a big bonus, CDI had recently diversified into the ownership and management of MRI centers — two in Philadelphia and one in New York with the Albert Einstein Hospital. CDI brought each of these MRI centers to profitability much faster than the industry norm, and their sterling reputation for good management built an excellent referral base. After the first MRI center opened in 1985, CDI's pretax income grew at a compounded annual rate of 31%. By 1989, MRI generated $5 million, or one-third of CDI revenues. CDI's management team hoped to stay on, and Raytel quickly negotiated a long-term employment contract with the president.

Question 4

Was the price of the CDI acquisition financially attractive to Raytel shareholders?

With Raytel/CDI now a merged entity, in October 1990 the board met to plan strategy. CDI had just finalized terms with a pacemaker monitoring company doing $1.3 million in revenues, and CDI would continue acquiring patient lists to expand its market share in pacemaker monitoring. Most important, the board believed that, even with the interest load from the leveraging, they could accelerate CDI's growth rate toward 25% by developing more MRI facilities.

Raytel/CDI pioneered a formula whereby it would do a joint venture with a radiology clinic or local hospital to create a new MRI center. For as little as $250,000 in cash plus the contribution of their management expertise, CDI got the majority interest in the new center. Each MRI center costs about $2.5 million — with equipment costing $1.7 million and a stand-alone building the rest. Centers could be financed with about one-third equity, mortgage debt for the building, and lease debt for the equipment. MRI equipment was easy leverage because it had a very high resale value. Depending on the usage rate of the new facility, after-tax return on equity ranged between 60% and 100% for the first year — from the combination of high pre-tax profit margin and leveraged acquisition cost — and a 50% compound rate of return on equity.

A complete review of Raytel/CDI pro formas showed amortization of its bank loan and subordinated debt by 1994. Any cash above the level needed for debt service could be used for more rapid opening of MRI centers. Two outside investors were willing to commit equity, above Raytel's resources, to finance these centers.

The MRI business was still risky — rife with technical obsolescence, proliferation of competition, cuts in Medicare reimbursements, and shifting politics of patient referrals. General Electric did a market study which concluded 4,000 MRI centers would service the total U.S. population. In 1990, 2,300 MRI centers were operating at 1,600 fixed sites and with 700 mobile units. In 1990 alone, 250 new sites opened. Raytel felt that they could either open new centers, or acquire centers that were managed badly. Because Congress passed laws preventing physicians from referring patients to MRI facilities in which they own an interest, several physician groups were looking to sell their MRI centers to companies like CDI. Raytel/CDI needed to grow quickly to justify an initial public offering, but the board decided they would contribute only $3 million to the acquisition of functioning MRI businesses. An MRI deal that placed the Raytel/CDI balance sheet at risk had to project a 60% return on equity; a deal that did not needed only a 30% return. Forecast was to add one new MRI facility in 1991, four in 1992, four in 1993, for a total of twelve.

With an MRI and cardiac monitoring strategy in place, Raytel proceeded to sell its imaging technology and its Olicon subsidiary. Olicon was a microfilm center, acquired in 1985 to service archives of cardiac images. Olicon was breaking even at $5 million in 1990 revenues, but its growth was slow and because it was located in Louisville it proved a drain on management time. Raytel took $600,000 in cash out of Olicon then, in October 1990, accepted a bid for $750,000 in cash. The sale of the Raytel imaging technology was to be Richard Bader's swan song. A key factor in looking for MRI centers to acquire would be finding one with a president who could lead Raytel into its new strategy. Bader agreed to this logic but, as the search continued, the board grew more convinced that Bader himself was doing an excellent job as president and CEO. He had especially proven his ability at fashioning deals, which would continue to be a primary part of Raytel's strategy.

By December 1990, ten months after the acquisition, Raytel/CDI looked very good. On consolidated calendar 1990 net revenues of $18.5 million (excluding Olicon revenues of $5 million) Raytel/CDI earned $4.0 million before interest, taxes, depreciation and amortization on the leveraged debt. They prepaid their bank loan by $1.25 million, and generated $500,000 surplus cash on the balance sheet. To make the numbers look even better, Raytel/CDI hoped to complete one major acquisition before 30 September 1991, then do the fiscal year audit of the combined companies. Once the audit was complete, Raytel could file for an IPO as early as January 1992.

In September 1991, Raytel/CDI agreed to acquire Merrill Lynch Imaging Partners (MIP). MIP was a limited partnership formed in 1985, when Merrill Lynch & Co., Inc. raised $25 million for investment in diagnostic imaging. Raytel/CDI had operated two of the six MIP facilities under management contract, were very familiar with their operations and knew how they could be improved. Furthermore, not all of the MIP centers were dedicated to MRI. Some centers offered a full range of outpatient diagnostic imaging, including computer tomography, nuclear medicine, ultrasound, x-rays, and mammography.

The combination of Raytel/CDI and MIP owned nine centers nationwide. Investment bankers valued the combined company at $60 million, and Merrill Lynch got 20% of Raytel for consideration of the merger. After the merger, HVF owned 4% of the combined entity, and HVF II owned 3%.

Soon after the merger, Raytel management had all entities operating in the black. Raytel/CDI management indeed found several ways to improve operations of the MIP facilities — better billing and collections, better unit pricing on supplies and equipment, better networking of referrals on a national basis. It looked to be on target for fiscal 1992 revenues of $29.5 million and EBITDA of $9.0 million (versus $17.5 million revenue in fiscal 1991 and EBITDA of $4.3 million). Soon other companies began suggesting themselves as acquisition candidates to the newly-renamed Raytel Medical Corporation.

CardioCare Acquisition

Raytel had already been approached by CardioCare, the servicing unit of Medtronic, Inc. Raytel expressed keen interest, but asked to delay discussions until completing the MIP merger. If Raytel did acquire CardioCare, which they initially considered a long shot, it would create a combined entity with $75 million in pro forma revenues and EBITDA of $15 million. More important, it would be a dominant force in cardiac care. Over 40,000 enrolled patients were supplied with CardioCare equipment that let them have their pacemakers and heart rhythms checked 24 hours a day by telephone. Another 30,000 other patients were enrolled in another CardioCare program to diagnose arrhythmia.[2] Raytel would become the largest pacemaker monitoring company in the United States, with 100,000 patients monitored, for a 50% market share. Furthermore, Raytel was well positioned to become a leader in monitoring the new implantable defibrillators.

Raytel acquired CardioCare on 1 March 1993, at terms that were later disclosed. The price was $14.5 million in cash and notes. CardioCare generated $25 million in revenues in 1992, with 300 employees working mostly at CardioCare headquarters in Forest Hills, New York. Raytel's Cardiac Datacorp subsidiary, located in Bloomfield, Connecticut, was merged into it. After the acquisition, HVF owned 3.53% of Raytel Medical, and HVF II owned 2.92%.

Raytel now positioned itself as a $100 million company offering diversified services to cardiac patients. Cardiac disease was the leading cause of death in the United States, with a 1992 treatment cost of $100 billion in 1992. Cardiac patients were the highest aggregate cost category for insured patients. In a recent study of large employers, 16.4% of their employee claim dollars were spent diagnosing and treating cardiac disease. With a business plan rich in cardiac service and diagnostic imaging, Raytel projected a very attractive 20% after-tax return on equity.

What strategy would you recommend for getting liquidity from an
investment in Raytel? What approaches are available for going public?
Would you restructure the company in any way?

The Raytel board drafted a plan to run the merged company to complete the fiscal 1993 audit, then gauge interest in an IPO. The timing
should be good, since Raytel's efforts to reduce health care costs was in
line with Clinton administration policies. However, changes to Medicare
might jeopardize the major source of Raytel reimbursements.
Uncertainty like this about the Clinton health care initiatives was driving down most health care stock. Even if the IPO was delayed, the shift
toward managed care would still boost Raytel's results.

In April 1994 the Raytel board heard presentations by three potential
underwriting groups — Ladenberg Thalman, Stephens & Co., and
Robertson, Stephens & Co. — then selected Stephens & Co. as the lead
underwriter. The board hoped for an IPO of $20 to $25 million, with a filing price range of $6 to $9 per share. Proceeds would go to pay off $17
million in existing bank debt, with the remainder for future acquisitions.
The S-1 registration statement would be ready for filing in July 1994. The
board wanted to bring Raytel public at the earliest possible moment, and
not a moment too soon.

While they were preparing for the IPO, Raytel saw a more efficient
way to go public. One company Raytel had studied as an acquisition candidate was Medical Diagnostics, Inc. MDI, based in Burlington,
Massachusetts, ran mobile MRI facilities throughout New England and
New York. Because MDI was listed on NASDAQ, Raytel could go public
via merger with a publicly-traded company. In December 1994, Raytel
formed an MDI Acquisition Corp. and made a hostile bid for Medical
Diagnostics shares. Raytel offered $5 per share, totalling $20 million cash.
Raytel extended its offer five times and receive tenders of 1.26 million
shares of MDI' s 3.57 million outstanding shares and 833,000 redeemable
options and warrants.[3] However, after many months of talking to Raytel
about boosting its bid over the $5 mark, on 1 May 1995 the MDI board
announced that they had instead reached merger terms with Advanced
NMR Systems, Inc.

Raytel Medical Corporation

Raytel had continued to grow its businesses while bidding for MDI, and simply retained a new underwriter to bring it public, at a valuation estimate of $80 million to $100 million. Raytel had started to get some very good press. It ranked 252 on *Inc.* magazine's list of America's 500 fastest growing companies. And Raytel provided trans-telephonic monitoring to over half the forty hospitals ranked by *U.S. News and World Report* as America's best.[4]

On 6 October 1995, Raytel filed with the SEC for an initial public offering to raise $39.6 million. Raytel would sell 2.3 million shares, and existing shareholders would sell 350,000. Though HVF had signed a six-month lock-up agreement, the IPO range of $11 to $13 per share valued the HVF investment in Raytel at $2.2 million.[5] Raytel was valued at $85 million on the IPO which occurred at $8.00 per share.

In the fall of 1995 Raytel officers did their road show, and the honing of Raytel's strategy became even clearer. Raytel would use the proceeds of the IPO to retire debt, redeem outstanding warrants, and for working capital on its expansion plans. Raytel now positioned itself as an advanced alternate site company, specializing in cardiology and diagnostic imaging. Expansion would focus on it cardiac catheterization laboratories.

In the spring of 1995, Raytel had acquired two catheterization laboratories in Texas, and created a subsidiary called Raytel Cardiovascular Laboratories, Inc. Raytel proclaimed that it was preparing itself for the consolidation sweeping through the health care industry. Raytel planned to transform these cath labs into a network of managed care heart centers, integrating the full range of diagnostic, catheterization, angioplasty, and therapeutic procedures the patient needed. Until then, cardiac care was a very expensive process delivered via a fragmented system. Once it proved its Texas model, Raytel hoped to develop new integrated heart centers. Raytel had signed a letter of intent with Stanford Health Services to develop a cardiac catheterization facility that would evolve into an integrated cardiac care center. They signed a similar agreement to manage cardiac patients for a hospital in Granada Hills, California.

However, investors were not entirely convinced that specialized managed care facilities was a high-growth industry. Raytel delayed its IPO until shares finally went public in December 1996 at $8 per share. The shares were snapped up but, amidst a feverish IPO market fueled by internet stocks, Raytel's stock remained relatively flat — closing about $9 throughout January 1996. Analysts remained quietly bullish on Raytel, as its stock rose to $15 per share. Henry remained fully invested in Raytel, and remained on its board until January 1997

Raytel continued to refine its strategy. On 5 May 1997, Raytel announced that it had retained Dillon, Read and Co. to help evaluate options for selling its diagnostic imaging business.[6] Bader said the unit was doing well, but that Raytel had to decide whether to focus on its strategy of integrated heart centers. On 12 August Raytel announced that it would indeed keep these centers and make some additional investment to expand their offerings of cardiology-oriented imaging modalities.

On 18 August 1997, Bader announced that Raytel had closed on acquisition of Cardiovascular Ventures, Inc. (CVI) of New Orleans. Raytel acquired CVI for $21.6 million figured as a combination of $15.78 million cash, 500,000 shares of Raytel common stock, and contingent notes in the aggregate principal amount of $820,000. To finance the acquisition and pay off certain CVI indebtedness, at the closing Raytel borrowed $19.3 million under its existing credit lines.

The CVI acquisition will boost Raytel's revenue run rate by one-third through eight cardiovascular diagnostic facilities in Florida, Texas, Louisiana, and Maryland. "CVI has pursued a strategy," noted Bader, "that is very similar to Raytel's integrated heart center strategy." CVI was profitable on about $24 million in 1996 revenues. (See Volpe Brown Research Report, page 471)

After many twists and turns, Raytel had built itself into a very different company from the one that began with a proprietary invention to convert x-ray films into digital images.

Epilogue

Raytel joined the ranks of the Living Dead after the acquisition of cardiology practices in 1997 eventually caused the company to lose over 90% of its public equity valuation as Raytel corporate performance drastically declined. Henry left the Raytel board in early 1997, and Henry Funds sold their stock at approximately $9 per share on the way down from Raytel's high water mark of $14 per share. As Raytel's performance continued to decline, its stock slumped to under $1.00 per share where NASDAQ threatened to delist the company. Raytel had lost 93% of its equity value in the public market by 2000.

Bader had difficult negotiations in separating Raytel from the cardiology business, but eventually managed to do so. The old reliable CDI pacemaker monitoring business was operating at breakeven, but Raytel was continuing to lose money in 2000, approximately 15 years after its founding.

At that time, Henry convinced Bader to participate in a management buyout attempt with Bader, the current CEO and Henry, the former director, forming the nucleus of a leveraged buyout attempt to take Raytel private. Bader and Henry bid $3/share to take Raytel private. Ironically, Raytel's current board, who were original Raytel directors with Bader and Henry initially 15 years earlier, thwarted the buyout attempt by bringing in an Israeli company to pay approximately $3.50 per Raytel share to acquire Raytel and take it private. Bader and Henry had accumulated a reasonable percentage of Raytel's stock, and they happily conveyed it to the Israeli company for cash at a very acceptable profit. Raytel then lurched into becoming a private division of an Israeli company nearly 20 years after its founding. Raytel still had significant operating problems, and Bader chose to not join the new acquirers, saying he thought he had stayed too long at Raytel. Raytel was still living, but it was dead as a stand alone company.

Citations

1. "Raytel Inc. (Acquisition Corp. to buy CDI Medical Services Inc. from Andersen Group Inc.)," *New York Times* 139 (21 November 1989) C4.

2. "Raytel Medical Corporation Acquires CardioCare," Press Release, 5 March 1993, Raytel Medical Corporation.

3. "Firm plans to launch offer to buy Medical Diagnostics," *Wall Street Journal* (30 November 1994) B4; "Medical Diagnostics, Inc." *Wall Street Journal* (6 December 1994) B8; "Raytel extends bid for Medical Diagnostics," *San Francisco Chronicle* (8March 1995) B3; "Raytel begins talks to acquire Medical Diagnostics," *New York Times* 144 (29 March 1995) C4.

4. "America's Best Hospitals," *U.S. News and World Report* (1995); "13th Annual Inc. 500," *Inc.* (1995)

5. Chris Rauber, "Cardiac testing company puts heart into $39M IPO," *San Francisco Business Times* (24 October 1995).

6. "Raytel Medical Corp." *New York Times* 146 (6 May 1997) C4.

Exhibit #1

Raytel Medical Corporation:
Private Placements and Valuations

	Feb. 1982	April 1984	May 1985	Oct. 1985	IPO Oct. 1995	Raytel Buyout 2001
Post-Money Valuation	$10.0m	$19.97m	$16.0m	$25.0m	$85.0m	$9.0m
Price per Share	—	$8.75	$7.00	$6.00	$9.00	$1.00
Number of Shares	417,000	914,000				
Amount of Placement	$m	$8.0m	$2m	$5m	$36m	$9.0m
Percent of Raytel Purchased	%	40%	%	19%	40% approx.	100%
Purchasers	Series A	Series B	Series C	NAP	Public Offering	Private Company
Investment Banker	Founders	Henry Humana et. al.	Existing Shareholders	—	Vector Securities	—
HVF Ownership	— 0 —	10%	10%	9%	3%	0%
Raytel Sales (Trailing 12 Months)	— 0 —	$1.0m	$4.1m	$4.1m	$63.5m	$60.0m
Raytel Earnings (Trailing 12 Months) (Loss)	— 0 —	($1.0m)	($3.7m)	($3.7m)	$4.4m	Loss

Exhibit #2-1

Statement of Operations:
Raytel Medical Imaging, Inc.

	1982 Nov 30	1983 Nov 30	1984 Sept 30 (ten months)	1985 Sept 30	1986 Sept 30	1987 Oct 3	1988 Oct 1	1989 Oct 1
Revenues:								
Product sales	$ —	$178,000	$955,550	$4,082,147	$8,121,277	$12,578,932		
Research contract fees	525,000	909,647	79,976	35,243	643,429	187,407		
Total revenues	525,000	1,087,647	1,035,526	4,117,390	8,764,706	12,766,339	8,123,107	4,009,126
Costs and Expenses:								
Cost of product sales	—	150,960	953,353	3,217,189	7,483,866	9,025,216	6,272,175	2,841,436
Research and development	509,942	1,569,399	913,020	1,810,796	1,851,551	1,768,798	1,899,014	1,298,276
Marketing, general & admin.	376,703	877,500	2,397,608	2,682,496	4,040,925	3,993,616	3,225,673	620,754
Interest income, net	(14,313)	(38,400)	32,226	(182,294)	(210,313)	(50,270)	(25,200)	94,277
Total costs and expenses	872,332	2,559,459	4,296,207	7,528,187	13,586,655	14,837,900	11,371,662	4,666,189
Settlement income								1,874,790
Net Loss	$347,332	$1,471,812	$3,196,229	$3,775,385	$4,821,949	$2,071,561	$3,298,955	$1,217,727

Exhibit #2-2

Consolidated Statements of Operations:
Raytel Medical Corporation
(000's omitted, except per share amounts)

	1990 Sept 30	1991 Sept 30
Revenues:		
Net patient revenues	$9,288	$17,878
Equity earnings from unconsolidated		
joint venture and partnership	54	11
Total revenues	9,342	17,889
Costs of operations:		
Operating expenses	2,955	5,936
Depreciation	204	345
Amortization	1,175	1,662
Total operating expenses	4,334	7,943
Gross margin	5,008	9,946
Selling, general and administrative	3,549	7,147
Interest expense	1,236	1,661
Amortization	509	1,385
Other income	(180)	(190)
Noncontrolling interest in income		
of consolidated entitites	519	1,142
Loss before income tax and		
discontinued operations	(625)	(1,194)
Provision for income taxes	18	24
Loss from continuing operations	(643)	(1,218)
Discontinued operations:		
Income from Olicon	169	
Loss on disposal of Olicon	5	
Loss from teleradiology equipment business	(530)	
Net loss	$(1,009)	$(1,218)
Net income per share	(.31)	(.28)
Weighted average common shares	3,871	3,624
and dilutive equivalents outstanding		

Exhibit #2-3

Consolidated Statements of Operations:
Raytel Medical Corporation

(years ended September 30)
(000's omitted, except per share amounts)

	1996	1995	1994	1993	1992
Revenues:					
Net patient and service revenues	$71,711	$63,087	$57,906	$44,957	$27,742
Other revenues	804	375	869	1,737	1,965
Total revenues	72,515	63,462	58,775	46,694	29,707
Costs and expenses:					
Operating costs	27,582	20,687	18,685	16,577	9,502
Selling, general, administrative	28,830	26,666	26,136	18,076	10,613
Depreciation and amortization	5,590	5,806	5,880	6,215	4,638
Write-off of intangibles					1,653
Non-recurring tender offer expense		1,050			
Total costs and expenses	62,002	54,209	50,701	40,868	26,406
Operating income	10,513	9,253	8,074	5,826	3,301
Interest expense	514	2,118	2,463	2,361	1,870
Other expense (income)	(591)	(347)	(305)	(106)	(282)
Minority interest	762	1,161	1,099	1,359	1,030
Income before taxes and item	9,828	6,321	4,817	2,212	683
Provision for income taxes	3,248	1,960	1,004	311	437
Extraordinary item, net of tax benefit	449				
Net income	6,131	4,361	3,813	1,901	246
Net income per share	.75	.78	.69	.35	.05
Weighted average common shares and dilutive equivalents outstanding	8,194	5,617	5,548	5,458	4,933

Exhibit #3-1

Balance Sheet Data
Raytel Medical Imaging, Inc.

(years ended September 30)
(000's omitted, except per share amounts)

Assets	1982 Nov 30	1983 Nov 30	1984 Sept 30	1985 Sept 30	1986 Sept 30
Current Assets:					
Cash and cash investments	$—	$199,730	2,650,121	408,198	378,555
Accounts receivable	—	178,779	194,716	2,083,898	1,598,268
Inventories	—	1,132,087	2,307,444	2,626,300	2,613,858
Due from affiliated companies					1,935,309
Prepaid expenses and other	41,365	5,112	52,137	80,869	72,434
Total current assets	41,365	1,515,708	5,204,421	5,199,265	6,598,424
Cost in excess of net assets acquired				689,227	
Property and Equipment:					
Furniture and fixtures	39,253	87,793	118,430	192,671	202,418
Machinery and equipment	129,030	510,895	1,303,802	1,765,007	2,214,856
Leasehold improvements	—	11,962	101,032	28,057	116,832
Accumulated depreciation	(12,230)	(86,132)	(589,455)	(230,206)	(1,089,518)
Total net property	156,053	524,518	1,220,206	1,469,255	1,444,588
Deposits:	34,700	74,205	173,935	252,734	329,531
Total Assets:	$232,118	$2,114,431	$6,598,444	$7,610,481	$8,372,543

Liabilities and Shareholder Equity

	1982 Nov 30	1983 Nov 30	1984 Sept 30	1985 Sept 30	1986 Sept 30
Current Liabilities:					
Bank overdraft	16,351	—			
Current portion of long term debt	$25,512	$56,479	158,670	353,799	272,789
Current portion of capital lease	97,000	620,000	70,290	230,050	349,162
Notes payable	155,472	920,157	1,051,177	1,009,620	435,400
Accounts payable	38,046	118,160	130,700	1,307,651	1,952,109
Accrued liabilities				490,667	900,276
Deferred revenues	100,000	45,049	173,870	13,700	223,850
Total current liabilities	432,381	1,759,845		3,565,657	4,133,586
Capital lease obligations, net	130,737	263,898	701,939	641,429	766,913
Long-term debt				2,316,396	83,009
Shareholder's Equity:					
Convertible preferred stock	—	1,500,000	8,996,199	8,996,199	11,136,800
Common stock	264,270	712,070	793,977	1,183,796	6,167,180
Deficit accumulated	(595,270)	(2,067,082)	(5,263,311)	(9,038,696)	(13,860,645)
Notes receivable from sale of stock		(54,300)	(54,300)	(54,300)	(54,300)
Total shareholders' equity	(331,000)	90,688	4,472,565	1,086,999	3,389,035
Total liabilities and shareholders equity	$232,118	$2,114,431	$6,598,444	$7,610,481	$8,372,543

Exhibit #3-2

Balance Sheet Data
Raytel Systems Corporation

Assets	1987 Oct 3	1988 Oct 2	1989 Oct 1
Current Assets:			
Cash and cash investments	$3,524,238	$2,203,360	$4,149,820
Accounts receivable	1,251,433	990,376	2,155,553
Inventories	2,933,072	2,062,281	446,659
Prepaid expenses and other	44,040	44,149	59,889
Current portion of net investment in sales-type lease		44,004	44,004
Due from affiliated companies	1,993,789	664,495	
Total current assets	9,746,572	6,008,665	6,855,925
Property and Equipment:			
Furniture and fixtures	218,273	230,238	229,024
Machinery and equipment	2,849,924	2,876,158	2,861,311
Leasehold improvements	137,594	54,800	49,133
Total net property	3,205,791	3,161,196	3,139,468
Accumulated depreciation and amortization	2,002,682	2,507,871	2,833,423
Deposits and other assets:	219,334	199,987	35,258
Net investment in sales type lease		165,211	111,477
Total Assets:	$11,169,015	$7,027,188	$7,308,705

Liabilities and Shareholder Equity	1987	1988	1989
Current Liabilities:			
Current portion of long-term debt	$182,452	$43,640	$234,071
Current portion of capital lease obligations	339,092	407,210	
Accounts payable	1,498,354	759,552	553,669
Accrued compensation and related liabilities	254,018	184,804	313,970
Deferred revenues	285,745	216,243	192,207
Other accrued expenses	855,307	1,004,932	689,183
Total current liabilities	3,414,968	2,616,381	1,983,100
Long-Term Debt:	60,125	79,788	34,585
Shareholder's Equity:			
Convertible preferred stock:			
Series A	1,500,000	1,500,000	1,500,000
Series B	7,496,199	7,496,199	7,496,199
Series C	2,140,601	2,140,601	2,140,601
Common stock	12,171,965	27,458	12,172
Additional paid-in capital		12,145,357	12,155,482
Deficit accumulated	(15,932,206)	(19,231,161)	(18,013,434)
Notes receivable from sale of stock	(10,700)	(10,700)	
Total shareholders' equity	7,365,859	4,067,754	5,291,020
Total liabilities and shareholders equity	$11,169,015	$7,027,188	$7,308,705

Exhibit #3-3

Consolidated Balance Sheet
Raytel Holding Corporation and Subsidiary
(000's omitted)

Assets	1990 Sept 30	1991 Sept 29	1992 Sept 30
Current Assets:			
Cash and cash investments	1,626	4,099	7,727
Receivables, net	3,766	3,804	
Prepaid expenses	91	147	
Net assets held for sale	755		
Total current assets	6,238	8,050	
Investment in unconsolidated joint venture and partnership	348	15	
Property and equipment, net of accumulated depreciation	804	681	
Intangible assets, net of accumulated amortization	17,198	14,874	
Total Assets:	$24,588	$23,620	$37,835

Liabilities and Shareholder Equity	1990	1991	1992
Current Liabilities:			
Current portion of long-term debt	850	1,738	
Accounts payable	985	1,054	
Accrued liabilities	1,743	1,957	
Total current liabilities	3,578	4,749	
Long-Term Debt:	12,412	10,567	
Redeemable warrants	620	620	
Noncontrolling interest in consolidated entities	1,045	1,727	
Series B stockholder's interest in Raytel Corporation	2,639	2,877	
Total liabilities	20,294	20,540	
Shareholder's Equity:			
Convertible preferred stock:			
Series A	1,500	1,500	
Series B	7,496	7,496	
Series C	2,141	2,141	
Common stock	12	12	
Additional paid-in capital	12,168	12,172	
Deficit accumulated	(19,023)	(20,241)	
Total shareholders' equity	4,294	3,080	5,166
Total liabilities and shareholders equity	$24,588	$23,620	

Exhibit #3-4

Consolidated Balance Sheet
Raytel Medical Corporation
(on 30 September; 000's omitted)

Assets	1993	1994	1995	1996
Current Assets:				
Cash and cash investments	3,993	5,847	$4,983	5,737
Receivables, net	20,477	21,325	22,415	21,753
Prepaid expenses and other	1,167	1,530	1,286	1,472
Total current assets	25,637	28,702	28,684	28,962
Investments in and advances to				
unconsolidated entities and partnerships	522	242	158	74
Property and equipment, less depreciation	12,462	10,172	8,598	9,156
Intangible assets, less accumulated amortization	12,782	11,129	9,328	29,838
Total assets	51,171	50,245	46,768	68,030

Liabilities and Shareholder Equity	1993	1994	1995	1996
Current liabilities:				
Current portion of long-term debt	6,194	4,895	4,275	2,703
Current portion of capital lease obligations	1,212	1,012	1,047	562
Accounts payable	2,273	2,417	2,189	2,861
Accrued liabilities	5,608	7,861	5,626	6,632
Total current liabilities	15,287	16,185	13,137	12,758

Long term debt, net	15,774	11,618	7,718	3,842
Capital lease obligations, net	3,146	2,105	984	469
Redeemable warrants	1,600	1,600	1,600	983
Deferred liabilities		224	749	
Minority interest in consolidated entities	1,831	1,353	1,081	1,100
Total liabilities	37,638	33,085	25,269	19,152
Stockholder's equity:				
Preferred stock	7	7	7	
Common stock	2	2	2	8
Additional paid-in capital	31,463	31,432	31,410	55,585
Common stock to be issued				852
Accumulated deficit	(17,707)	(14,281)	(9,920)	(7,567)
Total stockholder's equity	13,378	17,160	21,499	48,878
Total liabilities and shareholder's equity	$51,403	50,245	46,768	68,030

Case Solution

Question 1, page 434

You are a partner at HVF. Would you recommend an investment in Raytel? Describe your reasoning.

Answer:

Raytel would be a good candidate for a venture capital investment for the following reasons:

1. The potential market is large (3000 hospitals at perhaps $100,000 per instrument). Total market — $300 million.

2. Raytel's leading edge technology is an electronic breakthrough and represents a significant user benefit compared to viewing X-rays on a light box.

3. Cost savings to hospitals would result from use of the new technology.

4. The ability to store and transmit images to centers of excellence for diagnostic consultation is another significant user benefit.

Term Sheet & Purchase Agreement Differences

Question 2, page 434

Common Equivalent Shares Outstanding
12/83 Post Series B Financing (Actual Deal Closed)
Cap Table

			Percent Ownership
Series A (3.60/share)	417 thousand shares		18%
Series B	914 thousand shares	(Cv. 1/1)	40%
Common	951 thousand shares		20%
Total	2,282 thousand shares		100%

Valued at $8.75/share
Post B Total Value $19.97 million
Actual pre-money value was $19.9 - $7.5 = $12.4 million
Tangible net worth, post-financing $3.27/share

Question 2, page 434

Post-Series B Financing (Deal Sought and Not Closed)
$18.50 per share & 432 thousand shares to raise $8.0 million
Cap Table

		Percent Ownership
Series A	417 thousand shares	23%
Series B	432 thousand shares	24%
Common	951 thousand shares	53%
Total	1,800 thousand shares	100%

Valued at $18.50
Total value would have been $33.3 million post financing
Pre-money sought was $33.3 - $5.0 = $25.3 million

Question 2, page 434

Raytel Deal Difference — Series B Financing

	Actual Deal Closed	Deal Sought & Not Closed
Pre-money Value	$11.97 million	$25.3 million
Value per share, pre-money	$8.75	$18.50
Money Raised	$8.0 million	$8.0 million
Number of Shares Sold	914,000	432,432
Post-money Value	$19.97 million	$33.3 million

Term Sheet & Purchase Agreement Differences

Question 2, page 434

1) Price per share: $18.50 vs. $8.75

2) Shares issued: 432,434 vs. 914,402
   (Nearly twice the dilution to existing Raytel shareholders)

3) Dividend rate per share reduced from #2.57/share to $1.21. Aggregate amount same.

4) Redemption provision included in final deal. This is an offset to being diluted on price. It gives Raytel the opportunity to take out the Series B at $9.63/share. This caps the Series B upside. Realistically, Raytel is not likely to accumulate $9 million in surplus cash beyond normal working capital needs to accomplish redemption.

5) A minimum investment provision was included in the final Series B of $6,000,000.

6) A demand registration right is included in the final Series B.

Question 2, page 434

Is the reduction in Series B pre-money valuation between the closed financing and the projected financing a significant amount? Explain why or why not.

Yes. Very significant. The pre-money value sought by Raytel was $25.3 million in the financing not closed. The actual pre-money value received was $11.97 million in the financing which was closed. The percent ownership of Raytel of the Series B is 40% in the deal which closed.

The Series B were originally offered 24% ownership of Raytel for the same $8 million of invested proceeds.

The Series A percent ownership dropped to 18% in the deal which was closed as compared to 23% post-B financing in the deal not closed. Common shareholders had their ownership percentage reduced from 53% proposed in the Series B financing not closed to 42% ownership post-B financing which did close.

Question 2, page 434

If you were a venture capitalist on the Raytel board of directors, would you have voted to accept the Series B financing which was closed? Why or why not?

This venture capitalist voted to accept the Series B financing at $8.75 per share because LBKL had tested the market at the higher pre-money value of $25 million or $18.50 per share and had failed to raise any money at that valuation. HV II was the beneficiary of the reduced pre-money value accorded Raytel in the financing which closed. HV II invested approximately $2 million and acquired 10% ownership of Raytel as compared to a 6% ownership which would have been acquired for the $2 million investment at the higher pre-money value and higher per share value of $18.50.

Question 3, page 441

If you held preferred shares in Raytel, would you settle or fight?

Answer:

Settling is the most prudent choice. The main reason is that it would take five years to get a court decision. During that time the Raytel shareholders would have to finance Raytel and keep it out of bankruptcy as well. If Raytel were to fall into bankruptcy, NAP & ATT could buy Raytel's assets inexpensively. Settle and take the cash!

Question 4, page 444

Was the price of the Raytel acquisition of CDI financially attractive to Raytel shareholders?

Answer:

Yes. The EBITDA multiple is modest at 5.5 times for a company which has had a 31% compound growth rate (CGR) in pretax income since its inception. Also, the transaction required equity of only $6.5 million in the $22.2 million purchase price for relatively aggressive leverage of 3.41 times.

CDI Results FY 1990

Revenues $18.5 million

EBITDA $ 4.0 million

Raytel Paid

$22.2 million total

Provided by:

$2 million A/R line

$8 million Term loan

$6 million Sub. Debt

$6.5 million Equity cash

EBITDA multiple:

$22.2 million ÷ $4.0 million + 5.5 x

Leverage:

$22.2 million ÷ $6.5 million + 3.41 x

What strategy would you recommend for getting liquidity from an investment in Raytel? What approaches are available for going public? Would you restructure the company in any way?

Raytel Exit Strategy

Major considerations:

1. After 12 years as a private, venture-backed company, the venture shareholders sought partial liquidity through an IPO to get an external measure of valuation. There were very few selling shareholders.

2. A merger for cash or stock was not feasible because Raytel had a diverse mix of businesses (pacemaker monitoring and magnetic resonance imaging (MRI) patient therapy centers) which did not seem to fit with any acquirers. Raytel was built from acquisitions and was somewhat of a hybrid company. A merger or transfer premium (usually 30% over IPO valuation) would be difficult to achieve.

3. Investment bankers asked if Raytel wished to consider selling its business in two transactions with two potential buyers. The board decided this approach was too complicated.

4. It was similarly difficult for IPO investment bankers and ultimate IPO purchasers to value Raytel and understand the business synergies of pacemaker monitoring and MRI. The result was a somewhat lower valuation on IPO.

5. IPO was filed in the $9-$11/share price range ($82 million to $99 million total company valuation), and the stock was priced and brought to market at $8/share (total company valuation $72 million, which was 17% to 12% dilution from filing to pricing). IPO was done at a P/E of 10 which is low for a high rate of return company such as Raytel.

Raytel Medical Corporation

RTEK-NASDAQ $13
Announcement
Edward B. Keaney 415-274-4473 keaney@vbwco.com

VOLPE BROWN
WHELAN & CO.

EQUITY RESEARCH

October 13, 1997

EPS	1996A	1997E	1998E
Q1	$0.20	$0.21 A	$0.23
Q2	$0.19	$0.22 A	$0.26
Q3	$0.22	$0.22 A	$0.29
Q4	$0.20	$0.21	$0.32
Year (Sep)	$0.80	$0.87	$1.10
P/E	16.3x	14.9	11.8x
First Call		$0.87	$1.08
Revs. (M)	$73	$84	$119

Investment Opinion	BUY (2)
Price Target	$20
52-Week Price Range	$15-$7 3/4
Shares Out. (million)	90
Market Cap. (million)	$116.3
3-Year EPS Growth Rate	25%
CY98 P/E to Growth Rate	44%

Texas Heart Center Deal Validates Raytel's Growth Strategy

Last week, Raytel announced an agreement with the Baptist Hospital of Southeast Texas to open an integrated heart center. The Baptist Hospital is one of the three acute care facilities in the greater Beaumont market. It currently has a small heart program, encompassing 80-90 cases per year. Raytel's Beaumont-based cardiology group (Southeast Texas Cardiology Associates, or SETCA) refers about 50% of the open heart cases performed at Baptist. This relationship thus dovetails well with the Company's goal of developing heart centers in conjunction with hospitals familiar to its affiliated physicians.

Raytel expects to open the center by mid-Q2:98, following the build-out of a cardiac intensive care unit (CICU) within the hospital. Upon opening, we anticipate an initial revenue run rate of $6 million, ramping up to roughly $8 million within the first year. We believe that Raytel will be able to increase open heart case volume by 50% or more at Baptist within a reasonable timeframe. In addition to the CICU addition, Raytel has also enhanced its service capabilities in the Beaumont region by recently adding an electrophysiologist to SETCA. This will eliminate the need to outsource EP studies to a facility in Houston.

We are not revising our estimates at this time, since we included two new heart centers per year in our original projections. This announcement does lend greater visibility to our FY: 98 estimates. In its heart center/PPM segment, we now have visibility on almost 40% of the $20 million revenue run rate increase anticipated inFY:98. In addition, Raytel's pipeline is well-developed, and we believe the company's target of acquiring one cardiologist practice a quarter and two heart centers per fiscal year is eminently achievable.

Selling at only 12x forward EPS, we believe the current valuation of Raytel marks a compelling entry point for investors. As EPS gains accelerate=we project a ramp up from 10% yr/yr growth to more than 30% yr/yr increase as FY:98 progresses-we believe that recognition of the Company's achievements and prospects will result in substantial P/E expansion. We continue to rate the shares BUY (2) and note that our conservatively plotted price target of $20 per share represents potential appreciation of more than 50%

Date of previous comment: 10/09/97   Volpe Brown Whelan & Company, Member SIPC. c 1997